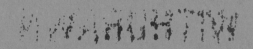

AUTHORITY AND POWER

WALTER ULLMANN

AUTHORITY AND POWER

STUDIES ON
MEDIEVAL LAW AND GOVERNMENT
PRESENTED TO WALTER ULLMANN ON
HIS SEVENTIETH BIRTHDAY

EDITED BY
BRIAN TIERNEY AND PETER LINEHAN

CAMBRIDGE UNIVERSITY PRESS

CAMBRIDGE

LONDON   NEW YORK   NEW ROCHELLE

MELBOURNE   SYDNEY

Published by the Press Syndicate of the University of Cambridge
The Pitt Building, Trumpington Street, Cambridge CB2 1RP
32 East 57th Street, New York, NY 10022, USA
296 Beaconsfield Parade, Middle Park, Melbourne 3206, Australia

First published 1980

Printed in Great Britain at the University Press, Cambridge

British Library Cataloguing in Publication Data
Authority and Power.
1. Law, Medieval – Addresses, essays, lectures
2. Law, Europe – Addresses, essays, lectures
3. Authority – Addresses, essays, lectures
4. Power (Social sciences) – Addresses, essays, lectures
I. Ullmann, Walter II. Tierney, Brian III. Linehan, Peter
340.5′5   Law   80-40587

ISBN 0 521 22275 3

CONTENTS

Contents

FOREWORD

Walter Ullmann first captivated a Cambridge audience with his Frederick William Maitland Memorial Lectures delivered in the Lent Term of 1948. For the next thirty years he stimulated, guided and instructed a whole generation of Cambridge undergraduates and research students. During those same years he was engaged in producing his own numerous and weighty contributions to medieval scholarship.

It will not seem surprising perhaps (if we recall the unhappy state of international affairs forty years ago) that Austria should have given to England a major scholar. But it does seem noteworthy that, as a result, Cambridge should have acquired a historian who has given a new depth and significance to a specifically Cambridge tradition of scholarship. Maitland himself, the greatest of legal historians, long ago called for a renewed study of medieval Roman and canon law in England. 'An educated Englishman may read and enjoy what Dante or Marsiglio has written. An English scholar may face Aquinas or Ockham or even the repellent Wycliff. But Baldus and Bartolus, Innocentius and Johannes Andreae, them he has not been taught to tackle, and they are not to be tackled by the untaught.' Walter Ullmann is the teacher who taught us to tackle them. Again, it was Maitland who wrote, 'In the Middle Ages the church was a state', and his disciple, Figgis, who put the point more emphatically: 'in the Middle Ages the church was the state'. Walter Ullmann's work can be seen as a richly rewarding inquiry into all the implications of these statements. His writings are exceptionally broad in range and varied in detail, but they have a common centre – the study of the medieval Church perceived as an organisation of government. In the work of so gifted a scholar this study has led on to endless new insights into the structure and development of Western institutions.

Our purpose here is not to explain in detail the importance and

vii

originality of Walter Ullmann's writings. The Bibliography at the end of the volume will serve that purpose better than could any words of ours. Rather we want to express our gratitude to a great teacher and kind friend whose love of his work and tireless zest in pursuing it have provided such an inspiring example for his pupils. Every research student will remember 'supervisions' that went on for hours, the passing of time forgotten by student and (we think) teacher alike, in the hunt for some fascinating truth, the true meaning of a difficult text, perhaps, or the true significance of a complex argument.

Those encounters invariably revealed Walter Ullmann's characteristic concern both for the *minutiae* of the subject and for the broad sweep. His formidable scholarship has illuminated so many aspects of the history of the medieval millennium – the papacy, the universities, canonistics, political theory – that any tribute to him must range widely too – from Visigothic Spain to fifteenth-century Poland. In their shared desire to express their deep affection and regard, his friends and former pupils have returned to topics which they formerly explored under his genial guidance. In seeking to do so they are all too conscious of the lapses and lacunae which their offerings may contain (not least because on this occasion they have not had the benefit of his advice). The collection comes as a present to mark two events – Walter Ullmann's retirement from the Chair of Medieval History in the University of Cambridge in September 1978, and his seventieth birthday in November 1980.

The Editors desire to thank all the contributors for their patient and willing collaboration, and the Syndics and staff of the Cambridge University Press for publishing the volume. They wish also to record their gratitude to Professor Michael Wilks for his original initiative in launching the enterprise.

BRIAN TIERNEY   PETER LINEHAN

ABBREVIATIONS

AC	Archivo de la Catedral
ALKG	*Archiv für Literatur und Kirchengeschichte des Mittelalters*
BL	British Library, London
BMCL	*Bulletin of Medieval Canon Law*, n.s.
BN	Bibliothèque Nationale, Paris
CHJ	*Cambridge Historical Journal*
CHR	*Catholic Historical Review*
Close Rolls	*Close Rolls of the Reign of Henry III* (14 vols., Record Publications, London, 1902–38)
CPL	*Calendar of Entries in the Papal Registers*, 1 (1198–1304), ed. W. H. Bliss (Record Publications, London, 1893)
CPR	*Calendar of Patent Rolls* (Record Publications, London, 1901–)
CR	*Cambridge Review*
CYS	Canterbury and York Society
EHR	*English Historical Review*
HZ	*Historische Zeitschrift*
JEH	*Journal of Ecclesiastical History*
JL	*Regesta pontificum Romanorum . . . ad annum* 1198, ed. P. Jaffé, 2nd edn S. Löwenfeld, etc. (2 vols., Leipzig, 1885–8)
JTS	*Journal of Theological Studies*
Ldl	*Libelli de lite*, ed. MGH (3 vols., Hanover, 1891–7)
LQR	*Law Quarterly Review*
LRS	Lincoln Record Society
Mansi	J. D. Mansi, *Sacrorum conciliorum nova et amplissima collectio*
MC	*Monumenta conciliorum generalium seculi decimi quinti, Concilium Basiliense, scriptorum*, ed. F. Palacky *et al.* (4 vols., Vienna-Basle 1857–1935)
MGH	Monumenta Germaniae Historica
	Auct. ant. Auctores antiquissimi
	Capit. Capitularia
	Conc. Concilia
	Const. Constitutiones
	DD Diplomata
	Epp. Epistolae
	Epp. sel. Epistolae selectae

Abbreviations

MGH	LL	Leges
	Poetae	Poetae Latini medii aevi
	Scr. rer. Germ.	Scriptores rerum Germanicarum in usum scholarum
	SS	Scriptores
	SS rer. Lang.	Scriptores rerum Langobardicarum et Italicarum saec. VI–X
	SS rer. Merov.	Scriptores rerum Merovingicarum
MIÖG		*Mitteilungen des Instituts für Österreichische Geschichtsforschung*
NA		*Neues Archiv der Gesellschaft für ältere deutsche Geschichtskunde*
OP		*Guillelmi de Ockham Opera Politica*, I–III (Manchester, 1940–)
PL		Migne, *Patrologia latina*
Potthast		Potthast, *Regesta pontificum romanorum*
RBPH		*Revue Belge de Philologie et d'Histoire*
RHD		*Revue d'Histoire du Droit/Tijdschrift voor Rechtsgeschiedenis*
RHE		*Revue d'histoire ecclésiastique*
R.S.		Rolls Series, London
SCH		*Studies in Church History*
ZRG		*Zeitschrift der Savigny–Stiftung für Rechtsgeschichte*
	Germ.	Germanistische ⎫
	Kan.	Kanonistische ⎬ Abteilung
	Rom.	Romanistische ⎭

THE ALLEGED TERRITORIALITY
OF VISIGOTHIC LAW

by P. D. KING

FOR ALL the difficulties and dangers into which their unconsidered use can lead the unwary, the secular legal monuments of the early Middle Ages stand unsurpassed in their evidentiary value for the historian. On the one hand – and the point has been made on a wider scale with no greater authority and assiduity than in the writings of Walter Ullmann himself – the laws reflect, and allow us therefore to perceive, the ideological principles and objectives of their creators; on the other, they furnish a rich fund of information on the more mundane realities of life within the societies in which they operated. In general, therefore, the more copious the quantity of legal material, the more plentiful the historical harvest which stands to be reaped; and not one of the barbarian kingdoms has more to offer in this respect than the Visigothic, from which an abundance of laws, promulgated by eleven or twelve different kings and over a period of some two and a quarter centuries, has survived. But one obviously essential preliminary to the correct employment of these sources is identification of the groups which they were intended to rule; and when the writer as a research student first lit upon the Visigoths – coming to them by a route, as deviously bewildering to himself as to a remarkably long-suffering supervisor, which had begun with Jonas of Orléans and Frankish episcopalism in the ninth century – it swiftly became apparent that precisely this matter was the subject of dispute.

Fundamental controversy was of relatively recent origin. Traditionally, Visigothic legal history had been explained in terms of development from an early 'national' stage, when Goths and Romans were ruled by separate bodies of law, to a later territorial one, when a single code governed both peoples. All had been agreed that the *Codex Euricianus* (CE), the compilation issued about 476 by the founder of the independent Visigothic kingdom and now surviving only in fragmentary form, was designed for the government of the Goths alone –

though it also contained certain provisions regulating the relations between them and the Romans and probably operated in mixed cases – and that Alaric II's celebrated *Lex Romana Visigothorum* (LRV), or Breviary, was promulgated in 506 for the internal use of the Romans, previously ruled by the Theodosian Code (CT) and other traditional sources of Roman law. A handful of scholars had maintained that a territorial regime was then introduced by the *Codex Revisus* (CR) of Leovigild (?568–86), the laws of which, though no longer extant, bulk large, as *Antiquae* and untitled texts, in the code (called here the LV) issued by Reccesvind, probably in 654, and still surviving; but the great majority had preferred to regard the CR as a simple 'national' substitute for the CE and the transition to territoriality as coming about rather with the publication of the LV itself. During the Second World War, however, a first radical challenge to this broad consensus had appeared. A lengthy article by the Spanish scholar Alfonso García Gallo had argued that the law of the independent Visigothic kingdom was territorial in scope from the very beginning: there was a succession of codes – the CE, the LRV, the CR, the LV – each abrogating its predecessor and wielding sole and universal sway over Goths and Romans alike. An important variation on this basic territorialist theme had been the work of Alvaro d'Ors in 1955. According to this distinguished Romanist, the CE was a collection of territorial law which stood in complement first to the variety of Roman legal and juristic sources which ruled towards the end of the fifth century and then to the LRV, a didascalic compilation: the CR replaced the CE but similarly coexisted with the Breviary until their conjoint territorial rule was abolished with the publication of Reccesvind's code.

The writer's research dissertation was eventually devoted to an examination of the whole question of the character of Visigothic legal development.[1] Its conclusion was that with regard to the CE and the LRV the traditional view – no justification of which, remarkably, had

[1] P. D. King, 'The character of Visigothic legislation' (unpublished doctoral dissertation: University of Cambridge, 1967), where pp. xxxix–xli describe the codes and pp. xlii–l the various views, including reactions to A. García Gallo, 'Nacionalidad y territorialidad del derecho en la época visigoda', *Anuario de historia del derecho español*, XIII (1936–41), pp. 168–264, and A. d'Ors, 'La territorialidad del derecho de los visigodos', *Estudios visigóticos*, I (Rome-Madrid, 1956), pp. 91–124 (also in *Settimane di studio del centro italiano di studi sull'alto medioevo*, III (1956), pp. 363–408). Brief comments in my *Law and Society in the Visigothic Kingdom*, Cambridge studies in medieval life and thought, 3rd series, v (Cambridge, 1972), pp. 6–10, 13, 18–19: cf. also my article cit. below, n. 3.

ever appeared[2] – must be retained but that the first territorial code was the work not of Leovigild or of Reccesvind but of the latter's father, Chindasvind, in 643/4.[3] The aim of the following pages is not to summarise the dissertation but to sketch the main lines of the case made there for the necessary rejection of both the territorialist verdicts concerning the relationship to each other of the different codes. This is a vital matter, for if it can be shown that neither García Gallo's 'abrogation' interpretation nor d'Ors's 'coexistence' thesis can conceivably be correct, then we are left with the very strongest of arguments for acceptance of the 'national' view: quite simply, what feasible alternative presents itself?

We may begin with the testimony of the two passages devoted to legal developments among the Goths in Isidore's *Historia Gothorum*:[4]

c. 35 Sub hoc rege (*scil.* Eurico) Gothi legum instituta scriptis habere coeperunt. Nam antea tantum moribus et consuetudine tenebantur.

c. 51 In legibus quoque ea quae ab Eurico incondite constituta videbantur correxit (*scil.* Leovigildus), plurimas leges praetermissas adiciens, plerasque superfluas auferens.

Now, whatever inaccuracy there may be in the first of these reports, the reliability of the second is beyond all challenge. Already of adult years when Leovigild died in 586, and moving in the highest circles even before he became bishop of Seville (*c.* 600), Isidore was admirably placed to know the truth. Moreover, the CR was still in force when he wrote his history in the mid-620s, for he would assuredly have mentioned the production of a new corpus if such had been the work of one or other of the Catholic kings since the Arian Leovigild: the *e silentio* argument, unusually strong in this instance, finds corroboration in the fact that of the 207 post-Leovigildian laws in the LV a mere five are attributable to these rulers. Nothing is more likely than that the promulgation decree of the CR, referring back to the CE, spelled out the changes being made in this, and that it is Isidore's use of this decree as a source which accounts for the precision of his report of the form

---

[2] With the single exception of the defence of the 'national' character of the LRV by F. de Cárdenas, *Estudios jurídicos*, I (Madrid, 1884), pp. 60–3 (remarks originally appearing in 1847/8).

[3] On this second matter see P. D. King, 'King Chindasvind and the first territorial law-code of the Visigothic kingdom', in E. F. James, ed., *Visigothic Spain: new approaches* (Oxford, 1980), pp. 131–57.

[4] MGH, Auct. ant., XI, ed. T. Mommsen (Berlin, 1894), pp. 281, 288.

3

taken by Leovigild's recasting – a form largely confirmed by a comparison of the Eurician texts with their corresponding *Antiquae*.[5]

Isidore's evidence strikes an important blow against the 'abrogation' thesis. For while he leaves no doubt that the CR was nothing but a revised edition of the CE, the irresistible implication of his language – the reference to Leovigild's correction of 'those things which seemed confusedly established by Euric', to his addition of laws 'overlooked' by his predecessor, to his removal of 'superfluous' laws – is that the revision was introduced precisely because Euric's code was still in force but marred by faults which rendered it inadequate for the changed legal needs of the time. To believe that the CE had been replaced by Alaric's Breviary as the exclusive law-code governing all the inhabitants of the kingdom and that it was the LRV which Leovigild's collection now replaced is to fly in the face of the natural sense of the bishop's report. Moreover, if the territorialist view has substance, how are we to explain Isidore's failure to mention the rule of the LRV over the Goths, even though this would have endured for some seventy years, have survived into his own early days at least, and have been in any case a matter of common knowledge among his older contemporaries? Isidore's evidence quite apart, the 'abrogation' argument involves the wholly untenable proposition that Leovigild took as the basis of his new code not the law which he found in force but a compilation which had been legally defunct for a lifetime[6] and which contained provisions frequently at striking variance, as we shall see, with those of the LRV. And as if all this were not enough, it so happens that the continued validity of the Breviary after the publication of the CR can be directly proved by seventh-century conciliar evidence.[7] Two of the canons of the Second Council of Seville, held in 619 (and presided over by Isidore), refer to *leges mundiales* which on grounds of terminology and content are indubitably to be identified with laws of the Breviary. Nineteen years later, a *sententia legum* read out and accepted in legal proceedings at the Sixth Council of Toledo turns out to be an exact rendering of one of Paulus's *Sententiae* from the LRV. It is out of the question that the fathers at Seville would have supported their canons by recourse to the rulings of an out-of-force compilation, the

---

[5] See, convincingly, K. Zeumer, 'Geschichte der westgothischen Gesetzgebung, I', *NA*, XXIII (1898), pp. 426ff., 476. Leovigild's omissions of Eurician texts cannot be proved, of course.

[6] García Gallo, 'Nacionalidad', p. 231, himself speaks of the 'disinterment' of the CE.

[7] Some details in King, 'Chindasvind', pp. 136–8: the much fuller account in *idem*, 'Legislation', pp. 119–36, draws attention also to highly probable and possible allusions.

use of which would assuredly have entailed severe penalty if the CR had been the exclusive legal authority of the kingdom, let alone that those at Toledo would have admitted the validity of one of these rulings in the resolution of a law-case: indeed, the use of the present tense – 'scribitur enim in lege mundiali' – in one of the Seville canons allows no possibility of doubt but that the 'worldly law' in question was currently in force.

The 'abrogation' argument fares no better when the pre-Leovigildian evidence is examined. Not only does this fail to offer a single jot of support for the view that the CE was abrogated in 506:[8] it shows that before that date the CE did not rule alone. It is the introductory *Commonitorium* to the LRV – the lone survivor from among the promulgation decrees of the pre-Reccesvindian codes – which is of central importance here.[9] If the territorialist interpretation were correct, we should naturally expect to find in this lengthy preamble explicit reference to the abrogation of the CE – the more so since the publica-tion of the Breviary was designed, like the calling to Agde earlier in 506 of the first-ever Catholic council of the kingdom, to win Roman support in the imminent struggle with the Franks,[10] and the implication of an alleged decision concomitantly to repeal the CE is thus Roman dissatisfaction with its laws: how could Alaric II in these circumstances have failed to make excellent propaganda-capital by direct allusion to its annulment? But there is nothing which by even the most elastic stretch of the imagination can be construed as such a reference. There are, it is true, various phrases of the *Commonitorium* which are in them-selves susceptible of a territorialist interpretation and might thus be held implicitly to indicate the CE's abrogation; but all these are also perfectly compatible with the traditional view of the LRV as a 'national' code for the Romans.[11]

The truth is that Alaric was totally unconcerned with the CE in the

[8] The lack of sixth-century references to the CE does not prove abrogation: where would we expect to find it mentioned? D'Ors, 'Territorialidad', p. 120, points out that the fragments, written in a sixth-century hand, almost certainly date from after 506 and that a defunct code is unlikely to have been copied.

[9] Ed. T. Mommsen in K. Zeumer, MGH, LL, I, Leges nationum Germanicarum, i: Leges Visigothorum (Hanover–Leipzig, 1902), pp. 465–7. References to the Visigothic laws are to Zeumer's edition or, in the case of the Breviary, to G. Haenel, *Lex Romana Visigothorum* (Leipzig, 1849).

[10] See King, *Law*, pp. 10–11, with the literature, especially Bruck, who is basic. Both García Gallo, 'Nacionalidad', pp. 261–2, and d'Ors, 'Territorialidad', p. 121, accept the Breviary's publication as politically inspired.

[11] On these, which cannot be discussed here, see King, 'Legislation', pp. 95–101.

publication of the LRV. He leaves us in no doubt about the purpose of his compilation:

Quod in legibus videbatur iniquum ... corrigimus, ut omnis legum Romanarum et antiqui iuris obscuritas ... in lucem intellegentiae melioris deducta resplendeat ac nihil habeatur ambiguum, unde se diuturna aut diversa iurgantium inpugnet obiectio.

Now, it is quite clear that the CE was not in mind here, for on no showing could it be regarded as a compilation of *ius antiquum* or *leges Romanae*. Alaric was referring rather to the removal of the obscurities in traditional Roman law and the ancient juristic pronouncements.[12] And far from being out of force already for a generation, as the 'abrogation' argument has it, this *lex* and *ius* was, the text makes plain, current: it was not a question of the resurrection and elucidation of law which was dead but of the clarification of that which was in constant use. Unless we care to assume that the CE had already been withdrawn *before* 506, then we are compelled to conclude that the legal regime of the Visigothic kingdom until that time was characterised by the dual rule of the CE and a complex of Roman laws and juristic *dicta*. It was Alaric's aim in the production of the Breviary to replace the variety of these latter with a single and definitive code which would contain the only authorities in future admissible: 'ut ... nulla alia lex neque iuris formula (*scil.* Romana) proferri vel recipi praesumatur'. This is the only interpretation to which the text of the *Commonitorium* lends itself, and it is entirely borne out by the contents of the Breviary which we find to be, exactly as we should expect, a collection of Roman juristic maxims and Roman laws, the latter without exception culled from the Theodosian code and later imperial novels. Not only is there no reference to the CE in the *Commonitorium*, but neither do the laws of the LRV owe any debt whatsoever to those of Euric. It is as if the CE had never existed.

But what problems this presents if the LRV abrogated the earlier code! To take but one example: how can we account for the omission of those Eurician laws which had dealt with the profoundly important issue of the division of lands? Are we to believe that this was a matter which required legal regulation before 506 and then again after the date of publication of the CR – in which the laws reappear, to remain also in the later codes – but not during the intervening period? No

---

[12] Thus also d'Ors, 'Territorialidad', p. 119, and P. Merêa, 'Uma tese revolucionária', *Anuario de historia del derecho español*, XIV (1942–3), p. 597.

great critical acumen is needed to recognise the force of this point alone as an argument against the 'abrogation' thesis. Just as the laws of the Breviary ignore certain matters handled in the CE and CR, so, it may be added, such basic Roman institutions as the colonate, the *curia* and the *dos ex muliere*, all of them figuring prominently in the CT and LRV and certainly still surviving in practice, find not a single mention in any of the Eurician or Leovigildian laws. Is it really credible that a legislator concerned to produce an exclusive territorial code could have omitted them, given that Romans formed the great bulk of the population?

Perhaps an even more fundamental objection to Professor García Gallo's interpretation lies in an associated matter: the sharp contrasts between the treatment of one and the same topic in the CE (and CR) on the one hand, and the LRV (and CT) on the other. It is clearly not feasible to examine these contrasts here,[13] but some of those which appear in the fields of matrimonial and successory law should be briefly noted. In the first place, the CE and CR freely allowed, as the Roman codes did not, donations between spouses during marriage.[14] Second, the rights of the Eurician or Leovigildian widow over property which had come to her from her husband were very much more extensive than those of the *vidua* of the LRV. Provided that she was not guilty of sexual misbehaviour, the widow of the CE enjoyed total liberty to dispose at will of all such property, whether or not she had issue; and even when Leovigild introduced restrictions on this liberal regime in the interests of the children of the union, the widow's freedom to do as she wished with her *dos*, or dowry, remained unaffected.[15] The widow of the Breviary, on the other hand, was limited to a simple usufructuary right over property which had devolved upon her *ex marito* – normally by way of *donatio ante nuptias*, the Roman equivalent of the Visigothic *dos*, or at her husband's death – when there were children born of the marriage.[16] Third, the CE and CR, in

---

[13] Some are dealt with in King, 'Legislation', pp. 183–233 – though much remains to be said.

[14] Compare especially CE 307 and 319 and the *Antiquae* v.2.4, v.2.5 and v.2.7 with LRV.P.Sent. II.24.2 (with *Interpretatio*), II.24.3, II.24.4 and LRV.Cod.Theod. III.13.3 (with *Int.*). Against the view of A. d'Ors, *El código de Eurico. Edición, palingenesia, índices*, Estudios visigóticos, II (Rome–Madrid, 1960) pp. 236–8, that the Eurician texts refer only to donations *mortis causa*, see King, 'Legislation', pp. 186–90. On Chindasvind's later compromise position in III.1.5, *idem, Law*, p. 236.

[15] All this emerges from a comparison of CE 319, the *Antiquae* v.2.4 and v.2.5 and the Chindasvindian laws IV.5.1 and IV.5.2: King, 'Legislation', pp. 192–5. For Chindasvind's amendment of the Leovigildian regime, see *idem, Law*, pp. 246–7.

[16] LRV.Nov.Sev.I.1, LRV.Nov.Theod.VII.1 (*Int.*) and King, 'Legislation', pp. 195–8.

contrast to the CT and LRV, allotted the widowed mother a usufructuary share, equal to that of each of the children, in the intestate
estate of her husband.[17] Fourth, the Breviary provided that a widowed
mother should be either partially or wholly excluded from succession
to a child who had died *sine prole* by the brothers or paternal uncles of
the deceased:[18] in the CE and CR her right to inherit took precedence
over theirs.[19] Despite the scanty remains of the CE, there are a number
of other differences between its regime and that of the LRV which can
be pointed to and which concern matters as diverse as the successory
claims of an unmarried daughter, the penalty for making a loan at an
illegal rate of interest, the period of prescription applicable in the case
of runaway slaves, the rights of a widower in the *res maternae* and so on,
but these cannot be detailed here.[20]

Enough will have been said, however, to show the impossibility of
accepting the 'abrogation' thesis. Quite apart from the difficulty of
explaining why Euric should have chosen to impose on his Roman
subjects a set of legal rulings which differed in certain vital regards
from those to which they were accustomed – an action bringing no
detectable advantages but likely to engender resentment at a time when
the Goths were dangerously over-extended – or why the Goths, if
these rulings had been what they wanted in 476(?), should have elected
not only to place themselves under a distinct regime in 506 but also to
remain ruled by this for a lifetime, or why then, suddenly and without
known reason, Leovigild should have decided to revive the laws
apparently found unsatisfactory seventy years before[21] – quite apart
from this, we are asked to believe that within just about a century the
Romans of the Visigothic kingdom were ruled by four separate codes
of law, the first and third of which were very much the same and
wholly Roman, the second and fourth of which were again much the
same but distinct in their provisions from the other two. The property
rights of a Roman widow would have been one thing before 476(?)
and between 506 and the year of publication of the CR, another
altogether between 476(?) and 506 and after the publication of
Leovigild's code! How often are legal developments, especially in the
private sphere, marked by revolution rather than evolution? Yet to

---

[17] CE 322 and the *Antiqua* IV.2.14.
[18] LRV.Cod.Theod. v.1.1 (*Int.*), v.1.2 (with *Int.*), v.1.7 and King, 'Legislation', pp. 200–6.
[19] CE 336 and the *Antiqua* IV.2.2: cf. CE 327, IV.2.18 and King, 'Legislation', pp. 207–11.
[20] For those mentioned, *ibid.*, pp. 212–32.
[21] Wholly unconvincing is García Gallo, 'Nacionalidad', pp. 260–3.

postulate that the CT was abrogated by the CE, this by the LRV and this in its turn by the CR is to postulate no less than three successive revolutions – or more accurately, a revolution and two counter-revolutions. It is frankly unbelievable that such violent *bouleversements* of the legal scene, involving reversions to previously abrogated regimes at that, could have taken place.

Although the various arguments above add up to what may be considered an impregnable case against the 'abrogation' interpretation, they do not serve to disprove the alternative 'coexistence' thesis. While this has the merit of accepting the evidence of the *Commonitorium*, Isidore and the councils that first the CE and the CT, then the CE and the LRV, and finally the CR and the LRV ruled alongside each other, it proposes that the two sets of laws in force at any one time did not govern one the Goths, one the Romans, but rather enjoyed conjoint rule over both peoples. 'Compatibility' is here the keyword.[22] Now, if all the codes concerned are held to be collections of positive law– law, that is, intended and able to be applied in practical fashion in the courts – there can quite certainly be no question of compatibility in the strict sense: juristically, as we have seen, the CE/CR and the CT/LRV went their separate ways. But Professor d'Ors rather regards the Breviary as a didascalic collection.[23] As a general characterisation, this cannot be sustained.[24] There is abundant evidence that the LRV was both intended as a code of real, applicable, law and later so treated. The *Commonitorium* makes it plain that the obscurities of the existing Roman *leges* and *ius* are not at all the subject of simple academic concern; they are the cause of constant practical problems for litigants: 'ac nihil habeatur ambiguum, unde se diuturna aut diversa iurgantium inpugnet obiectio'. The code produced to remedy this state of affairs is approved by a council of leading figures, called at a time of crisis – a circumstance hardly consonant with a view of the Breviary as a didascalic authority – and sent out so that all (Roman) cases may be judged according to its rulings: 'librum ... pro discingendis negotiis nostra iussit clementia destinari, ut iuxta eius seriem universa causarum sopiatur intentio'. The text is quite explicit: the code is to be *used* for the resolution of cases. Indeed, nothing else will do: 'nec aliud cuicumque aut de legibus aut de iure liceat in disceptatione proponere nisi quod directi libri ... ordo conplectitur'. The *disceptatio* itself is

---

[22] Thus d'Ors, 'Territorialidad', pp. 119, 121.   [23] *Ibid.*, pp. 121, 122 etc.
[24] Cf. A. García Gallo in discussion of d'Ors, *Settimane di Studio* (as n. 1), pp. 467–8, and E. Levy, *Gesammelte Schriften*, 1 (Cologne–Graz, 1963), p. 306, n. 10.

envisaged as a real dispute in the courtroom, not an academic one: 'ut in foro ... nulla alia lex neque iuris formula proferri vel recipi praesumatur'. Failure to obey Alaric's instructions may be punished by death – grotesquely over-severe as a penalty if the LRV is simply a didascalic authority. Certainly the code was not regarded in this light by King Theudis, who, in 546, ordered his new law concerning court costs – without question a law of positive application – to be incorporated into it,[25] or by the inhabitants of southern Gaul, whom it continued to serve, as their personal law, for centuries to come.[26]

Despite his frequent general designation of the LRV as didascalic, however, Professor d'Ors does in fact admit that its laws were intended to assist the judges in cases not covered by the provisions of the CE:[27] the Breviary is to be regarded, this must mean, as of amphibious character, partly positive, partly didascalic – the one when it is not the other. Regretfully, one is obliged to say that this interpretation has all the air of a hypothesis of convenience, devised as the only way of resolving the problems caused by the inviability of the 'abrogation' argument, the patent incompatibility of the laws of the CE and the LRV and the impossibility of considering the Breviary a didascalic collection pure and simple, when it is a precondition that the solution be reconcilable with a territorialist conception of Visigothic legislation. The hypothesis is to be rejected as arbitrary, not to say fanciful. Not a single argument is adduced in its favour, and none can be, so far as the writer can see. The great majority of the laws of the Breviary were laws capable of application: Professor d'Ors may know that only some of these were in fact meant to be applied, but how are the judges supposed to have been let in on the secret? Reference to the superior authority of the CE would have been quite indispensable, one might think, yet nowhere does even the most heavily veiled hint of this appear. On the contrary, the language of the *Commonitorium* offers decisive opposition to the thesis. *All* cases are to be judged in accordance with the provisions of the Breviary: 'ut iuxta eius seriem universa causarum sopiatur intentio'. Now, it is possible, though wrong, to interpret this phrase as witnessing the sole and territorial application of the LRV; it is equally possible – and this time correct – to maintain that it shows the LRV to have been the exclusive code of law for the

---

[25] *Lex Theudi* (pp. 467–9 in MGH, LL, I, i: Leges Visigothorum), lines 72–4.
[26] Generally on the career and influence of the Breviary, see A. de Wretschko, 'De usu Breviarii', in T. Mommsen and P. M. Meyer, *Theodosiani libri XVI* (etc.) (3rd edn, Berlin, 1962), I, part i, pp. cccvii–ccclx, esp. cccxiiiff. (Gaul).   [27] D'Ors, 'Territorialidad', p. 121.

Romans. What is certainly not permissible is to interpret 'all' here as meaning not 'all' but 'some'. It should be noted finally that the untitled text II.1.13, which is certainly Leovigildian and almost certainly Eurician,[28] quite explicitly forbids the judges to hear cases not dealt with in the code containing it: these are to be referred to the king.

There are other matters. Why, for example, do we find a whole chapter of the LRV taken over into the CR if the two codes ruled conjointly and territorially?[29] Why, once again, did Isidore not mention the rule of the LRV over the Goths? The strangeness of the omission has already been remarked upon; but how much stranger it is if the Breviary was still ruling the Goths when Isidore wrote, as Professor d'Ors believes! Enough has been said, however, to indicate why the 'coexistence' thesis is no more tenable than Professor García Gallo's. In a longer paper, of course, the case against both Spanish scholars would have been buttressed by a sketch of the grounds for rejection of their various particular arguments for the territorial character of certain periods or individual codes;[30] and account would have been taken of the considerable body of evidence, textual and circumstantial, which positively supports the 'national' view. But false arguments do not in themselves prove false theses, while to prove the theses false is in this instance to provide the strongest of arguments for the traditional interpretation. If two distinct codes were simultaneously in force but did not exercise joint territorial rule, what acceptable alternative is there but to think in terms of their separate rule over separate groups?[31] And what can these groups have been but Romans and Goths?[32] Acceptance of the 'national' standpoint, in short, is a necessary consequence of the invalidation of the rival interpretations.[33] The argument from elimination may not be as forceful or as satisfying as that based upon direct evidence: it is none the less compelling for that.

[28] Cf. K. Zeumer, 'Geschichte der westgothischen Gesetzgebung, II', *NA*, XXIV (1899), pp. 70–2, and R. de Ureña y Smenjaud, *La legislación gótico-hispana* (Madrid, 1905), p. 351. D'Ors, *Código*, p. 57, thinks the law 'entirely Leovigildian or even Reccesvindian'.

[29] See IV.1.1–7, and, on these and other borrowings from the LRV, Zeumer, 'Geschichte I', pp. 431–3: cf. Ureña, *La legislación*, p. 335, n. 2.

[30] Details of the particularly important critical articles by Schultze, Merêa and Sánchez-Albornoz in King, *Law*, p. 6, n. 4.

[31] The Eurician texts on successory matters suffice to show that the CE did not contain the law for mixed cases alone, for intermarriage between Romans and Goths was forbidden: *ibid.*, pp. 13–14.

[32] There is nothing in favour of the 'confessional' interpretation advanced by H. Mitteis, *Der Staat des hohen Mittelalters* (Weimar, 1948), pp. 27–8 but later abandoned, to judge by his review article in *ZRG Germ.* LXVIII (1951), pp. 531–2.

[33] All three other barbarian kingdoms about which we are informed were similarly characterised by a 'national' law system.

SOME CAROLINGIAN LAW-BOOKS
AND THEIR FUNCTION

by ROSAMOND MCKITTERICK

LEGISLATION in the Carolingian period was recorded and preserved in a number of different kinds of collection, each of which served a different purpose. Many of the codices which contain collections of Carolingian secular and ecclesiastical legislation, often combined with doctrinal, didactic and catechetical texts, were intended from the outset to serve as handbooks of reference for the ministering clergy. These I have classified elsewhere as episcopal handbooks.[1] There are also the books designed purely for secular use such as BN lat.10758, a collection of historical and legal texts honouring the Carolingian house, or Berlin 161 (Phillipps 1736) which contained an incomplete text of the *Lex Salica* and extracts from some of the capitularies Charlemagne addressed to his *missi dominici*, and which appears to have been intended for one of the king's regional officials.[2] These collections of secular law often differ greatly. Some were intended as books of reference for a count or royal official, others for everyday use in administering justice, and others to teach law in the schools. Most contained in various combinations the secular capitularies of the Franks, the 'barbarian' codes, and Roman law. Concerning some of these law books a number of things need to be considered.

In order to understand how Carolingian legislation was implemented one must first see what contemporary collections of this legislation can tell us. This applies as much to the dissemination of Germanic and Roman laws as it does to the capitularies and conciliar decrees of the Church. It is not only the promulgation and content of the law which is important, but also its transmission and influence, preservation and application. It has become customary when speaking of the survival of Roman law and the practice of Roman, Germanic and Frankish royal law side by side, to look at any one manuscript and the text of the laws

---

[1] Rosamond McKitterick, *The Frankish Church and the Carolingian Reforms, 789–895* (London, 1977), pp. 25–44.   [2] *Ibid.*, pp. 31 and 43.

it contains, not by itself, but in relation to a family of manuscripts in which one manuscript simply represents a set of variant readings. But it should also concern the historian how each legal compilation was read, for whom it may have been written, and what particular function any one book may have served. A study of some of the Carolingian codices containing laws may also provide a better understanding of how the law was conceived of by the Franks and how it was preserved in the various regions of the Frankish kingdoms.

The small number of manuscripts I propose to discuss deal more extensively with a particular aspect of the preservation of Carolingian legislation which it was not possible to include in my study of the Carolingian reforms and the Frankish church. They can be roughly divided into two groups: those containing the *Lex Romana Visigothorum* or *Breviarium Alarici*, sometimes with other codes, usually the Germanic ones, included; and those containing the *Lex Salica* of the Franks and other texts.

The Carolingian period witnessed a great effort to record the law in writing, and the authority of the written law, in whatever form, greatly increased.[3] In the eighth and ninth centuries the principle of the personality of the law prevailed; every man in the kingdom, which was by 814 made up of a number of different national groups, lived, at least in theory, according to the law peculiar to the particular national group to which he belonged. The Church on the other hand observed Roman law, and for some groups within the Frankish kingdoms, Roman law was their national law. As in every other sphere, the Carolingians made every effort to effect legal reforms. In 802 for example, Charlemagne provided for the revision and where possible the completion of existing texts of the laws and laws not recorded. He thus effectively upheld the legal validity of the Germanic codes.[4]

In court, both the defendant and the president of the court were expected to know under which national law they lived, and which would be applicable.[5] Counts and lesser officials were exhorted to acquire a knowledge of the law. This in many cases would simply be

---

[3] For example, *Capitulare missorum generale 802*, MGH, Capit., I, p. 96. c.26. *Ut iudices secundum scriptam legem iuste iudicent, non secundum arbitrium suum.*

[4] *Annales Laureshamenses an.* 802, MGH, SS, I, p. 38. See too F. L. Ganshof (trans. B. and M. Lyon), *Frankish Institutions under Charlemagne* (Providence, 1968), chs. 1 and 3.

[5] A good example is the familiar situation related by Adrevald in his *Miracula Sancti Benedicti*, MGH, SS, xv, 1, pp. 489–90, where a case had to be judged in the neighbouring region where the national law of the plaintiff was known. See too H. Brunner, *Deutsche Rechtsgeschichte*, I (Leipzig, 1906), p. 394, n. 6.

the law relevant for that official but a greater knowledge of the general principles of law as well as the actual precepts would also seem to have been deemed desirable. Both were certainly taught in the schools.[6] It is to the fulfilment of the king's requirement to acquire a knowledge of both the theory and practice of law that many Carolingian law-books can be related.

The *Breviarium Alarici* was the law code used by those of Gallo-Roman origin and for the remnants of the Visigothic populations of Septimania, Aquitaine and the Spanish Marches. Certainly it was the most systematic and popular collection of Roman law, and it was probably accepted as the authoritative code and principal source of Roman law within the Frankish kingdoms.[7]

The two principal elements in the *Breviarium Alarici* are the legislative and the theoretical; it was a book to be referred to both for actual prescriptions and for general legal principles. It was published in 506 (other digests of Roman law were published at later stages elsewhere), and is a compendium of Roman law, containing a much abridged version of the Theodosian Code, the *Novellae* of Valentinian III, Majorian, Marcian, and Severus, the *Liber* of Gaius, the *Sententiae* of Paul, which mostly outlined the principles of jurisdiction and the law, constitutions from the Gregorian code, an extract from the Hermogenian Code, and a fragment from the *Responsa* of Papinian. The code thus contains texts which deal with the various functions and duties of the officials at the palace and in the provinces, with the laws of the king and with fiscal, civil and municipal administration. The *Breviarium Alarici* omitted most of the financial clauses in the Theodosian Code which did not meet Visigothic arrangements. A selection of the laws for the Christian Church concerning bishops, the clergy, Jews and religion itself from Book XVI of the Theodosian Code was retained. Each section of the laws has an accompanying *Interpretatio*.

There exist a great many Carolingian copies of the *Breviarium*, which suggest that it – as did Roman legal principles generally – exerted considerable influence. Yet real evidence in support of the *Breviarium* is certainly lacking so far.[8] It is apparent from the occasional references

---

[6] See P. Riché, 'Enseignement du droit en Gaule du VIe au XIe siècle', *Ius Romanum Medii Aevi*, pars 1.5.b.bb. (Milan, 1965).

[7] J. Gaudemet, 'Le Bréviaire d'Alaric et les Épitomés', *Ius Romanum Medii Aevi*, pars 1.2.b.aa.β. (Milan, 1965). There is no proof that official recognition was ever accorded the *Breviarium* by Charlemagne or his successors.

[8] J. Gaudemet, 'Survivances romaines dans le droit de la monarchie franque du Ve au Xe siècles', *RHD*, XXIII (1955), pp. 149–206.

to use of Roman law that it gradually came to be considered more as a territorial than as a personal law, and moreover, that the Frankish laws made an attempt to adapt Roman law to new conditions. Yet, as Gaudemet has argued, although there are traces of Roman law in both the capitularies and conciliar decrees, as well as in canon law,[9] the citation of Roman law seems more important in theory than in practice. The actual position of Roman law and its effectiveness as living law remained rather weak; its greatest strength lay in its attractiveness to the Franks as a learned law, the law of Rome, an attraction enhanced no doubt by the revival of the notion of the Roman Emperor in the West. In other words, Roman law retained its influence as a model for legislation and procedure, and as an inspiration in formulating legal principles. The Church's role in the maintenance of Roman usage is undoubtedly of the utmost importance. Not only did the Church observe Roman law; clerics were responsible for providing instruction in the law. They also copied and selected the texts. Some clerics, furthermore, were instructed in the law as well as in the *trivium* of the seven Liberal Arts, in arithmetic and sacred learning, in order to train them to assist the abbot, bishop, count or king in his administrative functions.[10] Judging from the manuscripts containing digests of Roman law, moreover, most of which date from the reigns of Louis the Pious and Charles the Bald rather than earlier, it would seem that there was both a greater inspiration provided by and sought from Roman principles, as well as greater activity in recording the law then than there had been hitherto.

One of the earlier codices however is BN lat.4403[A], written in the middle of the eighth century, probably at Corbie.[11] Later it was in the library of Claude du Puy whose name is on the flyleaf. Even if the manuscript is not certainly from Corbie it was certainly produced and used in a monastic milieu. It is far from being a *de luxe* edition of the *Breviarium Alarici*, in contrast to BN lat.4404 or BN lat.4418, both

---

[9] See too J. Imbert, 'Le Droit romain dans les textes juridiques carolingiens', *Studi in onore Pietro de Francisci*, III (Milan, 1956), pp. 63–7. The Roman law which survived in the barbarian codes was for the most part the Roman law of the provinces.

[10] In 805, Charlemagne decreed that everyone in office had to have a notary, *Capitulare missorum in Theodonis villa datum primum*. *Mere ecclesiasticum* c.4, MGH, Capit., I, p. 121, in the recension in BN lat.9654 and Vat.Pal.lat.582 only.

[11] For a full palaeographical description of this manuscript see E. A. Lowe, *Codices Latini Antiquiores* (Oxford, 1934) V, 556. There remains some uncertainty concerning its origins. The list of contents on the flyleaf was certainly written at Corbie, and it could be the *Lex Gothorum* or more likely the *Libri Novellarum Sex Theodosiani I Valentiniani I Martiani I* of the oldest catalogue, but this fails to prove that the manuscript was there from the start.

written in the ninth century. It is written on fairly coarse, stout parchment, is not large, and the text, although clear, is not set out with the extravagance encountered in a more costly edition. It has a thoroughly utilitarian look; has, in fact, every appearance of being a school-book. It lacks ornament apart from one decorated initial with a fish motif on fo.163v, and the use of red uncials for the titles of each section of the laws and the chapters within each section. Lowe did not note that the codex actually contains two separate manuscripts, the first of four quires ending on fo.28v, while the next quire begins a new sequence of quires containing the *Breviarium Alarici*. The quire mark itself is also different, being an uncial q with a cross stroke through the shaft followed by a Roman numeral rather than the capital Q used on the first four quires. Both parts of the codex, however, come from the same scriptorium, and both texts occur in other manuscripts together as parts of the same book.[12] It is possible therefore that although written separately, the two parts of BN lat.4403[A] were bound together at a fairly early stage.

The first part of BN lat.4403[A] contains the extracts concerning law from the *Etymologiae* of Isidore of Seville.[13] In this copy it is entitled *Explanatio de legibus quem inter libros etomologiarum posuit (sic)*. The chapters, selected in this case from Books v, 1–27 and IX, 4–6 of the *Etymologiae*, provide a historical and theoretical exposition of the law, including Isidore's definitions concerning the authors of the law, divine and human law, that which distinguishes law from custom, natural, civil, military and public law, the function of the various officials who rule and govern by means of the law and the nature of the law itself. The ties of kinship are also fully explained. This *florilegium* is one of two forms the extracts take. The other is a succinct abridgment arranged in the question and answer form so popular in Carolingian didactic treatises.[14] Moreover it was invariably accompanied by a legal text, usually the *Breviarium Alarici*, and also, as in the cases of BN lat. 4626, 4628[A], 4631, 4730, 9653, 10758 and 18237, and Leiden 119, by texts of the Germanic laws, usually the *Lex Salica*. The appearance of either form of the text in a legal codex may well indicate that it was a school-book. Tardif suggested that the questionnaire form of this

---

[12] For example, manuscripts BN lat.4408, 4409, 4414, 4415, 9653 and 18237, Leiden 119, Vat.reg.lat. 1043 and Berne 263.

[13] J. Tardif, 'Un Abrégé juridique des Etymologiae d'Isidore de Séville', *Mélanges Julien Havet* (Paris, 1885), pp. 659–81.

[14] Printed by Tardif, *ibid.*, pp. 673–81.

didactic treatise was part of the judicial development of the northern part of the Frankish kingdoms, while the *florilegium* belonged to the south. BN lat. 4403[A] is, however, one notable exception, and it may be more accurate simply to state that this abridged text of Isidore on the law in either form is part of the judicial development and school curriculum of the Frankish kingdoms generally.

In a school text such as BN lat. 4403[A], it is to be assumed that the *Breviarium Alarici* would be regarded as the principal source for basic legal principles which would augment the simple definitions provided in the Isidore *florilegium*, as well as providing a substantial basis for instruction in the law. Thus the second part of the codex comprises the *Breviarium Alarici*. In most copies of this the sections of *Interpretatio* are included in the text, headed *Intp* or *Interpretatio*. In this copy, however, these sections have been indicated as such after the completion of the text, in order to make the arrangement of the text clearer to the un-initiated. The annotations are a further interesting feature of the book. There are two, possibly three, near contemporary annotators; a dark-brown annotator who also wrote in black ink, and the 'green' anno-tator. The annotations are written in a Merovingian cursive similar to – albeit less formal than – that on fos. 179–84 and 126v–127r.

The brown and black annotators insert explanation, and expansions of abbreviations, into the text, insertions which sometimes seem to imply a knowledge at first hand of another text of these laws. In the second column on fo.29v, for example, above the fourth chapter entitled *De denuntiatione vel edictione scribti* is written *H(oc) e(st) ut causae pupillor(um) ibi discutiantur ubi eoru(m)*. On fo.30v, *De corionum* is glossed *id est de curialium*. These and other additions are all made to the table of contents, thus making it more informative. There is also some attempt on the part of the annotator to clarify the meaning and make it more comprehensible for the social context within which the law would be applied. The chapters relating to clerical affairs pass unnoted, but at the section from Majorian entitled *De abrogatis capitibus*, the anno-tator has written *iniustis legis divi Maioriani*. The annotator also noted sections which had been omitted from the table of contents. Throughout the text are many *signes de renvoi*, an indication of attentive reading.

The most interesting annotations are those of the 'green' annotator, first appearing on fo.51r.[15] Most of these are of the summarising kind,

---

[15] G. Haenel, *Lex Romana Visigothorum* (Leipzig, 1849), describes all the manuscripts containing the *Breviarium Alarici* and the digests of it.

either describing the contents or in the form of a summary heading for a section. The chapter beginning *Clericos quoque praecepit ut negotiationes nullatenus exercere praesumant* on fo.144r, for example, is glossed *Ut clericus negotiator non sit*. Many of the green notes are in the sections dealing with litigations and the actual administration of the law, but it is especially significant that most of the green notes appear only in the *Pauli Sententiae*, that section of the *Breviarium* most concerned with general legal principles and procedures and thus most suited for the teaching of the law. Some of the green notes are simply glosses, but as they are selective, they indicate which texts were found interesting and important. Thus the section on female inheritance, the position of women within the law, the responsibilities of judges, military prescriptions, wills and testaments are all noted. Sections such as those on public works or on bishops, churches and clerics are not glossed at all. The notes cease after fo.202v. This manuscript therefore could well have been used for teaching law to potential clerks and notaries – whether at a monastic school or a layman's court cannot be determined, though the former is the more likely.

BN lat.4404 on the other hand is a *de luxe* edition of the *Breviarium Alarici*, the older, Merovingian, recension of the *Lex Salica*, the B text of the *Leges Alemannorum* and the A text of the *Lex Ribuaria*, which presumably belonged to a magnate or court official, probably in the south or south-east of the kingdom. It is a codex such as the Counts Eberhard of Friuli or Eccard of Mâcon might have possessed.[16]

A note by Étienne Baluze states that the manuscript came from *Gallia Narbonensis*, but there is no other clue concerning its origin. It is a large, handsome volume, measuring 340 mm × 233 mm, which has been savagely cropped by its binders so that the written page is close to the edge and some of the annotations as well as most of the running titles have been cut off. The text is written in a fine, clear, early ninth-century Caroline minuscule, whose clarity and grace accord ill with the primitive though charming figures with which it is illustrated. The illustrations are coloured brown, yellow and orange. On fo.1v, in the centre of the page, there is a full length portrait of Theodosius II, carrying his book of laws, flanked by Valentinian and two other anonymous legislators. A decorated border encloses these figures, and

---

[16] G. Becker, *Catalogi Bibliothecarum Antiqui* (Bonn, 1885), p. 29; and M. Prou and A. Vidier, *Receuil des chartes de l'Abbaye de Saint-Benoît-sur-Loire*, 1 (Paris, 1907), p. 59. See too P. Riché, 'Les Bibliothèques de trois aristocrates laïques', *Le Moyen Age*, LXIX (1963), pp. 87-104.

some birds resembling peacocks and geese frolic in the margins. The opposite page, fo.2r, has portraits of other compilers of the law included in the volume, namely Severus, Gaius, Paul and Hermogenianus. Birds decorating the margins are only visible from the neck up, the rest having been cut away. The chapter titles are written inside elegant decorated arches reminiscent of the canon tables of Carolingian Gospel Books. Here they are formed from the tongues, sprouting either leaves or feathers, of two animal heads at the base of each side of the arch. The illustrations generally resemble those of the Sacramentary of Gellone.[17]

After Alaric's preface to the *Breviarium* comes a short paragraph, presumably written by the compiler and scribe who calls himself *peregrinus*, informing the reader of all that he has put in the volume. He has, he states, included the extracts from Theodosius, the *Pauli Sententiae* and the other authors which make up the *Breviarium*, and is quite exact concerning their content. After these he has copied the *Pactus legis salicae*, the Alemannian and Ripuarian codes, the edicts of Childebert and Chlothar and of the 'lord Emperor Charles'. (These are the supplementary decrees of the *Lex Salica*.) He then exhorts the book's user:

Hos lege tu lector felix feliciter omnes, et tu qui legis peregrini mei in bonis memento dilectissimae frater.

The text of the laws starts on fo.14v, with the chapter titles from the table of contents repeated as headings for each chapter. There are some corrections in a slightly later hand. The manuscript has also been marked with various *nota* symbols, presumably by the owner. All those portions of the *Interpretationes* to the laws which he found interesting or relevant have been marked with the word *signum* or *signum titulis* in a notarial cursive with a very tall long-s. Sometimes he used a small capital s, sometimes both, one at the beginning and one at the end of the paragraph to be noted. Most of these signs are set against the clauses in the *Institutes* and *Novellae* concerning the duties and functions of various government officials, and in particular those clauses concerning judges and the administration of justice. For example, the reader has marked the chapters *De officio praefectorum, De officio rectoris provintiae* on fos. 16r and 16v, as well as the following section which discusses *iudices* at

[17] B. Teyssedre, *Le Sacrementaire de Gellone et la figure humaine dans les manuscrits francs du viiie siècle* (Toulouse, 1959).

length. On fo.19r the sign marks the clauses concerning jurisdiction, the places where cases should be heard and the obligations of judges when administering justice. The section on the hearings held by judges in criminal cases and the responsibility of the judge to uphold the authority of the written law was also noted. Further on in the text the sign is set against the paragraphs dealing with litigation, invalid witnesses and the various complexities of inheritance. The marriage laws, fos.28–30, are thickly marked with the *signum*. The section *De Iudiciis* itself, and the paragraphs defining crimes, punishments and accusations, together with the question of Christians with Jewish slaves and the Jewish Sabbath are all noted.

The next portions of the text to engage the reader's attention were those to do with possessions and their disposal on the death of the owner, and those on ecclesiastical matters such as the chapters *Lex haec speciali ordine praecepit ut de clericis non exactores non allectus facere* and *De Testamentis clericorum*. Many sections of the *Pauli Sententiae* are glossed too, such as the clauses dealing with the *via publica*, judgment and the taking of an oath.

The Roman laws are the only part of the codex to have been marked with the *signum*. The Germanic laws and edicts are devoid of any *nota* symbols. It is possible therefore that the magnate who owned the book was required to administer justice in an area where the majority of the population lived according to Roman law, and where there were, if one can deduce anything from the attention paid to references to Jews, some Jews as well. The inclusion of the Germanic codes suggests that these were required as well, but that the owner's principle interest was in the actual conduct of his office. It should be noted in particular that while the decoration of the opening pages of the *Lex Salica* and *Lex Ribuaria* is comparatively modest, the first page of the *Leges Alemannorum* is illustrated with a full-page portrait of *Lodhanri rex et dux Alemannorum* together with three little figures representing the thirty-three bishops, thirty-three dukes, seventy-two counts and the rest of the great multitude, again with the exhortation *Hos lege tu lector*. The Alemannian duke is thus represented in much the same way as Theodosius. Such a dignity accorded one barbarian leader suggests that the owner himself could have been an Alemannian and that a number of his subjects also lived according to the Alemannian code. The sheer size, weight and dignity of the codex suggest that the owner heard cases in his own court. Here at least is a judge who had every intention of being conscientious in his administration of justice.[18]

Another codex probably owned by a count or royal official is BN lat.4418. It is very large indeed, measuring 430 mm × 290 mm, possibly the size BN lat.4404 was before it was cropped. The manuscript has undergone extensive repairs, particularly to the edges of the pages. It was in de Thou's library before it came to the Royal library. Buchner dated it late ninth-century and suggested it came from the south of France.[19] Its elegant and large format, the care taken over its ruling and the preparation of the parchment, and the dignity of the script with full use of uncials and square capitals as display scripts make it a fine volume. It contains the *Epitome Aegidii*, a shortened form of the *Breviarium*, as well as the *Epitome Iuliani*, a digest of the constitutions of Justinian. The latter text is written in long lines in contrast to the double columns in the rest of the book. Within this section a *nota* symbol, a large capital N with a very long curved right-hand shaft, occurs. It is set opposite chapters XIII, XIV, and XVI which concern the procedures by which one becomes a monk and the length of the noviate, and what happens when someone who has entered a monastic community changes his mind and wishes to leave it. One may wonder at the train of thought of this annotator.

In the B text of the *Lex Ribuaria* there are some annotations on fos. 142v and 143r, but most of them have been cut away. What remains indicates that they are a note on sources, and in a much later hand. Corrections and glosses, possibly in a slightly later hand than the main text, have been made to the *Lex Salica* which follows. This is the corrected edition known as the *Karolina*.[20] In the section on pig-stealing, for example, a gloss is added to the effect that the *porcellum* is one of the house animals. Sometimes the glosses are of an even simpler nature. On fo.157v the phrase *si quis puellam quaedruchte* has *quaedruchte* underlined and glossed: *id est quam sponsatam duxerit*, and on fo.166v, *sigibarones* is glossed *dicuntur quasi senatores*.

On fo.191r there is a short tract very like the one in BN lat.4403[A]

<hr/>

[18] Unlike some of the judges described by Theodulph of Orleans in his *Versus contra Iudices*, MGH, Poet.lat.aevi.karol., I, pp. 493–517. See also his *Comparatio legis antiquae et modernae*, *ibid.*, pp. 517–20; and H. Liebeschütz, 'Theodulph of Orleans and the problem of the Carolingian Renaissance', in D. J. Gordon, ed., *Fritz Saxl 1890–1948* (London, 1957), pp. 77–93.

[19] F. Beyerle and R. Buchner, *Lex Ribuaria*, MGH, LL, nat.germ., III.ii., p. 36.

[20] K. A. Eckhardt, *Pactus Legis Salicae*, MGH, LL, nat.germ., IV.i., esp. pp. xviii–xxvi.

entitled *De instrumentis legalibus*, containing some extracts from Isidore, and which includes the following definition:

Lex est emula divinitatis antistitis religionis fons disciplinarum artifex iuris boni mores inveniens atque conponens gubernaculum civitatis iustitiae nuntia magistra vitae magis anima totius corporis populari.

BN lat.4417 may also have belonged to a royal official or a *missus dominicus*. It is a very fine codex, measuring 221 mm × 140 mm, written in an upright well-spaced minuscule probably of the last decades of the ninth century, and with some illuminated initials. It was given to Colbert in 1681.[21] Like the other codices, this one has been read assiduously and annotated in the margins, the most obvious sign being a distinctive *nota* symbol of a majuscule N with O and T super-imposed on the right-hand shaft. This sign answers a group of three dots in the text. The first part of the book contains again the *Epitome Aegidii*, and the *nota* sign first appears against a clause dealing with the rights of inheritance for daughters. Another comes in the section on administration, and negligence on the part of the *tutor*. The section on legitimate heirs has a great many *nota* symbols, particularly against those sections, curiously enough, which deal with the position of women.

A collection of the Germanic laws follows, including the B text of the *Lex Ribuaria*, the B text of the *Leges Alemannorum*[22] and the *emendata* text of the *Leges Baiuvariorum*. Frankish royal capitularies, written in a different hand in a new section, are appended. These include a Group I text of the capitulary collection of Ansegisus up to Book IV, 10,[23] and additional capitularies such as *Additamenta* to the *Lex Salica* and some of the decrees promulgated at Worms in 829. The prominence of the Ripuarian laws in this codex and the capitularies from Worms suggest that the manuscript was written for a count or royal official in Austrasia, who had a lively interest in the law insofar as it actually concerned him.

The next group of manuscripts to be discussed are those containing the *Lex Salica* and other Germanic codes, sometimes with some Roman law. The Germanic or barbarian laws are folk codes and personal codes given the force of law by the king. The king would often add pro-

[21] For a short description of the manuscript's contents see B. Krusch, *Die Lex Baiuvariorum* (Berlin, 1924), p. 102.
[22] K. Lehmann and K. A. Eckhardt, *Leges Alemannorum*, MGH, LL, nat. germ., v.i., pp. 55–157.
[23] K. Christ, 'Die Schlossbibliothek von Nikolsburg und die Überlieferung der Kapitularien-sammlung des Ansegis', *Deutsches Archiv*, I (1937), pp. 281–323.

visions to them; there are, for example, capitularies of Charlemagne and Louis the Pious which add clauses to the *Lex Salica*. They are pre-eminently penal codes with some clauses of civil and property law and information on procedure. It is probably this limitation in their application which led to their inclusion alongside both royal capitularies and Roman law in the codices. It was the *Lex Salica* which acquired a rather greater authority than the other codes, and a revised version of seventy chapters, the *Lex Salica Karolina*, was produced under Charlemagne after 800. Capitularies containing additions to the *Lex Salica* after Clovis, such as the *Pactum pro tenore pacis* of Childebert I and Chlothar I (511–58) and the *Edictum Chilperici* (561–84), were gradually incorporated into the main text.

BN nouv.acq.lat.204 is one of many codices containing the *Lex Salica Karolina*. It is a defective codex, large portions of the text having been extracted. Between fos.22v and 23r for example, four folios have been cut out. It measures 247 mm × 184 mm and contains, now, 95 folios. Its script is a well-written Caroline minuscule which could be of the middle decades of the ninth century, though some have wished to date it rather later. Appended to the *Lex Salica* are a number of the capitularies of Louis the Pious, followed by the B text of the *Leges Alemannorum*, the *emendata* text of the *Lex Baiuvariorum*, the *Lex Burgundionum*, a charter of Louis the Pious dated 822 and a formula for dues to be paid to a monastery from a Tours *formulae* collection. The last text is a portion of the *Epitome Aegidii* which has been associated with Tours.[24] This manuscript would appear then to be a compendium of the national laws of the *Regnum Francorum* written in the region of Tours.

BN lat.4628 is a fairly small late ninth-century book (220 mm × 160 mm); its pages are worn and the writing faded as if the book had been subject to constant use. There is some decoration, including a roughly ornamented initial on fo.1r. It contains the *Lex Salica Karolina*, the capitulary adding to the *Lex Salica* promulgated under Louis the Pious, and a capitulary addressed to the imperial *missi*, the first clause of which enjoins the *missi* to administer justice. On fo.49v are two rather drastic-sounding cures for epilepsy scrawled in a later hand, followed on fo.50r by the B texts of the *Lex Ribuaria* and the *Leges Alemannorum*. On fo.66v is an extraordinary drawing, possibly added later, of two standing figures with strange wild features and remarkable

[24] See Krusch, *Die Lex Baiuvariorum*, pp. 105–6.

head-dresses. One stands in the background, while the other expostulates to a suave, elegantly dressed count or *missus*, who sits calmly listening to him. This handbook of the national laws may once have belonged to a royal official in the northern parts of the kingdom.

Another small legal handbook is BN lat.4629, which includes a number of non-legal texts which suggest it was a school book. As well as the E text of the *Lex Salica* and the Edict of Childebert, there is a detailed explanation on fo.15r of the various additions made to the Salic law, a selection of the Carolingian additions to this law, and the A text of the *Lex Ribuaria*. On fo.15v there is a short treatise in the question and answer form entitled *Incipit questio de trinitate* and beginning *Quomodo credis dominum. Rep. Trinum et unum. Int. Quomodo trinum et quomodo unum. Rs. Trinum in personis et unum in deitate.* After it is a treatise on virtue beginning *Quid est initio virtutis. R. Non facere malum.* These same two pietistic and didactic texts occur in Berlin 161 (Phillipps 1736) referred to above, in which they form part of a royal official's legal handbook. At the end of the manuscript, however, but in a slightly later hand, is a short treatise on orthography. It is possible therefore that the manuscript was indeed originally in the possession of a lay royal official, but that additions were made to it when it was later used as a school text. This impression is reinforced by the nature of the additions themselves; these include a letter telling the recipient that this little manual has been prepared for his use so that he may attain a measure of goodness in his daily secular life, an epitaph in verse for an abbot, and a much later epigram on *caritas*.

BN lat.4788 is another book which possibly belonged to a count responsible for the administration of justice in an area where the *Lex Salica* was observed. It is so worn and mutilated as to be almost illegible, the pages full of holes and very thin. Enough writing remains to indicate that this little book, measuring only 140 mm × 120 mm is a pocket copy of the *Lex Salica*, with the possible addition of the *Capitula quae in legem Salicam mittenda sunt (sic)*.

A manuscript once in the possession of Antoine Loisel, on the other hand, BN lat.18237 (*olim* Notre Dame 252), appears to have been intended as a school book from the start. It is a small quarto of 144 folios, written in a careful Caroline minuscule of the second half of the ninth century, with titles in red rustic capitals. The parchment is fairly stout. It contains some annotations but these are of the eighteenth or nineteenth century. Large portions of the text are missing and paper leaves have been inserted to supply what is missing (though this they fall far short of doing). The manuscript contains the C text of the *Lex Salica*, a text closely related to the Merovingian recension and an incomplete text of the capitulary collection of Ansegisus starting at the chapter headed *De Iudicibus*. Most of these are the capitularies concerning ecclesiastical matters. Following the excerpts from Isidore of Seville on the law similar to those described in BN lat.4403[A], is a short *florilegium* on kinship, mostly from Isidore, and illustrated on fo.114v by a detailed diagram showing the familial relations.[25] This combination of texts, and the general appearance of the book, make it likely that it was indeed a school book, designed to teach general legal principles and the laws of the Frankish kings. The *Leges Alemannorum* at the end of the volume, fos.121r–126v, a fragment only, is from another manuscript. It was a fine one, written in large clear minuscule with a great many decorated initials.

The manuscripts here selected for discussion represent only a small number of the legal codices and the number of variant texts extant. Yet they are what was available to the Franks. However imperfect the texts and simplified the legal treatises and basic principles, these books were the only form in which the Carolingians could read their law, learn from it, teach with it, and resort to it for guidance in administration and passing judgment. Like the collections of capitularies and conciliar decrees which I have discussed elsewhere,[26] there is rarely an official code of either the Germanic or the Roman laws available in the Carolingian period. A reasonably successful attempt to produce such an official code can be seen in the revision of the *Lex Salica*; customary law was ultimately of greater influence and significance than Roman law. Generally, however, it is apparent that local needs determined what proportion of the laws available would be used, while the codification of these laws depended in great measure on personal initiative, on the acceptance of the authority of the written word promoted by Charlemagne, and on a knowledge of the law. In this respect the schools were crucially important. There both legal principles and familiarity with the texts were taught. With the gradual increase in knowledge and development of the law can be associated the treatises on government and kinship. The number of both legal codices and of

[25] A reproduction of this diagram is to be found in Liber XI, 28 of W. M. Lindsay, ed., *Isidori Hispalensis Episcopi Etymologiarum sive Originum* (Oxford, 1911).
[26] Rosamond McKitterick, *Frankish Church*, ch. 1.

Fürstenspiegel increases rapidly during the reign of Louis the Pious, and more notably, during that of Charles the Bald. BN nouv.acq.lat.1632, a mid-ninth-century codex possibly from Fleury, which contains two short treatises entitled *Quid sit proprie ministerium regis* and *Capitula diversarum sententiarum pro negociis rei publice consulendis*, is just one illustration of the absorbing interest in the theory of the law in the Carolingian period, and in particular, how ruling and government were seen to be, quite unequivocally, only feasible and honourable in terms of the law.

Because of the smallness of the group described here, it has not been possible to discuss the extent or type of legal book production in any one area at a given time. As knowledge of the date and provenance of the Carolingian law-books grows and is combined with the detailed information concerning each recension and type of text of all the laws, Germanic and Roman, it will be possible to have a clearer and more precise understanding of the law, its use, production and transmission in the Frankish kingdom in the eighth and ninth centuries.

THE EARLIEST SURVIVING ROYAL *ORDO*: SOME LITURGICAL AND HISTORICAL ASPECTS*

by JANET L. NELSON

IN HIS OWN CONTRIBUTION to the *Festschrift* for P. E. Schramm, Walter Ullmann wrote with characteristic generosity of Schramm's 'brilliant accomplishments' in the field of *Ordinesforschung*, and modestly offered his own remarkable paper as 'only a note' thereto.[1] I now offer the following further note, which consists in part of a revision of some of Schramm's work but would have been inconceivable without it, as a tribute to the no less brilliant accomplishments of Walter Ullmann himself. He will know just how much it owes to his inspiration.

Schramm began his study of the Anglo-Saxon *Ordines*[2] by distinguishing between, on the one hand, the date at which royal anointing was introduced and the king-making ritual in part assumed a liturgical form, and, on the other, the date at which a fixed rite was established and written down as an *Ordo*. While acknowledging the relevance of this distinction (in this paper I confine myself to the *Ordines*) and the possibility of such a time-lag, I would stress a further distinction between the date at which a fixed rite was used and the date of its earliest surviving manuscripts. That these may differ widely is the first and fundamental lesson that historians have to learn from liturgists. The *Ordo* Schramm identified as the earliest English one survives today in three manuscripts: Oxford, Bodleian MS 579 (the so-called Leofric Missal), Paris, Bibliothèque Nationale MS lat.10575 (the so-called Egbert Pontifical), and Rouen, Bibliothèque Municipale MS A.27 (the

* I am very grateful to Herr Josef Kirschner for kindly allowing me to draw on his work before it was published; to Mr Christopher Hohler for commenting on an earlier draft of this paper; and especially to Professor Dorothy Whitelock for her usual unstinting help.

[1] 'Der Souveränitätsgedanke in den mittelalterlichen Krönungsordines', in *Festschrift Schramm*, ed. P. Classen and P. Scheibert (2 vols., Wiesbaden, 1964), I, p. 72.

[2] 'Die Krönung bei den Westfranken und Angelsachsen von 878 bis um 1000', ZRG Kan., XXIII (1934), pp. 117–242, now reprinted with some additional references in Schramm's collected papers, *Kaiser, Könige und Päpste* (4 vols., Stuttgart, 1968), II, pp. 140–248. All my references below are to the latter reprint of the 1934 article.

Lanalet Pontifical).[3] In the case of the Egbert Pontifical, liturgists had long since pointed to a time-lag between the date of the manuscript, *c.*1000, and the date of its contents, allegedly the mid-eighth century; but because the arguments adduced in this case were unsound,[4] Schramm was able to ignore not only them but also their methodological implications for the treatment of liturgical materials in general. The Lanalet Pontifical is now usually assigned to the later tenth or early eleventh century. As for the Leofric Missal, Schramm followed its editor in believing this manuscript to have been written in Lotharingia *c.*900 but claimed, idiosyncratically, that its royal *Ordo* was among the additions made to the book in England *c.*969.[5]

Schramm's conclusions, which he emphasised were based on a manuscript tradition going back to 'the tenth century and no earlier', were first, that although royal anointing was practised in England 'from 787 onwards' no fixed rite existed until the 960s, and second, that the *Ordo* of the Leofric Missal (hereafter 'Leofric') represented a 'first draft' and the *Ordo* of the other two manuscripts (hereafter 'Egbert'/'Lanalet') a revised and amplified version of a royal *Ordo* drawn up by St Dunstan 'between 960 and 973' but never actually used. These two main conclusions, repeated in Schramm's *History of the English Coronation*

---

[3] The Leofric Missal was edited by F. E. Warren (Oxford, 1883), the *Benedictiones super regem noviter electum* there pp. 230–2 (I hope to justify below my application of the term *Ordo* to this series of benedictions, which form a full rite of royal inauguration including anointing); the Pontifical of Egbert by W. Greenwell, Surtees Society vol. XXVII (Durham, 1853), the consecration-rite (*Benedictio*) there pp. 100–5; the Lanalet Pontifical by G. H. Doble, Henry Bradshaw Society vol. LXXIV (London, 1937), the rite there (with only the *incipits* of the prayers appearing also in the *Benedictional of Archbishop Robert*, ed. H. A. Wilson, Henry Bradshaw Society vol. XXIV (London, 1903)) pp. 59–63. Schramm, *Kaiser*, pp. 223–33, gives further details and prints the *Ordo*, giving some (not all) variants of these three texts and of a fourth, the royal consecration-rite in the eleventh-century Pontifical of Milan, ed. M. Magistretti (Milan, 1897), pp. 112–19, in which a rite of the above type is spliced in with the West Frankish 'Seven-Forms'. C. A. Bouman, *Sacring and Crowning* (Groningen, 1957), pp. 9–15, 23–4, gives further details and supplies some corrections to Warren's and Greenwell's editions. Clearly, a new edition of the *Ordo* is urgently needed. I have been able to consult the Paris MS and photographs of the Oxford one. I dealt with this *Ordo* at length in my unpublished dissertation, 'Rituals of Royal Inauguration in Early Medieval Europe' (Cambridge, 1967), ch. 5, for which the inspiration and careful supervision of Walter Ullmann must here be gratefully acknowledged. I wish to make clear, however, that some of the views expressed therein, especially on the early English *Ordines* (briefly indicated in my paper in *SCH*, VII (1971) pp. 49–50), were wrong, and that I have thoroughly revised them in what follows.

[4] At the beginning of the Paris MS appears material from penitential canons once attributed to Archbishop Egbert of York (734–66). But the attribution is very questionable and, as Schramm saw, need have no bearing on the date of the Pontifical proper.

[5] For the most recent opinions on the date and character of all three books, see D. H. Turner, *The Claudius Pontificals*, Henry Bradshaw Society vol. XCVII (1971, issued for the year 1964), pp. xvi–xxviii, xxxiii; and C. Hohler, 'Some Service Books of the Later Saxon Church', in D. Parsons, ed., *Tenth-Century Studies* (London, 1975), pp. 60–83, 217–27 (notes).

(Oxford, 1937) and more recently in his collected papers, *Kaiser, Könige und Päpste*, continue to be accepted by leading historians of Anglo-Saxon England.[6] Yet work already published before 1934 (some of it then unknown to Schramm) as well as subsequent critical studies show both Schramm's conclusions to be untenable. They have survived partly through a regrettable lack of contact between liturgists and general historians, partly through the magic of Schramm's name reinforced, notably, by the magic of Sir Frank Stenton's, and partly through the coincidence that Schramm's two liturgist-critics, P. E. Ward[7] and C. A. Bouman (the latter unfortunately writing in ignorance of Ward's work), both abandoned academic life after publishing relatively little. It is now clear that the methods of *Diplomforschung*, which Schramm quite explicitly applied to the medieval *Ordines*, are simply not appropriate for liturgical documents.[8] In what follows, taking up some problems where Ward and Bouman left off and drawing on more recent liturgists' work, I attempt a long-overdue revision of Schramm's views and offer an alternative hypothesis which, whatever historical questionmarks it leaves, at least does no violence to the liturgical evidence.

I. THE 'LEOFRIC' 'ORDO' AND ITS RELATIONSHIP TO THE 'ORDO' OF JUDITH

Ward already observed against Schramm that the royal *Ordo* belongs to that part of the Leofric Missal which was written *c*.900.[9] 'Leofric' therefore could not have been Dunstan's work. But how much earlier than *c*.900 was such an *Ordo* in existence? The earliest securely dated royal *Ordo* is that used for Judith, Charles the Bald's daughter, as queen of the West Saxons when she married Æthelwulf in 856.[10] Schramm classed this *Ordo* as West Frankish,[11] not Anglo-Saxon,

[6] See F. M. Stenton, *Anglo-Saxon England*, 3rd edn (Oxford, 1971), p. 368; C. J. Godfrey, *The Church in Anglo-Saxon England* (Cambridge, 1962), p. 382; H. G. Richardson and G. O. Sayles, *The Governance of Medieval England* (Edinburgh, 1963), pp. 398-9.

[7] 'The Coronation Ceremony in Medieval England', *Speculum*, xiv (1939), pp. 160-78; 'An Early Version of the Anglo-Saxon Coronation Ceremony', *EHR*, lvii (1942), pp. 345-61.

[8] For excellent suggestions on method, see Bouman, *Sacring*, pp. 50-89; R. Elze, ed., *Ordines Coronationis Imperialis*, MGH, Fontes Iuris Germanici Antiqui, ix (Hanover, 1960), pp. xxiv-xxxv.

[9] Ward, 'Coronation Ceremony', pp. 162-3.

[10] *Benedictio super reginam quam Edelulfus rex accepit in uxorem*, ed. from a now lost Liège MS by J. Sirmond, *Hincmari archiepiscopi remensis opera* (Paris, 1645), I, pp. 741-4; reprinted in MGH, Capit. II, no. 296, pp. 425-7. (The couple were married at Verberie).

[11] 'Ordines-Studien II: die Krönung in Frankreich', *Archiv für Urkundenforschung*, xv (1938), p. 8.

attributing not only its structure but also its prayer-forms to Hincmar's authorship and ignoring the question of what sources Hincmar might have drawn on in existing regal liturgies, whether Frankish or English. Scholars have long been aware that 'Leofric' and 'Judith' are related. Schramm, asserting the priority of 'Judith', neglected the important article of Armitage Robinson, where the case for the priority of the king's *Ordo* was soundly based on careful comparison of the prayer-texts, showing the 'Judith' forms to be adaptations, those of 'Leofric' original.[12] Bouman produced some additional evidence pointing the same way, but he was very cautious about attributing a date pre-856 to 'the "Leofric" formulary as a whole', insisting only that some of the regal blessing-formulae which compose it were available in 856.[13]

As I hope to show, Robinson was substantially correct. But neither he nor Bouman really disposed of Schramm's main argument for the priority of a queen's *Ordo* over the king's: namely, the appearance in 'Leofric' of two passages which Schramm diagnosed as borrowings from the *Consecratio virginum* of the Gelasian Sacramentary[14] – proof enough, he claimed, of the dependence of 'Leofric' upon 'Judith', 'for how could anyone in the case of a king have conceived the idea of putting a prayer over virgins at the base of the *Ordo*?'[15] What are these alleged borrowings? First, Schramm observed that the *incipit* of the opening prayer of 'Leofric', 'Te invocamus domine sancte pater omnipotens aeterne deus', is paralleled in the Gelasian and Gregorian Sacramentaries only in the *Oratio super ancillas Dei*. Second, in the prayer 'Benedic domine hunc presulem principem', there are three clauses almost identical with a passage in the *Consecratio virginum*. (It was because these clauses do not in fact appear in 'Judith', as we have it, that Schramm felt forced to hypothesise a lost 'fuller version' – for whose existence there is otherwise no evidence at all.) Schramm's argument has, at first sight, considerable force: even if another possible source for *either* of the two passages in question could be found,

[12] J. A. Robinson, 'The Coronation Order in the Tenth Century', *JTS*, XIX (1918), pp. 56–72, esp. pp. 62–3. Schramm had discovered this article by 1938 when he listed it, without comment, in a bibliography in 'Ordines-Studien III: die Krönung in England', *Archiv für Urkunden-forschung*, XV (1938), p. 308. It is important to stress that in reprinting his 1934 paper in 1968, Schramm did not take the opportunity for any serious revision, merely citing Robinson's article, *Kaiser*, p. 169, n. 1, with the comment: 'seine Feststellungen sind – wie ich hoffe – durch meine Feststellungen überholt'(!).

[13] *Sacring*, pp. 100–3, 110–11, 153.

[14] Ed. L. C. Mohlberg, *Liber Sacramentorum Romanae Ecclesiae Ordinis Anni Circuli*. (*Sacramentarium Gelasianum*), Rerum Ecclesiasticarum Documenta, Series maior, Fontes IV (Rome, 1958), p. 126.   [15] 'Ordines-Studien III', p. 9, n. 3.

Schramm's explanation, relying on a single source as the model for *both*, would remain the most parsimonious one. But close examination of the liturgical sources shows Schramm's to be a false economy. In the borrowed clauses of 'Benedic domine', there are two critical variant readings, one of which occurs in the Gelasian *Consecratio virginum* but not in the Gregorian, the other in the Gregorian but not the Gelasian.[16] Only in the Leonine Sacramentary (*Veronense*) do both these variants occur: yet the *incipit* 'Te invocamus' does not appear in the Leonine virgins' prayer.[17] Thus, since we cannot in any event manage with fewer than two sources for these borrowings, we do better to deal separately with them.

'Te invocamus' is an *incipit* rare but not unparalleled in the Visigothic *Liber Ordinum*,[18] where it occurs, for instance, in the *Oratio ad barbas tondendas*, part of what in the Spanish book is still a coming-of-age rite adopted by the early church from pagan Rome.[19] In the Gelasian Sacramentary, a similar prayer has become associated with clerical orders. A comparison of these prayers with the opening benediction of 'Leofric' is suggestive:

Lib. Ord.	Gel.	'Leofric'
Te invocamus, aeterne omnipotens deus, ut abundantia fontis tuae benedicas hunc famulum tuum illum . . . Postea: Oratio . . . respice propitius . . . ut per huius benedictionis copiam ad iuvenilem se etatem pervenire congaudeat letabundus . . . ut . . . gratiam per manus inpositionem accipiat, sicut David per manus Samuelis accepit quod in apostolorum tuorum tipo prefiguratum est.	Deus cuius providentia creatura omnes crementes adulta congaudet, propitius super hunc famulum tuum iuvenilia aetatis decorem laetantem et florem primis auspiciis adtundentem . . .[20]	Te invocamus, d.s.p.o.a.d., ut hunc famulum tuum quem tuae divine dispensationis providentia . . . usque ad hunc presentem diem iuvenili flore laetantem crescere concessisti . . .

[16] Gregorian, ed. J. Deshusses, *Le Sacramentaire Grégorien*, Spicilegium Friburgense, XVI (Freiburg, 1971), p. 420: 'tu in merore solatium', where the Gelasian reads 'consolatio'. But the words 'In te habeat omnia' in the Gelasian have disappeared from the Gregorian version.

[17] Ed. C. Mohlberg, *Sacramentarium Veronense*, R.E.D., Fontes I (Rome, 1956), pp. 139–40.

[18] Ed. M. Férotin, *Monumenta Ecclesiae Liturgica*, V (Paris, 1904), p. 294. On such related expressions as 'Te rogamus', etc., see E. Bishop, 'Liturgical Note' to *The Book of Cerne*, ed. A. B. Kuypers (Cambridge, 1902), p. 258. See also Bouman, *Sacring*, p. 58, n. 1, for 'domine sancte pater . . .' etc. as 'a commonplace of euchology'.

[19] Ed. Férotin, p. 37. See A. Chavasse, *Le Sacramentaire Gélasien* (Tournai, 1958), pp. 451–2.

[20] Ed. Mohlberg, p. 229.

Regrettably, no comparable Leonine *Oratio* exists: if it did, we might have found here further evidence for the link which Coebergh traced between the sixth-century Roman liturgy and early Spanish texts.[21] In any case, it seems just as plausible to suggest that the author of the regal blessing drew on a coming-of-age rite as on a nun's consecration, especially if he were writing at a time and place in which Spanish texts could well have been available.

In fact the Spanish and insular affinities of the first two 'Leofric' prayers ('Te invocamus' and 'In diebus', Bouman suggests, were originally one)[22] are so obvious as to strike any open-minded reader. Spanish and insular 'symptoms' abound: *plasmatum*; *de die in diem . . . ad meliora proficere*; *pax et securitas*; the antithesis *cor–corpus*.[23] Relevant also are those Leonine affinities which C. Hohler now shows to be characteristic of insular as well as Spanish liturgies.[24] Schramm preferred to see 'In diebus' as a *Virtuosenstück* of a kind 'beloved by the age of Charles the Bald',[25] but he adduced no evidence in support of this statement, and the *liturgical* sources of that period will not, I think, afford any. Bouman was equally disinclined to see the obvious: noting the pronounced use of alliteration in these two prayers, he admitted that 'we might be tempted to regard the phenomenon . . . as an indication of their insular origin', but he resisted temptation by stalwartly concentrating on a literary tradition that linked Sidonius and Venantius with ninth-century Frankish writers, and finally by appealing to Schramm's comment on 'the age of Charles the Bald'. But Bouman, on his own admission, started from the assumption that these prayers were West Frankish of the mid-ninth century, and then proceeded to find an 'argument of style . . . entirely consistent with that conclusion'. Thus again, he described 'Te invocamus' as 'a wordy *oratio* of the Frankish–German pattern', and 'In diebus' as possibly designed to be pronounced 'as a "Gallican" benediction'.[26] What neither Schramm nor Bouman recognised is that not a literary but a *liturgical* context is of primary

---

[21] C. Coebergh, 'Sacramentaire léonien et liturgie mozarabe', in *Miscellanea liturgica in honorem L. C. Mohlberg* (2 vols., Rome, 1948–9), II, pp. 295–304.

[22] *Sacring*, p. 102.

[23] See F. E. Warren, *The Liturgy and Ritual of the Celtic Church* (Oxford, 1881), p. 168, n. 1; Bishop, 'Liturgical Note', pp. 252–3; G. Manz, *Ausdrucksformen der lateinischen Liturgiesprachen bis ins 11 Jht.* (Beuron, 1941), pp. 23–9; A. Dold and L. Eizenhoefer, eds., *Das Irische Palimpsestsakramentar im Clm. 14429* (Beuron, 1964), p. 88; H. Porter, 'The Origin of the Medieval Rite for Anointing the Sick', *JTS*, n.s. VII (1956), p. 219.

[24] 'Service Books', pp. 79–80. Compare *idem*, 'The Type of Sacramentary used by St Boniface', in *Sankt Bonifatius Gedenkgabe* (Fulda, 1964), pp. 89–93.

[25] *Kaiser*, p. 174. [26] *Sacring*, pp. 60–1, 102.

relevance here. In relation to that context, Bouman's mention only of Frankish and Gallican parallels is dangerously misleading when in fact extended alliteration, rhymed cola and rhythmic cursus are all well-known stylistic features of Spanish and insular liturgies par excellence.[27] There is one further piece of evidence for the insular origin of 'In diebus': the prayer 'Deus qui sub tuae maiestatis arbitrio', which appears in the rite for an abbot's consecration and which is clearly modelled on the king's prayer 'In diebus', is present in no fewer than seven liturgical books of English origin, and *only* in these.[28] Though none of them predates the tenth century, the fact that the abbot's prayer was then so widely used in England implies its considerably earlier adaptation, also in England, from the regal text.

The second alleged 'borrowing' by the 'Leofric' redactor from the *Consecratio virginum* consists of three clauses in the series of benedictions beginning 'Benedic domine hunc presulem principem'.[29] If, as the variants here suggest, the source of these clauses was a Leonine rather than a Gelasian or Gregorian Sacramentary, this would itself imply early date and the possibility of insular provenance.[30] Further, the whole passage beginning 'Sit in eis' (including all our borrowed clauses) in the Leonine virgins' prayer may originally have existed separately as 'a traditional form of blessing on solemn occasions',[31] and thus lacked any specific connection with virgins only. Certainly its wider suitability is shown by its use for the blessings of widows, kings and abbots. Thus we need not follow Schramm in regarding the presence of these clauses as proof of the dependence of the 'Leofric' king's *Ordo* on 'Judith'. Study of early Christian rites of passage as a group shows, not surprisingly, that these were felt to contain a common

---

[27] The fundamental work remains Bishop, *Liturgica Historica* (Oxford, 1918), esp. pp. 163–202. See also W. Meyer, *Gesammelte Abhandlungen zur mittellateinischen Rhythmik* (2 vols., Berlin, 1905), I, pp. 178, 192–3; K. Polheim, *Die lateinische Reimprosa* (Berlin, 1925), pp. 309–11; L. Brou, 'Problèmes liturgiques chez Saint Isidore', in *Isidoriana* (León, 1961), pp. 193–209; Dold and Eizenhoefer, *Palimpsestsakramentar*, pp. 87–9. For the background, see J. N. Hillgarth, 'The East, Visigothic Spain and the Irish', *Studia Patristica*, IV (1961), pp. 442–56; *idem*, 'Visigothic Spain and Early Christian Ireland', *Proceedings of the Royal Irish Academy*, CXII (1962), pp. 167–94.

[28] Turner, *Claudius Pontificals*, pp. xxxvi–xxxvii. V. Leroquais, *Les Pontificaux Manuscrits des bibliothèques publiques de France* (4 vols., Paris, 1937), notes no further instance of this prayer.

[29] Schramm, *Kaiser*, p. 229: clauses l., m., n. and the beginning of o. ('amore te timeat et timore diligat. Tu ei honor sis, tu gaudium, tu voluntas . . .' etc.).

[30] Above, p. 34.

[31] O. G. Harrison, 'The Formulas "Ad virgines sacras". A Study of the Sources', *Ephemerides Liturgicae*, LXVI (1952), pp. 260–1. But R. Metz, *La Consécration des vierges dans l'église romaine* (Paris, 1954), p. 160, n. 81, remains sceptical.

quality, such that borrowings from one to another were thought apt: from baptism to monastic profession, from the bishop's consecration to the king's to the abbot's, from the abbess's to the queen's, and so forth.[32]

If Schramm's case for the priority of 'Judith' must be rejected, can the priority of the 'Leofric' *Ordo* as such be affirmed? Bouman thought it 'easier to date some of the formulas ... than the formulary as a whole'.[33] But he was needlessly cautious. The near-identical ordering of the prayers in 'Leofric' and 'Judith' cannot be coincidental. The model which Hincmar had before him in 856 opened with 'Te invocamus', which needed relatively little adaptation for a queen; and if, on Bouman's own showing, this prayer and 'In diebus' which follows it in 'Leofric' originally 'belong together', Hincmar could have had both available but bypassed the second because he was using 'Te invocamus' as a *prooemium* to the consecration prayer which he was now casting as a Preface on the pattern of other major rites.[34] Then the model gave the 'Leofric' anointing-prayer, 'Deus electorum', which had to be adapted, in a characteristically Hincmarian style, for a royal lady.[35] It seems likely that the model next included the 'Leofric' benediction-series beginning 'Benedic domine hunc presulem principem': Hincmar adapted its first clause for Judith – a fact unnoticed by Bouman.[36] Next in the model came the blessings 'Omnipotens deus det tibi' and 'Benedic domine fortitudinem': in these prayers, which in 'Leofric' consist wholly of scriptural quotations, the adaptation for Judith is especially obvious. The only 'Leofric' prayer which cannot be shown to have influenced 'Judith' is the last, 'Deus perpetuitatis', but it was associated with an enthronement-ritual which would not have been required at Verberie.[37] Otherwise, the content and structure of

---

[32] For some detailed references, see my papers in *SCH*, VII (1971), p. 44, n. 4; and *ibid.*, XI (1975), p. 46, no. 19.

[33] *Sacring*, p. 153.
[34] *Ibid.*, pp. 100–3.

[35] Compare the Old Testament paradigms introduced here with those of the *consecratio* in Hincmar's *Ordo* of 877. Of the two 'quaint words' in the adapted section noted by Bouman, *Sacring*, pp. 60, n. 1, and 111, as 'not in keeping with the sober and traditional vocabulary of the rest of the formula', *lucifluam* was used by Hincmar in the *Annales Bertiniani, s.a.* 868, while *efferatum* is biblical.

[36] The 'Leofric' series is largely borrowed from two eighth-century Gelasian regal benedictions. A further argument for the priority of 'Leofric' is thus the improbability of Hincmar's having drawn directly on the eighth-century Gelasian source for just one clause of 'Judith'.

[37] It was also used as an *Oratio super militantes*, which might have been thought inappropriate for Judith. The prayer's earliest appearance under this rubric was not, as Schramm and, surprisingly, Bouman (*Sacring*, p. 67) seem to have believed, in the Sacramentary of Fulda (*c.*950), but in the Leofric Missal on the very same folio as the royal *Ordo* itself: its last three

'Judith' implies not only, as Bouman suggested, that Hincmar's sources in 856 included some regal benedictions like those of 'Leofric', but that Hincmar had before him a series in precisely 'Leofric's' order and with the anointing-prayer occupying the same central place. If we add the negative evidence that Hincmar had to compose a coronation-prayer for Judith presumably because his model lacked one, we need no longer leave open Bouman's possibility that 'the Order [of 'Leofric'] as such may have been composed at a later date than 856'. In other words, a full king's *Ordo* of 'Leofric' type was in existence by the mid-ninth century.

II. WHERE DOES THE 'LEOFRIC' 'ORDO' COME FROM?

The editor of the Leofric Missal, F. E. Warren, was convinced that this was a Lotharingian manuscript. More recently, Ward has claimed on 'paleographical grounds' that the 'Leofric' *Ordo* was evidence for 'Flanders *ca.*900'. Bouman, independently, inferred that the regal benedictions in the Leofric book 'are undoubtedly of West Frankish origin' though remaining 'no more than an "outsider"' on the continental side of the Channel, while Robinson having established the dependence of 'Judith' on 'Leofric' thought that this showed the latter to have been 'current in Rheims before 856'.[38] Now since the material in a liturgical (or any other) manuscript may originate in a different location from that in which the manuscript itself was written, it may seem odd that none of these three scholars seriously considered the possibility that 'Leofric' was English. Perhaps embarrassed or irritated by the chauvinism (real or imagined) of earlier and insular writers,[39] Robinson, Ward and Bouman, and I myself until recently, were very ready to accept indications of a continental origin for the earliest extant royal *Ordo*. Fortunately Hohler has now addressed the

lines immediately precede the *Ordo*'s opening rubric on fo.302v. The prayer reappears, along with the two benedictions preceding it in 'Leofric', to form a *Benedictio principis*, following blessings of banner and weapons, in a twelfth-century Cracow Pontifical, ed. W. Abraham, in *Polska Akademja: Umiejetuosci Hist.-Fil. Rozprawy*. Ser. II, 41, no. 1 (Cracow, 1927), pp. 1–17; but according to Ward, 'Anglo-Saxon Coronation', p. 346, n. 3, this pontifical was written in Lotharingia. The quite large variants in the texts of 'Deus perpetuitatis' suggest wide currency, but its history, whether English or continental, before *c.* 900 remains unknown: the Leofric Missal shows it in use for both warrior and king, but who borrowed from whom?

[38] Ward, 'Coronation Ceremony', p. 163; Bouman, *Sacring*, pp. 10; 154; Robinson, 'Coronation Order', p. 63.

[39] E.g. W. Maskell, *Monumenta ritualia ecclesiae Anglicanae*, 2nd edn (3 vols., Oxford, 1882), II, pp. x–xi; H. A. Wilson, 'The English Coronation Orders', *JTS*, II (1901), pp. 481–504.

problem without inhibitions: after demonstrating the extreme complexity of the make-up of early liturgical books, he has argued that the Leofric Missal, though it contains Lotharingian and West Frankish material and is written in a continental hand, is in fact an English book, and that parts of it, especially in its 'pontifical' section, may be as old as the 'sixth or seventh century'.[40] Although Hohler himself has been concerned with the book as a whole rather than with the royal *Ordo* as such, his conclusions at once require and enable us to take a fresh look at 'Leofric' and the problem of origins.[41]

Certain features of the 'Leofric' prayer-texts are suggestive of early date and/or insular provenance. First, 'Omnipotens deus det tibi' and 'Benedic fortitudinem', composed of quotations from the Old Testament, have only early parallels in regal liturgies, and they centre on the linked concepts of divine favour and the blessings of nature – identifiable themes of insular *Fürstenspiegel*.[42] Second, the Frankish benediction, 'Benedic domine hunc presulem principem', in my view of Merovingian origin, is adopted unchanged: since the use of the term *presul* for the king[43] was barely acceptable to ninth- and tenth-century clerics,[44] it had probably got into the English *Ordo* early enough to have become traditional by the end of the ninth century. Thirdly, the ideological content of 'Te invocamus', of 'In diebus' and of the

---

[40] 'Service Books', pp. 69–70, 78–80. The assertion, p. 80, that Bouman 'accepted' that 'the ['Leofric'] *Ordo* is English' is a little misleading, however: this may be, as Mr Hohler implies, the only reasonable inference from Bouman's work, but Bouman himself in fact repeatedly affirmed (*Sacring*, pp. 10, 61, 102, 144, 153–4) the West Frankish origin of both 'the formulary' and its component prayers and procedures. That is why the present paper still needed to be written.

[41] Since completing this paper, I have learned through the kindness of Professor Julian Brown of Mrs Elaine Drage's unpublished Oxford D.Phil. dissertation (1978), 'Bishop Leofric and Exeter Cathedral Chapter: a reassessment of the Manuscript Evidence'. Mrs Drage has produced very strong paleographical reasons for believing that the Leofric Missal was written in Lotharingia, at St Vaast, Arras, *c*.880. Nevertheless, in view of St Vaast's geographical position in the Rheims archdiocese, of ninth-century contacts between England and Flanders, and of the diverse origins of the liturgical material in the Leofric Missal, my arguments for the Anglo-Saxon origin of the king's *Ordo* itself will I hope stand independently of the MS's provenance. I am very grateful to Mrs Drage for discussion of all these points.

[42] H. H. Anton, *Fürstenspiegel und Herrscherethos in der Karolingerzeit* (Bonn, 1968), pp. 66–79.

[43] Aurelian of Arles addressed Theudebert as *praesul*: MGH, Epp. III, p. 124. For the late antique context, see J. Straub, 'Zur Ordination von Bischofen und Beamten in der christlichen Spätantike', in *Mullus. Festschrift T. Klauser* (Münster, 1964), pp. 336–45, at p. 342. Compare Isidore, *Sententiae*, PL LXXXIII. 721: 'Dedit deus principibus praesulatum.'

[44] See Bouman, *Sacring*, p. 164, for the original reading ('hos praesules principes') in the Sacramentary of Angoulême, and pp. 174 and 180, for alterations in West and East Frankish *Ordines* of the later ninth and tenth centuries. For 'hunc praeelectum principem' in the mature version of the Second English *Ordo*, see *Claudius Pontificals* II, ed. Turner, p. 94.

additional material in 'Deus electorum' and 'Benedic domine hunc presulem principem'[45] is reminiscent of such Spanish and insular texts as the Visigothic regal Mass,[46] the eighth-century Gelasian regal prayers 'Deus pater gloriae' and 'Christe deus oriens'[47] (both of these showing 'Spanish symptoms'), of Pseudo-Cyprian and the Irish *Collectio Canonum*, and of the letters of Boniface, Cathwulf and Alcuin.[48] In all these, the emphasis tends to be on the king as judge rather than as war-leader, on the king's protective function in relation to his people in general rather than to the Church and its ministers in particular, and on royal rights rather than royal duties.

It seems plausible for several reasons that an English *Ordo* should have provided the basis for Hincmar's *Ordo* of 856. The historical context is right. Charles the Bald had himself been anointed in 848, and his second son was anointed sub-king of Aquitaine in 855.[49] Charles and Hincmar would have planned the consecration of the thirteen-year-old Judith with a view to enhancing her status amongst the West Saxons, a people notorious in the ninth century for the scant respect they accorded kings' wives.[50] There was obviously no West Saxon queen's *Ordo* for Hincmar to borrow,[51] and neither, it seems, was there any West Frankish one: hence the need to adapt a king's *Ordo*, as in 856, or to compose a new rite, as for Ermentrude in 866.[52] But why should Hincmar not have adapted a West Frankish king's *ordo* in 856? It is possible that an English rite would in any case have been thought more apt for someone

---

[45] The material in these prayers for which no source has been identified amounts in 'Deus electorum' to the phrase: 'regnique fastigia in consiliis scientiae et aequitate iudicii semper assequi', and a reference to 'plebs commissa'; in 'Benedic domine' to nearly all of clause o. and all of p.: 'per tuam discat commissa sapientiam regni gubernacula moderari, ut semper felix, semper a te gaudens, de tuis mereatur beneficiis gratulari, et aeternis valeat commerciis copulari. Ut quem tu nobis hodie tua misericordia iucundum presentare dignatus es, tua facias multorum annorum curriculis protectione securum.' The stylistic similarities here are with eighth-century regal benedictions.

[46] *Liber Ordinum*, pp. 295–6.

[47] Ed. Bouman, p. 190, from the Sacramentary of Gellone. On the components and dating of the eighth-century Gelasian, see C. Vogel, *Introduction aux sources de l'histoire du culte chrétien* (Spoleto, 1966), pp. 58–67.

[48] For details of these insular texts, see Anton, *Fürstenspiegel*, pp. 67–131.

[49] *Annales Bertiniani*, s.a. 848, 855, ed. F. Grat *et al.*, pp. 55, 71.

[50] *Ann. Bertin.*, p. 73; Asser, *Vita Alfredi*, ed. W. Stevenson (repr. with introduction by D. Whitelock, Oxford, 1959), p. 11, with Stevenson's comments, pp. 200–2.

[51] It is just possible that a Mercian queen's *Ordo* existed: Professor Whitelock reminds me that in a charter of 869, W. G. Birch, *Cartularium Saxonicum* (3 vols., London, 1885–9) (hereafter cited as *BCS*), no. 524, Burgred's queen Æthelswith appears as 'pari coronata stemma regali', which could imply a consecration-rite for her, paralleling her husband's. But how could Hincmar have got hold of such an *Ordo*? Æthelwulf would be an unlikely middleman. In any event, Hincmar in 856 clearly adapted a *king's* rite.

[52] MGH, Capit., II, pp. 453–5.

becoming an English queen. But it is also likely that no fixed rite as yet existed in West Francia: there the *continuous* history of royal consecrations only begins in 848 and the *Ordines* tradition can be traced back no further than 869.[53] For England the picture is rather different. It is not so much that the virtual absence of liturgical evidence here,[54] as compared with the dozen or so surviving Frankish sacramentaries and pontificals of the later eighth and earlier ninth centuries,[55] precludes any argument from silence; for royal *Ordines* do not quickly become regular features of such books. (Equally, for the later tenth century when the English evidence becomes more plentiful, it would be easy to misinterpret the contrast between the regular appearance of a royal *Ordo* in Anglo-Saxon pontificals with the continuing rarity of such appearances in contemporary French books: the contrast is a symptom of varying degrees of royal power and ecclesiastical centralisation in the two realms.) It is rather that there is actually more English than Frankish evidence for the indigenous practice of royal consecration in the late eighth and early ninth centuries. Certainly the English evidence comes from Northumbria and Mercia,[56] not Wessex. But in view of the relations between the three kingdoms at this period, it seems unlikely that West Saxon kings would have neglected their

[53] See my comments in *EHR*, XCII (1977), p. 245, with nn. 3 and 4, for full bibliographical references. The consecration of 869 was a Lotharingian affair but the *Ordo* used, because of its influence on that of 877, is the fount of a West Frankish liturgical tradition. The Supplemented Gregorian, of course, unlike the eighth-century Gelasian, contained no formulas for royal consecration. Such formulae, and full *Ordines*, begin to reappear in sacramentaries and pontificals from the later ninth and tenth centuries onwards. For the *Ordo secundum occidentales*, see below, p. 42, n. 66.

[54] For the few mere fragments surviving, see K. Gamber, *Codices Liturgici Latini Antiquiores*, 2nd edn (Freiburg, 1968), pp. 150–1, 227–32.

[55] Vogel, *Introduction aux sources*, pp. 81–2, 185–6. For ninth-century MSS of the Gregorian, see now the edn of Deshusses, pp. 34–47.

[56] Northumbria: *Anglo-Saxon Chronicle*, s.a. 795 in the 'Northern' recension, ed. B. Thorpe, R.S. (London, 1861), p. 103, trans. D. Whitelock, *English Historical Documents* (London, 1955), p. 168; and Symeon of Durham, *Historia Regum*, ed. T. Arnold, R.S. (London, 1885), p. 58: both these draw on a lost set of Northumbrian annals nearly contemporary with the events they describe. Mercia: *Anglo-Saxon Chronicle*, s.a. 785 (for 787), ed. Thorpe, pp. 96–7, trans. Whitelock, *Documents*, p. 166 (the 'A' text here drawing on lost Mercian annals); *BCS* no. 370 (Ceolwulf I referring to his *consecratio* by the archbishop of Canterbury), on which see now K. Harrison, *The Framework of Anglo-Saxon History* (Cambridge, 1976), p. 115. J. M. Wallace-Hadrill, *Early Medieval History* (Oxford, 1976), pp. 158–9, is helpful, but in my view over-estimates Frankish influence. Of the decrees issued by the Synod of Chelsea (787), A. W. Haddan and W. Stubbs, eds., *Councils and Ecclesiastical Documents* (3 vols., Oxford, 1869–73), III, pp. 453f., c. 12, 'De ordinatione et honore regum', refers to the king as *christus domini*, but this need not imply *per se* a Mercian royal consecration-rite, as has sometimes been alleged. The novelty in 787, however, may well have lain in the pre-mortem succession, rather than the 'hallowing', of Offa's son: see my comment in 'Inauguration Rituals', in P. H. Sawyer and I. N. Wood, eds., *Early Medieval Kingship* (Leeds, 1977), p. 52.

neighbours' practice,[57] or that Æthelwulf and his advisers would have exported in 856 anything other than a West Saxon rite; unlikely too that Æthelwulf would have agreed to Judith's being anointed had he not been so himself, which could well mean taking the West Saxon fixed rite back at least to his accession in 839, if not to Egbert's in 802 or even Beorhtric's in 786.

How much older could 'Leofric' be? All its datable sources are considerably older than the mid-ninth century. The *Benedictio chrismatis* which forms the basis of 'Deus electorum' is Gelasian, and, like the Spanish sources discussed above, could have been available in England as early as the seventh century.[58] 'Benedic domine hunc presulem principem' is largely composed from two series of regal benedictions whose earliest extant source is eighth-century Gelasian but which themselves could fit very well in a Merovingian context. The origins of royal anointing in England cannot be explored here; nor can the further intriguing problem of possible Celtic precedents.[59] But if 'Leofric' represents an English fixed rite dating from the first half of the ninth century *at the latest*, then the search for origins could take us back a century or more before that.

III. 'LEOFRIC' IN RELATION TO 'EGBERT'/'LANALET'

If the 'Leofric' *Ordo* preserves the West Saxon usage of pre-856, what of its brother-*Ordo*, 'Egbert'/'Lanalet'? Here Schramm's view, that 'Egbert'/'Lanalet' is an 'amplification' of 'Leofric', has retained the assent of all subsequent scholars. Apart from the setting of the *Ordo* within the Mass, which even if a late feature[60] need not affect our view of the *Ordo* itself, the two characteristics of this alleged 'longer version'

---

[57] Compare the evidence for the elaboration of the West Saxon royal genealogy during the first half of the ninth century, probably to emulate that of the Mercian kings: see K. Sisam, 'Anglo-Saxon Royal Genealogies', *Proceedings of the British Academy*, XXXIX (1953), pp. 287–348. D. Dumville, 'Kingship, Genealogies and Regnal Lists', in Sawyer and Wood, *Early Medieval Kingship*, pp. 72–104, at p. 73, cites some later Scottish and Irish evidence for a link between genealogies and inauguration rituals (the recitation of the new king's genealogy is part of the king-making), and, pp. 74–5, shows the legitimising function of genealogies and king-lists on the continent.

[58] H. Mayr-Harting, *The Coming of Christianity to Anglo-Saxon England* (London, 1972), pp. 168–82, 272–5.

[59] For references, see my papers in *JEH*, XVIII (1967), p. 48, n. 4; and *SCH*, XIII (1976), p. 116. See now J. Prelog, 'Sind die Weihesalbungen insularen Ursprungs?', *Frühmittelalterliche Studien*, XIII (1979), pp. 303–56.

[60] See T. Klauser in *Jahrbuch für Liturgiewissenschaft*, XIV (1938), p. 461, though on pp. 289–91 of my dissertation, I adduced some evidence that early ninth-century Frankish inaugurations might have been set within the Mass.

are first, the insertion of the prayer 'Deus qui populis' between the first and second prayers of 'Leofric', and second, the presence of 'much more explicit rubrics'. But 'Deus qui populis' is clearly a late interpolation in an existing *Ordo*,[61] and therefore irrelevant to our dating problem. Neither do the 'more explicit rubrics' constitute in themselves an indication of later date by comparison with 'Leofric', any more than short or non-existent rubrics necessarily imply early date. We know that in the ninth century, the prayer texts for a major rite would be copied out in a *rotula*, while the detailed instructions on movement, gesture and so on would be set out separately in an *ordo*.[62] Although it was only from the tenth century onwards that it became normal practice to work from a single text, there are plenty of earlier examples, especially in baptismal and ordination rites, of detailed indications already being inserted in rubrics between the prayers. The very fact that the final, rather full rubrical direction of 'Egbert'/'Lanalet' actually appears in 'Leofric' too,[63] shows that the presence or absence of full rubrics will provide no sure criterion for relative datings. 'Leofric' may, indeed, have been intended for performance in just the same way as 'Egbert' or 'Lanalet', but with its officiants using a separate guidebook of ritual instructions.

'Archaic traits' were long since recognised in the 'Egbert'/'Lanalet' rubrics.[64] My own somewhat extended list runs as follows:

(i) In three rubrics, all the participating bishops are termed *pontifices*. Though this usage is extremely rare in early medieval liturgical sources, the word *pontifex* for 'bishop' does occur twice in rubrics in the Visigothic *Liber Ordinum*.[65] In the probably ninth-century *Ordo secundum occidentales*, the term will refer to an *arch*bishop,[66] but in other liturgical sources of this period it always denotes the pope. In the sixth and seventh centuries, writers used *pontifex* and *episcopus* interchange-

---

[61] The 'Egbert' scribe had no space to copy out the whole prayer, but seems to have been clumsily copying the rubric of his model (*req. in agapite libri*). See Bouman, *Sacring*, pp. 100–5.

[62] See Hincmar's letter to Adventius of Metz, and the excellent discussion of this evidence in M. Andrieu, 'Le Sacre épiscopal d'après Hincmar de Reims', *RHE*, XLVIII (1953), pp. 22–73.

[63] See below, pp. 46–7.

[64] G. Waitz, 'Die Formeln der deutschen Königs- und der römischen Kaiser-Krönung vom 10. bis zum 12. Jht.', *Abhandlungen der königlichen Gesellschaft der Wissenschaften zu Göttingen*, XVIII (1873), p. 21; E. Eichmann, 'Königs- und Bischofsweihe', *Sitzungsberichte der bayerischen Akademie der Wissenschaften, Phil.-Hist. Klasse*, VI (1928), p. 26.

[65] Ed. Férotin, pp. 61, 543.

[66] Ed. Elze, *Ordines*, pp. 3–5. I see no reason to link this *Ordo* with 816 and thus to interpret its *pontifex* as 'the pope'.

ably;[67] but thereafter there is a tendency (in Bede, for instance) for the latter term to be used for 'bishop', the former for 'archbishop' or 'pope'. The unspecialised sense of *pontifices* in our *Ordo* could thus be an indication of early date; and it may be worth noting that both *pontifex* and *episcopus* were translated by Anglo-Saxon *bisceop*.[68] The absence of early English liturgical material for comparison is very unfortunate.

(ii) The anointing-rubric shows the literal application of an Old Testament model: oil is to be poured out from a horn over the king's head, with the antiphon 'Uncserunt Salomonem'. As in contemporary rites of episcopal consecration, the emphasis is on the collective nature of the central act: one bishop pours the oil, the rest anoint.[69] There is no need to postulate a special link here with the circumstances of 751: the Solomon-model, well-attested in Merovingian sources, remained potent in the ninth century.[70] With Hincmar, the *modus* of royal anointing seems to have taken on new affinities with contemporary rites of baptism and of episcopal consecration. The very explicit Old Testament symbolism, which distinguishes 'Egbert'/'Lanalet' from all other western *Ordines* (and which finds parallels in the prayer texts too, as 'Leofric' showed) seems likely to be old.[71] It could also be insular, for Old Testament typology is at least as prominent in Anglo-Saxon historical and hagiographical writings of the seventh and eighth centuries as in contemporary Frankish products, and Fournier long ago drew attention to 'les tendances bibliques' in the Irish canons.[72]

[67] This is also true of 'Egbert'/'Lanalet', where in the final section the officiants are termed *episcopi*. See below, p. 46.
[68] Eddi, *Vita Wilfrithi*, ed. B. Colgrave (Cambridge, 1927) nearly always keeps *pontifex* for his hero Wilfrid (whom he occasionally also calls *episcopus*), and renders 'archbishop' by *archiepiscopus*, never *pontifex*. In M. Richter, ed., *The Canterbury Professions* (Torquay, 1973), there seems to be no case of *pontifex* for 'bishop', though nos. 1 and 19 contain rare appearances of *pontifex* for 'archbishop' in the late eighth and ninth centuries.
[69] The 'Egbert' rubric is perfectly clear: 'Unus ex pontificibus' is the subject of 'verget oleum'. I cannot see why Schramm and Bouman follow Greenwell in seeking to emend the text, and their punctuation has no manuscript support. The collective nature of Old Testament public king-makings was rightly stressed by J. De Pange, *Le Roi très chrétien* (Paris, 1949), pp. 49–50.
[70] Anton, *Fürstenspiegel*, pp. 51, with n. 31, 430–2, gives references.
[71] Eichmann, 'Die rechtliche und kirchenpolitische Bedeutung der Kaisersalbung im Mittelalter', *Festschrift G. Hertling* (Kempten, 1913), p. 264. For the possible modelling of the final section of the *Ordo* on Solomon's inauguration, see below, p. 47.
[72] P. Fournier, 'Le *Liber ex lege Moysi* et les tendances bibliques du droit canonique irlandais', *Revue Celtique*, XXX (1909), pp. 221–34; on Anglo-Saxon material, Mayr-Harting, *Coming of Christianity*, pp. 139–41, 204–19.

(iii) The *principes* join with the *pontifices* in handing over the sceptre. This surely represents a transitional phase in the evolution of a part of the inauguration ritual which, by the tenth century, would be monopolised by clergy. This is the only extant *Ordo* to prescribe the active participation of laymen within the liturgical rite proper[73] – in striking contrast with the West Frankish *Ordines* tradition from Hincmar onwards. Linking the appearance of the *principes* at this point with their and the people's role in the acclamation and enthronement which conclude the *Ordo*, I am tempted to compare the evidence for lay participation in the *deportatio ad cathedram* in Frankish episcopal consecration rituals.[74] Clearly, the sceptre is the central *Herrschaftszeichen* in our *Ordo* (there is, we recall, no coronation). This short sceptre has Old Testament and specifically Davidic connotations, signifying law as equity (as against the long *virga* – law as chastisement), but it also has Germanic ones.[75] Did early English kings have sceptres? Even if we leave the Sutton Hoo whetstone aside, we should perhaps treat the reference of Boniface to *sceptra imperii Anglorum* when writing to an English king[76] as more than rhetorical metonymy. The absence of any special tradition-prayer for the sceptre in the *Ordo* (compare Hincmar's 'Accipe sceptrum' and later similar formulae) is a further sign of early date.

(iv) The use of a helmet (*galea*)[77] rather than a crown has often been noted as archaic. While coronation was practised from at least the mid-ninth century in West Francia and the early tenth century in England, evidence for the helmet as a royal *Herrschaftszeichen* among Germanic peoples is considerably earlier.[78] Whether any regular

[73] That is, apart from their role in ritualised election procedures within the church.
[74] Bishops alone performed this at Wilfrid's ordination: Eddius, *Vita Wilfridi*, c. xii, ed. B. Colgrave (Cambridge, 1927), p. 26. But for lay participation, see Gregory of Tours, *Historiae Francorum*, III, 2, ed. B. Krusch and W. Levison, MGH, SS rer. Merov., I, i, p. 99; and the sources cited by E. Martène, *De Antiquis Ecclesiae Ritibus* (4 vols., Antwerp, 1736), II, pp. 80–1. Andrieu, 'Le Sacre épiscopal', p. 63, infers continuity in this usage from Merovingian times, though it is attested in liturgical books only from *c*.900.
[75] A. Gauert, 'Das "Szepter" von Sutton Hoo', in P. E. Schramm, *Herrschaftszeichen und Staatssymbolik* (3 vols., Stuttgart, 1954–6), I, pp. 260–80; and K. Hauck, 'Halsring und Ahnenstab als herrscherliche Würdezeichen', *ibid.*, pp. 145–212; S. L. Cohen, 'The Sutton Hoo Whetstone', *Speculum*, XLI (1966), pp. 466–70; R. L. S. Bruce-Mitford, *Aspects of Anglo-Saxon Archaeology* (London, 1974), pp. 6–7, 76–7.
[76] Boniface to Æthelbald of Mercia, ed. M. Tangl, MGH, Epp. sel., I, no. 73, p. 146.
[77] 'Egbert' gives: 'Hic omnes pontifices sumunt galeum [*sic*] et ponant super caput ipsius.'
[78] Paulus Diaconus, *Historia Langobardorum*, ed. G. Waitz, MGH, SS. rer. Lang., p. 59. See also H. Jankuhn, 'Herrschaftszeichen aus vor- und frühgeschichtlichen Funden Nordeuropas', in Schramm, *Herrschaftszeichen*, I, pp. 113–14.

Anglo-Saxon practice may be inferred from the Sutton Hoo helmet,[79] or from the dying Beowulf's handing-over of his gold-mounted helmet to his successor,[80] is debatable. But that a helmet did remain the prime royal headgear in ninth-century England is suggested by linguistic evidence which Josef Kirschner has expertly assembled.[81] Until about 900, the Latin *corona* was almost invariably translated by the Anglo-Saxon *beag*; but thereafter, West Saxon writers nearly always used *helm* and *cynehelm* instead to convey the concrete meaning of 'royal crown', *beag* being then restricted to religious contexts ('crown of glory', and so on). This change in linguistic usage may be seen as the outcome of a search for a more precise terminology, which itself reflected the reality of an Anglo-Saxon practice persisting throughout the ninth century: in other words, still around 900, the chief royal headgear actually was a *cynehelm* and not an open circlet (*beag*). We know, however, that precisely in the early tenth century a royal *Ordo* became current in England in which the use of a crown was prescribed[82] (though the crown did not necessarily immediately oust the helmet as an alternative *Herrschaftszeichen*); and it may also be relevant that the earliest numismatic portrayal of a crowned head in England dates from the reign of Athelstan.[83] It is possible that the *galea* of the Egbert and Lanalet books simply reflected the standard West Saxon terminology of the period when they were written, *corona* and *galea* being then perhaps treated as interchangeable (just as *cynehelm*, and even *helm*, were used to render 'crown of thorns'!).[84] But it seems more likely, in view of the 'Lanalet' scribe's possible difficulty with the word,[85] that *galea* in these two manuscripts faithfully reproduces a model dating from the period, that is, pre-900, when the helmet was

[79] Bruce-Mitford, *Anglo-Saxon Archaeology*, pp. 198–252.

[80] *Beowulf*, lines 2809–15.

[81] Herr Kirschner generously informed me of this material in a series of personal communications in 1973. I should stress that I alone am responsible for the historical inferences I have drawn from it. See now J. Kirschner, *Die Bezeichnungen für Kranz und Krone im Altenglischen*, Inaugural dissertation, Munich, 1975, esp. pp. 144ff., 177ff., 253ff.

[82] I accept the dating of the Second English *Ordo* by Turner, *Claudius Pontificals*, pp. xxxii–xxxiii. I hope to deal more fully with this *Ordo* in a forthcoming study.

[83] See C. E. Blunt, 'The Coinage of Athelstan', in *British Numismatic Journal*, XLII (1974), pp. 35–160. Hitherto kings had normally been shown wearing diadems. Mr Blunt interestingly notes (p. 47) the comparison with the similar crown worn by Athelstan in the frontispiece to the *Life of Cuthbert* in Corpus Christi College, Cambridge, MS 183, fo.1v (a contemporary picture). I am very grateful to Mr Blunt for kindly confirming this point.

[84] For instance by Ælfric: Herr Kirschner comments that this would seem 'an unlikely translator's choice, if not motivated by a rather old, strong and finally lexically "petrified" role of the Teutonic royal helmet'. See *Die Bezeichnungen*, pp. 187–8, 208–9, 252.

[85] According to Doble, p. 62, this word in the 'Lanalet' rubric is 'much blurred'.

the royal headgear. The rubric probably preserves the memory of a practice long outmoded by the time it was recorded: *galea* betokens both Englishness and antiquity.

The last and perhaps the most significant point in a comparison of 'Leofric' with 'Egbert'/'Lanalet' is the near-identity of their final sections, full rubrics and all. 'Leofric' in fact preserves in one passage what is evidently the original reading:

'Leofric'	'Egbert'	'Lanalet'
Tunc dicat omnis populus cum episcopis[86]. iii. vicibus	Et dicat omnis populus tribus vicibus cum episcopis et presbyteris	Et dicat omnis populus tribus vicibus cum episcopis et presbiteris
Vivat rex ill. in sempiternum. R. Amen.	Vivat rex .N. in sempiternum.	Vivat rex .N. in sempiternum. R.Amen. et venit omnis populus ad osculandum principem sempiternum.
Et confirmabitur cum benedictione omni populo in solio regni, et osculant principes in sempiternum dicentes Amen. Amen. Amen.	Tunc confirmabitur cum benedictione omnis populus et osculandum principem in sempiternum dicit. Amen. Amen. Amen. Tunc dicunt orationem septimam supra regem.	Tunc confirmabitur cum benedictione ista.
Deus perpetuitatis ... ... et defendas. Per.	Deus perpetuitatis ... Per. [Mass prayers] Primum mandatum regis ad populum hic videre potes.	Deus perpet ... [Mass prayers]
Rectitudo regis est noviter ordinati et in solium sublimati populo tria precepta sibi subdito precipere.	Rectitudo regis est noviter ordinati et in solium sublimati haec tria precepta populo christiano sibi subdito precipere.	

In primis ut ecclesia dei et omnis populus christianus veram pacem servent in omni tempore. R.Amen.[87]
Aliud est ut rapacitates et omnes iniquitates omnibus gradibus interdicat. R.Amen.
Tertium est ut in omnibus iudiciis aequitatem et misericordiam praecipiat ut per hoc[88] nobis indulgeat misericordiam suam[89] clemens et misericors deus. R.Amen.

Here is a discrete ritual bloc composed of acclamation and enthronement. Again the active participation of the *principes* here, and the

[86] Bouman, *Sacring*, p. 168, wrongly gives: 'cum episcopo'.
[87] 'Lanalet' omits 'R.Amen' here and after the second and third clauses. See Doble, p. 63.
[88] 'Lanalet' gives, instead of 'per hoc', 'sibi et'.
[89] 'Lanalet' gives 'suam misericordiam'; 'Leofric' omits 'suam'.

direct drawing on Old Testament models,[90] might indicate an early date: in later *Ordines*, clerically performed chants would take the place of this *collaudatio*.[91] That 'Leofric' preserves the correct technical sense of *confirmatio* = enthronement is borne out by the subsequent reference to the king as *in solium sublimatus*. The term *principes* reappears, evidently denoting a more restricted group than the whole acclaiming *populus*: those who took a hand in the tradition of the sceptre now come forward to kiss the new king in a ritual of recognition, not (as Schramm supposed) an act of feudal homage. The issuing of governmental *precepta* by the *rex noviter ordinatus* to his subjects was a natural corollary. The content of these *precepta* can be paralleled in insular sources – not only, as Schramm implied, in mid-tenth-century Anglo-Saxon laws, but in earlier laws,[92] and most notably in earlier Latin prose-writers: Pseudo-Cyprian, Boniface and Alcuin.[93] The programmatic formulation: 'rectitudo regis est . . . haec tria precipere' is reminiscent of the Irish canon-collection's: 'justitia regis justi haec est . . .' or 'sunt septem quae omni regi conveniunt . . .', Pseudo-Cyprian's 'Justitia regis est', and Alcuin's 'regis bonitas est . . .' and 'regis est'.[94]

CONCLUSION

Leaving open the problem of where royal anointings may first have been practised, I have tried merely to show good reasons for admitting Wilson's claim of 1901 that 'perhaps the earliest of all known western coronation [*sic*] orders is one contained in an English servicebook',[95] and for regarding that *Ordo* itself as English. I have also suggested that the *Ordo* is represented not only by 'Leofric' but by 'Egbert'/'Lanalet' too. Is it fortuitous that the earliest surviving *Ordo* should be an

[90] Schramm, *Kaiser*, p. 218, notes III Reg., 1. 39 and Dan., 2. 4 as models for the acclamation 'Vivat rex ill. in sempiternum'. But he neglected the much more significant I Paral. 29. 22–4, where the role of the *principes* is set out: 'Unxerunt . . . Salomonem . . . Seditque Salomon super solium Domini in regem pro David, patre suo; et cunctis placuit, et paruit illi omnis Israel. Sed et universi principes et potentes . . . dederunt manum, et subjecti fuerunt Salomoni regi.' Compare also II Paral. 23. 20.

[91] E. H. Kantorowicz, *Laudes Regiae* (Berkeley, 1946), pp. 78–80.

[92] Compare the preface and cap.1 of Ine's laws, ed. F. Liebermann, *Die Gesetze der Angelsachsen* (Halle, 1903–16), I, p. 88; also Alfred, cap.4,2, *ibid.*, p. 50, ('Swa we éac settað be eallum hadum' corresponding to the 'omnibus gradibus' of the *precepta*).

[93] Pseudo-Cyprian, ed. S. Hellmann, p. 51; Boniface, MGH, Epp. sel., I, p. 147; Alcuin, MGH, Epp., IV, pp. 51, 172, 293, etc.

[94] F. W. H. Wasserschleben, *Die Irische Kanonensammlung*, 2nd edn (Leipzig, 1885), pp. 77, 81; Pseudo-Cyprian and Alcuin as cited in preceding note.

[95] *JTS*, II (1901), p. 482.

English one? Perhaps – if a seventh-century Visigothic or Celtic rite ever existed. But in any case, this particular survival may have its own significance. Whatever the gap between the introduction of royal anointing in England, in the eighth century at the latest, and the establishment of a fixed rite, the liturgical tradition here seems to have been remarkably stable: if I am right, the same *Ordo* was used for West Saxon kings through most (if not all) the ninth century, and it was then very largely incorporated in the new *Ordo* current from the early tenth century until the close of the Anglo-Saxon period. In West Francia, by contrast, if a fixed rite existed before the mid-ninth century (and the evidence implies, rather, the continued use of Merovingian regal benedictions for early Carolingian king-makings) it was wholly abandoned by Hincmar whose *Ordines* seem to be quite original compositions; then a Sens tradition distinct from that of Rheims developed in the later ninth century; and a further break came in the tenth century with the importation of the English rite into West Francia.[96] If the relatively early introduction of a fixed rite in England may be explained in terms of the precocious political and ecclesiastical centralisation already achieved by the eighth century (had more evidence survived, Æthelheard of Canterbury might have appeared a figure comparable to Julian of Toledo or Hincmar of Rheims), the subsequent persistence of that rite through the ninth, tenth and most of the eleventh centuries reflects the continuity of English kingship and of the independent liturgical traditions of the English Church. As a witness to some of the political realities, as well as the political ideas, linking pre-Viking England with the age of the Conqueror, the first Anglo-Saxon *Ordo* can claim the attention of historians as well as liturgists. 'Leofric' and 'Egbert' have their origins in the world of *Beowulf*: they survive in the consecration-rite of 1066.[97]

[96] Turner, *Claudius Pontificals*, p. xxxiii.
[97] Corpus Christi College, Cambridge, MS 44, ed. J. Wickham Legg, *Three Coronation Orders*, Henry Bradshaw Society vol. XIX (London, 1900), pp. 53–61. For the association with William the Conqueror, see Schramm, *Archiv für Urkundenforschung*, XV (1938), pp. 317–18; and *idem*, *Kaiser*, pp. 180–2 – a characteristically brilliant and, in this case, plausible interpretation of textual variants in a liturgical document.

THE *EPISTOLA WIDONIS*,
ECCLESIASTICAL REFORM AND
CANONISTIC ENTERPRISE 1049–1141

by JOHN GILCHRIST

WHEN WALTER ULLMANN came to Leeds in 1947, he soon established a reputation for being an exacting scholar and teacher. As undergraduates we were somewhat overawed by his learning, but most of us survived the experience and it became a matter of quiet pride to say that one had been a student of Ullmann's. His example brought me into research and under his direction I began work on the political ideas of Cardinal Humbert of Silva-Candida (d. 1061). In time, I was confronted with the problem of Humbert's knowledge and expertise in the canon law. This presented many difficulties, for the canonical collection, *Diuersorum patrum sententie* (=74T), attributed to Humbert, was only partially edited, and that badly, in Friedrich Thaner's *Anselmi Episcopi Lucensis Collectio canonum una cum collectione minore* (Innsbruck 1906–1915). A definitive edition of the 74T was needed but Walter Ullmann warned of the difficulty of attempting such a task as part of the doctoral thesis.[1] In fact many years of work were needed before the edition was ready for publication in 1973, and by then Humbert's authorship of the collection was no longer accepted.[2]

The task of editing the 74T and dealing with related problems led to the conclusion that ecclesiastical reform in the eleventh century was more complex and less papally oriented than the title, *Gregorian Reform Movement*, suggested.[3] But the lack of printed texts of the canonical collections impeded the work of tracing the interrelationship of texts and ideas. It thus occurred to me quite early that, until suitable

---

[1] 'The Political Ideas of Cardinal Humbert of Silva-Candida (1050–61) with an edition of the Diuersorum Patrum Sententie' (thesis presented for the degree of Ph.D. in the University of Leeds, May 1957).

[2] On the authorship of the 74T see J. Gilchrist, ed., *Diuersorum patrum sententie siue Collectio in LXXIV titulos digesta*, Monumenta Iuris Canonici, Series B: Corpus Collectionum, 1 (Vatican City, 1973), pp. xx–xxvii, esp. nn. 33, 38, 42, 58, and p. xxxi, n. 88.

[3] For a recent summary see J. Gilchrist, 'The Reception of Pope Gregory VII into the Canon Law (1073–1141)', ZRG Kan., LIX (1973), pp. 35–82, esp. p. 73. A second part to this study will appear in the same journal.

editions were available, it might be a useful exercise to take a well-known text, such as the tract on simony known by the title *Epistola Paschasii pape* or *Epistola Widonis* (= Ep. W), and trace its influence and spread as fully as possible in canonical collections, papal letters, and polemical treatises produced in the reform period. This became a firm intention when I discovered a version of the Ep.W (in Florence, Biblioteca Laurenziana, MS Conventi soppressi 91 (formerly Badia 2685, fos.73r–79r = F) that was considerably longer than the commonly received version edited by Thaner in MGH, *Libelli de lite* 1.5–7 (= T), and which solved several problems raised by T.[4] Apart from minor variants, F and T are identical for the length of T. But the continuation in F, which I have labelled Ep.W(C), contains texts (some attributed to the Ep.W, others without inscription) found in other collections, the source of which puzzled the editors, including Thaner, because they were convinced that T was the complete text, at least so far as its *incipit* 'Fraterne mortis crimen incurrit' and *desinit* 'in futuro seculo remittatur' were concerned.

The importance of F led me to note down over the years references to the Ep.W, whenever the opportunities presented themselves. Recently, with support from the Canada Council, the research became more systematic and was completed. The major conclusions are presented in this paper and I feel honoured that they appear in a volume dedicated to Walter Ullmann.

The Ep.W opens with a respectful warning to the recipient that one cannot remain silent in face of rumoured abuses about the sale of holy orders. The author has heard that the recipient has indulged in such things and he warns that those who do so, are to be classed as heretics. Gregory I and St Augustine, as well as examples from the Sacred Scriptures such as Christ expelling the buyers and sellers from the Temple, are cited. This is followed by a text that became widespread in later works (*Inc.* 'Si quis autem obiecerit' . . . *des.* 'succidat'). The passage attacks the central defence put forward by simoniacs that 'they do not sell consecration but only its fruits'. This is mere rhetoric, argues the author, for just as the soul cannot live without the body, so can a bishopric not be separated into physical and spiritual properties, nor the one sold without the other.[5] If such agents of simony stand excommunicated and cut off from the church, it follows that the masses and

---

[4] On F see Gilchrist, *Diuersorum patrum sententie*, pp. xl–xli.
[5] See below, p. 56 and note 24.

prayers of simoniacal priests are harmful to the people, and those who hear them stand excommunicated as well. The author emphasises that simoniacal orders are not true orders and that simony is the worst of heresies. The short text concludes with an appeal to the addressee (Your excellency) and all the faithful in Christ to do their best to exterminate this widespread evil, lest they sin against the Holy Spirit to their eternal damnation.

In his edition Thaner used five MSS and reported three others (Regius, Colbertinus[1] and Colbertinus[2]) given by Étienne Baluze, but not identified by any catalogue numbers, in his version of the Ep.W published in 1678.[6] The Ep.W also occurs in Ivo of Chartres's *Decretum* 2.84 and in Deusdedit's *Collectio canonum* 4.93 and 94. To these must now be added some thirty other MSS. Although not all these MSS represent separate collections, they will be fully collated in the *apparatus criticus* of a new edition of F, to be published separately from the present paper. A new edition seems all the more necessary, when it is realised that Thaner's *apparatus* in the MGH has many errors.[7]

An examination of the MSS containing the Ep.W reveals a complicated interrelationship, which will not be easy to represent in a *stemma codicum*. But the broad tradition of the text seems clear enough: originating in Italy, in the diocese of Milan, the Ep.W was first incorporated into primitive collections of canonistic and patristic texts. For example, Bamberg Can. 4, P.I.8, which contains the Collection of Pseudo-Isidore (fos.1-2, 9-140) and the treatise of Auxilius, *Liber de ordinationibus a Formoso papa factis* (fos.141-146 = PL CXXIX. 1061-75), in a tenth-century hand, has the Ep.W inserted on fos.146v-147r, in an eleventh-century hand. Although Schafer Williams, in his study of the *Codices Pseudo-Isidoriani*, does not accept the *Katalog*'s attribution

---

[6] *Stephani Baluzii Tutelensis Miscellanea novo origine digesta ... opera ac studio Joannis Dominici Mansi Lucensis*: II (Lucca, 1761), pp. 114b-115a, reprinted in PL CLI. 637-40. On Baluze see J. Rambaud-Buhot, 'Baluze, bibliothécaire et canoniste', *Études d'Histoire du Droit Canonique dédiées à Gabriel Le Bras* (Paris, 1965), I, pp. 325-42. Baluze was in charge of the Colbert Library from 1667 to 1700 (*ibid.*, pp. 328-9).

[7] Thaner reports his variants according to the MSS numbered 1-5; 6 = the recension of Baluze, 7 = the different readings of the two Colbertine MSS. As examples of mistaken readings or misprints in Thaner, Ldl. 1.5-7 consider the following: Cod. 1 (St Gallen, Stiftsbibliothek 676, pp. 180-1) tam] tanti (Ldl.1.6.9) – no variant can be reported because the MS is damaged in this part; quid valet Arrianos, Sabellianos, Photinianos impurosque Manicheos *om.* 1 (Ldl. 1.7.7-8) – St Gallen 676 does *not* omit the text, but Cod. 2 (Vat. Barb. lat.581 fo.242v) does! Cod. 5 he gives as Lucca Plut. 1 32 but this MS does not contain the Ep.W. Thaner's variants correspond to the text in Lucca, Feliniana 124 fo.2v. Thaner misreads the text e.g. Ldl. 1.5.15 fundat] effundat, which results from a careless reading of 'sanguinē fundat', or 5.20 deglutiuit] glutinat, instead of the correct glutiuit, or 5.23 de quo] Deoque, where the MS reads 'de q̊'.

of this codex to the Cathedral Library of Milan as such, he does agree that 'there is no question that the script, format, and textual tradition ... relate it to a north Italian provenance'.[8]

From these primitive codices, the Ep.W became formally incorporated into a group of Italian collections, notably Deusdedit and the *Polycarpus*. Independently, it also found its way into Italian texts of the collection of Burchard of Worms: at first, it occurs as an addition at the end or beginning of the collection, and then more systematically it comes at the end of Book I or Book XIX.[9] Sometime before 1076 the Ep.W passed north of the Alps into Germany and France. In south-west Germany, we find it in MSS that relate very closely to the events of 1076–7 and to the works of reformers and canonists in the region of Constance, above all to Bernold of Constance himself.[10] St Gallen, Stiftsbibliothek, MS 676, which contains a text of the Swabian recension of the 74T, gives the Ep.W (pp. 180–1) under the rubric 'Decreta Paschasii pape ad archiepiscopum mediolanensem' but in the top margin appears the following anonymous gloss: 'Hanc epistolam non Paschasii pape fuisse qui nullus erat sed [text partly damaged] Epistola Widonis'.[11] Sélestat, Bibliothèque municipale MS 13 (formerly 99), originally belonged to the Abbey of Hirsau and it contains such reform texts as Bernold, *De prohibenda sacerdotum incontinentia* (fos.1–41r). This is followed by a collection of texts from Pope Gregory VII and others, on simoniacs and incontinent clerics (fos.41r–47r). Among these is the Ep.W (fos.45v–46v) with the rubric 'Decretum paschasii pp. [siue Paschalis pp. *suprascript*] ad archiepiscopum mediolanensem'. This last rubric illustrates the process by which the non-existent Pope Paschasius was transformed into a more meaningful, and thus more authoritative, Pope Paschal as the source of the text.[12]

In France, probably from a parent text found in the collection of

---

[8] *Codices Pseudo-Isidoriani: a Palaeographico-Historical Study*, Monumenta Iuris Canonici, Series C: Subsidia III (New York, 1971), pp. 8–9.

[9] Before Burchard: Lucca, Felin. 124 fo.2v. As an addition to Book XX: Florence, Bibl. Laurenziana, Plut. 16.21 fos.243v–244r; at the end of Book I: Monza, Archivio Capitolare (Biblioteca Capitolare) d–10/152 fos.27rb–28va; at the end of Book XIX: Monza h–5/154 fos.273ra–273vb, where it is numbered cap. cviiii.

[10] See J. Autenrieth, *Die Domschule von Konstanz zur Zeit des Investiturstreits* (Stuttgart, 1956), pp. 22, 26, 113–14.

[11] Gilchrist, *Diuersorum patrum sententie*, pp. lii–liii.

[12] On Sélestat 13 see *Catalogue général des manuscrits des bibliothèques publiques des départements*: III (Paris, 1861), pp. 590–1. More recently, P. Adam, *L'Humanisme à Sélestat: l'école, les humanistes, la bibliothèque* (Sélestat, 1962), p. 117 is faulty in its description. The best study is now I. S. Robinson, 'Zur Arbeitweise Bernolds von Konstanz und seines Kreises', *Deutsches Archiv*, XXXIV (1978), pp. 51–122, esp. pp. 56–8.

Burchard, the Ep.W became especially influential in a group of collections that comprised both the Poitevin texts and those based on the *Decretum* of Ivo of Chartres. This group has several significant variants that indicate the common parent, and accordingly, in the *apparatus criticus* to the new edition, I have given this version the siglum π.[13] These collections, which I consider to have been the last to incorporate the Ep.W with any significant changes in the text, bear witness to the final triumph and transformation of the text into a papal decretal. Almost without exception they inscribe the letter as a decree of Pope Paschal, omitting any indication that it had once been addressed to the archbishop of Milan. Gratian C.1 q.3 c.7 with the bare inscription 'Item Pascalis papa' epitomises this development.

An extensive study of the manuscript tradition of the Ep.W does not shed much new light on the question of authorship. Only two MSS (Vatican, Barb. lat.581 = V, and Regius(?) = R reported by Baluze in his edition) positively identify Guido or Wido, i.e. Guy of Arezzo, writing *c.*1031 to Archbishop Aribert II of Milan (1018–45), as the author: Epistola Widi (Guidoni V) (monachi contra simoniaca heresi laborantem *add.* V, ad Heribertum archiepiscopum *add.* R) = V fo.242v, R edit. Baluze (Lucca, 1761) 114b. Fortunately, we have the authority of the circle of the Constance canonists *c.*1076–88, especially of Bernold himself, that the tract was the work of Wido and no other.[14] The special connection between these canonists and the tradition of the Ep.W is demonstrated by the continuation found in the Florence MS. The significance lies in the fact that Ep.W(C) and *not* some stretched out version of Thaner's printed text is the source of three excerpts quoted by Bernard of Hildesheim and Deusdedit as belonging to the tract, but not found therein by their editors.[15] Thus Thaner, and after him Sackur and Saltet, none of whom was aware of Ep.W(C), spent much time in conjecturing whether the excerpts were later inter-

---

[13] On the Poitevin collections see R. E. Reynolds, 'The Turin Collection in Seven Books: A Poitevin Canonical Collection', *Traditio*, xxv (1969), pp. 508–14. As examples of the variants of π see Ldl. 5.5 impiorum iniquitatem] impietatem iniquorum π; 6.1 consecrationes] emi *add.*; 6.2 uendi, uidetur, quidem aliquid dicere, nichil autem penitus sapere] penitus desipere probatur; 6.9 succidat] incidat.

[14] Bernold, *De Statutis Ecclesiasticis Sobrie Legendis*; 'Sunt autem multa sanctorum patrum statutis falso ascripta, ut scriptum Widonis musici de symoniacis' (Ldl. 2.157.5–6). See Autenrieth, *Domschule*, pp. 113–14, 139.

[15] The excerpts are De damn. scis. (Ldl. 2.41.24 *inc.* 'Quicumque sacros' . . . *des.* 36 'uendere'; 42.10 *inc.* 'Numquid maledictus' . . . *des.* 17 'dampnatam'. In F these two excerpts are reversed and form a sequence); Deusdedit, *Libellus contra Invasores et Symoniacos* cap. 2 (Ldl. 2.318 *inc.* 'Omnes autem uendentes' . . . *des.* 'benedictionibus uestris').

polations into Ep.W or had been deleted for some reason from the original. Thaner preferred the explanation that they had been cut from the original because they were too extreme in their absolute condemnation of the validity of simoniacal orders. He gives the excerpts at the foot of the printed edition and indicates by asterisks where he thinks they have been deleted from the text. Although the place of the deletions and the explanation thereof were rather forced, no subsequent historian questioned their appropriateness or suggested an alternative solution.[16]

Of course, Ep.W(C) provides the correct source of these texts. It also provides the source for two fragments, capp. 93 & 94, found in the collection (1130-9) of Milan, Archivio Capitolare di S. Ambrogio, M 11 fo.21rv, inscribed 'Beatus Gregorius papa' and 'Augustinus' respectively. Picasso, the editor of this collection, prints the two texts in an appendix but without any indication that they were apocryphal as far as Augustine and Gregory were concerned.[17] In the Ep.W(C) the two excerpts form one continuous text. The explanation of these errors lies in the carelessness with which the author of the Milanese collection transcribed his sources: for example, the chapter immediately preceding the two excerpts from Ep.W(C) is correctly identified by Picasso as Nicholas II, Lateran Council (1060) but the bare inscription in the collection itself is 'Augustinus'.[18]

Ep.W(C) is about four times the length of the tract edited by Thaner in the MGH. It is surely in the inordinate length of the letter rather than in some sensitivity to the expression of extreme views about the validity of simoniacal orders that we find the explanation for the canonists' adoption into their collections of the short form. For several reasons the continuation may be considered an integral part of the original text: 1) there is little break in the style of the letter from the first to the second part; 2) the excerpts from the continuation cited by Bernard and Deusdedit are attributed to the same author as those from the first part;[19] 3) Bernold and the anonymous glossators, who point to Bernard's false attribution of the text to Pope Paschal, do not question that the excerpts also belonged to the Epistola Widonis; and 4) one of the earliest known uses of the Ep.W (1076) coincided with the appearance of the continuation.

[16] Thaner, Ldl. 1.4; Sackur, Ldl. 2.318; L. Saltet, Les Réordinations (Paris, 1907), pp. 180-1.
[17] G. Picasso, Collezioni canoniche milanesi del secolo XII (Milan, 1969), pp. 227-8.
[18] Picasso, Collezioni, p. 53, cap. 92.
[19] See De damn. scis. Ldl. 2.41.23 Audi Paschalem papam; Deusdedit, Contra Invasores Ldl. 2.318.14.

The continuation opens with the comment that God became Man in order to provide us with an antidote to the poison of the Leviathan.[20] Christ drove the buyers and sellers of doves from the Temple but not those of sheep and oxen. This had a mystical significance, i.e. the *cathedra* of the sellers of doves stands for the faith of heretics. The doves signify the Holy Spirit, and the sellers of doves are the simoniacs. The Lord's judgment: *Maledicam benedictionibus vestris* is upon them. The author then asks rhetorically whether a person guilty of this crime is not excommunicated and cannot be received back without penance? What can we say about priests who, not for the love of religion but for the sake of avoiding penury, presume through simoniacal heresy to ascend to consecrating the eucharist of our salvation? Can an accursed priest convert bread into the flesh of Christ? From the analogy of certain scriptural texts he concludes that if Christ forbids the lesser (of two things), how can the greater, i.e. a simoniacal priest conferring valid orders, be allowed? Such men are like Judas Iscariot. The donor and the donee have received nothing, the one does not have the payment, nor the other Christ. If unrepentant, they lose Christ. Judas gained eternal fire, so what do they, the simoniacs, gain? If Judas's prayers on his own behalf were not heard, how shall theirs be heard on behalf of others? The betrayer of Christ and the betrayers of the Paraclete are equal in guilt and therefore equal in punishment.[21] As for the defence that the simoniac acts in ignorance, he dismisses this summarily: those who so act gain nothing nor do they avoid the fires of eternal damnation. The sincere Catholic who wishes to extirpate this heresy will do well to equip himself with weapons 'de armario bibliothece'. By way of illustration the author takes the example of Simon Magus in the Acts of the Apostles. The special penalty attached to him applies to all men who are his followers. If he were alive today and said the mass, he would be shunned. So what can be said of his disciples? The mass of simoniacs cannot stand against the Lord's curse. Nor is there any validity in the argument that a person who pays nothing for his ordination by a simoniac can receive it, for the sin is not just a matter of money but of the mind. The civil law allows for different

---

[20] F, fo.75r 'Referentibus illis proceribus qui fidem catholicam corde, ore, manu cruoreque fundauerunt, agnouimus quod⟨ut⟩ altitonans Deus leviathan crudelissimi detestabile os perforaret hamo passionis, dignatus sit induere uidelicet factus homo carnem nostre mortalitatis. Et ut auferret ab eius faucibus iniuste preuaricatione prothoplausti dampnatos, contra mortifera illius uenena nequitie propinauit nobis antidotum penitentie.'

[21] F, fo.76v 'Numquid non pares sunt in ultione, qui pares sunt in crimine? Ille filium Dei uendidit, isti, quantum in ipsis est, Spiritum Sanctum conantur uendere.'

degrees of guilt and punishment, depending on the nature of the crime, the status and intention of the criminal, but in the case of simoniacs the matters of will, act and guilt are foreknown and are heretical. Thus an equal punishment and similar impotency applies to these heretics.[22]

From the two summaries given in this paper it becomes clear that the *Epistola Widonis* in its full form deserves study simply on the grounds that it is an outstanding example of the eleventh-century attack upon the heresy of simony and that it is uncompromising in its rejection of all acts in any way tainted with this guilt, whether given or received with or without knowledge, freely or conditionally. On simony the *Libri tres adversus simoniacos* does not say more, nor does Humbert's work, which has left hardly any trace in later collections and treatises, have an influence anywhere near that of the Ep.W.[23] It is not too rash to say that the Ep.W had an *extraordinary* influence, in three ways: first, through its incorporation into canonical collections as a complete text; second, through excerpts taken into the collections and polemical treatises; and third, through brief notices that refer to its authority, found in the treatises and papal letters. These will all be documented when the edition is published, but as a conclusion to this paper I have chosen to illustrate the spread of the Ep.W by citing *in extenso* the tradition of one excerpt. This is the text 'Si quis obiecerit . . . derelinquit' (= Gratian C.1 q.3 c.7 with an addition) or the slightly longer form that ends 'mucrone succidat [*var.* incidat]'. The popularity of this text is understandable for it rejects the main argument of the simoniacs that they sell not the spiritual office but only its fruits.[24]

The variants indicate two traditions of this excerpt, which I have called the Italian and French versions:

I. ITALIAN

Florence, Ashburnham 1554, fo.32v 'Ex epistola Pascalis pape Mediolanensibus missa. Si quis obiecerit . . . succidat'. The MS is early twelfth-century, but the collection on fos.12–72, which consists of a rearranged 74T, with additional texts, probably

[22] F, fo.79v 'Cum igitur simoniacis uoluntas et opus sint heretica et culpa prenota, sicut adultera paria sunt, ita par pena premat hereticos et similis inpotentia.'

[23] J. Gilchrist, ' "Simoniaca Haeresis" and the Problem of Orders from Leo IX to Gratian', *Proceedings of the Second International Congress of Medieval Canon Law* (Vatican City, 1965), pp. 209–35, here 213 and note 14.

[24] F, fos.73v–74r (= Ldl. 1.6.1–6) 'Si quis autem obiecerit non consecrationes sed res ipsas que ex consecratione proueniunt, uendunt, uidetur quidem aliquid dicere, nichil autem penitus sapere. Nam cum corporalis ecclesie aut episcopus aut abbas aut tale aliquid sine rebus corporalibus et exterioribus in nullo proficiat, sicut nec anima sine corpore corporaliter uiuit, quisquis eorum alterum uendit, sine quo alterum habere non prouenit, neutrum uenditum derelinquit.'

dates from the time of Gregory VII and is Roman in origin. The excerpt has some affinity with the Ep.W found (earlier?) in Deusdedit's collection.

Paris, BN lat.3858C, fo.15v 'Ex epistola Pascalis pape Mediolanensibus missa. Si quis obiecerit ... succidat'. The excerpt is cap. 169 of a collection of 482 capp. (fos. 11–50r), of Italian origin, closely related to Ashburnham 1554 but neither is the parent of the other.

Vatican, Cod. lat.3831, fo.34rb 'Pascalis papa. Si quis obiecerit ... derelinquit' = cap. 2.9.6 of the Italian Collection in Three Books (*c.*1112). This collection receives capp. from the *Polycarpus* and Burchard (via Ivo's *Decretum*) but our cap. has variants that link it with the same source as the Ep.W in Deusdedit.

Vatican, Basilica di San Pietro C.118, fo.31rb 'Pascalis papa. Si quis obiecerit ... derelinquit' = 3.7 of the Collection in Nine Books (*c.*1125), which is a revision of IIII in Vat. lat.3831.

Vatican, Cod. lat.5715, fo.17va 'Pascalis .i. mediolanensibus. Si quis obiecerit ... succidat' = 4.43 of the *Caesaraugustana* (1125 and 1139). Although this collection is from Northern Spain, Aquitaine or Burgundy and uses Ivo's *Decretum*, the excerpt from the Ep.W is probably from Deusdedit or a related source.

II. FRENCH

Florence, Ashburnham 53, fo.140vb 'Ex decretis Pascasii pape c. xviii. Si quis autem obiecerit ... incidat' = cap. 7 of a series of ten chapters on simony added to the end of Book VIII of this copy of the Collection of Anselm of Lucca. The collection is Italian but the addition is probably from Ivo or the same source.

Vatican, Cod. lat.4977, fo.32r 'Ex decretis pape Pascalis. Si quis autem obiecerit ... incidat'. This MS, written post-Gratian, 'offers significant evidence for the continuing interest in copying "antiquated" collections of the eleventh century – 74T and the "Corporis canonum aliud fragmentum" (Coll. II: fo.23ff.) – at a time when Gratian's *Concordia* was already in use'.[25] The Coll. II uses the Collection in Five Books, composed in Italy between 1014 and 1023, with additions such as our excerpt. The original of Coll. II probably dates from the pontificate of Urban II (1088–99).

Alger of Liège, *Liber de misericordia et justitia* (before 1094) 2.39 (PL CLXXX. 949C/D) 'testatur papa Paschasius: Si quis objecerit ... derelinquit'.

Ivo of Chartres, *Panormia* (*c.*1094–5) 3.123 (PL CLXI. 1156D–1157A) 'Ex decretis Paschalis papae c. 18 Si quis autem objecerit ... incidat'.

Paris, BN lat.3881, fo.224v 'Ex decretis Paschasii. Si quis obiecerit ... incidat' = *Polycarpus* (1104–6) Roman origin but this cap. comes via the *Panormia* of Ivo.

Collection in Ten Parts (*c.*1123) (Berlin, Phillipps 1746 fo.55ra; Paris, BN lat.10743 fo.170v; Vienna, Österreichische Nationalbibliothek MS 2178 (juris canonici 91) fo.67ra). Part III de simoniacis cap. 36 = *Panormia* 3.123.

Châlons sur Marne, Bibliothèque municipale 75, fo.29v cap. xxv 'Ex decretis Paschalis pape. c. xviii. Si quis autem obiecerit ... incidat'. This Collection in Thirteen Parts

[25] S. Kuttner, 'Some Roman Manuscripts of Canonical Collections', *BMCL*, I (1971), pp. 7–29, here p. 9.

(1130–9) was based on the collection of Châlons MS 47, the *Tripartita*, and the Collection in Ten Parts (above). The Ep.W excerpt is from the *Panormia* 3.123 via the Collection in Ten Parts.

Paris, BN lat.4286, fos.31v–32r 'Ex decretis Paschasii pape. Quod nulla sit eorum excusatio qui dicunt se in ecclesia res emere non spiritum nam sicut corpus et anima coniuncta vel adiuncta sunt ita temporale et spirituale et si quis horum alterum uendit neutrum inuenditum derelinquit' = *Summa Haimonis* (*c.*1130–5) of the Collection in Ten Parts (above) based on the *Panormia* of Ivo.

Gratian C.1 q.3 c.7 'Item Pascalis papa. Si quis obiecerit ... derelinquit. Nullus ergo emat ecclesiam uel prebendam, uel aliquid ecclesiasticum, nec pastellum, nec pastum ante uel postea pro huiusmodi soluat.'

So far as my own research goes, the first known use of the Ep.W was in the exchange of letters between Alboin and Bernold, *De prohibenda sacerdotum incontinentia*, which took place 1074–6.[26] From that time onwards there is a continuous history of the influence of the text on popes, canonists, and polemicists, including the imperialist Wido, bishop of Ferrara.[27] Its ultimate significance lay not in its rejection of the validity of simoniacal transactions but in the argument that there was no distinction between the spiritual and corporal goods attached to things ecclesiastical. This simple message, stripped of all the surrounding gloss, supported by other authorities and itself elevated to the rank of a papal decretal, penetrated deeply the Western clerical mind in the century of reform that led to Gratian and contributed much to the great debate between the two orders in Christian society. Perhaps the humble Wido of Arezzo, if indeed he were the author, deserved the honour unwittingly accorded him as Pope Paschal, by Gerhoh of Reichersberg, who joined him to Pope Leo the Great and cited the letter sent to the clergy of Milan as confirming even St Augustine himself![28]

[26] Ldl. 2.14.43–6 'Horum, inquam, pudenda, et a te, et ab omnibus zelum Dei habentibus sunt detegenda, ne *fraterne mortis crimen incurratis* . . .' (my italics – see Ldl. 1.5.2 'Fraternae mortis crimen incurrit quisquis . . .'). For the date see Autenrieth, *Die Domschule*, p. 133.

[27] *Wido episcopus Ferrariensis de scismate Hildebrandi*, ed. R. Wilmans and E. Dümmler, in MGH, Ldl. 1.532–67 cf. 537.15–17 (under the title cap. IV *Quare eum excommunicaverit*, p. 533) 'Huc mihi veterum monimenta priorum. Hinc agat Ambrosius, astipuletur Gelasius, loquatur Pascasius . . .' and again 538.6 (cap. V *Quod eum non absurde maledicto perculerit, sed autentice*, p. 533) 'Verum ne id absurde factum quisquam existimet, quae secuntur sanctorum patrum constitutiones et exempla perspiciat et oculo vigilanti percurrat, nec erit ulterius, quod ambigere debeat. Inquit beatus papa Pascasius inter alia: Si quis obiecerit ... *des.* succidat.'

[28] *Liber de simoniacis* Ldl. 3.266.17–20 'Si autem aliquae auctoritates requiruntur a sede apostolica promulgatae nostris assertionibus consone, poterunt sufficere auctoritates premisse de scriptis Leonis Magni et pape Pascalis excerptae ... alter in epistola Mediolanensibus directa illud beati Augustini dictum comprobat.'

RALPH DE DICETO, HENRY II AND BECKET WITH AN APPENDIX ON DECRETAL LETTERS

by CHARLES DUGGAN and ANNE DUGGAN

THROUGH MANY YEARS' REFLECTION on the reign of Henry II and the Becket dispute, the unique value of Ralph de Diceto's historical writings has become ever more apparent. It is not surprising that Dr Beryl Smalley has made the well-judged comment in her volume on the intellectual background of the controversy: 'The dean of St Paul's is jogging my elbow. Master Ralph of Diss has a right to the last word, since he crops up at each stage of the conflict, and then he narrated it in his *Histories*.'[1] The indispensable starting point for a fresh evaluation of Diceto's work is still the erudite two-volume edition published by Stubbs almost exactly one hundred years ago.[2] But, despite his characteristic learning in introductions and textual presentation, there are evident limitations in the deductions he drew from Diceto's personal associations, and more importantly in his knowledge of the sources available to the author, and the complex intellectual and psychological insights which the *opera omnia* disclose. It would indeed be strange if some restatement were not now necessary, in view of the many relevant monographs published meanwhile by political historians, experts in textual transmission, biblical and canonical scholars, and paleographers studying anew the superb surviving manuscripts, two of which were almost certainly products of the St Paul's scriptorium in the closing years of Diceto's own administration (as Stubbs himself showed), the Lambeth MS 8 being in all probability a transcription of the author's final revision, and perhaps his personal possession.[3] Happily, the necessary reappraisal is making rapid progress. In two studies Dr Smalley has discussed Diceto's stance in the Becket affair, with special emphasis on his historical method and technique, and on his place in

---

[1] B. Smalley, *The Becket Conflict and the Schools* (Oxford, 1973), pp. 230–4.
[2] *Radulfi de Diceto decani Lundoniensis Opera Historica* (hereafter Diceto), ed. W. Stubbs, R.S. (2 vols., London, 1876).
[3] *Ibid.*, I, pp. lxxxviii–c, esp. lxxxviii–xc.

the writing of history.[4] And Dr Grover Zinn has followed further one of her suggestions to demonstrate Diceto's indebtedness to Hugh of St Victor's *Chronicon* in his own *Abbreviationes Chronicorum*.[5] The purpose of the present essay is to give notice of a broad revision of Diceto's treatment of the Becket dispute, which will seek to determine his principal literary, epistolary and legal sources, and so to evaluate more surely his record of the causes, course and consequences of the affair.[6]

The conventional view of Diceto's standpoint as historian of Becket's career and martyrdom is that of an essentially moderate and conciliatory observer. As Dr Chibnall has well expressed it, despite his Angevin leanings, he gave a very fair and balanced account of the controversy.[7] But any such simple statement must conceal the subtle and elusive character of his writings, and particularly of his principal historical composition, the *Ymagines Historiarum*.[8] His scholarly formation was completed in the schools of Paris, and his skill in administration was secured in the chapter of St Paul's, where he was archdeacon of Middlesex from 1152 and dean from 1180 until his death in 1202.[9] He was a man of intelligence, keen perception, sensitivity and all-round ability, with an innate concern for order and a respect for authority. He seems above all a man who withdrew by natural inclination from confrontation and radical positions. Circumstances placed him at a delicate intersecting point of many lines of contrasting influences and ideologies, and found in him an unusual confluence of

[4] Smalley, *Becket Conflict*, pp. 230–4, and *Historians in the Middle Ages* (London, 1974), pp. 114–19.

[5] Grover A. Zinn, Jr, 'The Influence of Hugh of St Victor's *Chronicon* on the *Abbreviationes Chronicorum* by Ralph of Diceto', *Speculum*, LII (1977), pp. 38–61. There is an excellent recent survey of Diceto's life and works in A. Gransden, *Historical Writing in England c.550 to c.1317* (London, 1974), esp. pp. 230–6 and Plate VII, in which several points are touched upon which concern the special emphasis of this essay. See also C. N. L. Brooke and G. Keir, *London 800–1216: the Shaping of a City* (London, 1975), pp. 350–6 and Plate 51.

[6] For a brief survey of the controversy, cf. C. Duggan, 'The Significance of the Becket Dispute in the History of the English Church', *Ampleforth Journal*, LXXV (1970), pp. 365–75. The best recent biography of the archbishop is by D. Knowles, *Thomas Becket* (London, 1970). The largest and most learned survey of the whole subject is still that by R. Foreville, *L'Église et la royauté en Angleterre sous Henri II Plantagenet* (Paris, 1943).

[7] M. M. Chibnall, 'Ralph of Diceto', *New Catholic Encyclopedia* (15 vols., New York, 1967), XII, pp. 70–1.

[8] Diceto, I, pp. 289–440, and II, pp. 1–174.

[9] *Ibid.*, I, pp. x–lxxxiii, *passim*; Smalley, *Becket Conflict*, p. 230 and n. 53; A. Morey and C. N. L. Brooke, *Gilbert Foliot and his Letters* (Cambridge, 1965), and *The Letters and Charters of Gilbert Foliot* (Cambridge, 1967), *passim*; D. E. Greenway, 'The Succession to Ralph de Diceto, Dean of St Paul's', *Bulletin of the Institute of Historical Research*, XXXIX (1966), pp. 86–95, and *John Le Neve, Fasti Ecclesiae Anglicanae, 1066–1300: I. St Paul's, London* (London, 1968), *passim*.

personal relationships. His wide circle of patrons and friends included partisans both of Henry II and of Becket, as well as others who avoided with prudence a positive or exclusive attachment to either.[10] His close links with Foliot, bishop of London and most hostile of Becket's episcopal colleagues, did not unduly colour his record of their quarrel.[11] He shared the doctrinal orthodoxy of the English Church of the period, and accepted axiomatically the ascendant jurisdictional authority of the papacy. He wrote 'de fide nostra' as a matter of course in connection with the refutation of heresy,[12] and in his short treatise *De Dupplici Potestate* he distinguished in a familiar contemporary fashion the two swords of spiritual and temporal power, while duly stressing the inherited Petrine character of the papal office, with its superior faculty of binding and loosing, 'quoniam anima dignior est quam corpus'.[13] At the same time, his loyalty and fidelity to his lawful secular lord were deeply rooted, and he was on intimate terms with the king's most powerful and familiar supporters.[14]

Despite his discretion and his ability to treat of divisive matters with circumspection, he was a man of very positive attitudes. His multiplex loyalties and antipathies are seldom concealed. As a leading ecclesiastic, he reveals an implicit acceptance of the unity of Western Christendom under the pope, a concern for clerical privilege in general and for the rights of the Church in England, commitment to the pre-eminence of the Canterbury province within the English Church, and anxious care for the precedence of his own London diocese.[15] In secular matters, his loyalty was manifestly secured to the English Crown, and very

---

[10] Cf. C. Duggan, 'Richard of Ilchester, Royal Servant and Bishop', *Transactions of the Royal Historical Society*, 5th series, XVI (1966), pp. 1–21, esp. pp. 1–2 and 8–14.

[11] Note his inclusion in the *Ymagines Historiarum* of items 8, 9, 14 and 15, Appendix I, below; all four letters contain material critical of Foliot's actions.

[12] Diceto, I, p. 295. It should be emphasised that Diceto's work is highly derivative: the passage cited is taken verbatim from Robert of Torigni; cf. *Chronicles of the Reigns of Stephen, Henry II, and Richard I: Chronica Roberti de Torigneio, abbatis Monasterii Sancti Michaelis in Periculo Maris*, ed. R. Howlett, R.S. (4 vols., London, 1884–9), IV (1889), p. 168.

[13] Diceto, II, p. 180.

[14] *Ibid.*, introductions to vols. I and II, *passim*; note especially II, pp. xxxi–xxxii; cf. C. Duggan, 'Richard of Ilchester', as in n. 10, above.

[15] Examples of all these basic attitudes are found too frequently to list here. The exercise of papal authority within the Western Church is taken for granted, rather than expounded enthusiastically, in the summoning of councils, the granting of the pallium, the confirming of appointments, the canonisation of Becket, the reception of appeals, the commissioning of legates and judges, and in numerous other ways (the brief treatise *De Dupplici Potestate* is already cited in n. 13 above, and an indented reference at the 1175 'concilium regionale' of Westminster notes: 'Solius papae est concilium generale, Romanae ecclesiae et Constantinopolitanae est concilium universale', Diceto, I, p. 399). A striking example of Diceto's recognition of the Petrine

strikingly to Henry II in person, to established political authority, and to a regime of social law and order. In a more personal way, his stability and reliability are witnessed in his relations with colleagues and friends, who appear to have valued his counsel – his letter of restraint to Richard of Ilchester at an emotional moment of crisis in 1166 is a notable instance of these qualities.[16] But his prejudices are no less evident. His comments unfold the Canterbury subject's condescension to the province of York, the London dean's circumscription of the aspirations of the bishops of Winchester and Rochester, and an English contempt for the French monarchy and the French people, from whom he seemingly excludes the continental subjects of the Angevin king of England.[17] The Becket dispute brought into sharp focus the problems arising from such diverse and sometimes conflicting sentiments, at a time of exceptional crisis in relations between ecclesiastical and secular interests in a unitary Christian society, and his version of that crisis is found in the *Ymagines Historiarum* and more compactly in the *Series Causae inter Henricum Regem et Thomam Archiepiscopum*, the latter providing an unusually clear and brief survey of the controversy on the basis of a sequence of texts distributed through the relevant years in the larger work.[18]

From the plateau of relative tranquillity when the *Ymagines* was completed, Diceto portrays the conflict in a deceptively detached manner, in contrast with the emotive atmosphere captured in the hagiographical and epistolary sources, an atmosphere often charged

doctrine of papal power, together with his willingness to criticise a particular papal decision, occurs *ibid.*, II, p. 165. The records of the dispute at Clarendon in 1164 and the reconciliations of 1172 and 1175- 6 reveal a concern for clerical rights, *ibid.*, pp. 312–13, 351–2, 402–3 and 410. Assertions of the pre-eminence of Canterbury within the English Church are evident in the record of the Council of Tours in 1163 and the triple dignity acquired by Archbishop Richard in 1174, *ibid.*, pp. 310 and 390; indeed one of Diceto's special *signa in margine posita* identifies important sections 'De privilegiis Cantuariensis ecclesiae', *ibid.*, p. 4. His assumption of the distinction of London is nowhere better illustrated than in a passage on episcopal precedence at Becket's consecration, or in another on Foliot's translation from Hereford to London, the 'civitas regalis sedes' as Alexander III's letter describes it, *ibid.*, pp. 306–7 and 309.

16 *Ibid.*, pp. 319–20.

17 For ecclesiastical matters, cf. n. 15, above. Stubbs discussed the possibility that Diceto was himself of French origins (cf. *ibid.*, xvii–xx), but concluded nevertheless that 'Ralph was an Englishman of the period of amalgamation'. There is no doubt that Ralph speaks disparagingly of the French king and his subjects on many occasions, notably during the war of 1173–4: cf. *ibid.*, pp. 372, 375, 386–7, 394 *et passim*; but a more favourable comment appears at times, as when Louis VII visited the martyr's tomb at Canterbury in 1179: *ibid.*, pp. 432–4. For a note on loyalty to Henry II in Maine and Anjou, cf. *ibid.*, pp. 379–80.

18 For the distributed passages in the *Ymagines*, cf. *ibid.*, pp. 307–14, 329 and 337; for the *Series Causae*, cf. *ibid.*, II, pp. 279–85.

with tensions, drama, tragedy and terror.[19] It is certain that he reconstructed the earlier part of the *Ymagines* from sources already existing. He used the *Chronica* of Robert of Torigni for material down to 1162.[20] For the Becket conflict he drew on archival material available to him, selecting from hagiographical works and letter collections, perhaps to some extent from his own records preserved from that time, and from the experience and files of his many influential friends. It is essentially a work of editing and selection, composed retrospectively by one who was personally involved in the situation he is recreating, and who was present on some of the occasions to which he refers.[21] It is only later, from *c.*1180 when he became dean of St Paul's, that his history acquires a quality of immediacy and takes on a more personal and more complete character. And herein lies the fascination of his handling of the Becket question. It is difficult to penetrate with any sense of certainty into his own thoughts on the matter, whether at the time of the original crisis or at the moment of his choosing and dissecting the documents many years later. To take a single example: his account of Becket's distress at Northampton in October 1164 is admittedly expressed in terms of sympathetic sorrow for the archbishop, but we would not suspect that this was the occasion of which William FitzStephen wrote: 'Similiter et Radulphus de Dicito . . . plurimum ea die ibi lacrymatus est.'[22] This element of self-effacement increases the character of ambivalent detachment in Diceto's treatment of delicate areas of conflict.

Yet there is no concealment of his loyalty to Henry II, or of his admiration of the king's qualities, energy and statesmanlike policies. And this devotion is a necessary backcloth to his view of the conflict between Henry and Becket. The king is the very pattern of the just and clement ruler – 'a tyrannide semper oculos deflexit et animum'.[23] He is shrewd in evaluation of his adversaries' motives, but ready to act

---

[19] A striking example of the sense of terror created at points of crisis is recorded in the letter *Mandatum vestrum*, which envoys of Thomas sent him from England before his return in late 1170 (note especially its postscript): *Materials for the History of Thomas Becket* (hereafter *Materials*), eds. J. C. Robertson and J. B. Sheppard, R.S. (7 vols., London, 1875–85), VII (1885), pp. 389–93, ep. 717.

[20] Diceto, II, pp. x–xii and 291–306; Chibnall, above, n.7, pp. 70–1.

[21] He was involved in negotiations leading to Foliot's translation in 1163 (Diceto, I, pp. xxxviii–xxxix and 309), was present at Northampton in 1164 (*ibid.*, pp. xlii–xliii), and was consulted by Richard of Ilchester on the latter's excommunication in 1166 (*ibid.*, pp. xliii–xliv and 319–20); and numerous similar examples can be cited throughout Diceto's career. The point is well discussed in Stubbs's introduction: I, introd., *passim*.

[22] Cf. Diceto, I, pp. 313–14, and FitzStephen, *Materials*, III (1877), p. 59.

[23] Diceto, I, p. 394.

to his own disadvantage for the general good or through family piety –
'Francos igitur vel dona ferentes evitasse debuerat' (a double thrust
here in adapting the Virgilian phrase to scorn the French).[24] So great
is his power and skill in government that the young King Philip of
France is reportedly advised to model himself upon him – 'ut igitur in
amministratione regni tanti principis informaretur exemplo'.[25] Lengthy
panegyrics extol the king's thirst and quest for justice, as also his
devoted care for the welfare and education of his children.[26] In a passage
of exceptional interest, Diceto attributes to the king both strength of
character and psychological insights, reflected in a conscious assumption of outward confidence in the face of heightening perils.[27] This is
the ruler whom he sees in hostility to his own spiritual father. Even in
this context, he registered important points in Henry's favour. Thus,
as Diceto has it, Henry won the approbation of many by his offer to
submit the quarrel to arbitration (though on his own terms) in 1169 –
'ita rex Angliae, qui prius odium in se plurimorum conflaverat, in hoc
verbo plurium favorem adeptus est'.[28] Likewise, he accepts from his
epistolary sources that, on hearing of Becket's murder, Henry offered
forthwith to submit to the Church's judgment and accept its verdict.[29]

There is no need to doubt the sincerity of Diceto's high praise of the
king. It would be over-simple to attribute it either to regard for a
powerful patron or to fear of retribution. Diceto's final draft was
completed after Henry's death, though the work of composition
was begun earlier. Other contemporary writers, notably Giraldus
Cambrensis and Ralph Niger, spoke without inhibition on the king's
public and private conduct. For Giraldus, the king was a notorious
adulterer, lacking in respect for God, a hammer of the Church and
born to its destruction – 'ecclesiae malleus et filius in perniciem natus'.[30]
The fair-minded William of Newburgh attributed a measure of blame
to archbishop and king alike, judging that no advantage came from
Becket's actions, but that rather they inflamed the wrath of the king
and brought many misfortunes in their train.[31] He concluded that the
acts of 'that venerable man' were not to be praised, though they
resulted from commendable zeal; but Henry's attitude to Becket

[24] Ibid., p. 394.
[25] Ibid., II, pp. 7–8.
[26] Ibid., I, pp. 434–7, and II, pp. 17–18.
[27] Ibid., I, pp. 373–4.
[28] Ibid., pp. 336–7.
[29] Ibid., p. 345.
[30] Giraldi Cambrensis Opera, edd. J. S. Brewer, J. F. Dimock and G. F. Warner, R.S. (8 vols.,
London, 1861–91), VIII (1891), De principis instructione liber, p. 160.
[31] Chronicles of the Reigns of Stephen, Henry II, and Richard I, ed. Howlett, I (1884), Willelmi Parvi,
canonici de Novoburgo, Historia Rerum Anglicarum, pp. 142–3 and 281.

also exceeded the bounds of moderation in its unreasoned rage – 'in absentem irrationabiliter saeviens, et plusquam deceret principem, effrenato furori indulgens'. In his general survey of the reign, William reflected that Henry's later misfortunes were in part the result of his failure to the end to abate the fierceness of his unhappy hostility to Becket (an unusually truthful record of the king's implacable enmity), and hoped that a happier fortune would be Henry's in another life.[32] Diceto's appraisal of the dispute stands quite apart from such positive statements, and in seeking to bridge the gulf between the two protagonists he presents an enigma. In a subtle passage, Professor Warren speaks of Diceto's doing his best for his friend, the king, and concludes that 'he seems to be writing on the defensive, as if he knew men would find it hard to believe him'.[33]

Indeed it is in his narrative treatment of Becket, both as a person and as the unflinching upholder of principle, that Diceto is most elusive and perplexing. If his position *vis-à-vis* the king was one of loyalty and admiration, his account of Becket's long ordeal and death is expressed with respect and reverence, though without evident warmth. Again, it would be over-simple to explain this approach as simply sharing in a general *ex post facto* devotion to the martyr and canonised saint. He had an expert knowledge of ecclesiastical law and the rights of the Church, which he himself defended on occasions; he clearly knew when customary policies or exceptional incidents were infringements of canon law, even if he sometimes considered a deviation from the strict law to be a matter of common sense or wisdom. There is no reason to doubt that he agreed with Becket on the controverted juristic principles, as did the English bishops in general. On single issues emerging in the course of the quarrel, he may well have seen in Becket a champion of claims close to his own heart, as in the rivalry between Canterbury and York. He did not believe in the subjection of the Church to secular domination, and such phrases as the *libertas ecclesiae* were not without important meaning to him. But he did not seek or support emotional and violent solutions to difficult problems, above all when he felt sympathy for both sides in the great dispute. If it is a truism that all men are to some extent the products of their age and environment, Diceto is nevertheless a striking example. He was a well-favoured member of the privileged strata in the English society

---

[32] *Ibid.*, p. 281.
[33] W. L. Warren, *Henry II* (London, 1973), pp. 214–15.

of his day, and a product of that network of family and social connections which provided many of the influential English ecclesiastics in his period – the ramifications of patronage by the Belmeis and Foliot families in his own London chapter clearly illustrate this factor.[34] To such a man, the growing tension between the ever more confident claims of canonists and theologians on the one hand, and the consolidation of traditional secular kingship, with its politico-theological infrastructure, on the other, was unwelcome and feared, and imperfectly understood.[35] This is a familiar and recurring predicament in Christian society, which must be recognised as the essential framework of the Becket dispute in its deepest sense, but as the explanation also of the minor part played within it by a clerk like the dean of St Paul's.

It was entirely natural to Diceto that secular and ecclesiastical leaders should work in harmony. It was familiar and customary, and mutually beneficial. He knew that canon law placed limitations on the secular activities of clerks, but Becket's refusal to continue in the office of chancellor on becoming archbishop in 1162 not only alienated the king – 'quod altius in cor regis ascendit' – but contrasted with the dual roles of the archbishops of Mainz and Cologne, who functioned also as arch-chancellors in the Empire.[36] In the same way, Henry's choice of the bishops of Winchester, Ely and Norwich as arch-justiciars of the realm in 1179 was admittedly 'contra canonum instituta', but seemed justified by the king's pursuit of incorruptible judges and followed a precedent in the career of Roger of Salisbury in the reign of Henry I.[37] Diceto's comments on the appointments of 1179 may well appear ingenuous to some, and he was certainly treading a razor's edge in describing Richard of Ilchester, Geoffrey Ridel and John of Oxford

---

[34] Diceto, I, pp. xx–xxx and xxxv–xl; C. N. L. Brooke, 'The Composition of the Chapter of St Paul's, 1086–1163', *Cambridge Historical Journal*, x (1951), pp. 111–32; *idem*, 'The Deans of St Paul's, c.1090–1499', *Bulletin of the Institute of Historical Research*, xxix (1956), pp. 231–44; *idem* and Morey, *Gilbert Foliot and his Letters*, and *Letters and Charters of Gilbert Foliot, passim*. Cf. A. T. Bannister, *The Cathedral Church of Hereford* (London, 1924), pp. 37–46, on 'The Rule of the Foliots' at Hereford.

[35] For the complex theological and ideological background, cf. Smalley, *Becket Conflict*. See now the important volume of essays: R. Foreville, ed., *Thomas Becket*, Actes du Colloque International de Sédières, August 1973 (Paris, 1975), e.g., J. Châtillon, 'Thomas Becket et les Victorins', pp. 89–101; and A. Graboïs, 'L'Idéal de la royauté biblique dans la pensée de Thomas Becket', pp. 103–10, together with discussions of both papers, *ibid.*, pp. 127–32. In a wider context, the studies by P. Classen are of outstanding importance: cf. his *Gerhoch von Reichersberg* (Wiesbaden, 1960); see also S. Chodorow, *Christian Political Theory and Church Politics in the Mid-Twelfth Century* (Berkeley, 1972).

[36] Diceto, I, pp. 307–8.

[37] *Ibid.*, pp. 434–5; this passage is discussed in C. Duggan, *Richard of Ilchester*, pp. 1–2.

(the bishops in question) as standing for the 'sanctuariam Dei'; but his general argument is readily understandable and was widespread among his contemporaries. In view of the central importance of canonical questions in the Becket dispute, Diceto's interest in canon law is clearly crucial. He was at once alert when some unusual point of law arose, or where infractions of basic principles cut across his own experience or that of his associates. In some such cases he cited in the *Ymagines* relevant precedents culled from the *Decretum* of Ivo of Chartres, and made cross-references to these same topics in a transcription of Ivo's preface, incorporated in his own *Abbreviationes Chronicorum*.[38] A few problems drew his special attention: the consecration of priests' sons and their succeeding in their fathers' churches, ecclesiastical restoration after deposition, and the translation of bishops from one see to another.[39] This last question was of immediate interest to him, by reason of Foliot's translation from Hereford to London, in which Diceto was himself involved, and other problems were familiar to him in the exercise of his office.[40] Yet he reveals in the *Ymagines* less direct concern with canon law and ecclesiastical legislation than we might expect. His treatment of the important conciliar business at Tours (1163), Westminster (1175) and the Lateran (1179) is surprisingly slight.[41]

The principal stages of the quarrel between Henry II and Becket are well known and need not be restated here, but Diceto's selection of texts and details requires evaluation, and provides at the same time an unusually succinct account. His record is set out most clearly in the *Series Causae inter Henricum Regem et Thomam Archiepiscopum*, devoted exclusively to the dispute and sent by him to the religious of Saint Colombe at Sens, which had provided a refuge for Becket in exile, after his departure from Pontigny. The work opens with Thomas's elevation to Canterbury and his resignation of the chancellorship in 1162, proceeds through the crisis and its aftermath to the canonisation in 1173, and concludes with a postilla on the devotion shown to the saint by magnates and prelates of France.[42] As noted already, the *Series*

---

[38] Diceto, I, pp. 32-3, esp. *ad finem*.   [39] *Ibid.*, pp. 305, 298, 309 and 413.
[40] *Ibid.*, pp. xxxviii–xl and 309, for the Foliot translation.
[41] *Ibid.*, pp. 310, 399 and 429-30. He provides no information on the canons of the 1163 council; of the Westminster Council, he says with brief significance 'Statuta concilii si bene revolveris perpauca reperies quae tibi corpus canonum incorporare non possit'; and of the important 1179 Lateran Council, he comments 'plurima memoriae plurimum commendanda statuta sunt ibi, de quibus saltem inseramus paucissima', adding merely two brief extracts dealing respectively with plurality and the privilege of Templars and Hospitallers in interdicted churches.
[42] *Ibid.*, II, pp. 279-85, for the *Series Causae*; cf. *Ymagines, ibid.*, I, pp. 307-14, 329 and 337.

Causae is in effect an integration of numerous relevant passages distributed through the annalistic strata of the *Ymagines*. In each work, high points of crisis are numbered in order of chronology and marked with the special symbol of two letters C, linked back to back, and defined in a prefatory table to the *Abbreviationes Chronicorum* by the phrase 'De controversiis inter regnum et sacerdotium'.[43] Thirteen passages are picked out in this way in the edition of the *Series Causae*, with one further and later item similarly designated in the *Ymagines*.[44] The phrase is apt in one obvious sense, but the use of the sign (one of Diceto's 'signa in margine posita') is limited, denoting a choice of incidents confined to the Becket dispute, almost entirely to its early phases, and wholly within the limits 1162-9. This is a narrower vision than the phrase suggests. The topics signalised are these: the voluntary resignation of the chancellorship by Becket, his enforced resignation of the Canterbury archdeaconry, resistance to his authority by Clarembald of St Augustine's, tenurial disputes between the archbishop and Earl Roger de Clare and William de Ros (concerning holdings in Kent), the king's reaction to the excommunication of William of Eynsford in an advowson dispute, his efforts to win to his side the pope in exile in France, the Council of Clarendon, the debate over criminous clerks, Thomas's abortive attempt to leave England after Clarendon, his dispute with John the Marshal over a property matter, and the ensuing crisis at the Council of Northampton. These first twelve stages mark the evolving crisis to October 1164, and thereafter the marginal sign is used only twice: once for a garbled reference to papal legates in 1166 (an apparent confusion of names and dates), and finally for the failure of attempts at reconciliation between the king and archbishop in 1169.[45] It could hardly be said that Diceto's use of his own marking device is comprehensive, yet it is strikingly effective in disclosing the nature of the quarrel and its diverse facets in the opening phases, as

[43] For Diceto's explanation and list of his *signa in margine posita*, cf. the preface to his *Abbreviationes Chronicorum, ibid.*, pp. 3-4. For Dr Smalley's discussion of this device, cf. references in n. 4, above.

[44] Diceto, I, p. 337; the symbol is not given at the corresponding position in II, p. 283.

[45] Diceto's account of the failure of negotiations for a reconciliation in 1166 is inaccurate, *ibid.*, I, p. 329. He refers to an abortive meeting of the papal legates William of Pavia and John of Naples with Henry and Becket at Montmirail in that year. William and John are not otherwise recorded as acting jointly, though William and Otto were involved in two meetings in late 1167 (firstly between Gisors and Trie, and secondly at Argentan); and there was a conference at Montmirail in January 1169, but the papal representatives there were Bernard de Corilo and Prior Simon of Mont Dieu. For a general discussion of Diceto's dating (excluding the present example), cf. *ibid.*, II, pp. xxxii-xlv.

these appeared to a closely-involved observer. Though couched in the language of a neutral record, his account reveals the devious methods adopted by the king in his response to Becket's stand. Diceto's narrative clearly shows how both ecclesiastical and secular persons, especially in Kent, seized the opportunity afforded by Becket's fall from royal favour to resist his authority or lordship, to advance their own interests and contribute to his distress and humiliation; and it is evident that they could count on the king's support in this. Diceto's narrative in general is of exceptional value in combining evidence both of the jurisdictional problems involved in the dispute (advowsons, clerical privilege, excommunication of tenants-in-chief and so forth) and the numerous personal and material factors which helped to shape the actual course of events. And the sequence of paragraphs marked for special emphasis presents such evidence even more directly.

But, in assessing Diceto's role as historian of the Becket dispute, it is at once apparent that many essential features are omitted or insufficiently explained. From his record, we should have a wholly inadequate knowledge of the complex legal arguments advanced at Clarendon in 1164 and no evidence at all of the *in terrorem* constitutions of 1169, to mention just two examples.[46] On the other hand, we find a fair and accurate summary of the points of agreement reached at Avranches in 1172 and the unique survival of Henry II's letter to Alexander III in 1176, following Pierleoni's mission as papal legate and marking the second decisive stage of reconciliation after Becket's death.[47] Diceto was much dependent on epistolary records for his reconstruction of the story, and his selection from the very large number of letters available was limited and fragmentary, but without partisan emphasis. Some letters are set out formally as such, with addresses and *incipits*, and transcribed verbatim, though not always in full. Others are adapted in a paraphrased version and incorporated without identification of source into his own composition. Many passages of seeming narrative or comment can be shown to be derived from letters in this way. At critical phases, he appears to seek a balance in the choice of texts, to

---

[46] *Ibid.*, I, pp. 312–13, for the Council of Clarendon; the record is extremely brief, but important for the criminous clerks dispute. The latest discussion (with texts) of the 1169 constitutions is by M. D. Knowles, A. J. Duggan and C. N. L. Brooke, 'Henry II's Supplement to the Constitutions of Clarendon', *EHR*, LXXXVII (1972), pp. 757–71.

[47] Diceto, I, pp. 351–2, 402–3 and 410. For the Avranches settlement, Diceto was probably using the text of a communication from the papal legates, Albert and Theodwin, to Henry II (cf. item 30, Appendix I, below), but his letter from Henry II to the pope in 1176 is among the most valuable of his records not otherwise known.

disclose the arguments of each side, as in his account of representations made to the pope in 1164, or in the selection of important letters from the year 1166.[48] The latter include Becket's famous and didactic *Desiderio desideravi* to the king, a letter of profound ideological interest, and his condemnatory *Mirandum et vehementer* to Gilbert Foliot.[49] These are hardly matched in power by the Canterbury suffragans' *Quae vestro pater*, reproachfully addressed to Becket, and Diceto omits Foliot's *Multiplicem*, the most important of all epistolary attacks on the archbishop.[50] The author's own letter to Richard of Ilchester in the same year, *Si tactus inconsulto*, perfectly exemplifies his personal moderation and respect for the due process of law, in advising Richard to accept with humility the sentence of excommunication imposed by Becket on Richard and others at Vézelay, though he dates the sentence inaccurately.[51] The letter is of further interest, since its contextual commentary makes no mention of the presence of the excommunicates at the schismatical council at Würzburg in 1165, which was specifically stressed in their condemnation. This *suppressio veri*, like the omission of *Multiplicem*, may well reflect the exercise of editorial tact.[52]

As far as the strictly jurisdictional issues are concerned, there can be little doubt that Diceto judged Becket's canonical arguments to be well grounded. His passage on the criminous clerks debate is of the utmost value in its brevity and precision. He makes crystal clear the king's procedural proposals for dealing with felonous clerks, and states the general episcopal dissent from this policy – 'Rex Anglorum volens in singulis ... In contrarium sentiebant episcopi *etc.*' There is no hint here of peculiarity in Becket's opposition to the king's plan.[53] And he

[48] Diceto, I, pp. 314–17 (cf. items 3 and 4, Appendix I, below), and 319–28 (cf. items 5–9, Appendix I, below).

[49] Diceto, I, pp. 320–1 and 323–5.

[50] *Ibid.*, pp. 321–3. For *Multiplicem*, cf. Knowles, *The Episcopal Colleagues of Archbishop Thomas Becket* (Cambridge, 1951), pp 171–80; Morey and Brooke, *Gilbert Foliot and his Letters*, pp. 166–87; and for the text, *eidem, Letters and Charters of Gilbert Foliot*, pp. 229–43, ep. 170.

[51] Diceto, I, pp. 318–20. Diceto records that the excommunications were promulgated on Ascension Day, whereas the correct dating is Whit Sunday. The *Ymagines* preserves the letter *Si tactus inconsulto* as addressed to Richard of Ilchester 'ab amico' (*ibid.*, p. 319, with editorial note 'Possibly by our author himself'), but the *Series Causae* places the matter beyond dispute with the addition 'Radulfo scilicet de Diceto' (*ibid.*, II, p. 282).

[52] *Ibid.*, I, p. 318. Diceto records that the excommunicates were condemned as observers, defenders and instigators of the *avitae consuetudines*; it is a serious omission that the presence of some at the schismatical council is not recorded by Diceto, since the verdict linked the interests of both Alexander III and Becket, of the Roman and the English Churches.

[53] *Ibid.*, p. 313. For discussion of the criminous clerks dispute in its canonical setting, cf. C. Duggan, 'The Becket Dispute and the Criminous Clerks', *Bulletin of the Institute of Historical Research*, XXXV (1962), pp. 1–28; *idem*, 'The Becket Dispute: William of Canterbury and

alone completes the story of this issue with a transcription of Henry's formal statement of the terms of the compromise in 1176.[54] Despite his friendship for the king and Foliot, he inserts letters of papal and archiepiscopal reproach to both, and his documented narrative of the circumstances of the Young King's coronation in 1170 and of the gathering storms preceding Becket's murder tilt the balance of sympathy rather in Thomas's favour.[55] But his ambivalence and caution are seen once more, when speaking of Henry's reactions to Becket's death. He records a measure of blame attributed by some personally to the king for the outrage, quoting the aged Henry of Winchester's stern rebuke to the king – 'qui eum pro morte gloriosi martyris increpavit durissime' – as well as the impassioned denunciation of the murder by Archbishop William of Sens.[56] At the same time, there is an unconvincing note in his statement of Henry's remorse at the moment of hearing of Becket's fate: even among conventional claims of the king's regrets, credulity is taken beyond reasonable limits by such excusatory comments as that Henry was blameless – 'nisi forte in hoc delictum sit, quod adhuc minus diligere credebatur archiepiscopum'.[57] This is an almost stunning understatement, but in this passage he is closely following a well-known letter by Arnulf of Lisieux, his old friend and Becket's adversary: the language is Arnulf's, not his own.[58] A seldom-noticed letter from the king proves that his immediate chief anxiety was that harmful repercussions should not adversely affect himself. The letter is entirely devoid of compassion for the victim, who indeed continues to be censured even in death.[59] Nevertheless, it is clear that Diceto strove to tread a path between contentious and prejudiced positions. It was earlier remarked that he achieved a notably objective summation, the more so in view of the complications of loyalties and

Clerical Privilege', in *The Reception of Canon Law in England in the Later-Twelfth Century*, Monumenta Iuris Canonici, Series C: Subsidia I (Vatican City, 1965), pp. 359–65 and 378–82; *idem*, 'Bishop John and Archdeacon Richard of Poitiers: Their Roles in the Becket Dispute and its Aftermath', in Foreville, ed., *Thomas Becket*, pp. 71–83, esp. pp. 76–8. For varied recent judgments, cf. Knowles, *Thomas Becket*, pp. 77–87; Smalley, *Becket Conflict*, pp. 124–37; Warren, *Henry II*, pp. 459–70, 480–1 and 537–42.   [54] Diceto, I, p. 410.

[55] *Ibid.*, pp. 332–5 and 338–41 (cf. items 13–16, 20, 22 and 23, Appendix I, below). On the coronation, cf. A. J. Duggan (A. J. Heslin), 'The Coronation of the Young King in 1170', *SCH*, II (1965), pp. 165–78.

[56] Diceto, I, pp. 347–8.   [57] *Ibid.*, p. 345.

[58] *Materials*, VII, pp. 438–9, ep. 738 (cf. item 25, Appendix I, below).

[59] *Materials*, VII, p. 440, ep. 739. This letter was not known in the collections of Becket correspondence, but is found inserted at the foot of a folio in the Avranches decretal collection (from Mont St Michel), Avranches, Bibl. de la Ville, MS 149; its significance and authenticity are discussed by C. Duggan, in Foreville, ed., *Thomas Becket*, pp. 192–3.

duties briefly discussed in this essay. It must be recognised that his silences and omissions are as significant as his assertions, and that he composed his account largely on a basis of documents selected from epistolary archives, documents which he dismembered and dissected at will.[60] Yet, if we had Diceto's version of the Becket dispute in isolation, none other surviving, the more favourable verdict between the opposing parties would be awarded to Becket, and with some reluctance against our author's friends. But it would be a finely balanced judgment.

APPENDIX I

LIST OF LETTERS, SPEECHES AND RELATED DOCUMENTS, USED IN THE 'YMAGINES HISTORIARUM' FOR THE PERIOD 1163–73

It is plain that Diceto relied extensively on epistolary sources for the years from Becket's elevation as archbishop to his canonisation. Substantial sections are composed almost entirely of transcriptions, abbreviations or paraphrases of letters, sometimes very freely rendered. The list below cites such letters, whether they have been clearly set out as documents or have been identified as sources of seemingly narrative passages, together with a small number of allocutions or reports. Others may yet be discovered by further research. The list is drawn up as follows: where a letter is formally transcribed as such, its *incipit* in Diceto's version is stated first, followed by the true *incipit* in parentheses if the opening has been truncated. Where a letter has been adapted or woven into the narrative, the opening and closing phrases of Diceto's adaptation are given first, and the item is marked with an asterisk; the original letter is then identified. The sender and recipient are named wherever possible, the page location in the first volume of the printed edition (RD) is noted, with the year in which Diceto places the item. Where appropriate, the number of the original in Robertson's edition of the Becket Materials (BM) is given, and its number in Jaffé's *Regesta Pontificum Romanorum* (JL) in the case of a papal letter. Finally, the correct date is noted, or the closest approximation to the true date is suggested on the basis of internal and circumstantial evidence. More exact dating may be achieved later in some cases. The list is set out in order of appearance in the *Ymagines*, but Diceto's dating is not always correct; a few items are seriously misplaced.

1. *Ex litteris karissimi:* Alexander III to the London chapter, RD 309 (1163), JL 10838, 19 March 1163.
2. *Ex antiqua Romanorum:* Alexander III to Louis VII, RD 310–11 (1163), JL 10826, 1 March 1163.

[60] Diceto's access to the archives of Gilbert Foliot has been frequently assumed, and will be further discussed by A. Duggan; see also *eadem, Thomas Becket: a textual history of his letters* (Oxford, 1980). For collections of papal letters, cf. C. Duggan, *Twelfth-Century Decretal Collections and their Importance in English History*, University of London Historical Studies XII (London, 1963).

3. 'Inter Thomam ... parentaret' (*Medicinae potius*): royal envoys to the pope in consistory at Sens, RD 314–15 (1164); extract from *Medicinae potius:* 'enemies of Thomas' to Alexander III and cardinals, BM ep.73; allocution in the papal consistory, early November 1164 (perhaps drafted in England, late October).

4. 'Ad audientiam tuam ... repertor': allocution by Thomas in the presence of Alexander III, RD 316–17 (1164), BM ep.74, mid-November 1164.

5. *Si tactus inconsulto:* Diceto to Richard of Ilchester, RD 319–20 (1166), BM ep.211, in or shortly after late June 1166.

6. *Desiderio desideravi:* Thomas to Henry II, RD 320–1 (1166), BM ep.154, April–May 1166.

7. *Quae vestro pater:* Canterbury suffragans *et al.* to Thomas, RD 321–3 (1166), BM ep.205, *c.*24 June 1166.

8. *Mirandum et vehementer:* Thomas to Gilbert Foliot, RD 323–5 (1166), BM ep.224, in or after July 1166.

9. *Fraternitatis vestrae:* Thomas to his suffragans, RD 326–8 (1166), BM ep.223, in or after July 1166.

10. *Praedecessorum nostrorum* (*In apostolicae sedis*): Alexander III to Thomas, RD 330 (1167), BM ep.170, JL 11268, 8 April 1166.

11. *Cum clerum plurimum:* anonymous report on council of Würzburg, RD 331 (1168): to Alexander III; BM ep.99: 'De schismatis innovatione'. RD address and text appropriate for letter to the pope, but BM text suggests this improbable; cf. BM ep.98, *Imperator cum principes*, letter of similar content from a friend to Alexander III. End of May 1165 or (more probably) soon after.

12. *Mandatum vestrum:* Gilbert Foliot to Alexander III, RD 331–2 (1168), BM ep.108, late July or early August 1165.

13. *Quam paterne:* Alexander III to Henry II, RD 332–3 (1169), BM ep.423, JL 11404, 22 May 1168.

14. *Excessus vestros:* Thomas to Gilbert Foliot, RD 333 (1169), BM ep.479, *c.*April 1169.

15. *Vestram non debet:* Thomas to the dean, archdeacon and clergy of London, RD 334 (1169), BM ep.488, 13 April 1169.

16. *Serenitatem tuam* (*Ex naturali ratione*): Alexander III to Henry II, RD 334–5 (1169), BM ep.492, JL 11621, 10 May 1169.

*17. 'Siquidem dignitas ... consequatur' (*Nuntios et litteras*): Norman bishops and clergy to Alexander III, RD 336 (18 November 1169), BM ep.567, after 8 September 1169.

18. 'Hoc petimus ... permittat': petition of Thomas to Henry II, presented at Montmartre, RD 336 (18 November 1169), BM ep.604, 18 November 1169; incorporated also in *Omnem operam*, report on the Montmartre conference by Vivian to Alexander III, BM ep.607.

19. *Rotomagensi archiepiscopo* (*Quod tibi ad praesens*): Alexander III to Gilbert Foliot, RD 337–8 (1170), BM ep.627, JL 11716, 12 February 1170.

20. *Illius dignitatis:* Alexander III to the archbishop of York and all the bishops of England, RD 338 (before June 1170), BM ep.169, JL 11267, 5 April 1166.

21. *Sciatis quod Thomas:* Henry II to the Young King, RD 339 (1170), BM ep.690, *c.*15 October 1170.

22. *Cum filium suum* (*Licet commendabiles*): Alexander III to Roger of York and Hugh of Durham, RD 339-40 (1170), BM ep.701, JL 11836, 16 September 1170.

23. *Cum karissimus filius* (*Oportuerat vos*): Alexander III to the bishops of London, Salisbury, Exeter, Chester, Rochester, St Asaph and Llandaff, RD 340-1 (1170), BM ep.700, JL 11835, 16 September 1170.

24. *Adductus est* (*Quam iustis*): Thomas to Alexander III, RD 341-2 (1170), BM ep.723, early December 1170; extracted also from *Quam iustis:* 'Evocavit rex . . . episcoporum', RD 342.

★25. 'Rex Anglorum . . . repromisit' (*Cum apud regem*): Arnulf of Lisieux to Alexander III, RD 345 (1171), BM ep.738, early January 1171.

★26. 'Missi sunt nuncii . . . foverent', RD 345-6 (1171), constructed largely from passages in *Noverit vestra,* BM ep.750, 28 March 1171 and *Qui fuerint primi,* BM ep.751, April 1171: respectively, royal envoys' report to Henry II and royal envoy's letter to Richard of Ilchester.

27. *Vestro apostolatui:* William of Sens to Alexander III, RD 347-8 (1171), BM ep.740, January 1171.

★28. 'Rotro Rotomagensis . . . restitutus', RD 348 (1171), probably paraphrased from *Et ipsa loci:* Alexander III to Rotrou of Rouen and the bishop of Amiens, BM ep.763, JL 11908, 23 October 1171.

★29. 'Rotro Rotomagensis . . . ecclesiam', RD 351 (1172), probably paraphrased from *Fraternitati vestrae:* Alexander III to Rotrou of Rouen and the bishop of Amiens, BM ep.767, JL 12143, 28 February 1172.

★30. 'Post longos . . . promisit', RD 351-2 (1172), probably paraphrased from *Ne in dubium:* Albert and Theodwin to Henry II, BM ep.772, on or after 21 May 1172.

31. *Inspirante Illo:* Albert and Theodwin to clerks and monks of vacant churches in England, RD 366-7 (1173), BM ep.789, late 1172 or early 1173.

32. *Redolet Anglia:* Alexander III to the prelates, clergy and people of England, RD 369-70 (13 March 1173), BM ep.785 (12 March 1173); cf. JL 12203 and 12204, 12 and 13 March 1173; cf. also JL 12218, 2 April 1173: Alexander III to William of Sens.

APPENDIX II

DICETO AND THE SOURCES OF CANON LAW, WITH PARTICULAR REFERENCE TO DECRETAL LETTERS[61]

The present essay has indicated only very briefly the interest of Ralph de Diceto in questions of canon law and his use of canonical sources. This is a major topic which will be explored in a separate study. Meanwhile, the importance of the *Ymagines Historiarum* for the criminous clerks controversy and for the two principal phases of

---

[61] This section is appended in recognition of the special debt owed by CD to Walter Ullmann, under whose guidance his interest in the decretal collections first began.

reconciliation following Becket's death, in 1172 and 1175-6, should be emphasised. Likewise, his comments on the jurisdictional conflicts and on problems arising from a strict application of canonical principles in the political climate of his day are most illuminating. It is necessary to investigate further his use of the more formative books of canon law, of Gratian and the new decretal collections, with which it must be assumed he was familiar, and his approach to conciliar edicts. But it will be revealing also to examine the extent of his personal involvement in the administration of canon law. His duties as archdeacon of Middlesex and later as dean of St Paul's drew him into the routine business of the Church courts, but he was also the recipient of papal mandates and commissions, and acted occasionally as a papal judge delegate. A few examples must suffice here to illustrate both his own use of papal decretals as a chronicler and also the importance of letters which he himself received.

(a) *Nos attendentes* (JL 13106) and *Causam que inter* (JL 14002)

The mandate *Nos attendentes*, from Alexander III to the bishops of London and Winchester, is found in the *Ymagines Historiarum* under the date 1 October 1178. This date establishes the recipients as Gilbert Foliot and Richard of Ilchester, both of whom were on terms of close familiarity with Diceto. It is a brief passage which asserts that questions of property are subject to the king's jurisdiction, not to that of the Church. Noting that King Henry has been much disturbed in this matter, the pope orders the bishops to leave the judgment of possessions to the king. Stubbs remarked that this was an original document, not otherwise known, and it was listed in the *Regesta* from this single source (JL 13106). The papal ruling is of such evident importance for the history of jurisdictional conflicts that scholars have frequently been drawn to its evaluation. Its context has remained unknown. One striking theory is that Alexander III here laid down a general principle of law, advisedly to two English prelates of special influence.[62] But it can now be shown that *Nos attendentes* is an excerpt from the marriage decretal *Causam que inter*, which Alexander III sent to Gilbert and Richard. The decretal records one phase in a great marriage dispute involving the Arderne (or de Ardenna) family. It is found in sixteen decretal collections, including the *Appendix Concilii Lateranensis* (33.4) and the Gregorian *Decretales* (4.17.7). It is separately registered in the *Regesta* (JL 14002), and must be read with a further decretal, *Causam que vertitur*, to the Bishops Bartholomew of Exeter and Richard of Winchester and Abbot Baldwin of Ford (JL 13932: in thirteen decretal collections; cf. *Decretales* 1.29.17, 4.17.4, and 2.14.3). *Causam que vertitur* records a later stage in the same dispute, and includes a new papal ruling notwithstanding previous references to the question of possession and the king's court.[63] It is therefore clear that Diceto's *Nos attendentes* is misleadingly abbreviated, since it records a judgment in a particular case and was not devised as a considered statement of general principle. Neither marriage decretal was dated more narrowly than 1159-81 in the *Regesta*, though Holtzmann in

---

[62] Cf. C. Duggan, *Richard of Ilchester*, p. 16.
[63] The Arderne case is discussed in A. Morey, *Bartholomew of Exeter: bishop and canonist* (Cambridge, 1937), pp. 68-70.

his unpublished index reduced the limits to 1174–81, the *terminus a quo* being decided by Richard's consecration as bishop of Winchester in 1174.[64] The combined evidence of the decretal collections and Diceto's entry shows that *Nos attendentes* is part of *Causam que inter*, that JL 13106 and 14002 are therefore one and the same letter, whose date is 1 October 1178, and that *Causam que vertitur* (JL 13932) was issued between that date and Alexander III's death in 1181. The identity of the core of *Causam que inter* and *Nos attendentes* is made clear in Document A, below.

(b) *Audito laudabili* (JL 13897) and *Dignum est* (JL 14183)

The papal dispensation *Audito laudabili* is placed by Diceto at the close of December 1189, though it was issued by Alexander III, and cannot therefore be later than 1181. It is addressed to the Archdeacon Richard of Ely, and grants that he could by papal indulgence proceed to an ecclesiastical benefice or dignity, despite his illegitimacy. It was doubtless inserted at that point as an appropriate preface to the record of Richard's consecration as bishop of London on 31 December 1189.[65] Stubbs noted that the letter could not have been issued after 1181, and concluded that it came into Diceto's hands at the time of Richard's consecration, which is indeed one possible explanation. Richard was the famous FitzNeal, treasurer to King Henry II and author of the *Dialogus de Scaccario*. He was archdeacon of Ely from *c*.1158, a canon of London by 1181, and dean of Lincoln from *c*.December 1183. He was nominated for the bishopric of Lincoln in 1186, but unsuccessfully, and became bishop of London in 1189, as noted here.[66] At which stage in his career Richard obtained the papal dispensation has not been determined. Charles Johnson argued that Richard became archdeacon about 1160 and 'must have received his dispensation from Alexander III' at that time.[67] If the more recent view is correct that Richard was archdeacon from *c*.1158, he could not have been granted the indulgence to proceed to that office by Alexander III (1159–81). Moreover, the form of address in Diceto's record raises a query, since it names Richard as archdeacon in a letter granting him permission to accept an ecclesiastical benefice and rank in the future. This problem lies open for further study, but it may be conjectured that Richard secured the papal letter in expectation of higher preferment. The address and dating could point to the London canonry, which might also explain Diceto's possession of a copy. In the absence of firmer evidence, the grant can be dated only by the limits of Alexander III's pontificate, as it is listed from this source in the *Regesta* (JL 13897).

[64] For this reference and other decretal discussions, thanks are due to Professor Stephan Kuttner for generous access to the Holtzmann papers in the Institute of Medieval Canon Law in the University of California at Berkeley. Full details of all known decretal collections of the twelfth century, their manuscript locations, editions, analyses and secondary literature are now provided in C. R. Cheney and Mary G. Cheney, eds., *Studies in the Collections of Twelfth-Century Decretals: from the papers of the late Walther Holtzmann* (Vatican City, 1979). All collections cited in the present paper are fully documented in this volume.   [65] Diceto, II, pp. 74–5.

[66] For the most recent details of Richard's career, cf. D. E. Greenway, *John Le Neve, Fasti Ecclesiae Anglicanae, 1066–1300: Lincoln* (London, 1977), p. 9. His various offices were noted by Diceto, II, p. 69.

[67] *Dialogus de Scaccario*, ed. Charles Johnson (Nelson's Medieval Texts: London, 1950), p. xv.

Now *Audito laudabili* should be compared with the decretal *Dignum est*, which deals with an identical dispensation and is found only in the three systematic collections *Tanner* (3.12.5), *Francofortana* (12.7), and *Compilatio Prima* (1.9.9), which latter affords an edited text.[68] This letter is also listed in the *Regesta* for Alexander III's pontifical years, its recipient being uncertain (JL 14183: 'Cuidam' and 'Eboracensi archiepiscopo perperam inscribitur'). It was not part of the main transcription in *Tanner*, where it was inserted later with a shortened text, and was added to one codex of *Compilatio Prima*. Both these sources record an address from Alexander III to the archbishop of York, which cannot be reconciled with the dispensation. The evidence of the *Francofortana* codices is unhelpful – one has an uncertain reading, except that Alexander is named as the sender, and the others associate the text with the 1179 Lateran Council, which is seemingly a scribal error. In these circumstances the context of *Dignum est* has lacked a solution. Holtzmann pondered the election of Geoffrey, illegitimate son of Henry II, to York in 1191 as a possible solution, but rightly decided against it. The presence of the letter in the *Francofortana* collections would rule out a date as late as Geoffrey's election to York, and the York address cannot be accurate. Nor is an address to Lincoln acceptable. Geoffrey was elected to Lincoln in 1173, when he was already an archdeacon, but he was also then under age, and Diceto records that Alexander III granted a delayed dispensation 'tam aetatis quam nativitatis' in 1175 (RD I, 392–3 and 401). A collation of the decretal *Dignum est* with Diceto's text *Audito laudabili* provides a very convincing explanation. The FitzNeal dispensation is almost certainly part of the decretal *Dignum est*. By the same reasoning, JL 13897 and 14183 are one and the same letter, recording variants of the papal dispensation sent to Richard of Ely sometime within the limits of Alexander III's pontificate. The false address to York could conceivably spring from a scribe's misreading of Archdeacon Richard of Ely as Archbishop Roger of York (cf. 'R. elien. archi.' and 'R. eboracen. archi.'). Similarities in the careers of Richard and Geoffrey could likewise give rise to a mistake. The possibility must be allowed that Alexander III issued identically phrased letters to meet comparable situations, and therefore that two distinct letters are in consideration. But the collation of *Dignum est* and *Audito laudabili* in Document B, below, reveals their striking similarity, and justifies the proposal that they are derivatives from a single text.

(c) *Retulit nobis* and *Indignum est* (JL 15172 and 15177)

The foregoing examples have shown how Diceto's excerpts from papal letters may be freshly examined in the light of more recent studies on the decretals. The latter also disclose his involvement in delegated jurisdiction. He was quite possibly the Archdeacon R. of London commissioned with Gilbert Foliot by Alexander III in the letter *Significatum est nobis* (JL 14222: 1163–81), but the identification is uncertain, since there were other Archdeacons R. in the London diocese at that time. The decretal mandated action against clerical and lay incontinence in the area subject to

68 E. Friedberg, *Quinque Compilationes Antiquae necnon Compilatio Lipsiensis* (Leipzig, 1882), p. 5.

them.[69] He was certainly the recipient of a number of commissions by Lucius III (1181–5), when he was dean of St Paul's. Jointly with his Archdeacon Nicholas, he settled a dispute between St Bartholomew's Hospital and Peter of Wakering over the church of Little Wakering in Essex, in the years c.1182–6.[70] Among the letters which he received from Lucius, the decretal *Retulit nobis* is of exceptional interest. As noted already, Dr Smalley remarked that Diceto 'has a right to the last word' on the Becket dispute.[71] By a strange chance, he was quite literally a recipient of the last word in the Gregorian *Decretales*, the most important official collection of canon law in the middle ages, though his identity there would pass unnoticed. The closing entry in the *Decretales* appears under the title 'De regulis iuris', with a chapter rubric 'Pro spiritualibus homagium non praestatur' (5.41.11). The total entry under these headings is 'Lucius III. Indignum est et a Romanae ecclesiae consuetudine alienum, ut pro spiritualibus facere quis homagium compellatur.' It is found in this form both in the sixteenth-century edition by the *Correctores Romani* and in the standard nineteenth-century edition by Friedberg. But Friedberg drew on the evidence of additional manuscripts and other collections, which provided a fuller text and a further *incipit*, *Retulit nobis*. His critical apparatus recorded the discovery of various corrupted versions of the address: 'decano Bidea et abbati de Fi', 'Eborac. archiep. et Lendon. decano et abb. de Filien.' and 'Eborac. archiep. et decano Lundon. et abb. de Fi.'. From these sources the letter was listed in the *Regesta* (JL 15172), with both *incipits*, *Retulit nobis* and *Indignum est*. But a further entry in the *Regesta* (JL 15177) refers to a letter *Retulit nobis*, transcribed in the Paris B.N. MS 16992, fo.220. This letter deals with the same matter as the decretal, with an address 'Episcopo Herefordensi et abbati de Faversham'. From this evidence it seemed likely that the archbishop of York, the bishop of Hereford, the dean of London and the abbot of Faversham provided a list of possible recipients, that JL 15172 and 15177 were derived from a single letter, and that *Indignum est* is a fragment of *Retulit nobis*, stating an important juristic principle excerpted from a longer letter dealing with an individual case. These conjectures prove mostly correct, except that the inclusion of the archbishop of York is an error and his name must be deleted. The letter is found in ten decretal collections. The complete text is preserved only in *Cheltenhamensis* (14.7), but mostly also in *Sangermanensis* (3.9.2 and 10.78), *Abrincensis* (3.6.1), *Alanus* (5.14.1) and *Fuldensis* (5.17.2). The correct address is 'Lucius III Herefordensi episcopo et decano Londoniensi et abbati de Faversham', and the decretal is 'Retulit nobis . . . appellavit', concerning an important dispute between the bishop of Chichester and his archdeacon. The complete letter is printed for the first time in Document C, below.[72] Since the dating limits are determined by Lucius III's pontificate, the recipients were

---

[69] The latter is found only in the *Belverensis* decretal collection, contained in an important volume of Foliot materials: cf. C. Duggan, *Twelfth-Century Decretal Collections*, pp. 71–3 and 155–62: cf. no.2.6, p. 158.

[70] Morey and Brooke, *Letters and Charters of Gilbert Foliot*, pp. 452–3.

[71] Smalley, *Becket Conflict*, p. 230.

[72] The case is discussed in its historical setting in *The Acta of the Bishops of Chichester*, ed. H. Mayr-Harting, Canterbury and York Society cxxx (Torquay, 1962), pp. 50–1.

Bishop Robert Foliot of Hereford, Dean Ralph de Diceto of St Paul's, and Abbot Guerric of Faversham. The disputants in the case were Bishop Seffrid II of Chichester and Archdeacon Jocelin of Lewes.[73]

APPENDIX III

DOCUMENTS

A Collation of *Causam que inter* and *Nos attendentes*; cf. Appendix IIa above. The version of *Causam que inter* supplied here is a composite text, based principally on *Wigorniensis* (7.9), with improved personal names derived from *Roffensis* (60). The greater part of the letter was transmitted to the *Decretales* (4.17.7). The text of *Nos attendentes* is reproduced from the edition of the *Ymagines Historiarum* (RD 1.427–8).

Causam que inter	*Nos attendentes*
Causam, que inter *ᵃFrancum et R. de Ardena super eo quod Agathaᵃ* mater iamdicti R. dicitur non fuisse de legitimo matrimonio nata agitari dinoscitur, experientie vestre commisimus terminandam. Verum quoniam litteris nostris inseri fecimus ut predicto R. possessionem omnium eorum quorum possessor extitit quando avus suus iter Ierosolimam proficiendiᵇ arripuit ante principalis cause ingressum feceritisᶜ appellatione cessante restitui, si eadem possessione fuisset per violentiam spoliatus, nosᵈ attendentes quod ad regem pertineat, non ad ecclesiam, de talibus possessionibus iudicare, ne videamur iuri ᵉet dignitati carissimi in Christo filii nostri Henriciᵉ regis Anglorum detrahere, qui sicut accepimus commotus est et turbatus, quod de possessionibus scripsimus, ᶠcum ipsarum iudicium ad se asserat pertinere,ᶠ volumus et fraternitati vestre mandamus ut regi possessionum iudicium relinquentes de causa principali, videlicet utrum predicta mulier de legitimo	Nos attendentes quod ad regem pertineat, nonecclesiam, de possessionibus iudicare, ne videamur iuri et dignitati karissimi in Christo filii nostri H. illustris Anglorum regis detrahere, qui sicut accepimus commotus est et turbatur, quod de possessionibus scripsimus, cum earum iudicium ad se asserat pertinere, volumus et fraternitati vestre mandamus, ut regi possessionum iudicium relinquatis.

a–a R. et F. super eo quod *Wig.* and *Decretales* (X); Francum et R. de Ardena super nativitate ipsius R. . . . utrum Agath(a) mater R. *etc Roff.* *b* proficiscendi X *c* faceretis X *d* om. *Wig.* *e–e* om. *Wig.* *f–f* om. Wig.

73 *Ibid.*, and pp. 209–13.

matrimonio fuerat nata, plenius
cognoscatis et appellatione remota
secundum formam aliarum litterarum
nostrarum terminetis, licet videatur
incongruum quod matrimonium matris
prefati R. impetatur,ᵍ quod ea vivente
non fuit ut dicitur impetitum.

Data Tusculani kalendis Octobris.

ᵍ impretatur *Wig.*

B Collation of *Dignum est* and *Audito laudabili*; cf. Appendix IIb above. The text of
Dignum est is taken from the *Francofortana codices* (12.7). *Audito laudabili* is repro-
duced from the edition of the *Ymagines Historiarum* (RD 2.74–5: 'Alexander papa
IIIᵗⁱᵘˢ Ricardo Elyensi archidiacono').

<table>
<tr><td>

ᵃDignum est

Dignum est et rationi consentaneum
ut qui litterarum scientia sunt prediti
et honestatis moribus ornati preroga-
tivam favoris et gratie nostre obtineant
et speciali privilegio decorentur honoris.
Inde est quod de te laudabili multorum
testimonio audito, quod videlicet
scientia litterarum et honestatis moribus
sis ornatus, tibi de consueta clementia
et benignitate apostolice sedis indul-
gemus ut, si aliqua ecclesia annuente
domino te ad beneficium vel dignitatem
quamlibet vocaverit, non obstante quia
non es de legitimo matrimonio natus,
libere valeas ad beneficium vel digni-
tatem assumi. Ita tamen ut, que tibi de
speciali beneficio indulgemus, non
debeant aliis in posterum legem
prefigere, nec in exemplum deduci,
statuentes ut nulli omnino homini
liceat hanc paginam nostre concess-
ionis infringere et ei aliquatenus
contraire. Si quis etc.

</td><td>

Audito laudabili

Audito laudabili multorum
testimonio, quod
scientia litterarum et honestatis moribus
sis adornatus, tibi de consueta clementia
et benignitate sedis apostolice indul-
gemus ut, si aliqua ecclesia annuente
Deo te ad beneficium vel dignitatem
quamlibet vocaverit, non obstante quia
non es de legitimo matrimonio natus,
libere valeas ad beneficium vel digni-
tatem assumi.

</td></tr>
</table>

ᵃ inscription in *Tanner* (3.12.5): Al. III Ebor. arch.; in *Compilatio Prima* (1.9.9): Idem (*scil.*
Alexander III) Eboracensi archiepiscopo; in the Frankfurt, Troyes, and St Maximin codices of
Francofortana (12.7): ex concilio Lateranensi; the Rouen codex has the ambiguous reading: li alex̄.
III. An adjacent letter in *Tanner* (3.12.6) and *Francofortana* (12.6) is addressed to the bishop-elect
(Geoffrey) of Lincoln: JL 13982. As noted already, the text is a later addition in *Tanner*, trans-
cribed at the foot of the folio; it stops short at 'legem prefigere'. Friedberg's edition of *Compilatio*

C The text of *Retulit nobis*; cf. Appendix IIc above. This text is based on *Chelten-hamensis* (14.7), *Sangermanensis* (3.9.2 and 10.78), *Abrincensis* (3.6.1), *Frag. Riccar-dianum* (55), and *Compilatio Secunda* (5.13.2). Among decretal sources, the complete text is found only in *Chelt.*; only paragraph [b] was transmitted to the *Decretales*; and paragraph [c] has not been found elsewhere in print.*

Retulit nobis

Lucius III Herefordensi episcopo et decano Lundoniensi et abbati de Faversham.

1181-5

[a] Retulit nobis dilectus filius noster Jocelinus archidiaconus Cicestrensis quod, cum canonice archidiaconatum Cicestrensem possideat, eius episcopus pro eo quod decanatum tanquam quem sibi credit de iure competere vendicare laborat, ipsi prorsus infestus iura ipsius minuere et que ad archidiaconatum de consuetudine et iure spectare noscuntur turbare et subtrahere post appellationem ad sedem apostolicam factam non desistit. Preterea homagium ab eo et fidelitatem novam pro sua voluntate requirit. Volentes igitur paci et iustitie ipsius archidiaconi paterna dilectione providere, discretioni vestre per apostolica scripta precipiendo mandamus quatinus inquisita diligentius veritate, si eum predecessori episcopo et successoribus eius fidelitatem iurasse constiterit, iam dictum episcopum ex parte nostra moneatis et ecclesiastica censura nullius appellatione obstante auctoritate nostra cogatis ut iura archidiaconatus integra archidiaconum sine contradictione possidere permittat, et ab exactione homagii et fidelitatis omnino desistat.

[b] Indignum siquidem est et a Romane ecclesie consuetudine alienum ut pro spiritualibus facere homagium quisquam compellatur.

[c] Si que vero post appellationem factam vel postquam archidiaconus iter arripuit ad sedem apostolicam veniendi circa eum vel possessiones suas videritis innovata vel mutata, omnia in eum statum appellatione remota reducatis in quo fuisse constiterit quando archidiaconus appellavit.

Prima notes that the text is in the Augustiniana edition but otherwise missing, except that it appears as a marginal addition in cod. Friburgensis 361a. The transmission of the text in the decretal collections merits further study.

* In addition to the collections listed above, the following also contain parts of the decretal: *Dunelmensis Secunda* (151b), *Alanus* (5.14.1), *Fuldensis* (5.17.2), *Compilatio Prima* (5.37.13), and *Decretales* (5.41.11).

FIDES ET CULPA: THE USE OF ROMAN LAW IN ECCLESIASTICAL IDEOLOGY

by E. F. VODOLA

HISTORIANS are always concerned with the bond which links the individual to society and its institutions, and with the ideology which surrounds this bond. In his work Walter Ullmann has shown that the legal and theological tracts of the Middle Ages offer an unusually full and articulate documentation of medieval social attitudes, enabling us to examine the ideology of ecclesiastical authority in considerable detail. In my own research under Professor Ullmann's supervision I studied the relationship between the individual and the society of the *ecclesia* in the two crucial rites of baptism and excommunication.

Excommunication was the principal sanction of the legal system of the Church, and its consequences, social, legal, and political, were both far-reaching and severe. One could not appreciate the versatility of this sanction without wondering from where it derived its strength; for the entire system of ecclesiastical law was imposed upon a society which was already governed by at least one system of public law, and sometimes, where for example both feudal and communal laws obtained, by several. Why should the ordinary individual have felt himself to be bound also by the laws of the Church?

At least part of the answer lay in baptism, since it was in baptism that the individual became subject to ecclesiastical authority. Although the canon law of baptism itself is chiefly theological and liturgical in its orientation, the significance of the sacrament in the public sphere is more apparent in the penal legislation through which the Church exerted its authority. Nowhere is this more evident than in Boniface VIII's decretal *Contra Christianos*, which declared that Christians or converted Jews who apostasised to Judaism should be treated as heretics.[1] *Contra Christianos* treated baptism as an event in the life of the individual which could be considered quite independently from the subjective question of faith: those baptised as infants and those bap-

[1] VI.5.2.13.

tised under threat of death were alike fully subject to ecclesiastical authority and liable to be charged with heresy.

Innocent III had laid the groundwork for this principle in the decretal *Maiores*.[2] Written in response to heretics who denied the efficacy of infant baptism on the grounds that sin could not be dismissed without faith and charity, *Maiores* declared that the inability of the infant to 'believe' did not impede the effect of the sacrament. Linked with the problem of infant baptism was that of adults who had not given their consent to the rite, either because they were comatose or mad or because they were baptised under duress. Innocent decided that those who were comatose or mad could be said to be baptised validly if they had been catechumens before falling ill. But the problem of those baptised under duress was almost insoluble for an institution based on faith. Innocent referred to the canon *De Iudeis* in the *Decretum*, taken from the Fourth Council of Toledo, which seemed to confer *de facto* validity upon forcible baptisms, since it declared that certain Jews who had been coerced into receiving the sacrament should be compelled to uphold the faith. Enlarging upon this canon, Innocent drew a distinction between conditional and total coercion, and determined that only the individual who had been literally dragged through the ceremony could be excused from the obligation of faith. In other words any sign of free-will was sufficient for the validity of the sacrament: even the individual who accepted baptism only under torture and threat was the subject of ecclesiastical authority.

Maiores and *Contra Christianos* are convincing testimony of the penetration of fundamentally legal concepts into the doctrine of baptism. The cavalier treatment of the whole problem of the subjectivity of faith and belief suggests that theological considerations were subordinated to the directives of the law. In itself this is not very surprising; for the use of the sanction of excommunication, especially against heretics, seems to have been predicated on the assumption that the psychological entity of belief was subservient to the strong arm of the law.[3] What is surprising, however, is that this legalistic approach to baptism had come to dominate doctrine as early as 1201, the year in which *Maiores* was promulgated. While the theologians had only begun to debate the psychological effects of baptism the jurists had evidently accomplished the task of assimilating baptism into the field of law.

[2] x.3.42.3; cf. *Clem.1.1.uni.*
[3] See in the *Decretum* C. 23–6, and for Gratian's own cogent arguments see especially *d. p. c. 4*, C. 23 q. 6.

In this paper we shall be examining both the origins of this doctrinal development among the canonists and the mature expression of the legalistic approach to baptism in the *Glossa Palatina* of Laurentius Hispanus, which was published a little more than a decade after the promulgation of *Maiores*.

'FIDES' IN THE DECRETIST PERIOD

The speed with which the canonists assimilated baptism into the realm of law is the more surprising because the first generation of decretists seems to have taken very little interest in the sacrament. Yet the mainly theological texts of *De consecratione* D. 4, the section of the *Decretum* which deals with baptism, provide even in themselves some foundation for a legalistic interpretation of baptism because of the patristic exploitation of the vocabulary of Roman law. The term *sacramentum* itself had several specific legal uses in Roman law, and in a general sense referred to any act which was sealed with an oath.[4] Over and above vocabulary, the rite of baptism from a very early time incorporated a confession of faith which, in its format of question and response, seems to have been based upon the formula of the Roman verbal contract *stipulatio* ('Spondesne?' 'Spondeo').[5] In the *Decretum* this link was suggested in *De cons.* D. 4 c. 73, a pseudo-Augustinian excerpt which referred to the baptismal promise to renounce the devil as *certissima cautio*: a *cautio* was a document used to record the forging of *stipulatio*, if any written record was made.

Other chapters also bear the stamp of legal influence. In *De cons.* D. 4 c. 105, another pseudo-Augustinian excerpt, the godparents were called *fideiussores apud Deum* for the infant *baptizatus*. In c. 74 the *parvulus* was linked with others who had to be baptised through the offices of others: this category of individuals, the deaf, the dumb, and the diseased, calls to mind the similar category of those whom the *Digest* forbade to enter into *stipulatio*.[6]

---

[4] A recent study which has excellent references to the literature on the subject is D. Michaélides, *Sacramentum chez Tertullien* (Paris, 1970). For the earliest legal usages of the term see Gaius, *Institutes*, ed. and trans. by F. de Zulueta (2 vols., Oxford 1946–53), IV.11–14, vol. I, pp. 234–6; and Sextus Pompeius Festus, *De verborum significatu quae supersunt cum Pauli epitome*, ed. W. M. Lindsay (Leipzig, 1913), *s. v.* 'sacramento', p. 466.

[5] See A. Ehrhardt, 'Christian baptism and Roman law' in *Festschrift Guido Kisch* (Stuttgart, 1955), pp. 147–66 at 147–53. On *stipulatio* in Roman law see especially Gaius, *Institutes*, III.92–3, vol. I, p. 180; and *Dig.* XLV *passim*.

[6] See *Dig.* XLV.I.I.

For one trained in law the thematic presentation of texts on baptism, punctuated by patristic allusions to Roman law, cannot have failed to raise the question of exactly how the unknowing infant could be said to make the promises necessary for a valid baptism. Nonetheless, no canonist of note took up the problem before Huguccio, who finished his *Summa* around 1188. It was doubtless no coincidence that Huguccio was also the first canonist whose work takes into account the significance of the legal terms used in the canons. In his commentary on *De cons.* D. 4 c. 73 Huguccio dealt squarely with the ambiguous status of the baptismal promise. Since strictly speaking neither the godparents nor the *parvulus* could be held for the ensuing obligation, the former because the promise was not made on their own behalf and the latter because he was incapable of promising, Huguccio drew the conclusion that there was no real promise in infant baptism. In place of the complex concepts of belief and promise Huguccio substituted the concrete *sacramentum fidei*. Even for an adult, Huguccio decided, the reception of the sacrament stood for the less tangible commitment of faith, so that, for example, the question, 'Credis in deum?' could be more accurately phrased, 'Vis recipere sacramentum fidei ex qua creditur in deum?'[7]

Huguccio's legal assessment of baptism also prompted him to apply a distinction drawn from the decretists' doctrine on perjury to the interpretation of the canon *De Iudeis*. While *De Iudeis* was used by other canonists to endorse the principle that Jews who had been converted through the use of force, and who had subsequently associated with the faithful in the sacraments, should be compelled to uphold the faith, Huguccio distinguished between conditional and total coercion.[8]

---

[7] Huguccio, *Summa, ad De cons.* D. 4 c. 73, *v.* 'Emissa . . .', Admont Stiftsbibl. MS 7, fo. 458rb: 'Set si puer . . . non observaverit (promissionem) cum venerit ad adultam etatem quis tenebitur, scilicet puer an sponsor? Et videtur quod neuter. Sponsor enim non tenetur quia non pro se set pro puero fit illa sponsio. Nec puer videtur teneri cum eo ignorante et non consentiente fit illa sponsio. . . . Set difficile est videre quomodo puer ex tali sponsione obligetur et ideo securius dicitur quod non obligatur ex tali sponsione set tantum ex sacramenti susceptione . . .' See also *ad De cons.* D. 4 c. 73, *v.* 'Credis . . .', fo. 458va: 'Et secundum hoc est sensus: "quid petis ad ecclesiam?" respondeo "fidem", id est sacramentum fidei. . . .' Readings from Huguccio's *Summa* have been corrected with the aid of Vatican MS Vat. lat.2280.

[8] Huguccio, *Summa, ad* D. 45 c. 5, *v.* 'Associatos . . .', Admont Stiftsbibl. MS 7, fo. 61va–b: '. . . distinguo aut est absoluta aut est conditionalis. Si absoluta coactione quis baptizetur puta unus tenet eum ligatum et alius superfundit aquam nisi postea consentiat non debet cogi ad fidem christianam tenendam . . . Si vero coactione conditionali quis baptizetur puta te verbabo vel spoliabo vel interficiam vel ledam nisi baptizeris debet cogi ut fidem teneat quia per talem coactionem de volente efficitur quis volens et volens baptizatur. Voluntas enim coacta voluntas est et volentem facit.' For the development of the similar doctrine on perjury see Rufinus,

This distinction, obviously the basis for Innocent III's doctrine in *Maiores*, was drawn from the purely legal sphere of the canonists' commentary on C. 22, the *causa* on perjury. The decretists developed the principle that an act was voluntary if there had been even the slightest expression of free-will: 'Voluntas coacta voluntas est.' The implication of Huguccio's application of this principle was that perjury and heresy were related as analogous transgressions of oaths.

For the beginnings of a detailed legal analysis of baptism, however, one must look to the period immediately following the publication of Huguccio's *Summa*. The first apparatus whose glosses offer any legal insights into *De consecratione* seems to have been Alanus Anglicus's, of which the second recension was completed in 1202. Alanus for the first time included the appropriate legal citations, thus bringing the baptismal promise directly into the realm of law. On the one hand Alanus argued that the baptismal promise could be called *certissima cautio* because it was made in relation to the faith of the Church, which we are always held to serve.[9] But in his commentary on c. 105 Alanus denied that the godparents could enter into a valid obligation on behalf of the infant *baptizatus*, and adduced a law from Justinian's *Institutes* which declared that no such *stipulatio* could be valid.[10] In the French *summa* 'Animal est Substantia', which was nearly contemporary with Alanus's apparatus, the author similarly drew attention to the fact that the baptismal promise did not observe the rules of the *Digest* for *stipulatio*.[11]

In short, a straightforward use of the Roman citations seemed only

---

Summa decretorum, ed. H. Singer (Paderborn, 1902; repr. 1963), ad C. 22 q. 5 c. 1, *v.* 'Qui compulsus', p. 400; and for discussion see S. Kuttner, *Kanonistische Schuldlehre von Gratian bis auf die Dekretalen Gregors IX*, Studi e testi, LXIV (Vatican City, 1935), pp. 301–7 and 314–33.

[9] Alanus Anglicus, 'Expleto tractatu de matrimonio', ad De cons. D. 4 c. 73, *v.* 'Certissima', Vatican MS Ross. 595, fo.296vb: 'Nota simplicem promissionem appellari certissimam cautionem. Quod immo dicitur quia de servanda fide emittit, quam firmissime tenemur servare.' On the tract 'Expleto', see my article 'Legal precision in the decretist period', *BMCL*, VI (1976), n. 19, which has references to the other MSS against which readings have been checked.

[10] Alanus, 'Expleto', ad De cons. D. 4 c. 105, *v.* 'Fideiussores', Vatican MS Ross. 595, fo.298ra: 'Quasi. Non enim promittunt eum fore iustum, ut infra eodem distinctione, Queris a me (c. 129). Et si alienum factum promitterent non obligarentur, ut Instit. de inuti. sti. §Si quis alium (*Inst.* III.19.3).'

[11] *Summa* 'Animal est substantia', ad De cons. D. 4 c. 73, Liège Univ. MS 127 E, fo.302ra: 'Ergo per alium obligari possit et alios etiam obligare, ff. rem pupilli sal. fo. l. ii (*Dig.* XLVI.6.2). Sed alias non valet stipulatio per aliud (!) quia liber homo non potest alii stipulari. Ad hoc enim invente sunt stipulationes ut quilibet alius non alii sed sibi stipuletur, ut ff. de ver.ob. Stipulatio ita (*Dig.* XLV.1.38).' For the date see S. Kuttner, *Repertorium der Kanonistik (1140–1234)*, Studi e testi, LXXI (Vatican City, 1937), pp. 157–8.

to jeopardise the status of the baptismal promise. If it was too late to retreat from the new methodology, then what was needed was a more imaginative approach to the entire problem of the legal analysis of baptism. Laurentius Hispanus seems to have been the first canonist whose work achieved this mastery of Roman law. Even in his apparatus on the *Decretum* Laurentius anticipated the solutions which he perfected in the *Glossa Palatina*. The baptismal promise was indeed binding, Laurentius insisted, whether made by the *baptizatus* himself or by godparents. In order to obviate the difficulty which ensued in strict law, however, Laurentius introduced the theological notion that baptism signified not an obligation but a liberation, a notion which had deep roots in the tradition of the Pauline epistles.[12] For support Laurentius referred to a chapter in *De consecratione* in which Augustine had used similar reasoning to contrast the negligible effects of parental sacrifice to demons with the beneficial effects of baptism. Having shown the way to a solution by subordinating legal principles to theological doctrine, Laurentius added yet another tool to the methodological analysis of baptism by citing a recent decretal which dealt not with any theological or doctrinal issue but with procedural law, a decretal of Lucius III which stated that the law is always more ready to absolve than to condemn. This principle seemed to justify the deficient legal status of the promise made for the infant, since the baptismal promise absolved the infant from the guilt of original sin. This was supplemented with a reference to the same effect from the *Digest*. In short, the challenge of Roman law had been met and overcome with the resources of the canon law itself.

ROMAN LAW IN THE 'GLOSSA PALATINA' ON 'DE CONSECRATIONE' D. 4

So far our investigation has been selective: although the earlier decretist sources were valuable in showing that the exploration of the baptismal

[12] Laurentius Hispanus, *Apparatus ad Decretum*, ad De cons. D. 4 c. 73, *v.* 'Cautione', Paris B.N. MS lat.15393, fo.293vb: 'Et ita obligantur illi qui non respondent pro se in baptismo. Eodem modo videtur quod per voces eorum qui pro puero respondent obligetur puer. Quod non est verum. Pocius enim ibi est obligi(!) absolutio quam obligatio quia liberatur a vinculis diaboli, quod potest fieri. Per alium ignorans enim bene absolvitur.' Cf. *ad De cons.* D. 4 c. 129 (the Augustinian passage), *v.* 'Sic', fo.296vb: 'Quia aliud est in absolutione quam obligatione, ff. de actio. et obli. Arrianus (*Dig.* XLIV.7.47). Quia prom⟨pti⟩ora sint iura etc., extra de prob., Ex literis (*Ia.*2.12.2, = *X.*2.19.3).' On Laurentius's apparatus see A. M. Stickler, 'Il decretista Laurentius Hispanus', *Studia Gratiana*, IX (1966), pp. 461–550, at 474–98, which has references to earlier literature.

promise focused attention upon the problems of faith and obligation, these sources were too sketchy to justify a systematic approach to our topic. But the *Glossa Palatina* is rich enough to permit a much more exhaustive study of the use of Roman law in the interpretation of theological doctrine.

The *Palatina* is appropriate for such a study because it provides a very graphic link between the earlier glosses of the decretists, which Laurentius compiled in such a way as to preserve their integrity to a marked degree, and the *Glossa Ordinaria* on the *Decretum*, which was one of the most important sources of canon law throughout the Middle Ages.[13]

The *Palatina* is vastly richer in Roman citations than any of the major apparatus on the *Decretum* which preceded it, including Laurentius's own apparatus on the *Decretum*. There are, by my count, eighty-nine references to Roman law in the *Palatina*'s commentary on *De consecratione* D. 4.[14] Since no systematic study has been made of Roman law in the *Palatina* we shall sample briefly each of the categories into which the citations tend to fall, although our chief interest is in the use of Roman law to illustrate the concepts of faith and guilt.

The citations can be roughly divided into six categories: 'clever' applications of Roman law to problems which are not in themselves important (6); explication of legal principles inspired by the baptismal material (18); description of the liturgical properties of the sacrament (13); direct citation of Imperial laws (3); exposition of the problem of faith in baptism, developed from the glosses already examined (22); and exposition of the theological problem of guilt (27).

The 'clever' applications of Roman law show that the canonists took pleasure in an imaginative and even whimsical exploitation of the *Corpus iuris civilis* once they had set aside the convention against citing the *leges* in sacramental discussion. Thus the *Palatina* pointed out that

---

[13] On the *Glossa Palatina* see Stickler, 'Il decretista', *passim*, with references to earlier literature. One can give here only a brief example of Laurentius's method in the *Palatina*. In its commentary on two of the chapters in *De cons.* D. 4 (cc. 28 and 74) the *Palatina* did not refer to the decretal *Maiores* (discussed in the text) in discussions in which such a reference would have been not only appropriate but even necessary, and was indeed made in the *Glossa Ordinaria*. On the other hand the references which were made to *Maiores* indicate that Laurentius used glosses which referred to *Maiores* in at least two different canonical compilations, without editorial standardisation; see *ad De cons.* D. 4 c. 5, *v*. 'Quod apud', Vatican MS Pal. lat.658, fo. 100va (which refers to *Maiores* in the compilation of Alanus Anglicus), and *ad De cons.* D. 4 c. 76, *v*. 'Nichil', fo.101vb (which refers to *Maiores* in the *Comp. Ia*). Readings from the *Palatina* have been corrected with the aid of Vatican MS Reg. lat. 977.

[14] For some comparisons, see my article 'Precision', n. 25.

the *leges* differed from the canons in that according to the *leges* baptism would not be valid if another liquid were added to the baptismal water, citing a law in the *Digest* which dealt with the conversion of raw materials in manufacture.[15] The *Palatina* implied that the mixture of another liquid would produce a wholly different species, and thereby invalidate the rite if the *leges* were to be applied to the problem. This rather far-fetched analogy sheds more light upon the author's extra-canonical reading than on the nature of the baptismal water, which could, by tradition, be supplemented by other liquids if necessary.

Not too different is the category of citations used to draw attention to a legal principle arising from the canons. For example the *Palatina* used four chapters in *De cons.* D. 4, which determined that an infant baptised in the womb of its mother must be rebaptised after birth, as the occasion for a debate on the problem of whether an embryo may be said to have a legal personality. Laurentius drew into the discussion several of the laws on manumission which, although opposed to the canons in principle (since they conceded that if a pregnant woman was manumitted the *partus* should be regarded as free) nonetheless recalled the link which he made in the earlier *Decretum* apparatus between baptism and liberation.[16]

Another category comprised the citations used to recast liturgical matters in a juristic form. For example, to elucidate the principle that baptism by heretics was valid (if performed in the form prescribed by the Church), the *Palatina* adduced a law from Justinian's *Institutes* which showed that it is sometimes possible to alienate property over which one does not have true *dominium*, as a creditor can, by prior pact, sell off the security given by his debtor if the debt is not paid.[17]

---

[15] *Glossa Palatina, ad De cons.* D. 4 c. 1, *v.* 'Sacramentum', Vatican MS Pal. lat.658, fo.100rb: 'Item si alius liquor admisceatur ipsi aque nunquid baptiçatur puer? Secundum leges videtur quod non quia desinit esse aqua, ff. de acqui. rerum dominio. Adeo. § Voluntas (*Dig.* XLI.1.7.8). Secundum canones secus.'

[16] See for example *Glossa Palatina, ad De cons.* D. 4 c. 114, *v.* 'Si ad matris', Vatican MS Pal. lat.658, fo.102rb: 'Pone casum infra eodem, Si qua mulier (c. 116). Quia forte dicebat Julianus quod mulier pregnans non debet baptiçari propter iuris impossibilitatem quia baptiçaretur puer in utero et iterum postquam esset editus debet baptiçari propter illud "Nisi quis renatus fuerit etc." (John 3.5). Videtur tamen quod bene dicat quia si mater manumittitur et partus, Instit. de ingenuis § ii (*nunc Inst.* 1.4. *in princ.*). Et quia partus pars est viscerum, ff. de ventre inspici. l. i (*Dig.* XXV.4.1). Sed ad primum dic baptismum esse personalem beneficium. Nec personam egreditur. Secus in manumissione.' The relevant chapters in *De cons.* D. 4 are 35 and 114–16.

[17] *Glossa Palatina, ad De cons.* D. 4 c. 23, *v.* 'Romanus', Vatican MS Pal. lat.658, fo.100vb: 'Contra. Ibi enim dicitur quod nemo dare potest quod non habet, ut infra eodem. Quomodo ergo baptismum paganus tradere dicitur? Sed creditor dominium rei sibi obligate post biennium in alium transfert quod tamen non habet, Instit. quibus ali. licet vel non § i (*Inst.* II.8.1).

In a similar way, the *Palatina* pointed out, a heretic could confer the grace of the *spiritus sanctus* even though his own ministry was not founded on that grace.

Only three Roman citations were used to refer to Imperial laws which were directly relevant to the ecclesiastical issues at hand.[18] Two are citations from the *Code* on the punishment of Jews who circumcised Christians or others over whom they held authority, while the third cited the law which imposed the death penalty upon heretics who rebaptised Christians. The latter reference was in fact cited to defend a canon which forbade Christians to rebaptise those who had already been baptised by heretics in the form of the Church, a reversal of the Imperial law, although in the same title in the *Code* the first law (with a lesser penalty) forbade Christians to rebaptise.

In contrast to this reluctance to apply Imperial laws which would have been directly relevant, the preponderance of Roman citations in the *Palatina* were used to elucidate the theological issues of faith and guilt. The *Palatina* drew together the themes tentatively explored in the earlier decretist sources to present a much more mature and coherent study of the problem of *fides* than had hitherto been attempted, treating both the issue of consent and the role of the godparents in considerable detail. For the first time in the *Palatina* there was an explicit recognition that the contract lay at the heart of the baptismal ritual: in its commentary on c. 73 the *Palatina* noted: 'Hic ergo intercedit stipulatio.'[19] The consequence of this *stipulatio*, the *Palatina* went on, was that infants were held by their godparents' promise even though they understood nothing of the transaction. As a result of the baptismal contract baptised infants were obligated to uphold the faith of the Church when they became adults: the *Palatina* referred to the canon *De Iudeis* in support of the principle that the baptismal obligation should be enforced through ecclesiastical discipline, a principle which

---

[18] *Glossa Palatina, ad De cons.* D. 4 c. 94, *v.* 'Separentur',Vatican MS Pal. lat.658, fo.102ra: 'Et bonorum prescriptione et perpetuo auxilio (!) dampnabuntur, ut C. de iudeis et ce. Iudei (*Cod.* 1.9.16). Sed hoc cum sue secte mancipium ⟨sit⟩ (?). Alias capite punitur, C. ne mancipium christianum. l. una (*Cod.* 1.10.1), C. de eunuchis. l. i (*Cod.* IV.42.1)'; and *ad De cons.* D. 4 c. 108, *v.* 'Inanissimum', Vatican MS Pal. lat.658, fo.102rb: 'Et capite punitur, C. ne sanctum bap. reiteretur. l. ii (*Cod.* 1.6.2).'

[19] *Glossa Palatina, ad De cons.* D. 4 c. 73, *v.* 'Cautione', Vatican MS Pal. lat.658, fo.101vb: 'Hic ergo intercedit stipulatio et obligantur pueri ex promissione patrini licet non intelligant, quod speciale est in baptismo. Illud autem est loco stipulationis: "Credis in deum?" Tenetur ergo observare puer factus adultus, xlv. De iudeis (D. 45 c. 5). Et obligantur licet nihil intelligant, C. de fal. mo. l. i (*Cod.* IX.24.1). Immo si bene inspexerimus potius liberatur a diabolo quam obligetur. Ac ignorans bene per alium liberatur.' See also n. 20, and on the same point in Laurentius's apparatus, n. 12.

arose from the contractual nature of the sacrament. In contrast to earlier glossators, who tried to use the *leges* selectively to buttress various aspects of baptism, Laurentius admitted that the baptismal obligation could never be fully justified in juristic terms, and that this form of contracting an obligation was unique to baptism: 'Obligantur pueri ex promissione patrini, licet non intelligant, quod speciale est in baptismo'. This unapologetic admission marked the confidence with which Laurentius dealt with legal rules, and indeed the contrast between the *leges* and the canons was heightened by a reference to a law in the *Code* which excused *impuberes* from the penalties for counterfeiting even if they were well aware of what was going on, on the grounds that 'Aetas eorum quid videat ignorat'. Of course the very opposite rule obtained in baptism, in which infants incurred an obligation even though they were wholly unaware of what was being done on their behalf. Laurentius reinforced this account of the baptismal transaction by reformulating the theme developed earlier in his apparatus, that baptism conferred not an obligation but a liberation from the power of the devil.

The same themes of liberation and obligation recurred in the *Palatina*'s discussion of the role of the godparents. Laurentius did not try to suppress the fact that on the mundane level baptism did impose an obligation: this was abundantly evident in the citation of *De Iudeis* in the same passage in which attention was drawn to the presence of *stipulatio* in the baptismal ritual. But the theme of liberation was used to balance the theme of obligation, just as the invisible effects of baptism balanced the visible effect, the obligation of faith. In its commentary on c. 74, which stated that children and others who could not speak for themselves were baptised *alio profitente*, the *Palatina* concluded that it was appropriate that an individual who was liberated through the offices of another should also be obligated through the offices of another.[20] The statement summarises several familiar theological themes: in transcendent terms any man was obligated by the debt imposed for the sin of Adam and was liberated through the death of Christ, while on a more mundane level the *baptizatus* was freed from the burdens of sin but held by an obligation to submit to ecclesiastical authority.

[20] *Glossa Palatina, ad De cons.* D. 4 c. 74, *v.* 'Quorum vice', Vatican MS Pal. lat.658, fo.101vb: 'Nam satis conveniens est ut qui per alium liberatur per alium obligetur, infra eodem, Queris (c. 129). Item dicit lex pro ignorante fideiubere possunt, ff. de fideiuss. Fideiubere (*Dig.* XLVI.1.30). Et ignoranti etiam accio acquiri. Item ff. si certum pe. Si a furioso (*Dig.* XII.1.12).'

The *Palatina* hesitated to refer to the godparents as *fideiussores* on the grounds that they could not guarantee that the *baptizatus* would lead a virtuous life. The term *quasi fideiussores*, borrowed from the *Digest*, might be more appropriate.[21] But the promise of faith was not itself jeopardised, moral questions aside. The *Palatina* implied that the tutorial principle which bound a tutor to protect the estate of his pupil was part of the fidejussory role of the godparents. The reality of the baptismal obligation was affirmed by a reference to a law in the *Digest* which stated that a *fideiussor* could not be sued before the principal party was sued: the personal responsibility of the *baptizatus* exceeded the responsibility of the godparents. But the tutorial principles were more valuable in explaining how the obligation came about in the first place: the *Palatina* cited a law which declared that a father could not act to recover the dowry of his divorced daughter without her permission, although such an action would have been of benefit to her, but declared that the daughter's failure to contradict her father's action in some manifest way could be taken as consent. In the same way the non-contradiction of the infant *baptizatus* could be taken for consent, since baptism would be of benefit to him.

Having established that the essence of the baptismal interrogations was the contract *stipulatio*, the *Palatina* gave careful attention to the *intentio* of the minister as well as to the problem of the consent of the *baptizatus*. The words of the baptismal formula were to be understood as instruments of the intention of the minister, just as, according to a law in the *Digest*, the interpretation of wills of household goods was based upon common usage.[22] Nonetheless a law in the *Digest* stated that the validity of a *stipulatio* was not jeopardised by the inclusion of superfluous words or by variations in the nominations of persons or things: thus for example the *stipulatio* 'Arma virumque cano, spondeo' would be valid, as would a *stipulatio* in which several different names

[21] *Glossa Palatina, ad De cons.* D. 4 c. 105, *v.* 'Fideiussores', Vatican MS Pal. lat.658, fo.102ra: 'Sed non videtur quod sint fideiussores pro puero. Quia si queratur ab eis: "Eritne iste bonus?" non dicerent sic vel non. . . . Sed sunt quasi fideiussores, ar. ff. ad municipalem. l. ii (*Dig.* L.1.2). Et sufficit quod puer non contradicat, ff. solu. matrim. l. ii §ult. (*Dig.* XXIV.3.2.2). Nam infans furioso comparatur, xv. q. ult. (!). Illud. pereque (*immo* C. 15 q. 1 c. 2). Et ita eo ipso tenentur parvuli quod non contradicunt, infra eodem. Queris. Alias enim non tenentur fideiussores, ff. de fideius. Fideiussor (*Dig.* XLVI.1.57). b.'

[22] *Glossa Palatina, ad De cons.* D. 4 c. 31, *v.* 'Exploratum', Vatican MS Pal. lat.658, fo.101ra: 'Ubi ergo totum mimice agitur non est baptismus, ar. ff. de act. et o. Obli. §ult. (*Dig.* XLIV.7.3.2). Unde dicimus quod semper exigitur intentio baptiçantis. . . . Sed verba serviunt intentioni, xxii. q. v. Humane (c. 11), ff. de suppel. l. Labeo (*Dig.* XXXIII.10.7).'

were used to refer to the same persons or things.[23] Despite its usual rigour the *Palatina* stretched this point to affirm the validity of baptism even if the devil were included with the Trinity in the formula, presumably as a superfluity rather than as a variation in the nomination.

For the first time in the *Palatina* the legal assessment of the *fides* of baptism was balanced by an almost equally thorough juristic scrutiny of the problems of guilt and redemption. Perhaps it was Laurentius's stress upon the liberation conferred by baptism which led him to focus upon the gains of the promiser.

Most of the *Palatina*'s analogies turned on comparisons with the legal actions which arose from contracts. The grace conferred by the Holy Spirit was compared with a remedy granted by the law. For example, several chapters in *De cons.* D. 4 enunciated the doctrine that the concupiscence which is a result of original sin remains in the individual even after baptism, but in a debilitated form. The *Palatina* drew an analogy between the baptismal debilitation of concupiscence and the legal effects of a *pactum de non petendo*, a pact in which a creditor agreed not to sue his debtor.[24] In both cases the *obligatio* (concupiscence) remains, but the creditor's right to sue (the power of the devil) becomes ineffectual.

The *Palatina* also drew a comparison between the grace of baptism and the legal *actio* itself. For example, in a gloss which referred to the law which forbade women (from the middle of the first century A.D.) to undertake liability for anyone, the *Palatina* compared the deceptive power of the devil over man with the deception practised by a man who tried to make a woman surety for his debt in contravention of the law: in the one case baptism, in the other a legal action, were granted

---

[23] *Glossa Palatina, ad De cons.* D. 4 c. 72, *v.* 'Contra fidem', Vatican MS Pal. lat.658, fo.101vb: 'Ex hoc capitulo colligitur quod non vitiatur forma baptismi si quid in ea apponatur contra fidem vel preter. Quod admitto si sequatur. Ut si dicatur "Baptiço te in nomine patris et filii et spiritussancti et diaboli. Vel arma virumque cano, vel quicquid sequatur baptiçatus est, ar. ff. de ver. o. Que extrinsecus (*Dig.* XLV.1.65).' These lengthy deliberations, of which this excerpt is only a small fragment, could seemingly have been avoided by the application of the Imperial legislation which simplified the requirements for *stipulationes*, on which see B. Nicholas, 'The form of the stipulation in Roman law', *LQR*, LXIX (1953), pp. 63–79 and 233–52. The *Palatina* did in fact refer to *Cod.* VI.23.25 in the course of its discussion.

[24] *Glossa Palatina, ad De cons.* D. 4 c. 2, *v.* 'Ne obsit', Vatican MS Pal. lat.658, fo.100rb: 'Immo etiam ut profit. Quia ubi maior pugna maior corona, de pe. di. iii. Ille rex (c. 25). Similiter remanet accio sed inefficax facto pacto de non petendo, Instit. de except. § Preterea (*Inst.* IV.13.3). Vel cum opponitur exceptio sententie, ar. ff. solut. matrim. Viro (*Dig.* XXIV.3.39). Ita et hic originale transit reatu sed remanet actu.' The relevant chapters in *De cons.* D. 4 are 145–6.

as remedies against the deceiver.[25] Once again Laurentius pointed out that it did not matter that the infant *baptizatus* did not consent, since the right of action, unlike obligation, could arise without consent: thus even a lunatic might acquire a right of action if someone borrowed money from him in the belief that he was sane, and then tried to steal the money.[26]

The *Palatina* posited a third analogy in procedural law in the legal *exceptio*, the right granted to a defendant to delay the proceedings being conducted against him. The benefits of baptism were compared with an *exceptio* granted to a defendant against the execution of a judicial sentence.[27] This analogy was even more subtly suited to the doctrine of sin and redemption than was that of the legal *actio*: its implication was that baptism gave the *fidelis* the right to delay the sentence which would otherwise condemn him for original sin, while the possibility remained that the sentence might yet be executed for actual sin. While the guilt of original sin was deleted in baptism, the potentiality for sin endured: 'Originale transit reatu sed remanet actu'. Similarly the effect of a legal *exceptio* was that the right of action against the defendant remained, but only in a latent form: 'Licet ... maneat actio dormit tamen'.

The influence of the requirements for legal precision was evident in the treatment of the concept of grace in Innocent's decretal *Maiores*. Innocent argued that a comatose person could not normally receive valid baptism because of the contradiction which would ensue: having been relieved of the guilt of original sin he would be worthy of the vision of God, but as a penalty for his (necessarily) unrepented actual sins he would still be worthy of eternal damnation. Innocent pointed out that it was impossible that the vision of God should be enjoyed in hell.

The *Palatina* used the Roman citations to give a far more effective resolution of the problem, albeit in the piecemeal glossarial fashion.

---

[25] *Glossa Palatina, ad De cons.* D. 4 c. 62, *v.* 'Que decepit', Vatican MS Pal. lat.658, fo.101va: 'Et ideo fuit restitutus. Nam deceptis etc., ff. ad Velleianum l. i (*Dig.* XVI.1.1., but see XVI.1.2.3).' For the two remedies given to a woman see *Dig.* XVI.1.1.2.

[26] See n. 20.

[27] See *Glossa Palatina, ad De cons.* D. 4 c. 146, *v.* 'Peremptum', Vatican MS Pal. lat.658, fo.102vb: 'Ita dicit lex de eo qui habet exceptionem efficacem. Licet enim maneat actio dormit tamen, ff. de regul. iur. Marcellus (*Dig.* L.17.66). Et sicut peccatum reviviscit hic propter culpam sic et quandoque actio reviviscit propter culpam . . .'; see also *v.* 'Dicta', fo.102vb: 'Differentia hic notatur inter originale peccatum et actuale, quia illa transeunt actu et remanent reatu donec per baptismum vel penitentiam ex toto deleantur. Originale vero in baptismo remanet actu sed transit reatu.'

Thus in one of the chapters in *De cons*. D. 4 Augustine declared that the grace of baptism dismissed sins 'quae facta sunt' and helped the *fidelis* to abstain from future sin. The *Palatina* pointed out that grace redeemed original sin once for all, just as, according to a law in the *Digest*, a judge's interest in a case should end with the judgment, and he should not exact interest from a debtor for the time which elapsed after the appointed time of execution in a judgment of good faith.[28] Similarly, Laurentius noted, a *pactum de non petendo* in which the right of action was actually destroyed by the pact could not be supplanted by a later pact recreating the right of action. In another place the *Palatina* emphasised this point by citing a law which declared that once a debtor had discharged his debt it could not be revived, as long as payment had been made in the agreed fashion.[29] The implication was that the grace of baptism shifted the individual to a different plane from that of his natural birth and entitled him to expect salvation. In short, if baptism was a contract one could justly demand stability in the *intentio* of the Church: this might indeed have been the significance of Innocent's reasoning that the vision of God, once granted, could not be rescinded, so that a contradiction arose between the enjoyment of the vision of God and the suffering of hell. Nonetheless this view required some qualification, and the *Palatina* clarified its exposition of grace with a citation of a law in the *Digest* which stated that a seemingly contradictory act by a testator could be proven valid if it could be shown that the act arose *ex nova voluntate*. Similarly the penalty of the withdrawal of grace followed upon the commission of actual sins *ex nova voluntate* after baptism. Thus the penal system of the Church supplied the means for the renewal of grace for the sinner, who had recreated the debt of sin for himself.

CONCLUSION

Our investigation suggests that the canonistic revival of Roman law had important consequences in the field of ecclesiastical ideology. The contractual nature of baptism, latent in the terminology and in the

[28] *Glossa Palatina*, ad *De cons*. D. 4 c. 141, *v*. 'Que facta sunt', Vatican MS Pal. lat.658, fo.102vb: 'In futura. Quia tractatus futuri temporis etc., ff. de usurur. l. i. §i (*nunc Dig.* XXII.1.2). Nec de futura iniuria pacisci possumus, ff. de pactis. Si unus §Pacta (*Dig.* II.14.27.2).'

[29] *Glossa Palatina*, ad *De cons*. D. 4 c. 129, *v*. 'Contrahitur', Vatican MS Pal. lat.658, fo.102va: 'Vires enim obligationis evacuate reperari nequeunt, C. de solut. l. iiii (*Cod.* VIII.42.4), xxiii. q. iiii. Si illic (c. 29). Arguunt contra ff. de leg. Si chorus §ult. (*Dig.* XXXII.1.79.3) et ff. de con. et demon. Filie sue §Attia (*Dig.* XXXV.1.28.1). Sed illud exaudi ex nova voluntate peti posse, alias non, ff. de adim. leg. Cum servus (*Dig.* XXXIV.4.15) et l. Si servus (!) (*Dig.* XXXIV.4.26.1).'

ritual of the sacrament, had come to dominate the canonists' interpretation of baptismal theology by the early thirteenth century. The *fides* which the individual promised the Church in baptism now resembled the objective legal obligation which arose from a contract, isolated from the psychological complexities of the theological concepts of faith and belief. The fundamental metaphor of *sacramentum* as contract gave rise to a series of others in which the faith of the individual was adjudicated as the terms of a contract would be in the eyes of the law.

Further analysis of this material should consider both its historical and its anthropological dimensions. In particular one would want to explore more deeply the relationship between the sacrament which linked the individual to society and the sanction of excommunication which excluded him. The increasing legal refinement of the concept of *fides* suggests that the transgression of the baptismal promise was regarded as an extremely grave form of perjury, heresy being the most flagrant and the most contumacious possible abuse of divine witness. Yet, although many of the penalties associated with excommunication were taken over from Roman law, which itself created certain categories of legal outcast like the *infamis*, and, under earlier religious law, the *homo sacer*, Roman law did not punish perjury as such.[30] In the religious law it seems that divine and human sanctions were seen as co-operating in the punishment of certain grave crimes by parallel religious and social sanctions, but the punishment of perjury as such was reserved for the gods. Hence it appears that in ecclesiastical ideology one must take care to discern when old and familiar concepts are being recast in new forms and for new purposes. Yet the threads of continuity, such as they are, suggest that the Church might have been tapping some very deep social impulse which came to be crystallised in the regulations surrounding the sacraments. In a society so dependent upon bonds of faith, the ultimate transcendence of the sacrament of baptism made its transgression an act of extreme antisociability.

[30] See J. L. Strachan-Davidson, *Problems of the Roman Criminal Law* (2 vols., Oxford, 1912), I, pp. 48–9.

HOSTIENSIS ON *PER VENERABILEM*:
THE ROLE OF
THE COLLEGE OF CARDINALS

by J. A. WATT

TO THE MEDIEVAL CANONISTS, Innocent III's decretal *Per venerabilem* (1202) was *difficile et multum famosum*.[1] What gave it its particular difficulty and notoriety was its argument, or apparent argument, that the legitimation of bastards *ad sacra* brought in its train legitimation *in temporalibus*, particularly legitimation so far as hereditary succession was concerned. Since this claim conflicted with established ideas about the autonomy of the lay power in civil jurisdiction, it demanded discussion, explanation and qualification and this it received in abundance, to make of the decretal the focus of an on-going analysis of the relations of the two powers.[2] The arguments advanced by the pope in support of his legitimation of the two children born of the union of Philip Augustus and Agnes of Meran depended in part on the recognition that the king of France knew no temporal superior to whom recourse might be had. The canonists further began to discuss in this context the reality of the theoretical universalism of the authority of the Holy Roman Empire, with all the implications for the development of a theory of the national sovereign state that this involved.[3] Nor did this exhaust the interest of the decretal so far as the analysis of authority

---

[1] *Glossa Ordinaria* (Paris, 1561) on 4.17.13: 'In terris ecclesie papa potest libere illegitimos legitimare, in terris vero alienis non, nisi ex causis multum arduis, vel nisi in spiritualibus; tunc tamen indirecte et per quandam consequentiam intelligitur legitimare quo ad temporalia. Hoc tamen ultimum non est sine scrupulo; hoc dicitur secundum intellectum qui placet Panormitano et est capitulum difficile et multum famosum.'

[2] About which modern historians have tended to draw different conclusions: M. Maccarrone, *Chiesa e stato nella dottrina di Papa Innocenzo III* (Rome, 1940), pp. 118–23; F. Kempf, *Papsttum und Kaisertum bei Innocenz III: die geistigen und rechtlichen Grundlagen seiner Thronstreitpolitik* (Rome, 1954), pp. 256–69; B. Tierney, ' "Tria quippe distinguit iudicia ..." A note on Innocent III's decretal *Per venerabilem*', *Speculum*, XXXVII (1962), pp. 48–59; A. R. Damas, *Pensamiento político de Hostiensis* (Zürich, 1964), pp. 73–82, 221–4; J. A. Watt, *The Theory of Papal Monarchy in the Thirteenth Century. The Contribution of the Canonists* (New York–London, 1965), pp. 41–4, 53–6, 98–9, 108–17; K. Pennington, 'Innocent III's views on Church and State: a gloss to *Per Venerabilem*', in K. Pennington and R. Somerville (eds.), *Essays in honor of Stephan Kuttner* (Pennsylvania, 1977), pp. 49–67.

[3] W. Ullmann, *Law and Politics in the Middle Ages. An Introduction to the Sources of Medieval Political Ideas* (London, 1975), pp. 102–3, 181–2, 222.

was concerned. Innocent III, in an extended exegesis of Deuteronomy 17.8–12, which is the very heart of *Per venerabilem*, described those 'priests of the Levitical race' of whom the text spoke, as 'our brothers who, by Levitical right, stand with us as our assistants in the exercise of our priestly function' ('... fratres nostri, qui nobis iure Levitico in executione sacerdotalis officii coadiutores existunt'). The reference was manifestly to the College of Cardinals and, in due course, it aroused the interest of decretalists in the authority of the cardinalate, 'than which', the Cardinal Bishop of Ostia was to write shortly before his death in 1271, 'the Roman Church knows no higher dignity since the cardinals together with the pope judge all and can be judged by no one but the pope and his colleagues'.[4] Thus *Per venerabilem* is a primary *locus* for canonist discussion of many types of authority: of the pope, of the emperor, of cardinals, of national kings, of bishops. It was as a student of Walter Ullmann that I first came to appreciate its intrinsic fascination, as well as its significance. In returning to it, I recall with great gratitude the dynamism of his teaching and his inimitable enthusiasm, ranging over so many topics in the history of ideas about authority.

Hostiensis reached saturation point in his analysis of *Per venerabilem*, as one of his canonist successors was to observe.[5] His was certainly the most lengthy commentary to appear in the thirteenth century, occupying some five and a half columns of the printed version of his *Summa* (written 1250–3) and nine and a half columns of his *Apparatus* (1268–71). And his was to prove one of the most influential in the later evolution of the canonist tradition. His round assertion that, in strict law, only the pope could legitimise – since marriage was exclusively of ecclesiastical jurisdiction and therefore he who had cognisance of the principal matter had cognisance of the accessory – guaranteed his place in all subsequent discussion of legitimation. His lively sense of the majesty of the emperor – *dominus mundi, vicarius Dei in temporalibus*, holder of the *plenitudo potestatis in temporalibus* – kept alive, against current trends of decretalist thought, the *de iure* imperial claim to

---

[4] 'Hoc tamen hodie tenet romana ecclesia quod nulla sit dignitas maior cardinalatu, cum ipsi cardinales una cum papa omnes iudicent, nec iudicari possint ab alio quam a papa et collegis suis, argu. ix.q.iii. Nemo (C.9.q.3 c.13) et capitulis sequentibus. Argumentum tamen contra in eo quod legitur et notatur supra, de cleri. non resi. c.ii (3.4.2).' *Apparatus*, 3.5.19 *s.v. episcopi Prenestinensis*. The 'argumentum contra' refers to discussion as to whether the pope alone could judge cardinals. This issue is examined later in this article.

[5] 'Ad saturitatem' was the phrase of Joannes Andreae in a marginal comment to G. Durantis, *Speculum iuris* (Venice, 1499), II fo.508va.

universal authority. His forceful, even indignant, refutation of those who would maintain 'nihil ad papam de temporalibus' constituted a *locus classicus* of canonist discussion of the theory of the relations of the two powers. Hostiensis implanted his own distinctive personal point of view on the discussion of each of these themes. But he was never more individual than when he came to discuss the 'priests of the Levitical race', the pope's *coadiutores*. He was not the first canonist to make observations about the College of Cardinals but he was the first to acknowledge the importance of *Per venerabilem* for this subject. The earliest decretalists, glossing this decretal when it appeared in *Compilatio IIIa*, showed a lively interest in the legitimation issue and the principles of the relations of the two powers. They showed no interest in the papal *coadiutores*[6] and this neglect was reflected in the *glossa ordinaria*, produced by Bernard of Parma in the period 1241–63. Innocent IV, to whom Hostiensis always referred as 'dominus meus', likewise ignored this context, though some observations about the cardinalate are to be found elsewhere in his *Apparatus*. It was left to Hostiensis to accept the opportunity to discuss the carefully nuanced words of Innocent III about the participation of others in papal government. Relatively little further reading in the *Apparatus* is needed to see that his commentary on this section of *Per venerabilem* is but a part of his writing on the cardinalate, a subject on which he had come to evince no little interest and even concern.[7]

The significance of this subject is not in doubt. The Sacred College was still, in the thirteenth century, a developing institution. It was primarily in the canonist literature that established constitutional theory, such as it was, encountered the problems posed by the actual exercise of power by the cardinals – problems like their role as papal assistants, their function as electors of popes, the scope of their jurisdiction during papal vacancies. All these matters were very live issues in the second half of the thirteenth century. Hostiensis was of course a leading member of the College, having been created cardinal, in a memorable reconstruction of its depleted ranks, by Urban IV in 1261.[8] What explains

---

[6] I have examined a representative selection of this commentary especially in the mixed gloss compilations of BM Royal MS 11.C.vi and Durham Cathedral MS C.iii.4.

[7] B. Tierney, *Foundations of the Conciliar Theory* (Cambridge, 1955), pp. 149–53; J. A. Watt, 'The constitutional law of the College of Cardinals from Hostiensis to Joannes Andreae', *Mediaeval Studies*, xxxiii (1971), pp. 127–57. This article includes an Appendix containing all the relevant texts of Hostiensis.

[8] E. Jordan. 'Les Promotions de cardinaux sous Urbain IV', *Revue d'histoire et de littérature religieuses*, v (1900), pp. 322–34.

the somewhat defensive tone of part of his writing about the cardinalate was his awareness that in his own day the College had come under severe criticism. There can be little doubt that the cause of the odium incurred by the cardinals was the electoral deadlock which, after the death of Clement IV in 1268, kept the papacy vacant for a record two years and nine months. It was precisely in the period of this vacancy that Hostiensis was completing his *Apparatus*. His defence of the College, and his understandable disposition to maximise its role, was linked to a prudent awareness of the need to reform the canon law governing papal elections and vacancies.

This subject has its significance not only for the better understanding of the medieval papacy. It must be noticed that it is not without relevance for contemporary theology. The recent renewal of interest in the history of ecclesiological doctrine, in the wake of *Lumen gentium* of Vatican II, has brought *Per venerabilem* and the cardinalate into the study of the doctrine of episcopal collegiality.[9]

The importance of Hostiensis in all this discussion has been clearly recognised in modern scholarship. But the precise interpretation of his position is still, to some degree, in dispute. It is the purpose of this essay to attempt, by way of a reappraisal of the sources, to achieve a *concordia* from the dialectic of recent analyses. Since the first duty of a decretalist was to expound a papal text, the logic and form of which would condition the nature of his commentary, it is as well to begin with *Per venerabilem* itself.

The canonists found it convenient for purposes of analysis to divide the decretal into four parts. In the first part, Innocent III reproduced arguments concerning the validity of papal legitimation *in temporalibus*. He proceeded to explain, in the second part, why, having consented to legitimise the children of Philip Augustus, he could not do the same for the children of his petitioner, William, Count of Montpellier. The fourth part was devoted to further observations about this refusal. In the third part, the pope had deliberately widened the scope of the decretal from the narrow issue of legitimation, to enunciate certain general considerations governing the exercise of papal authority in temporal affairs. He attempted to demonstrate that the occasional

---

[9] Y. M.-J. Congar, 'Notes sur le destin de l'idée de collégialité épiscopale en Occident au moyen âge (VIIe–XVIe siècles)', in *La Collégialité épiscopale. Histoire et théologie*, Unam sanctam, LII (Paris, 1965), pp. 99–129; G. Alberigo, *Cardinalato e collegialità. Studi sull' ecclesiologia tra l'XI e il XIV secolo* (Florence, 1969); B. Tierney, 'Hostiensis and collegiality', *Proceedings of the Fourth International Congress of Medieval Canon Law* (Vatican City, 1976), pp. 401–9.

exercise of papal jurisdiction in the temporal order in emergency situations, and where the rights of others were not infringed, was justified by the authority of both Old and New Testaments. The central text of the Old Testament dimension of his proof was Deuteronomy 17.8–12, of which this was the passage relevant to discussion of the cardinalate:

If thou perceive that there be among you a hard and doubtful matter in judgment between blood and blood, cause and cause, leprosy and leprosy, and thou see that the words of the judges within thy gates do vary ... thou shalt come to the priests of the Levitical race, and to the judge that shall be at that time ... who will show thee the truth of the judgment and thou shalt do whatsoever they shall say that preside in the place which the Lord shall choose ... and thou shalt follow their sentence ...

There followed an exegesis of this text, the objective of which was to link it with complementary New Testament teaching. Hence 'the place which the Lord shall choose' referred to the apostolic see established by Christ as the Church's foundation stone. The 'priests of the Levitical race' are 'our brothers who by Levitical right stand with us as our coadjutors in the exercise of our priestly function'. These assistants are distinguished from 'the judge that shall be at that time'. For

He indeed is above them (*superest*) as priest and judge to whom the Lord said through Peter: 'Whatsoever thou shalt bind on earth will be bound also in heaven'; his vicar who is priest for ever according to the order of Melchisedech, appointed by God judge of the living and the dead.

Innocent III was here making a carefully nuanced expression both of a notion of fraternal participation in papal government and a principle of Petrine superiority, which included personal superiority over his *coadiutores*. We should be cautious about making any assessment of Hostiensis's opinion which ran *contra textum*. The pope's exegetical exposition then went on to explain what he understood by the three types of judgment which the text distinguished, postulating that when there were doubts and difficulties in any of the three, recourse should be had to the apostolic see for their resolution. He then concluded his commentary with an audacious adaptation of I Cor. 6.3:

Paul to explain the plenitude of power, writing to the Corinthians says: 'Know you not that you shall judge angels? How much more the things of this world?'

It was by way of explanation of the term 'plenitude of power' that Hostiensis contrived to say most of what he had to say about papal primacy. The third part of *Per venerabilem*, and this reference to St Paul, inspired him to his most detailed exposition, with a slant towards the political implications of the term. Something of its rhetorical flavour is exemplified in its opening paragraph:

Plenitude of power. Here it appears sufficiently clearly from the very force of the expression that the pope stands above all and commands them; although here I may seem to add brightness to the sun, for fullness needs no addition, *vi. q. i. c. si omnia,* yet I am unable to keep silent and I acknowledge that this supreme and surpassing superiority and power and authority has been granted to him without reservation in all matters, through every means and over all Christians of the whole world, referring to what has been fully noted above, *de conces. preben. c. proposuit* (3.8.4.). For the pope himself has plenitude of power, as is stated here and above, *de electio. c. illa, de usu pal. c. ad honorem* (1.8.4). And he is greater than and superior to all Christians as can be proved by many evident and convincing reasons.[10]

There follow nine such reasons which are not here our main concern. What must be noted, however, are two points. The first is methodological: Hostiensis singled out two other decretals of Innocent III, *Proposuit* (3.8.4) and *Ad honorem* (1.8.4) as supporting authorities for the most generalised description of the plenitude of power. Secondly, it is to be remarked that in this passage, Hostiensis attached the plenitude of power to the pope personally: 'Habet enim *papa ipse* plenitudinem potestatis.' In emphasising that this power resides in the pope individually (monarchically, as we may say), Hostiensis was being consistent with related glosses both on *Per venerabilem* and elsewhere in his work.[11]

However, this was not to be his last word in the *Per venerabilem* context on the subject of the plenitude of power. He concluded his gloss on 'our brothers' with the comment that the text did not use the singular but the plural 'you will judge' in order to indicate that not only the pope but also the cardinals 'should be included even in the expression of the plenitude of power'. He added a reference to something he had written in another context: 'I write this to put to silence

---

[10] '*Plenitudinem potestatis.* Hic satis patet ex vi locutionis quod papa superest et preest omnibus; quamvis videar solem faciebus adiuvare, quia nulla adiectione indiget plenitudo, vi. q.i.c. si omnia (C.6.q.1.c.7, which has 'quoniam diuine gratie plenitudo adiectione humana non indiget') tamen silere nequeo et hanc maioritatem et potestatem et auctoritatem in omnibus et per omnia et super omnibus christianis totius mundi indistincte sibi datam concedo secundum ea quod plene notatur supra de conces. preben. Proposuit. Habet enim papa ipse plenitudinem potestatis, ut hic, et supra, de electio. c. Illa (1.6.39), supra, de usu pal. Ad honorem. Et maior et superior est omnibus christianis, quod potest probari multis rationibus nimis dilucidis et effacibus' (ed. Paris, 1512; Venice, 1581).

[11] I have collected the relevant texts, in 'The use of the term plenitudo potestatis by Hostiensis', *Proceedings of the Second International Congress of Medieval Canon Law* (Vatican City, 1965), pp. 162–87.

those who seem to reduce the power of the cardinals to nothing.'[12]
Then, returning to the verb in the plural form (*iudicabitis*), he reiterated
his earlier view of the cardinals' involvement in papal government:
'they participated in the plenitude of power'.

How is this opinion to be reconciled with his insistence that it was
papa ipse who held the plenitude of power? What precisely did
Hostiensis have in mind when he spoke of the cardinals' inclusion and
participation in the papal sovereignty?

From one point of view, to speak of the College participating in
papal government was a simple statement of fact. Everyone in
Christendom knew the cardinals had a part in the routine day-to-day
work of the curia. In practice the cardinals were just what Innocent III
in *Per venerabilem* said they were, the pope's *coadiutores*: 'they who
assisted him continually, and on whose advice (*consilium*) he acted',[13]
explained Hostiensis. Elaborating further on the Innocentian text, he
declared that 'it was fitting for the pope to seek the advice of his
brothers, for a judgment was the firmer for being sought of many ...
thus it is said that they are his coadjutors in the exercise of the priestly
function'.[14] Hence the inclusion of the cardinals in the plenitude of
power seems to mean, in practical terms, participation in papal government especially in an advisory capacity. 'Do thou nothing without
counsel and thou shalt not repent when thou hast done', Hostiensis
advised popes in the words of Solomon (Ecclesiasticus 32.24). He was
adamant that popes should never act without advice, that the cardinals
were their natural advisers, and that to give counsel was to participate
in government. Did Hostiensis mean anything more than this when he
spoke of including the cardinals in the expression of the plenitude of
power?

---

[12] 'Unde et dictum est non "iudicabis" in singulari, sed "iudicabitis" in plurali, ut non solum
papa sed et cardinales includerentur etiam in expressione plenitudinis potestatis, infra, eo.para
v.fi., de quo tamen dic ut plene notatur infra, de peniten. Cum ex eo (5.38.14). para. fi.' The
first of these references is to a later gloss on *Per venerabilem*: '*iudicabitis*: scilicet, tu et cardinales.
Participant ergo cardinales plenitudini potestatis ...' The second reference is to the concluding
part of a long gloss about the powers of the College during a papal vacancy: 'Hec scribo ad
confutandos illos qui potestatem cardinalium quasi omnino adnihilare videntur ...' The full
text is printed in my 'Constitutional law of the College of Cardinals', pp. 155–7.

[13] '*Fratres nostri*. Ergo omnes episcopi ... qui et vocati sunt in partem sollicitudinis, supra, de usu
pal. c. Ad honorem (1.8.4). Cardinales tamen continue ei assistunt de quorum consilio procedit
... et de ipsis (i.e. cardinalibus) hoc specialiter est intelligendum, sed de aliis (i.e. episcopis)
generaliter.'

[14] 'Multo fortius ergo decet papam consilia fratrum suorum requirere, nam et firmius est iudicium
quod a pluribus queritur, xx. dist. De quibus (D.20 c.3): ideo et dicitur hic quod in executione
sacerdotalis officii sibi coadiutores existunt.'

If we were to confine our attention simply to the context of *Per venerabilem* we might quite properly doubt it. But there were glosses elsewhere in the *Apparatus* which suggested that Hostiensis's zeal to confound his critics had brought him to a more radical position, making the Sacred College, rather than the pope, the residuary of supreme power in the Church. The cardinals, Hostiensis repeated on a number of occasions, were part of the pope's body.[15] The expression had been adapted from Roman law terminology concerning the relationship of emperor and senators. To speak of a papal senate, even if the term is not very specific, was to emphasise the corporate nature of papal government. The accepted etymology of the word cardinal promoted a similar line of thought.[16] Both arguments reinforced the conclusion that there existed a 'college supreme and superior over all so united with the pope as to be one and the same with him'.[17] In brief, 'pope and cardinals together constituted the Roman Church'.[18]

It thus appears that there can be identified in Hostiensis's writing about the cardinalate a double trend of interpretation: one where the pope personally is seen as holder of the plenitude of power, with the role of the cardinals that of counsellors, and the other where pope and cardinals together form an integral headship of the Church. It is, perhaps, not to be expected that the two positions will be brought to perfect harmony and at least one good judge thinks that it is not possible to come to a convincingly safe conclusion about Hostiensis's views on the cardinalate.[19] Certainly some inconsistency or unresolved tension between differing views is discernible in another aspect of his

[15] '... et pars corporis domini pape sunt, C. ad leg. iul. maiesta' (2.24.4 *s.v. Romane ecclesie*); 'Sunt enim cardinales pars corporis domini pape qui super omnes est nec ab aliis iudicatur, ix.q.iii. Aliorum et c.seq. (C.9 q.3 c.14, 15), sed et cum eo orbem iudicant et disponunt ...' (3.4.2 *s.v. In sinodo*); 'Sed et maior est cardinalis, inquantum est pars corporis generalis vicarii iesu christi ...' (3.5.19 *s.v. episcopi*); 'Ab aliis ergo recipiat papa iuramentum ut ab extraneis, a cardinalibus uero non recipit, tanquam sibi inuisceratis, unde ob hoc dicuntur mitti de ipsius latere ...' (5.33.23 *s.v. iuramento*).

[16] '... sic dicti a cardine, quia sicut cardine regitur ostium, ita per istos regi debet officium ecclesie; inde dicti sunt cardinales quia per eos regitur totus mundus; inde papa cardo omnium ecclesiarum appellatur ...' (1.24.2 *s.v. cardinalium*); 'Unde et dicti sunt cardinales a cardine, quasi cum papa mundum regentes ...' (4.17.13 *s.v. fratres nostri*).

[17] 'Estque summum et excellens collegium super omnia alia unitum adeo [not 'a Deo'] quod cum ipso unum et idem est ...' (5.6.17 *s.v. sancte Romane ecclesie*); '... licet papa sit generale caput universalis ecclesie et singuli fideles eius membra generalia, est tamen speciale caput cardinalium' et ipsi eius specialia membra respectu aliorum: quod corpus adeo debet esse unitum, quod ab his specialibus membris papa fidelitatem vel obedientiam non exigit, sicut nec a seipso ...' (5.33.23 *s.v. iuramento*).

[18] '... quia papa et ipsi romanam ecclesiam constituunt' (2.24.4 *s.v. Romane ecclesie*).

[19] 'Non credo sia possibile concludere in modo sicuro e convincente sulla posizione dell' Ostiense rispetto al cardinalato.' Alberigo, *Cardinalato e collegialità*, p. 106.

teaching on the papacy,[20] while it is a recognised characteristic of canonist writing in general that it knew 'a real uncertainty in the face of fundamental problems concerning the juristic structure of the Church and the interrelations of its various organs of government'.[21] But it is possible to go further by asking of Hostiensis certain questions about the apportioning of power between pope and cardinals. These are questions suggested by canonists and cardinals themselves and they bear especially on the practical implications of any general principle suggestive of a papal constitutional monarchy. Did Hostiensis envisage the possibility of papal power being in any way limited by the cardinals' part in government?

Certain of his decretist predecessors, who also had defined the *ecclesia romana* as pope with cardinals, had done so. In the early decades of the thirteenth century, a period of revitalised scholarship which was to produce the *glossa ordinaria* on Gratian's *Decretum*, there was adventurous speculation on papal authority in general, on the supreme legislative power in particular, and, more specifically still, on the subject of the cardinals' role in the promulgation of new canons. This latter problem was suggested especially by a canon which spoke of its being lawful for the pope to issue new laws. Could the pope alone do so, without the participation of the cardinals? Opinion was divided. Laurentius Hispanus argued that he could not promulgate a general law for the universal Church without them.[22] Alanus Anglicus, on the other hand, argued that he could (though his choice of supporting authority for his view, the Donation of Constantine, was an odd one). He considered, however, that it would be better if the pope did in fact consult them when introducing something new.[23] The discussion remained of interest to canonists. Guido de Baysio put the two viewpoints together as a *quaestio* at the end of the century.[24] Hostiensis, however,

[20] Watt, *Theory of Papal Monarchy*, pp. 142–3.   [21] Tierney, *Foundations*, p. 218.

[22] *Glossa Palatina*: 'Quero utrum solus papa possit condere canones. Videtur quod sic, ar. xcvi, in palea Constantinus . . . Solutio, generalem legem de universali statu ecclesie non potest sine cardinalibus condere'. Text published by Tierney, *Foundations*, p. 81. That this work was written by Laurentius has been established by A. M. Stickler, 'Il decretista Laurentius Hispanus', *Studia Gratiana*, IX (1966), pp. 463–549.

[23] *Apparatus* 'Ius naturale': 'Sed numquid papa solus sine cardinalibus potest condere nouos canones? Utique, ar. xcvi. di. Constantinus, C. de legibus, Si imperialis: melius tamen faciat si fratres cardinales adiciat si aliquod nouum uelit introducere.' C.25 q.1 c.6 *s.v. nouas condere leges* BN 15393, fo.207rb.

[24] 'Dicit Laurentius quod generalem legem de universali statu ecclesie condere non potest papa sine cardinalibus, sed particularem sic, ar. xi. di. Catholica (D.11 c.8); sed videtur quod solus papa possit condere canones, ar. xcvi. di. Constantinus, palea est (D.96 c.14), licet sit argumentum contra, C. de le., Si imperialis et l. Humanum.' *Rosarium* C.25 q.1 c.6 *s.v. sunt quidam.*

kept a discreet silence in this debate, thus passing up an opportunity of explaining one at least of the practical implications of the cardinals' participation in the plenitude of power. In default of any explicit statement about whether the consent of the cardinals was a necessary part of the papal legislative process, is it possible to surmise from other glosses which of the early decretist opinions he favoured?

There is an obvious link between this aspect of papal power and the phrase so often encountered in decretals: that the judicial decision had been taken *de fratrum nostrum consilio*. Its frequent appearance in the Gregorian decretals was a standing invitation for the term to be discussed in a purely academic way. But in fact it was in the world of affairs that it was to have its first major airing. In the first place, it figured prominently in the *plaidoyer* of the Colonna cardinals in their denunciations of the pope who had expelled them from the Sacred College. Secondly, it was to be discussed in terms of actual curial practice in the rather less polemical context of commentary on *Liber Sextus* (1298). The Colonnas argued that in all difficult matters, especially in alienations of church property, even a true pope (here contrasted with *iste pseudoprefectus*, Benedict Gaetani) was accustomed to seek the counsel and consent of the cardinals and was indeed under obligation to do so. The obligation was not simply to seek advice but to follow it. Their participation was 'necessary' in the sense that what was done without them was illegal.[25] Behind what the Colonnas were saying about consultation lay a decretal of Alexander III (3.10.4: c. *Novit*). In it he had reminded the Latin patriarch of Jerusalem that he and his chapter were one body, he the head, they the members, and it was not therefore fitting that he should neglect their advice in the conduct of the business of their church, for this was to violate the decrees of the fathers. It had come to the pope's ears that the patriarch had collated to and deprived from ecclesiastical offices without the advice of his brothers. All such acts were by apostolic authority declared null. The *glossa ordinaria* summarised: 'Thus a prelate must (*debet*) conduct the business of his church on the advice of his brothers and especially particular matters of the kind specified, otherwise the acts are void (*non tenent*).' By considering the relationship of pope and cardinals analogous to that of bishop and chapter, it was possible to

---

[25] 'Porro cum in quibuslibet arduis peragendis, maxime in alienationibus rerum ecclesie, etiam verum pontifex cardinalium consilia petere et sequi consensus nichilominus consueverit et etiam teneatur . . .' H. Denifle, 'Die Denkschriften der Colonna gegen Bonifaz VIII und der Cardinale gegen die Colonna', *ALKG*, ix (1889), p. 521.

relate, as the Colonna pamphlet did, the consultation doctrine of *Novit* to the cardinals' participation in the papal decision-making process. This Hostiensis had done too, in the *Per venerabilem* context. But before we turn to his comment in order to determine whether or not he read it in the same way as the Colonna cardinals, let us see *Novit* in another canonist context.

In his *Apparatus* on the *Liber Sextus*, Cardinal Jean Lemoine reported on a consistory in which Boniface VIII and the cardinals were discussing the validity of some of the appointments made by the recently abdicated Celestine V. He had nominated many abbots, bishops and other high dignitaries without consulting the cardinals. When this point was made, Lemoine gave it as his opinion 'that it was proper that what the pope in his canon ordered should be observed by others, should not be neglected by himself: for he commands that bishops, abbots and superiors should order the business of their churches, at least in difficult matters, with the advice of their brothers, otherwise what is done is invalid'. He then noted that he was arguing from *Novit*. The collations were in fact quashed, Lemoine reported, especially because the cardinals were in the position that difficult questions were not to be discussed or decided without their advice. Thus papal practice conformed to the well-known Roman law maxim that though the prince was above the law, he should himself live according to it.[26] The Cardinal developed his argument that advice was a necessary constituent for the validity of a papal act by recalling a second occasion when actual papal practice pointed in that direction. He reported that Benedict XI had suspended statutes which Boniface VIII had issued for the Marches because they concerned difficult matters and were promulgated without the advice of the cardinals. There being a defect in the required procedure (*in modo necessario*), what had been done was invalid.[27]

[26] 'Quero an hec (*scil.* 'de fratrum nostrum consilio') sint uerba uoluntatis, congruencie, decencie vel necessitatis? Scio quod Celestinus papa quintus multas abbatias, episcopatus et superiores dignitates contulit sine fratrum consilio, et coram successore (*scil.* Bonifatius) fuit iste articulus in dubium revocatus; et dixi tunc, decet ut quod papa mandat in suo canone ab aliis observari, illud non negligat: mandat enim quod episcopi, abbates et superiores saltem in ardua suarum ecclesiarum ordinent de consilio fratrum suorum; aliter non teneatur quod agitur, supra, de his que fiunt a prelatis sine consensu capituli, Nouit (3.10.4) ... Et scio quod dicte collationes fuerunt cassate, presertim quia cetus cardinalium erat in hac possessione quod ardua negocia erant de eorum consilio tractanda et terminanda, et in multis iuribus dicitur "de fratrum nostrorum consilio" et licet princeps sit solutus legibus, tamen secundum legem ipse viuere decet ...' *Apparatus* VI° 5.2.4 (Paris, 1535; Pembroke College, Cambridge, MS 165).

[27] 'A Benedicto papa xi. statuta que dedit marchianis Bonifacius papa absque consilio fratrum, quia ardua tangebant, fuerunt suspensa, licet multa iusta fuissent in dictis statutis contenta. Nam defectus in persona facientis vel modo necessario reddit factum inutile ...'

If the trend of Lemoine's argument was to establish that *consilium* was a matter of obligation, another canonist, equally distinguished and also drawing on his experience in the curia, was coming to a contrary conclusion. Guido de Baysio noted that he had often heard questioning in the papal curia about the effect of the expression 'with the advice of our brothers', and sought an explanation of his own. He too discussed *Novit* and noted that the pope, just as he wished his inferiors to do, should use advice in framing decisions, especially in major issues. But such consultation, so far as the pope was concerned, Guido said specifically, was not of obligation: *non quantum in necessitatem.*[28]

Thus, some thirty years after the death of Hostiensis, there was no received opinion among canonists as to the precise nature of the papal obligation to consult the cardinals. Let us turn back to *Per venerabilem* to determine, if possible, whether it was Lemoine or Guido de Baysio who most closely followed in his footsteps. Hostiensis before them had attached particular importance to *Novit*. He argued that the bond between pope and cardinals was even stronger than the bond between any other prelate and his chapter. Since, as *Novit* urged on the patriarch of Jerusalem, the advice of the chapter was needed for the transaction of the important business of his church, because of the stronger bond, 'so much the more therefore was it fitting for the pope to require the counsels of his brothers'.[29] Was that requirement *quantum in necessitatem?* Hostiensis did not definitely say so and the question remains an open one. His choice of the word *decet* rather than *tenet* or *debet* (which *Novit* used) does not suggest insistence on the necessity rather than the eminent desirability of consultation. It is also not without significance that, when Hostiensis discussed the general topic of what a prelate might do without the consent of his chapter, he went to some trouble

[28] 'Sepius vidi in curia queri quid operentur ista verba "de fratrum nostrorum consilio". Dici potest quod sunt ad bonam ordinationem pape qui habet uti consilio potissime fratrum, unde in multis iuribus antiquis et novis dicitur "habito fratrum nostrorum consilio": sed non quantum ad necessitatem ... Sed potissime in magnis negociis tali debet uti consilio, cum alios inferiores velit ita facere, ut infra, de his que fi. a pre., Novit (3.10.4) ...' *Apparatus* VI° 1.16.8 s.v. *consilio* (Venice, 1577).

[29] 'Inter cardinales quippe et papam tanta est unio ut sibi omnia communicare deceat, sicut enim inter episcopum et capitulum suum maior est communio quam inter eundem episcopum et ceteras ecclesias sue dyocesis ... sic multo magis et multo excellentius est unio inter papam et collegium romane ecclesie quam etiam inter aliquem alium patriarcham et capitulum suum ... et tamen patriarcha sine consilio fratrum non debet ardua expedire, ut patet in his que leguntur et notantur supra, de his que fiunt a prela. Novit et c. Quanto (3.10.4,5). Multo fortius ergo decet papam consilia fratrum suorum requirere ...' 4.17.13 s.v. *fratres nostri.*

to make of the word *consilium* a technical term to be sharply distinguished from another technical term, *consensus*. Where *consensus* was required, what was done without it was void. On *consilium* he noted: 'he who requires advice can follow it if he wishes: if he does not wish to do so, he is under no necessity'.[30] The *Per venerabilem* gloss used the word *consilium* throughout.

In fact, Hostiensis seems to have used the word *consensus* only once in relation to the cardinals' participation in papal government. And then it was as part of the opinion of someone else, which he himself rejected. The context is an important one.

A decretal of Pope Leo III, which found its place in the Gregorian decretals in that title which was concerned with clerical non-residence, recorded how a certain cardinal priest had been deposed in a synod for persistent absenteeism. That the deposition took place in the Roman synod prompted the canonists to enquire whether the deposition was pronounced by the synod and if so, whether the pope alone could depose a cardinal. The *glossa ordinaria* said unambiguously that when the text spoke of the sentence as issuing 'from all' it meant that 'all those present approved the act, since it was the pope alone who deposed him'.[31] Hostiensis discussed this problem afresh. He advanced the argument that cardinals, because of their special relationship with the pope, had a valid claim to enjoy a special position when there was question of their being disciplined. Hence, he stated, it was the custom for the pope, when preparing legal action against a cardinal, to consult the other members of the College. Some went further, he stated, to argue that the pope was bound to consult the others if he wanted to excommunicate one of them or indeed to issue any sort of command. They also argued that no general sentence applied against cardinals unless there was included in the decree a special proviso making it so applicable. Others, reported Hostiensis, were of a contrary opinion. 'But whatever is said', he declared roundly by way of conclusion, 'this I clearly acknowledge, that the plenitude of power rests in the pope alone, as is stated above, *de usu pal. c. Ad honorem*, against which I do not purpose

---

[30] 'Alii dicunt quod consilium requiritur, id est consensus: et his verbis consilio et consensu promiscue utuntur et secundum ipsos nulla est differentia inter consensum et consilium ...' *Summa* 3.10 (ed. Cologne, 1612) col. 802. Hostiensis had already (col. 801) made his position clear: 'Sed que est differentia inter consensum et consilium? Respondeo, ubi consensus requiritur, non valet quod agitur, nisi consensus habeatur ... potest sequi consilium si vult, is qui ipsum requirit: si non vult, non habet necesse (*recte*: necessitas).'

[31] 'Ab omnibus: id est, omnibus approbantibus suam depositionem: quoniam solus ipsum deposuit.' *Gl. ord. ad* 3.4.2. (Paris, 1561).

to write, as appears in what is noted below, *de conces. preben. c. Proposuit.*[32]

That is to say, he did not intend to detract from the personal power of the pope to expel a cardinal from the College, to excommunicate him or command him in any other way. But the protestation went further than that. By citing the text of the decretal *Ad honorem* and of *Proposuit* with his commentary thereon, Hostiensis was manifestly referring to the supreme and universal power of the pope himself and not just to one specific application of it. For these texts, both of Pope Innocent III, were standard authorities for the principle of plenitude of power *in se*. It was the supreme power itself, inherent in the pope alone, that Hostiensis was declaring he did not wish to impugn.

Ad honorem was concerned with the wearing of the *pallium* by archbishops. The context required the pope to make comparisons between episcopal and papal usages. The comparison gave him an opportunity to repeat the classical distinction between the pope, who alone held plenitude of power, and bishops who were called *in partem sollicitudinis*. *Ad honorem* was, then, a particularly important assertion of traditional terminology, and Hostiensis frequently referred to it precisely when he was emphasising the general principle of the papal plenitude of power.[33]

Proposuit was also much cited in discussion of the primacy because it contained another of the classical formulations of papal sovereignty: '(nos) qui secundum plenitudinum potestatis de iure supra ius dispensare'. Because of this formula, Hostiensis's commentary was

---

[32] 'Inde est quod papa non consueuit, nec etiam potest secundum quosdam, aliquem de cardinalibus excommunicare vel ei aliquod preceptum facere sine aliorum suorum fratrum consilio et consensu ... Sed et dicunt quod cardinales non incurrunt aliquam sententiam canonis vel aliam generalem, nisi in canone vel sententia de ipsis specialis mentio habeatur ... Alii vero contrarium tenent. Quicquid tamen dicitur, hoc de plano fateor quod in solum papam plenitudo residet potestatis, supra de usu pal. Ad honorem (1.8.4), contra (quam) scribere non intendo, ut patet in eo quod notatur, infra de conces. preben. Proposuit (3.8.4).' *Apparatus,* 3.4.2 *s.v. In synodo.*

[33] The decretal figures in twelve of the glosses I have printed in the Appendix to 'Use of the term plenitudo potestatis by Hostiensis', pp. 178–87. These three reveal his characteristic usage of *Ad honorem:* '(Papa) plenus vicarius (Christi) extat ... plenus, id est, habens plenitudinem potestatis, ad quam vocatus est, alii vero in partem sollicitudinis, supra, de usu pal. Ad honorem ...' *Summa* 1.32.3 col. 286. 'Ab hac vero generalitate excipitur papa ad quem appellari potest a quolibet ordinario omisso medio, ut ii.q.vi.c.i.et ii (C.2.q.6 cc.1,2). Et hoc est propter plenitudinem potestatis quam habet, supra, de usu pal. Ad honorem, et quia ordinarius est singulorum ...' *Apparatus,* 2.28.66 *s.v. non tenere.* 'Ideo et dicitur de papa quod habet non solum potestatem, sed etiam plenitudinem potestatis, supra, de usu pal. Ad honorem, quia Petro et successoribus claves regni celorum dedit dicens, "Quodcunque ligaueris etc." et iterum, "Pasce oues meas etc.": oues autem non solum fideles, sed infideles ...' *Apparatus* 3.34.8 *s.v. pro defensione.*

primarily about dispensation, about the papal *potestas absoluta*, i.e. being *solutus a legibus*, about the supreme legislative power.[34] It then considered other aspects of sovereignty, such as the obedience owed by subjects and the pope's being subject to no human jurisdiction. *Proposuit* itself, then, and Hostiensis's commentary thereon, with *Ad honorem* and his usage of that text, amount to a substantial statement about the plenitude of power in itself. Accordingly, it was plenitude of power understood in its general sense, and not in some particular one, that Hostiensis was confessing he believed to reside in the pope alone. It is within the perspective of that categorical assertion that any statement about the cardinals participating in supreme power must be read.

Hostiensis wrote no treatise on the cardinalate, and his views on it can only be recovered after an arduous search through his voluminous *Apparatus* and a minutely critical study of each gloss, read carefully in conjunction with both the text of the decretal which had prompted it, and the decretals cited in support or against any proposition. As all the texts in which Hostiensis spoke both of the plenitude of power and of the cardinals are duly weighed, it would seem that the balance tips towards an interpretation on these lines: the Sacred College held a uniquely important advisory and coadjutory position in the government of the Church, without giving this body authority to limit papal authority. The College participated, with the pope, in the exercise of the plenitude of power, but the power itself belonged to him alone. It shared his governmental function but not his primacy. Was not Innocent III saying just this in *Per venerabilem*? The papacy had not been transformed into a constitutional monarchy, but the pope should do 'little or nothing' without the advice of his senate. In practice, this was how the Church was ruled in the thirteenth century and Hostiensis was defending the *status quo*, not promoting some new concept of papal primacy.

[34] The lengthy gloss is printed in 'Use of the term plenitudo potestatis by Hostiensis', pp. 183–4. Notice: '*supra ius*, quasi dicat, nullo iure astringimur, immo sumus positi supra omnia iura atque concilia ... Sed tamen perraro a iure communi volumus deviare; hoc enim decet nos, licet non astringat.' *Apparatus*, 3.8.4 *s.v. supra ius*.

CENTRE AND LOCALITY: ASPECTS OF PAPAL ADMINISTRATION IN ENGLAND IN THE LATER THIRTEENTH CENTURY

by JANE SAYERS

LIKE THE ENGLISH ROYAL COURT, the papal court was peripatetic. The restless nature of royal and papal government was partly imposed by the difficulties of staying put in one place. The justices-in-eyre and the judges-delegate were the expedients of the twelfth century – administration on the move – reaching their zenith in the mid-thirteenth century. The new demand was for a settled place of administration and justice, a demand which was met more successfully by the royal government in England (although the baronial activities caused temporary dislocations) with the settlement of the bench and its professional judges at Westminster, than by the papal court of audience which was never able to remain in Rome for long. Rome in the thirteenth century presented a panorama of fortified residences and castellated towers, sheltering barons as turbulent as any in Europe. Many popes spent time in their native cities, where their landed influence provided stability: Innocent IV at Genoa, for example, and Boniface VIII at Anagni. The two French popes, Urban IV (1261–4) and Clement IV (1265–8), never entered the papal city of Rome. Of the thirteenth-century popes, Gregory IX spent much time at Anagni, Innocent IV at Genoa and Lyons, Clement IV at Perugia and Viterbo, and Gregory X at Orvieto and Lyons.

A political elite and a professional civil service were responsible for both the papal and English royal administrations, centring on the household. We do not need Namier to show that it was family connection, rather than any kind of specific party alliance, that determined selection and entry into the household, whether it was the household of pope, king, cardinal, bishop or earl. The paternalistic nature of curial government – papal, royal, episcopal – extended the conception of the family into a wider field. A pope, king or bishop, who did not provide for his own 'especially for those of his own house', as Adam Marsh reminded Grosseteste, citing I Timothy 5.8, 'had denied the faith and

115

was worse than an infidel'.[1] The reliance on family and friends filled an otherwise unsupplied need in the administrative system.

Nowhere is this better shown in the late thirteenth century than by examining the family of Fieschi. The Fieschi were a noble family from Lavagna near Genoa, whose influence on thirteenth-century politics was comparable with that of the Bonapartes in nineteenth-century Europe or the Kennedys in twentieth-century America. In origin the family was probably Germanic (as were the Conti). They were married into most of the royal families of Europe and were connected with the Marquises of Carreti and of Pallavicini and later with the Este, Gonzaga and Visconti families. Their accession to the papal throne in the person of Innocent IV signalised their first major entry into papal politics, although there had been two earlier Fieschi cardinals.[2] The difficulty of staying in Rome meant that Innocent IV had to create his own power base elsewhere and the exile of this pope from the city exalted the house of Fieschi perhaps more than would otherwise have been the case.

There was, indeed, during the years of their influence, scarcely a diocese or cathedral chapter in Europe where the Fieschi were not represented. In Italy, they were, of course, strong in Genoa, and also in other cathedral churches, such as Parma. In France and the Low Countries, they held office in Bayeux, Beauvais, Cambrai, Meaux, Narbonne, Paris, Rheims, Rouen and St Brieuc. In England they had prebends in York, Lincoln, Salisbury and Lichfield, and various benefices. By far the most influential of the Fieschi in touch with England was Innocent IV's nephew, the legate Ottobon, but the family also produced at least two royal clerks – Master Tedisius (who was also a papal scribe) and Master Rowland, who served as a royal proctor – and numerous papal chaplains. Master Rowland of Lavagna, brother of the legate, occurs as a king's clerk between 1258 and 1267, and in 1259 was presented to the church of Steeple Morden by the king, during a vacancy in the see of Winchester. Two other Fieschi were engaged on the king's business – Percival in 1268, and Luke, cardinal deacon of St Mary in Via Lata, who in 1301 was granted a pension of fifty marks at the Exchequer 'in consideration of his good offices in the king's affairs'. Luke was Edward I's kinsman, the son of Nicholas, the elder

---

[1] Cited by C. R. Cheney, *Pope Innocent III and England*, Päpste und Papsttum, IX (Stuttgart, 1976), pp. 82–3.

[2] F. Federici, *Della famiglia Fiesco trattato* (Genoa, ?1650) deals (somewhat inaccurately) with the family.

brother of Ottobon, whose sister had married into the house of Savoy.[3] If, indeed, we had to find a parallel for the Fieschi at this period, in filling offices in Church and State, it would surely be the house of Savoy.

Payment of the increasing bureaucracy presented a severe problem. The benefice was the most common reward, for all the officers with whom we are concerned were in orders of some kind, usually deacon's, but there is evidence of a growing shortage of benefices at this time due to increased appropriation by the monasteries. No doubt the payment of a papal civil service had already exercised the mind of Honorius III, as chamberlain and vice-chancellor, before his accession to the papacy. Indeed the pope's letter putting forward a scheme in 1225 refers to an earlier proposal which had been discussed at the Fourth Lateran Council, when it was suggested that a tenth should be levied on the revenues of all cathedral churches. Honorius said that he had heard of complaints about financial excesses in Rome, which he believed to be not wholly warranted because many proctors spent their expenses on good living, and then lied to their employers about the amounts necessary for the conduct of business. However, the pope thought that reform was desirable and therefore he wished to obtain a permanent income for the curial officers. If such a revenue could be assured, he would impose heavy penalties on those in the curia who took bribes, and would eliminate not only the customary gratuities but also all fees, with the one exception of that charged by the chancery for the application of the *bulla*. To provide a fixed income for the curial officials, the pope proposed that the bishops should hand over a prebend in each cathedral and prebendal church, that the monasteries and collegiate churches should provide a sum relative to their resources, and that bishops personally should provide some long-term gift to form a common fund. The plan was not accepted, nor was a renewed form of it in 1244.[4] In the face of such a negative response, the curia was left with no alternative but to continue with the old system of revenue-raising to pay its officers, and to operate the system of provision to foreign benefices for which it was so severely criticised. To understand clearly why the scheme was rejected it is necessary to consider the channels of communication to the papal court.

[3] F. M. Powicke, *King Henry III and the Lord Edward*, 1 vol. edn (Oxford, 1966), p. 526.
[4] *Regesta Honorii Papae III*, ed. P. Pressutti (Rome, 1888–95), no. 5285. For the full text see *Register of S. Osmund*, I, ed. W. H. Rich Jones, R.S. (London, 1883), p. 366; and see W. E. Lunt, *Financial Relations of the Papacy with England to 1327* (Cambridge, Mass., 1939), pp. 178, 213.

Much of the work of papal government operated through the cardinals' households. There was usually one English-born cardinal in the curia: in the latter part of the century, John of Toledo (1244–75), Robert Kilwardby (1278–9) and Hugh of Evesham (1281–7). There were also those whose legations and assignments brought them into touch with England and English affairs, who were the natural targets for English petitioners and placemen in search of provision – Ottobon, cardinal from 1252–76 and legate from 1265–8, and among the cardinals of foreign origin, Cardinal Richard Annibaldi (1238–76).

It is unknown how the English-born John of Toledo, cardinal from 1244–75, entered the curia, but if the chronicler is correct when he states on John's death in 1275 that he had been in the curia for some sixty years some further *curriculum vitae* is necessary for him. So far as is known he was not in Langton's household nor in the royal service, but had, like Adrian IV before him, entered a foreign religious house, in this case Clairvaux, from where he had come to prominence, possibly as a proctor. The influence of the Cistercians within the curia is apparent from the mid-twelfth century, and it had certainly not died by the time of John of Toledo, the 'Cardinal Albus', protector of the Order in all but name. He had in his youth studied medicine at Toledo and another possible channel of his influence is as a doctor. His households as cardinal priest and later as cardinal bishop contained some fifty-eight members, of whom eighteen to nineteen were apparently English, two were Scots, thirteen to fourteen Italian, eight to nine French, one Spanish and one from Tortosa (fourteen unknown).[5] Fourteen were beneficed in England, and two deserve some short comment. William de Lexington, a chaplain of the cardinal, came from the Nottinghamshire family of Laxton, and was a relative of Stephen de Lexington, Abbot of Clairvaux from 1243 to 1255.[6] When, on 16 March 1247, William was authorised to have an additional benefice with cure of souls – the one he already held was probably Whaddon, Cambs. – the letter was endorsed 'To the Abbot of Clairvaux (Stephen de Lexington) at the instance of J(ohn of Toledo) cardinal priest of St Laurence in Lucina by Master William de Buttona, Archdeacon of Wells'. William de Lexington's future was to be identi-

---

[5] Based on A. Paravicini Bagliani, *Cardinali di curia e 'familiae' cardinalizie dal 1227 al 1254*, Italia Sacra XVIII, XIX (Padua, 1972), pp. 242–55.

[6] On the family see *Rufford Charters*, I, ed. C. J. Holdsworth, Thoroton Soc. Rec. Ser. XXIX (1972), pp. xcii–xcix; and *Rolls and Register of Bishop Oliver Sutton*, III, ed. R. M. T. Hill, LRS, XLVIII (1954), p. xiv.

fied with his home region of Lincoln. He was a canon of Lincoln by 1259 and prebendary of Langford manor (this prebend had been held consecutively by Henry de Lexington and Richard Gravesend), precentor, and elected dean in 1262.[7] Master Richard Gravesend who occurs as a chaplain of the cardinal in August 1254 was already treasurer of Hereford cathedral. Nine years earlier, in 1245, he had objected to residence, enforced by a papal bull, in order to draw from the common fund.[8] He was archdeacon of Oxford by 1249, and, on the occasion when he is referred to as chaplain, he was dispensed to hold both the rectory of Ross (Herefordshire) and the deanery of Lincoln.[9] He was consecrated bishop of Lincoln in 1258, on the death of Henry de Lexington.[10] He supported the baronial party and hence was *persona non grata* with the legate, Ottobon.

Through the good offices of the 'Cardinal Albus', during the years of his influence at the curia, especially under Alexander IV (1254–61), many members of his household and others were provided to benefices. His own clerk, the king's clerk and papal chaplain, Roger Lovel, was 'at the cardinal's request' dispensed for plurality, as was Roger's brother Philip, papal chaplain and royal treasurer, while the canonist, Master Roger Marmion, prebendary of York, was appointed papal chaplain on the cardinal's recommendation.[11] There were also dispensations for illegitimacy, issued at John's request, and licences to appropriate livings, for the English Cistercian houses of Newenham and Roche, and the Benedictine nuns of Elstow (Beds.). In 1258, through John's influence, Waverley, and all the English Cistercian houses, were exempted from contributing to the tenth of church revenues, granted by the pope to the king; and the papal registers abound with references to John's activities on behalf of English petitioners and the Cistercian College in Paris.[12]

The two other most influential cardinals at this time, Cardinal Richard Annibaldi and Cardinal Ottobon Fieschi, were both closely attached to the English. Cardinal Richard Annibaldi (1238–76) came from the great Roman family of Annibaldi and was a nephew of Innocent III. Cardinal Richard's household had some thirty-eight members, two of whom were English: John of Somercotes and Roger

---

[7] BL Harley Ch. III A 7; and see *John Le Neve, Fasti Ecclesiae Anglicanae 1066–1300: III. Lincoln*, comp. D. E. Greenway (London, 1977), pp. 11, 14, 76.

[8] Hereford D. and C. Ch. 2515.

[9] *Les Registres d'Innocent IV*, ed. E. Berger (4 vols., Paris, 1884–1911), no. 7974.

[10] See introduction by A. Hamilton Thompson to *Rotuli Ricardi Gravesend episcopi Lincolniensis*, ed. F. N. Davis, LRS, xx (1925).

[11] *CPL* pp. 324, 330, 336, 349.   [12] *Ibid.*, pp. 331, 348, 351–2, 359–60.

Lovel, who transferred to John of Toledo's household in 1252. Mainly the cardinal's associates were Italian, two at least of whom had English benefices: Roffredus of Ferentino, rector of Holland, and John de Panormo, rector of Wandsworth. Richard's activities in English government were concerned with the candidature of Henry III's son, Edmund, for the *Regno* in 1252 and the election of Richard of Cornwall as senator of Rome in 1261. His support for Edmund was canvassed by John of Toledo, and, in recognition of his activities, the English crown granted him a yearly salary of thirty marks. He was a highly respected papal auditor during nearly forty years of influence, and protector of the Augustinians.[13] His nephew, the papal subdeacon and notary, Richard, held several English benefices, including Dorking, and another nephew, Stephen Surdus, held the prebend of Scamblesby and the living of Kirkby Thore.[14] Both Richard and John Annibaldi, who occur at the turn of the century, beneficed in Lincoln, were probably great-nephews.

Cardinal Ottobon Fieschi, nephew of Innocent IV, and later Pope Adrian V, was legate in England from 1265 to 1268. He had close associations with the royal house – indeed his mission was to provide a political settlement – and, in a stay of two-and-a-half years, his influence was bound to be felt in favour of his family and *familia* on English benefices. He had come to England with Otto's legation in 1237 and had held the churches of Twywell (Northants) (patrons, Thorney), and St Nicholas, Durham, to which he had been presented by the king during a vacancy.[15] In 1257, on his petition to the papal court, William son of Mussus, his cousin, was dispensed to hold another benefice besides St Mary-in-the-castle, Chester, and St Eval (Cornwall).[16] His household included two men provided to prebends in Hereford cathedral – the Englishman John le Berton, canon of Merton, his chaplain, and Ardicio de Comite, his chancellor, from the Conti family, and later papal collector in England.[17] Master James de Portubus, canon of Syracuse, living in England from 1263, was his clerk during the English legation. It also included Alfred the Englishman in 1271, Gilbert of St Léofard, in his service in March 1266, and Geoffrey de

---

[13] F. Roth, 'Cardinal Richard Annibaldi', *Augustiniana*, II (1952), pp. 26–60, 108–49, 283–313; IV (1954), pp. 5–24.

[14] *CPL* pp. 377, 417, 492.

[15] *Rotuli Roberti Grosseteste*, ed. F. N. Davis, LRS, XI (1914), p. 182; and *Register or Rolls of Walter Gray*, ed. J. Raine, Surtees Society, LVI (1870), no. 382.

[16] *CPL* p. 345.

[17] *Diplomatic Documents*, I, ed. P. Chaplais (London, 1964), no. 412.

Sancta Agatha (?Easby), rector of Houghton and incumbent of Lazonby (Cumb.) (patrons, Lanercost), chaplain from October 1258. His secretary during the English legation was Benedict Gaetani, the future Boniface VIII.

Finally, Hugh of Evesham, cardinal from 1281 to 1287 ('Anglicus cardinalis'), previously prebendary of Bugthorpe, proctor of the archbishop of York in 1280, and archdeacon of Worcester, deserves some attention. Overtures, softly made to him in those years, speak discreetly from the bishops' registers – thirty marks from Bishop Cantelupe in June 1281,[18] for example – as they had done to others in the 1230s and 1240s. Even Bishop Grosseteste had felt no compunction about writing to Cardinal Robert of Somercotes on his elevation to the cardinalate, congratulating him, and asking his favour in current business in the curia, though he got his name wrong, calling him Cardinal Raymond, and hence perhaps reaped little harvest, but the cardinal after all was beneficed in his diocese, and could be expected to repay those who had sped him on his way).[19] When Archbishop Giffard sent a present to Cardinal Richard Annibaldi, he rather archly apologised for the smallness of it.[20] But a Giffard could at least offer a present to an Annibaldi, without fear of rebuff.

On the promotion of Hugh of Evesham to the cardinalate, indeed, English spirits must have risen, and the papal registers show his activities on behalf of his family, English petitioners and his household. Richard de Duriard, a relative, was to have a prebend of Lichfield when one came vacant,[21] Master Henry of Somerset, rector of Curry Rivel, 'at the request of the cardinal' was to have another benefice. Master Walter of Bath, king's clerk and doctor of civil law, was to be ordained and hold a benefice, although he was illegitimate.[22] With Cardinal Hugh's chaplain, Master Stefano di San Giorgio, who was a papal scribe in 1288,[23] we touch on an important royal clerk of the wardrobe, who first appears in the royal court in 1274, was proctor of Edward I at the papal court in 1283 and was still employed by the king in 1290.[24]

[18] *Registrum Thome de Cantilupo*, ed. R. G. Griffiths and W. W. Capes, CYS, II (1907), p. 274.
[19] *Roberti Grosseteste . . . Epistolae*, ed. H. R. Luard, R.S. (London, 1861), no. lxv.
[20] *Register of Walter Giffard*, Surtees Society, CIX (1904), p. 244.
[21] *Les Registres d'Honorius IV*, ed. M. Prou (Paris, 1886–8), no. 342.
[22] *Ibid.*, no. 54.
[23] CPL p. 492.
[24] T. F. Tout, *Chapters in . . . Administrative History*, II (Manchester, 1937), pp. 23–4; CPR (1272–81), pp. 61, 76, 209, 242, 295; and CPR (1281–92), pp. 86, 374, 447. He had acted as proctor of M. Robert of Lavagna, king's clerk (see below, p. 125).

How easily such men moved between the royal court, the papal court and the cardinals' households!

This brings us to new realms of connection in the curia's business, but, before following them, we must consider the extent of provision for curialists in English secular cathedrals and benefices. The bishops, who were expected in Honorius's scheme to make gifts to the Roman church, were doubtless continuing to do so, into the hands of those whom *they* chose. They surrendered prebends for curial officers (sometimes more than the required one) when *they* chose. That way they played their own cards: no faceless Roman pope did it for them and absorbed their contributions into a common sinking fund where none knew from whence they came. When Innocent III appointed his nephew, Leonard, to York, he did not hesitate to point out to the chapter the benefits which might accrue to it, but he was forced to ask and persuade them and explain his action.[25] Bishop Hugh Nonant of Coventry, who assigned prebends in his projected secular chapter to Roman cardinals, is said to have done so with the definite purpose of securing defenders of the new constitution in the curia.[26]

If we look at three out of the nine English secular cathedral chapters in the thirteenth century, the evidence is as follows. Of the thirty-six prebends of York, twenty-one identified prebends, i.e. two-thirds, were in the hands of foreigners (mainly Italians from the great papal families) at some point in the century. Three prebends were occupied by the Fieschi, two by the Savelli, three by the Orsini, two by the Gaetani, one by a Conti and one by a Ceccano. Rufinus, the nephew of the legate Guala, and prebendary of Strensall, who had a multitude of benefices, was forced in 1233 to be content with those to a value of 200 marks, but he kept Cropredy in Lincoln. Eight of the thirty-six prebends had more than one foreign occupant in succession.

Fifteen of the fifty-six prebends of Lincoln had foreign occupants. Lincoln supported five Colonnas, two Fieschi, two Conti, two Savelli, two Annibaldi, and various relatives of these families, such as a Surdi related to the Annibaldi. Cropredy, described by Grosseteste as one of the best prebends, represents the most interesting succession: Rufinus, Master Adenulf dei Conti of Anagni (nephew of Gregory IX, prebendary of Salisbury, canon of St Paul's, and canon and prebendary of

[25] *York Minster Fasti*, II, ed. C. T. Clay, Yorks. Archaeol. Soc. Rec. Ser., CXXIV (1958), p. 47.
[26] 'Chronicle of Richard of Devizes', *Chronicles of the Reigns of . . . Stephen, Henry II and Richard I*, III, ed. R. Howlett, R.S. (London, 1886), pp. 440–1.

122

York), Odo de Colonna and John Annibaldi. Pandulph de Savelli, son of Luke, who succeeded Cinthius de Pinea de Urbe in the prebend of Farndon-cum-Balderton, was a papal notary and prebendary of Hereford, Salisbury and York, and of several French cathedrals.

London (St Paul's) had an establishment of thirty canons and twelve minor canons. Five of the prebends were held by eight Italians (nine foreigners) during the thirteenth century. There were two Italian archdeacons of Essex. The prebend of Rugmere invites comparison with Cropredy. Master Cinthius the Roman was followed by the Gascon, Master Rostand, papal nuncio, and in the service of the king, and also beneficed in York, who was succeeded by two further Romans, Jordan Piruntus dei Conti, papal vice-chancellor, and Osbert. Brownswood nurtured Henry de Sarracenis, while Cantlers provided for Antony de Camilla (a branch of the Fieschi family). The church of St Paul was called upon apparently more frequently to supply prebends for distinctly royal, rather than papal, curial servants.[27]

There were heavy losses for both Lincoln and York with Percival of Lavagna, canon of Bayeux, canon of Paris, papal chaplain, and described in 1268 as in the service of the king. He acquired during his brother Ottobon's legation a prebend of Ripon, the sacristy of the chapel of St Mary and the Holy Angels, York (to which belonged thirteen parish churches), the rich prebend of Aylesbury, for which he gladly surrendered Brampton, and in 1270 the archdeaconry of Buckingham.[28] Disenchantment with Percival was apparent at Lincoln by 1269. Bishop Gravesend offered Percival, whom he addressed as 'immensely reverent man', 350 marks for the prebend. Percival, however, took the matter before a papal auditor who decreed 400 marks for the farm, and later in the relations between Percival and Lincoln, the Lincoln clerk described him, now the pope's brother, as the pope's eye.[29] The Lincoln bishop and chapter were not alone in feeling dissatisfied with the lack of services by Percival. Archbishop Giffard, who, having himself collated Percival to the sacristy, doubtless expected his help and intervention on behalf of the church of York, by 1271 was lamenting his action and describing Percival as 'brought up almost

---

[27] See *John Le Neve, Fasti Ecclesiae Anglicanae 1066–1300: I St Paul's, London*, comp. D. E. Greenway (London 1968).

[28] *Les Registres d'Urbain IV*, ed. J. Guiraud, (4 vols., Paris, 1899–1958), nos. 362, 1602; *Reg. Walter Giffard*, pp. 148–9, 230–1, 233–4; *Close Rolls (1256–9)*, p. 176; and Greenway, *Fasti . . . Lincoln*, pp. 40–1, 49.

[29] Lincoln, D. & C. Dij 66/2/30, 31, 74.

from infancy on the goods of the Church' and 'like a child that hangs at its mother's breast, living upon the food and doing no good'.[30]

The papal schemes to pay for the activities of the papal court had suggested that each religious house might contribute a benefice, and Innocent IV had proposed one worth not less than forty marks per annum. In refusing the papal request, the monasteries, like the cathedral chapters and the bishops, almost certainly fared worse financially than if they had accepted. But in doing so they retained a direct channel of influence to the papal court, which might be needed in the event of litigation or when some other business was pending, such as the procurement of a privilege or a dispensation. Undoubtedly the cathedral chapters and the monasteries found it advantageous to be able to distribute largesse on the pope's behalf, through which means they might make personal contact with powerful papal officials. It is, of course, impossible actually to see these influences and pressures at work, but we can trace certain benefices which continued in the hands of papal clerks when once a curial person had been presented. Scotter church (Lincs.), of which Peterborough were the patrons, was held by Master John of Ferentino, papal chamberlain, and archdeacon of Norwich, in 1236–7, and then by Richard Annibaldi by papal provision in 1238.[31] Conisborough vicarage (Yorks.), belonging to Lewes priory, was given to John, cardinal deacon of St Mary in Cosmedin, papal chancellor, and Innocent III's brother, in 1205, and then to Ptolemy, clerk, also a kinsman of Innocent III, in 1213.[32] Sibsey, belonging to the prior and convent of Spalding, passed from Robert of Somercotes to Tedisius of Lavagna in 1251.[33] Ombersley, belonging to Evesham, had been given by the legate Nicholas of Tusculum to one of his clerks before passing to Master Marinus, papal vice-chancellor and chamberlain, and in 1249 to Tedisius of Lavagna.[34] Tedisius's provision to Ombersley took effect before he ceased to be a papal scribe in the chancery of his uncle Innocent IV[35] and in this capacity and as a royal clerk (perhaps as early as 1258) and papal chaplain from 1265 to 1268 – Ottobon's legation[36] – he must have been of use to Evesham. But

[30] *Memorials of the Church of . . . Ripon*, ed. J. T. Fowler, Surtees Society, LXXVIII (1884), II, pp. 5–7.
[31] *Rot. Grosseteste*, pp. 136, 137; *Rot. Gravesend*, p. 96.   [32] *York Minster Fasti*, II, p. 47.
[33] *Rot. Grosseteste*, pp. 70, 165; and see *Rot. Gravesend*, p. 51.
[34] BL Harley MS 3763 fo.13r–v.
[35] P. Herde, *Beiträge zum Päpstlichen Kanzlei- und Urkundenwesen im 13. Jahrhundert*, 2nd edn (Kallmünz, 1967), pp. 22, 44–5, 47, 55.
[36] *Close Rolls (1264–8)*, p. 138; *CPR (1266–72)*, pp. 259, 306; and see *CPR (1247–58)*, p. 626.

when the dispute about the ownership of the church broke out in 1284, Tedisius being now in Genoa, the abbot and convent were naturally keen to regain the living.[37]

Strenuous efforts were made in some instances to get the benefices back, particularly when the occupant was no longer useful to the provider. Richard de Burstall got Sibson rectory (patrons, Lyre) probably on the death or retirement of M. Andrew de Mevagna. Master Giles of Spoleto was probably succeeded by Peterborough's clerk, Adam de Bretegat, at Warmington in 1243–4, and Master Gregory, Otto's chancellor, was succeeded in the living of Berkhampstead (patrons, Grestein) by John de Merse. When the future Cardinal Ottobon relinquished Twywell (patrons, Thorney) it was held by John de Hengham.[38] The living of Gainford (patrons, St Mary's, York) was held by Master Godfrey de Trani in 1240 and by Opizo of San Vitale, canon of Parma, and nephew of Innocent IV, in 1245, but the pope promised that when Opizo vacated the living it would return to St Mary's.[39]

The king did not hesitate to squeeze in his own servants during vacancies – and often this right worked in favour of the Church's servants who were also his own – men such as Master Peter de Burdegal, clerk of the legate Otto, who was presented by the king to the church of West Wycombe during a vacancy in the see of Winchester. Master Peter had been on the king's business in 1242. The church of Kirkby Thore (Westmorland) in the patronage of the Vipont family, is found in the possession of Master Peter de Piperno, papal chaplain, and chancellor of Percival of Lavagna.[40] On the death of Master Peter, Urban IV provided Stephen Surdus, nephew of Cardinal Richard Annibaldi, to the church, and a dispute about possession ensued between Stephen and a clerk who was probably Master Robert of Lavagna, king's clerk, and a member of the Fieschi family, presented by the king on behalf of Roger de Clifford (husband of one of the Vipont heiresses) whose heir and lands were in the king's hands.[41]

[37] *Register of Bishop Godfrey Giffard*, ed. J. W. Willis Bund, Worcestershire Historical Society (1902), II, pp. 264, 284, 299; and *Les Registres de Boniface VIII*, ed. G. Digard and R. Fawtier, (4 vols., Paris, 1904–39), no. 1758. There were persistent rumours that he was dead by 1272 but he was in fact at Bologna from 1270.

[38] *Rot. Grosseteste*, p. 182; *Rot. Gravesend*, p. 136.

[39] *Les Registres de Grégoire IX*, ed. L. Auvray (Paris, 1896–1910), no. 5250; *Reg. Walter Gray*, p. 77; and *Reg. Inn. IV*, no. 1460.

[40] See G. F. Nüske, 'Untersuchungen über das Personal der päpstlichen Kanzlei 1254–1304', *Archiv für Diplomatik*, XX (1974), p. 74, and *CPL* pp. 369, 382.

[41] *CPL* pp. 492, 588; and see *CPR (1272–81)*, pp. 427, 456; *CPR (1280–92)*, p. 56.

Much work remains to be done on the king's clerks – their powers and position. Many who were in the king's service, both Englishmen and foreigners, were also papal chaplains – Henry of Wingham, Philip Lovel, king's treasurer, and Albert, chancellor of Milan, beneficed in Salisbury cathedral, who as such made requests for petitioners (for plurality, for example)[42] and effected provisions. Some were (besides being papal chaplains and royal clerks) royal proctors, such as Roger Lovel and Master Rostand. There were legists, too, such as the canonist, Master Roger Marmion, and the civilian, William Arnaldi de Mota, against whom apparently, amongst the counsellors and royal clerks of Henry III, the bishops and chapters felt most dislike. Matthew Paris says that of these the king had a 'large pack which he uncoupled as a huntsman uncouples his dogs, and let loose upon the electors of prelates'.[43]

The advantages of a confidential royal clerk being also in the papal service were apparent to king and pope. Such dual appointments allowed the wheels of government to turn. A common identity for many of the royal servants and papal officers and provisees meant less friction between crown and papacy than between national Church (bishops, deans and chapters and monasteries) and papacy at this time. Rights of advowson were dear to all parties, but often king and pope might be mutually suited in the appointment of candidates to benefices, for the personnel of the papal and of the royal service frequently overlapped.

[42] E.g. *CPL* p. 349: William de Wendling, dispensed for plurality in 1257 at the request of Master Nicholas, archdeacon of Ely and papal chaplain.
[43] Powicke, *King Henry III*, p. 297.

THE SPANISH CHURCH REVISITED:
THE EPISCOPAL *GRAVAMINA* OF 1279

by PETER LINEHAN

IN OCTOBER 1310 Archbishop Rodrigo of Compostela and various of his suffragans assembled at Salamanca and agreed upon a number of measures designed to preserve *libertas ecclesiastica*. They bound themselves to make common cause should any of their number come under attack thereafter. They would establish a fighting fund and share the expense of legal representation at the papal curia, and they would hold annual councils; but they did not call them councils, preferring the vaguer *tractatus* and *congregationes*. Nor did they define the enemy, except to insist that their resolve to assist one another did not lead them to contemplate the use of canonical sentences against members of the royal families of Castile–León and Portugal. Indeed they specifically excluded the possibility of employing the canon law against their monarchs. Errant kings would be visited not with spiritual penalties but by persuasive prelates.[1] These then were the heirs to the achievements of the thirteenth century – the century of Innocent III, Innocent IV and Boniface VIII, and the century of false starts in self-defence for the peninsular churches. Before them lay an equally sombre future. They had accepted the royal view of ecclesiastical councils as mitred *hermandades*. Eugenius IV was preaching to the converted in the Spanish kingdoms when in 1436 he alerted the estate of Catholic princes to the dangerous implications of the conciliarism of Basle.[2] The kings of Portugal, Aragon and Castile had survived relatively unscathed the century which followed the Fourth Lateran Council. The king of Castile in particular had been spared an Archbishop Pecham.

[1] H. Flórez, *España Sagrada*, XVIII (Madrid, 1764), pp. 372 ff. Cf. A. García y García, 'La "Summa de Libertate Ecclesiastica" de D. Egas de Viseu', in *Estudios sobre la canonística portuguesa medieval* (Madrid, 1976), pp. 242–3.

[2] 'In exactly the same way their own peoples, by assembling together, could claim power over *them*. This would turn upside down at once the episcopal order and the Christian polity – which is both unspeakable and insufferable': cit. A. J. Black, *Monarchy and Community: Political Ideas in the Later Conciliar Controversy 1430–1450* (Cambridge, 1970), p. 88. Cf. J. Gimeno Casalduero, *La imagen del monarca en la Castilla del siglo XIV* (Madrid, 1972), pp. 193–200.

PETER LINEHAN

Control over potential political opposition, however, was only one aspect of the Castilian monarch's mastery of his Church. The recently discovered correspondence of Pedro de Casis, Alfonso XI's agent at Avignon in the 1340s, has drawn attention to another enduring feature – the king's remote control of the traffic in ecclesiastical benefices – and has provided a reminder of the need always to distinguish the material well-being of individual churchmen from the well-being of the Church at large.[3] As was shown in some of the reviews of the work first done during that memorable period spent under Walter Ullmann's supervision, the sombre side of the story – the getting and spending, the illiteracy, the concubinage – was not the whole story. Nor was it ever intended to be.[4] Rodrigo of Toledo's many and illustrious achievements as warrior and scholar may be taken for granted.[5] The deplorable state of the peninsular clergy (deplored, that is, by contemporaries, from Diego García to Álvaro Pais) did not hamper unduly the careers of individual luminaries who distinguished themselves in the schools both at home and abroad.[6] Contemporary criticism must be weighed, however, and in the weighing a historian will ask questions about the assumed preponderance of churchmen *and of the Church* during this period. It may be time to jettison, after due scrutiny, the age-old assumptions which historians elsewhere have questioned; in this case the view of the Age of the Reconquest as the history of the Spanish Church militant, inexorably triumphant, and richly rewarded for her efforts.[7] We stand in need of scores of local

[3] A. García y García, 'Notas sobre la política eclesiástica de Alfonso XI de Castilla', *Miscelanea José Zunzunegui (1911–1974)* (Vitoria, 1975), pp. 163–82.

[4] See the prefatory remarks to Linehan, *La iglesia española y el papado en el siglo XIII* (Salamanca, 1975).

[5] See now H. Grassotti, 'Don Rodrigo Ximénez de Rada, gran señor y hombre de negocios en la Castilla del siglo XIII', *Cuadernos de Historia de España*, LVII–LVIII (1973), pp. 1–302; M. Nieto Cumplido. 'La "Cronica Omnium Pontificum et Imperatorum Romanorum" de Rodrigo Jiménez de Rada', *Historia. Instituciones. Documentos*, I (1974), pp. 391–415. The attribution to Rodrigo of the authorship of the *Cronica latina anónima* (ed. M. D. Cabanés Pecourt (Valencia, 1964)) is, however, surely mistaken. Cf. Linehan, *La iglesia*, p. 18.

[6] Peter Linehan, *The Spanish Church and the Papacy in the Thirteenth Century* (Cambridge, 1971), pp. 12, 239–40. The strictures of Álvaro Pais are conveniently summarised in A.D. de Sousa Costa, *Estudos sobre Álvaro Pais* (Lisbon, 1966), pp. 41–51. One such figure who has recently been shown to have held the office of 'ultramontanorum scolarium rector' at Bologna in 1252 was Abril, archdeacon of Salamanca, and subsequently bishop of Urgel. See D. Maffei, 'Un trattato di Bonaccorso degli Elisei e i più antichi Statuti dello Studio di Bologna nel manoscritto 22 della Robbins Collection', *BMCL*, n.s. V (1975), pp. 85–7; P. A. Linehan, 'La carrera del obispo Abril de Urgel: la Iglesia española en el siglo XIII', *Anuario de Estudios Medievales*, VIII (1972–3), pp. 143–97.

[7] Linehan, *Spanish Church*, p. 102; R. S. Lopez, 'Hard Times and Investment in Culture' in W. K. Ferguson, ed., *The Renaissance, a Symposium* (New York, 1953), pp. 19–32. Cf. M.

128

studies which are both institutional and revealing.[8] Meanwhile we may be confident that the hypothesis of a connection between the supine posture of the Spanish bishops and the reported condition of their dioceses is one which will not unduly disconcert the scholars on the spot. Although the coincidence of conciliar activity and pastoral activity (as in the province of Tarragona in the 1240s) would be difficult to explain away, it would be hazardous either to state it in simple terms of cause and effect, or without qualification to ascribe to the Aragonese prelates any measure of disinterested zeal for the notion of *libertas ecclesiastica*. The bishops present at the Tarragona Council of 1244 were anxious to defend the Aragonese Church against royal depredations, but they did not scruple to exempt themselves from the measures which they prescribed against *raptores ecclesiarum*.[9] Still, no such collective measures seem even to have been attempted during the 1240s in Castile, where, appropriately enough, it was the son of the man whose *Planeta* had subjected the bishops to such merciless criticism a generation earlier who superintended Fernando III's taxation of the churches for military purposes.[10]

Hernández Villaescusa, *Recaredo y la unidad católica* (Barcelona, 1890), p. 343, cit. Linehan, *La iglesia*, p. 1, n. 5. T. F. Ruiz has recently advanced, as if it were revolutionary, the proposition 'que l'expansion en Andalousie au XIIIᵉ siècle fut une cause majeure de la crise économique, sociale et institutionelle qui affecta la Castille pour la plus grande partie du siècle qui suivit la chute de Séville en 1248', and has chided historians for not having pursued this line of inquiry: 'Expansion et changement: la conquête de Séville et la société castillane (1248–1350)' *Annales – Économies – Sociétés – Civilisations*, XXXIV (1979), pp. 548, 549.

[8] See B. de Gaiffier, 'Hispania et Lusitana VII', *Analecta Bollandiana*, XCIV (1976), p. 407, reviewing T. Villacorta Rodríguez, *El cabildo catedral de León: estudio histórico-jurídico, siglo XII–XIX* (León, 1974). T. F. Ruiz has traced the decline of the chapter of Burgos as a land-purchasing agent in the second half of the thirteenth century: 'The transformation of the Castilian municipalities: the case of Burgos 1248–1350', *Past & Present*, LXXVII (1977), pp. 14–15. A highly revealing study of conditions in the city of Toledo is that of R. Gonzálvez, 'El arcediano Joffre de Loaysa y las parroquias urbanas de Toledo en 1300', *Historia Mozárabe* (Primer Congreso Internacional de Estudios Mozárabes, 1975) (Toledo, 1978), pp. 91–148.

[9] A. Durán Gudiol, 'Vidal de Canellas, obispo de Huesca', *Estudios de Edad Media de la Corona de Aragón*, IX (1973), p. 285; Linehan, *Spanish Church*, p. 81, n. 7. An edition of the conciliar legislation of the Aragonese Church has been initiated by J. M. Pons Guri, 'Constitucions conciliars Tarraconenses (1229–1330)', *Analecta Sacra Tarraconensia*, XLVII (1974), pp. 65–128. Cf. J. A. Brundage, 'The Provincial Council of Tarragona, 1239: a new text', *BMCL*, n.s. VIII (1978), pp. 21–7.

[10] P. Fernández Martín, 'El obispo de Osma Don Juan Díaz, canciller de Fernando III el Santo, no se llamaba Don Juan Domínguez', *Celtiberia*, XXVII (1964), pp. 90–5; Linehan, *Spanish Church*, p. 111, n. 8. Bishop Juan's role as prelate and royal chancellor is aptly illustrated by the terms of the letter sent to the chapter of Osma regarding the appointment of a successor as sacrist to Fr. Gonzalo: 'si possumus sacristianam dilecto clerico nostro J. Guterii contulimus [et si non possumus commendamus: *insert.*] viro discreto...per quem speramus multa provenire ecclesie tam in temporalibus quam in spiritualibus profutura' (dated 7 April, no year, but 1234 × 1240): Burgo de Osma, Biblioteca del Cabildo, cód. 89, fo. 1r.

Throughout the century the papacy generally stood aloof from these events. Apprehensive of the dire consequences of Islamic counter-attack – an apprehension which the kings of Castile tended to encourage – successive pontiffs acquiesced in the fate of peninsular churches and churchmen. Castile's alleged vulnerability to the Moors was Alfonso X's surest safeguard against papal interference. Registered drafts of Clement IV's correspondence during the summer of 1265 when the king of Granada was in rebellion against Alfonso show the pope progressively de-emphasising the king's personal responsibility for the baneful effects of retention of the *tercias decimarum*.[11] So much a feature of the century was papal acceptance of royal control of the churches, and so intermittent the attempts to check it, that by 1328 Alfonso XI was able to represent his willingness to contemplate some limitation on his fiscal policies as a gratuitous concession and an act of royal magnanimity in favour of Pope John XXII. Because then, as in the later period investigated by Professor Domínguez Ortiz, papal–royal disputes so often had the appearance of mere family squabbles, sig-nalising an underlying stability, any evidence of concerted papal-episcopal resistance to the king deserves very careful consideration.[12]

Episcopal opposition in the portentous decade after the re-conquest of Seville was betrayed by the king's brother, Archbishop Sancho of Toledo in 1257–9. The story has already been told[13] and need be recapitulated only to indicate the effectiveness of royal sub-version of ecclesiastical unity. Whether or not Alexander IV's quin-quennial grant to Sancho in January 1259 of *duas partes tertie decimarum* of the city, province and diocese of Toledo (*Affectu benevolentie*) was held to extend to the tithe income of the cathedral churches,[14] none of the archbishop's neighbours and erstwhile friends was unaffected by Sancho's ecclesiastical imperialism and Alexander's acquiescence in

---

[11] E. Pásztor, 'Per la storia dei Registri Pontifici nel Duecento', *Archivum Historiae Pontificiae*, VI (1968), pp. 85–6; Linehan, *Spanish Church*, p. 208.

[12] L. Serrano, 'Alfonso XI y el papa Clemente VI durante el cerco de Algeciras', *Escuela Española de arqueología e historia en Roma: Cuadernos de trabajos*, III (1915), p. 4. Cf. A. Domínguez Ortiz, 'Iglesia y estado en el siglo XVII español', in M. Andrés *et al.*, eds., *Aproximación a la historia social de la Iglesia española contemporánea* (El Escorial, 1978), p. x: 'Incluso cuando más amargos eran los reproches entre los papas y los reyes de España no dejaron de tener un aire de disputas de familia, cuya unidad esencial no estaba en cuestión.'

[13] Linehan, *Spanish Church*, pp. 152–72.

[14] AC Toledo, V.3.A.1.7 (26 Jan. 1259). Cf. the view of Bonaguida de Aretio cited by G. Barraclough, 'The English royal chancery and the papal chancery in the reign of Henry III', *MIÖG*, LXII (1954), p. 376, n. 16.

it.[15] In April 1259 the grant of *tercias* was reinforced by a papal licence (*Inducunt nos*) entitling Sancho to the entire receipts of one tithe-collector of his own nomination in each and every parish of his province for the same five-year period, as a contribution towards the building expenses of Toledo Cathedral.[16] Alexander's prompt cancellation of *Inducunt nos* 'ex certa causa' and the reduction from five years to three of the terms of *Affectu benevolentie*[17] highlight the confusion and division fostered by recent events. So too does the recorded action of one of Sancho's suffragans, Bishop Fernando of Palencia, who while seeking exemption on his own account did not hesitate to instruct his diocesan clergy to comply with the terms of *Inducunt nos*.[18] As pope and primate combined against the churches of Castile the bishops exposed their flocks to the storm and blamed the tempest on the papacy.[19] Of their feelings towards the real cause of their misfortunes only meagre evidence has survived. Archbishop Sancho II of Toledo and his bishops met at Brioca in 1267, but the unique record of the *acta* of that assembly is barely legible.[20] It would of course be fanciful to associate Sancho II's willingness to allow dissent its voice with the fact of his Aragonese origin. However, eight years later he again protested, together with his episcopal colleagues, this time to Alfonso

---

[15] *Devotionis tue:* sole appointment of two clerics to Toledo benefices collation to which was shared *de jure* with the chapter: AC Toledo, Z.1.G.1.5 (22 Nov. 1257); *Cum sicut:* benefices for eight of his clerics in the churches of Castile–León: AC Toledo, V.2.D.1.5 (7 Feb. 1259). Objections were entered by both the archbishop of Tarragona and the bishop of Zaragoza to the inclusion of the church of Segorbe in Alexander's solemn privilege of 17 June 1259 confirming the rights of the church of Toledo: Linehan, *Spanish Church*, p. 170; Zaragoza, Archivo Diocesano, 2/2/13 (*Venerabili fratri nostro*, 29 July 1259=Potthast, 17646 *mutatis mutandis*).

[16] AC Toledo, X.3.A.1.2 (2 April 1259). For some indications as to the mechanics of tithe-collection see José Luís Martín, 'Diezmos eclesiásticos: notas sobre la economía de la sede zamorana (s. XII–XIII)' *Actas de las I Jornadas de Metodología aplicada de las ciencias históricas*, II (Santiago de Compostela, 1975), pp. 69–78; A. García Sanz, 'Los diezmos del obispado de Segovia del siglo XV al XIX', *Estudios Segovianos*, XXV (1973), p. 14.

[17] AC Toledo, V.3.A.1.16: *Inter alia* (ed. of executor's copy in P. A. Linehan, 'The *gravamina* of the Castilian Church in 1262–3', *EHR*, LXXXV (1970), p. 750). On 7 Sept. 1260 Alexander decreed that the three-year period commence on 1 October next: *Cum sicut:* AC Toledo, V.3.A.1.22; O.12.A.1.27.

[18] AC Toledo, X.3.A.1.8; Linehan, *Spanish Church*, p. 171.

[19] Linehan, '*Gravamina*', p. 731ff.

[20] AC Palencia, 4/1/3; Linehan, *Spanish Church*, pp. 175–6. The *Crónica del Rey Don Alfonso Décimo*, ed. C. Rosell (Madrid, 1953), pp. 22–3, while charging the prelates at the Burgos Cortes of 1272 with having sought to sow dissension between king and nobles, states that Alfonso 'quisiera los echar del reino', but that for certain reasons (including that of 'non aver contra sí al Papa') he held back from doing so. Cf. A. Ballesteros y Beretta, *Alfonso X el Sabio* (Barcelona, 1963), p. 584. Sancho II's role in these years remains enigmatic. Cf. R. Gonzálvez, 'El Infante D. Sancho de Aragón, arzobispo de Toledo (1266–1275)', *Escritos del Vedat*, VII (1977), pp. 97–121.

X's heir Fernando de la Cerda. Their complaints were certainly specific, but they were directed at the secular authorities in the localities, not at the king or his advisers, and the Infante's response – that custom be observed – is not revealing.[21] For a clearer view of the churchmen's case what is needed is an extended account of their *gravamina*, together with some response from the king's side. A document which provides some of this evidence has recently been discovered, and in view of its singular interest it is published below.

The document belongs to the year 1279, when Nicholas III sent a legate, Bishop Pietro of Rieti, to Castile to investigate a list of complaints against Alfonso X and his agents, which had been submitted by Castilian and Leonese prelates, and notably by two exiles, Archbishop Gonzalo García of Compostela and Bishop Martín Fernández of León.[22] The Spanish Church was leaderless, the see of Toledo having remained vacant since the death of Archbishop Sancho II in October 1275, with the pope refusing to approve the election of the abbot of Covarrubias, Fernán Rodríguez de Cabañas, on the grounds that he had alienated ecclesiastical property to, amongst others, Alfonso's clerk – and his emissary to the Infante Sancho in July 1270 – Pay Dacana. Prelates who had been ousted from the positions that they regarded as traditionally theirs looked on helplessly as Alfonso's creatures – a French bishop, Fredulus of Oviedo, and a foreign medic, 'Maestre P. de Marsella cirurgiano dela camara del rey' – toured the country unlawfully exacting *decima*. Two years earlier Alfonso had threatened Nicholas's predecessor John XXI with the Moors; now, with Alfonso's imperial ambitions liquidated, the pope felt able to launch a frontal attack on the king's policy of exploiting ecclesiastics

[21] R. Menéndez Pidal, *Documentos lingüísticos de España*, I (Madrid, 1919), pp. 300–2. The letter transcribed in Madrid, Academia de la Historia, Col. Salazar, vol. o–8, fos. 8ov–81r, is a garbled abbreviated version of this letter (dated 13 April 1275), and not as described in *Índice de la Colección de D. Luís de Salazar y Castro*, formado por el Marqués de Siete Iglesias y B. Cuartero y Huerta, I– (Madrid, 1949–), no. 65977. (I am grateful to Miss Driana Wybourne for verifying this for me.) See also J. L. Martín Martín, L. M. Villar García, F. Marcos Rodríguez, M. Sánchez Rodríguez, *Documentos de los archivos catedralicio y diocesano de Salamanca (siglos XII–XIII)* (Salamanca, 1979), no. 349.
[22] For Gonzalo's exile see Linehan, *Spanish Church*, p. 140. That of Martín Fernández does not seem to have been noticed previously. Twenty-five years earlier he had enjoyed Alfonso's friendship, but since then he and his church had been at odds with the *conceio* of León over rights of jurisdiction: P. A. Linehan, 'La iglesia de León a mediados del siglo XIII', in *León y su historia: Miscelanea histórica*, III (León, 1975), p. 19; *España Sagrada*, XXXV (Madrid, 1786), pp. 323, 434–49. See also E. S. Procter, *The Judicial Use of 'Pesquisa' in Leon and Castile 1157–1369* (London, 1966), p. 7, and sections B' and B" of the document published below.

and ecclesiastical resources.[23] What was at issue, as Nicholas stressed in a letter addressed to the king's bastard son, Alfonso Fernández, was *conculcatio ecclesiastice libertatis.*[24] The king himself was treated to a letter of unexampled peremptoriness, *Prepara quaesumus*, and urged to provide real not fictitious remedies.[25] A text of the legate's commission entitled *Memoriale secretum* is preserved in the papal register, together with detailed tactical instructions which were evidently based on expert knowledge of the political realities of Alfonso's court and of the difficulties which the legate was likely to encounter there. But the *gravamina* are listed only summarily and in no logical order.[26] The *memoriale* (which was for the legate's eyes only) states that Bishop Pietro bore with him more detailed evidence relating to the charges against the king ('quosdam alios articulos prolixiores ... in quibus seriosius gravamina exprimuntur'). This more detailed evidence, if not the full charge-sheet, has now emerged in the archive of Toledo Cathedral. Written on paper, the *folleto* AC Toledo X.1.B.1.4 contains a Spanish translation of the *gravamina* together with the Latin text of some of these as sent by Alfonso with a covering letter, here transcribed, to the Infante Sancho of 29 July 1279, four months after the pope had despatched his legate.[27] The king was seeking his son's advice, and appended is what appears to be an incomplete draft, undated, of the reply prepared either by Sancho or on his behalf. It cannot be assumed that this draft, or indeed any later version of it, was ever sent to

---

23 *Reg. Nicholas III*, nos. 27–41, 649; L. Serrano, *Cartulario del Infantado de Covarrubias*(Valladolid, 1907), p. 119; Linehan, *Spanish Church*, pp. 214–15, 217–20; AC Toledo, V.3.A.1.31 (11 May 1277); J. M. E. de la P., 'Variedades', *Revista de Archivos, Bibliotecas y Museos*, II (1872), pp. 58–60; Ballesteros, *Alfonso X*, p. 837.

24 *Reg. Nicholas III*, no. 740. The address of this letter in the papal register (R.V. 40, fo. 55r) is, as given in the edition of J. Gay, 'dilecto filio nobili viro A. nato carissimi in Christo filii nostri ... regis Castelle ac Legionis'. It is perhaps surprising that the pope should have written to Alfonso Fernández, for whom see H. Flórez, *Memorias de las reynas cathólicas*, 3rd edn (Madrid, 1790), pp. 537–9.

25 *Reg. Nicholas III*, no. 739: 'non verbalem tantummodo set realem ... veritatem'.

26 *Ibid.*, no. 743; Linehan, *Spanish Church*, pp. 218–19.

27 'Don Alffonsso & c. avos Don Sancho & c. Sepades que el Legado me dio escriptos unos articulos en razon dequellas cosas por quel embio el papa ami. Et yo embio vos el traslado ende con maestre M. abbat de sant Quirze e con Gomez Garcia canonigo de Toledo vuestros clerigos. Onde vos ruego e vos mando por aquella fe que vos devedes adios e ami que vos que lo mostredes a essos omnes buenos que son y connusco tan bien clerigos como legos a aquellos que vos entendieredes que vos sabran conseiar en tal fecho como este. Et otrossi que lo embiedes mostrar alos prelados e alos otros omnes buenos dy dela tierra que ellos que vos conseien en esta razon, e aquell conseio que vos diese embiarme lo dezir por vuestra carta e gradescer vos lo e mucho. Dada en Sevilla. xxix dias de julio.' Cf. Ballesteros, *Alfonso X*, p. 1117. According to Gil de Zamora, *De Preconiis Civitatis Numantine* (ed. F. Fita, *Boletín de la R. Academia de la Historia*, v (1884), p. 146), Sancho 'incipit coregnare' in 1278.

Alfonso. Its presence in the archive of Toledo Cathedral (the repository, it may be conjectured, of sections at least of the 'lost' Castilian archives) is best explained in terms of its direct transmission thither by Sancho himself and, in view of its contents, probably before rather than after his accession to the throne in 1284.

The *Memoriale secretum* lists the charges against the king under five headings: 1. *tercias*; 2. royal custody of vacant churches; 3–4. the king's persecution of the prelates of Compostela and León; 5. *gravamina prelatorum*. (A sixth item, a request for Alfonso's good offices in securing the liberty of the Portuguese Church, is not mentioned in the Toledo document.) No response from Sancho to items 3 or 4 is preserved. He and his advisers refer only to 1, 2 and various of the issues raised under 5 which the scribe identifies by the letters A, B, C as far as K.[28] If what has survived is the complete dossier sent by Alfonso then it would appear that it was on item 5, the *gravamina prelatorum*, that he particularly desired advice, for only of item 5 is the Latin (*prolixior*) text of the legate's charges provided. The draft gives Sancho's answers on 1 (= A), 2 (= B) and part of 5 (= C–F), at which point it ends abruptly. On the last sheet of the *folleto* the *gravamina* G–K are stated, and after each there is a gap unfilled (except in the case of I) by any response or attempt at justification. Here then either the ingenuity of Sancho's advisers deserted them or their work was interrupted or abandoned. Whatever the reason, this is the more regrettable in view of the interest of these *gravamina*, and particularly of those collected under *M*.

Because it provides both an extended version of the episcopal *gravamina* expressing exceptional bitterness against Alfonso X, and a sketch of his son's handling of them, the document possesses a twofold interest and is doubly revealing of the condition of one sector of the kingdom of Castile on the eve of Sancho's rebellion against his father's rule. The Infante, on this evidence, wished it to be known that he shared the conventional and incorrect view that, by courtesy of *la eglesia* (undefined), Alfonso was entitled to the *tercias* for life,[29] as well as to the use of ecclesiastical property during vacancies (which in the recent past had become increasingly numerous).[30] Otherwise the tone,

---

[28] For convenience of reference the subsequent items have been lettered *L*, *M* etc. in the edition below.

[29] Item A. Cf. Linehan, *Spanish Church*, pp. 207–8.

[30] Item B. For the king's view of his rights during episcopal vacancies, see *Primera Partida*, tit. v, *ley* XVIII in *Alfonso X el Sabio Primera Partida* (*manuscrito Add. 20787 del British Museum*), ed. J. A. Arias Bonet (Valladolid, 1975), p. 77. In January 1273 nine out of twenty-nine of the sees

where not positively evasive, is markedly conciliatory to the protesting churchmen, but conciliatory only as to principle and falling short of admission as to fact. On article C the text of the reply is not entirely clear. It seems to state that royal interference in episcopal elections ought to be discontinued. Similarly, with regard to D, the events of the previous thirty years notwithstanding, Sancho opines that *de jure* churchmen and their vassals could not be subjected to fiscal demands. The same bland response is given to the complaint regarding the excesses of the secular justices (E) which had been reported to Fernando de la Cerda in 1275.[31] It is perhaps only in the distinctions made in the carefully phrased treatment of item F relating to alleged infringements of churchmen's landed rights, with its reference to the much debated Ordenamiento de Nájera, that Sancho appears conscious of his responsibilities as a future ruler rather than of the advantages available to the party politician.[32] The reply to I amounts to no more than a statement of fact that any restriction on free episcopal assembly and movement[33] is 'contra libertad de sancta eglesia e grand servidumbre delos clerigos e grand periudicio dela eglesia de Roma' while offering no comment on the justice of the allegations themselves.

The remaining unanswered articles, intriguing though they are, may be rapidly reviewed. The reference (G) to 'novum ordinem *seu* religionem' is even more enigmatic in its translated form 'nueva orden *a* religion'.[34] The accusation of using papal privileges *ultra tempus* can be proved (H).[35] Mention of Jewish influence in public affairs (K) echoes

of Castile–León had been vacant: L. Sánchez Belda, ed., *Privilegios reales y viejos documentos de Baeza* (Madrid, 1964), doc. IV. The *gravamina* of 1279 do not, however, charge Alfonso with having a consistent policy on this score.

[31] Menéndez Pidal, *loc. cit.* For Alfonso's centralisation of law codes in the 1270s, and secular reaction to his policies, see A. Iglesia Ferreirós, 'Las Cortes de Zamora de 1274 y los Casos de Corte', *Anuario de Historia del Derecho Español*, XLI (1971), pp. 945–71.

[32] See C. Sánchez-Albornoz, 'Dudas sobre el Ordenamiento de Nájera', *Cuadernos de Historia de España*, XXXV–XXXVI (1962), pp. 315–36; idem, 'Menos dudas sobre el Ordenamiento de Nájera', *Anuario de Estudios Medievales*, III (1966), pp. 465–7 (jointly reprinted in his *Investigaciones y documentos sobre las instituciones hispanas* (Santiago de Chile, 1970), pp. 514–33). Cf. J. González, 'Sobre la fecha de las Cortes de Nájera', *Cuadernos de Historia de España*, LXI–LXII (1977), pp. 357–61.

[33] That Spanish churchmen did indeed travel abroad, and especially to the papal curia, cannot be doubted. See Linehan, *Spanish Church, passim*; idem, 'Spanish litigants and their agents at the thirteenth-century papal curia', *Proceedings of the Fifth International Congress of Medieval Canon Law* 1976 (Vatican City, 1980), pp. 487–501; idem, 'Proctors representing Spanish interests at the papal court, 1216–1303', *Archivum Historiae Pontificiae*, XVII (1979), pp. 69–123.

[34] I am now doubtful whether this is a reference to the mendicant Orders. Cf. Linehan, *Spanish Church*, p. 223.

[35] Ibid., p. 243, n. 1; AC Toledo, O.4.L.1.10 (use by Sancho IV, 1288–90, of privileges of Innocent III, Clement IV and Innocent V: Potthast 5012, 21135, *Reg. Clement IV*, 15).

one of the complaints of the Brioca assembly of 1267.[36] It was precisely at this time that Alfonso's chief *almojarife* in León–Castile, Çag de la Maleha, fell from grace after the Infante Sancho had fraudulently appropriated the monies collected by him for the king's troops at the siege of Algeciras – a fall from grace which dragged his co-religionists down with him.[37] The allegedly false charges of usury brought by Alfonso as a further means of raising revenue (*L*) belong to the same context,[38] as presumably does that charge in *M* which appears to have been designed to draw attention to current theological controversy in terms which may have been calculated to remind the pope of recent events in the University of Paris.[39] Significantly perhaps, no translation is furnished of *M* which, reflecting as it does contemporary suspicions regarding the orthodoxy of Alfonso (and of Sancho for that matter),[40]

[36] AC Palencia, 4/1/3: 'nephas est ut blasfemantibus (?) Christi iudeis maior habeatur fides quam christifidelibus christianis'.

[37] Y. Baer, *A History of the Jews in Christian Spain*, I (Philadelphia, 1961), p. 129–30; Ballesteros, *Alfonso X*, p. 896. In May 1282 the rebellious Sancho adopted anti-Jewish measures apparently in order to attract churchmen to his cause: D. Mansilla Reoyo, *Catálogo documental del Archivo Catedral de Burgos (804–1416)* (Madrid–Barcelona, 1971), no. 855.

[38] Ballesteros, *Alfonso X*, p. 853; P. León Tello, 'Legislación sobre judios en las Cortes de los antiguos reinos de León y Castilla', *Fourth World Congress of Jewish Studies*, II (Jerusalem, 1968), p. 59. The legislation of the Zamora Cortes of 1301 refers (c. 11) to the other complaint ventilated in *L* – royal prohibition of spiritual penalties – during Alfonso X's reign: *Cortes de León y de Castilla*, I (Madrid, 1861), pp. 154–5. The bishops could not necessarily count on papal support in this matter: just two years later Martin IV instructed the dean of Ávila not to impose sentences of excommunication or interdict on the nobleman Martinus Aldefonsi, if convicted of property offences against the bishop of Zamora, 'nisi a nobis super hoc mandatum receperis speciale': rescript *Conquestus est*, 7 May 1281: AC Zamora, 11(D–1)i.10.

[39] Cf. Thomas Aquinas, *Summa Theologiae*, 1a2ae. 35, 6; J. Guttmann (trans. D. W. Silverman), *Philosophies of Judaism* (London, 1964), pp. 170, 212ff; D. J. Silver, *Maimonidean Criticism and the Maimonidean Controversy 1180–1240* (Leiden, 1965); M. Alonso, *Teología de Averroes* (Madrid–Granada, 1947), pp. 228, 283ff. For the genesis of the terminology employed, see H. A. Lucks, 'Natura Naturans – Natura Naturata', *The New Scholasticism*, IX (1935), pp. 1–24, and O. Weijers, ed., *Pseudo-Boèce: De Disciplina Scolarium* (Leiden, 1976), pp. 169–70, who traces it back to the *Liber Introductorius* of Michael Scot, *c.*1230. (I owe these references to the Rev. Dr Edward Booth O.P. and Dr Charles Burnett.) An unnoticed earlier usage of Spanish provenance occurs in a literary exercise of Archbishop Rodrigo of Toledo *c.*1218: M. Alonso, ed., *Diego García: Planeta* (Madrid, 1943), p. 463. For the condemnation of the naturalistic propositions at Paris in 1277 – especially regarding 'libros, rotulos seu quaternos nigromanticos aut continentes experimenta sortilegiorum, invocationes demonum, sive coniurationes in periculum animarum', see P. Mandonnet, *Siger de Brabant et l'averroïsme latin au XIIIe siècle* (Louvain, 1908), II, p. 176; R. Hissette, *Enquête sur les 219 articles condamnés à Paris le 7 mars 1277* (Louvain–Paris, 1977), esp. pp. 32–4, 147–60; J. F. Wippel, 'The condemnations of 1270 and 1277 at Paris', *Journal of Medieval and Renaissance Studies*, VII (1977), pp. 169–201, esp. pp. 175–6.

[40] In the mid-fourteenth-century Silos Chronicle (ed. D. W. Lomax, *Homenaje a Fray Justo Pérez de Urbel O.S.B.*, I (Silos, 1976), p. 335), Alfonso is alleged to have boasted that had he been present at the Creation 'muchas menguas se y fiçieron que non se fiçieran'. But our knowledge of the literary remains of the king's circle of translators (who were particularly active during the years 1276–9): M. Rico y Sanobas, *Libros del Saber de Astronomia del rey D. Alfonso X*, I

contains a hint of mounting hysteria. It was not the last time that Castilian churchmen would claim that royal policies were resulting in the promotion of totally unsuitable prelates ('immo viles et ydiote'): the clergy of Jaén had the same tale to tell in December 1283.[41] By then, however, they had at least learnt to remain silent on that other issue raised under *M, matrimonia illicita*: eighteen months earlier the Infante Sancho had openly contracted such a union, with no audible protest from his ecclesiastical supporters.[42]

Alfonso X's accusers represented him as a barely Christian tyrant manipulated by Jewish counsellors, intent upon subjecting churchmen to an intolerable yoke of persecution and servitude. In the recent past Alfonso had effortlessly shrugged off the occasional mild reproof from Rome. Now, however, he may have been conscious of the imminent risk of ecclesiastical sanctions – a risk the reality of which was confirmed by the pope's anxiety that no publicity be given to the episcopal *gravamina*.[43] (In neighbouring Portugal Afonso III had died only a month before the legate's departure for Castile, having incurred excommunication and brought interdict upon his kingdom by ecclesiastical policies hardly distinguishable from those of Alfonso X.[44] Afonso III of course no longer had the alibi of the Reconquest with which to

(Madrid, 1863), pp. lxiii–lxxxiv; v.i (1867), pp. 9–10; E. S. Procter, 'The scientific works of the court of Alfonso X of Castile: the king and his collaborators', *Modern Language Review*, XL (1946), p. 27) does not bear out the bishops' charge: see J. Fernández Montaña, ed., *Lapidario del rey D. Alfonso X* (Madrid, 1881), p. 1; J. A. Sánchez Pérez, 'El Libro de las Cruces', *Isis*, XIV (1930), p. 80; J. Domínguez Bordona, 'El "Libro de los Juicios de las Estrellas" traducido para Alfonso el Sabio', *Rev. de la Biblioteca, Archivo y Museo*, VIII (1931), p. 174 (AvenRagel's prologue). The testimony of *Partida*, VII, 23, 1 ('Adevinanza tanto quiere decir como quier tomar poder de Dios para saber las cosas que son por venir') is cited by A. G. Solalinde, 'Alfonso X astrólogo: noticia del MS Vat. Reg. Lat. 1283', *Rev. Filología Española*, XIII (1926), p. 354. Attention is drawn to 'the confrontation of Christianity with the apparently naturalistic interpretation of reality represented by Greek philosophy in Semitic dress' in the *Lucidario* attributed to Sancho IV ('Ca dos saberes son que son el vno contra el otro e estos son la theologia e las naturas . . .') by R. B. Tate and I. R. Macpherson in their edition of Juan Manuel *Libro de los Estados* (Oxford, 1974), p. xxx, n. 32.

41 Linehan, *Spanish Church*, p. 235.

42 A. Marcos Pous, 'Los dos matrimonios de Sancho IV de Castilla', *Escuela Española de arqueología e historia en Roma: Cuadernos de trabajos*, VIII (1956), p. 43. Cf. Flórez, *Memorias*, p. 548.

43 *Reg. Nicholas III*, no. 739: the legate would refer *viva voce* to various matters 'que propter honorem tuum et presentis conditionis regnorum eorundem qualitate pensata non inserere distincte patentibus nostris litteris ex cautela providimus nec illa in vulgarem voluimus notitiam derivare.' Cf. the note (not translated) which prefaces item C, below ('Hic intermititur . . .').

44 The Castilian *gravamina* of 1279 are evidently related to the Portuguese *gravamina* of 1268 and 1289–92. The nature of the relationship merits careful study. The Portuguese evidence is considerably more abundant than the Castilian. See García y García, *Canonística portuguesa*, pp. 222–6; Linehan, *Spanish Church*, p. 220; *As Gavetas da Torre do Tombo* (Centro de Estudos Históricos Ultramarinos, Lisbon, 1968), VII, pp. 23–36.

ward off a determined pontiff.) In seeking the assistance of Sancho, Alfonso betrayed a measure of anxiety upon which his son may well have chosen to capitalise. Sancho did not content himself with attempting to comply with his father's request for advice. As requested, he consulted widely. Thirty years ago Antonio Ballesteros published evidence of the Infante's activity in the autumn and winter of 1279 summoning meetings of the *conceios* of Castile 'sobre aquellas cosas que el legado dixo al rey de parte del Papa'. However, Ballesteros misunderstood the purpose of the bishop of Rieti's legation, assuming that it was connected with Alfonso's diplomatic conflict with France – despite the fact that the *Memoriale secretum* and the pope's letters had been in print since 1932.[45] A further piece of evidence, hitherto unnoticed, shows that Sancho was casting even further afield than Ballesteros knew. On a spare leaf of a manuscript of the *Panormia* of Ivo of Chartres in the cathedral library of Burgo de Osma is copied the reply of that church, dated 14 October 1279, to Sancho's invitation to comment on 'the articles sent by the pope to the king concerning the state of the Church and of the land'. Osma's reply breathes defiance of Alfonso. Their spokesmen were charged to bear witness to the truth of the *gravamina*, even if they found themselves alone in this.[46]

This further text should serve to remove the suspicion that the episcopal *gravamina* of 1279 were merely those of the prelates of

[45] A. Ballesteros y Beretta, 'Burgos y la rebelión del Infante Don Sancho', *Boletín de la R. Academia de la Historia*, CXIX (1946), pp. 141–5 (where a connection with the siege of Algeciras is suggested); *idem, Alfonso X*, pp. 909–12. J. F. O'Callaghan, although aware of the *Memoriale secretum*, interprets Sancho's autumnal activity as having to do with a projected campaign against Granada: 'The Cortes and royal taxation in the reign of Alfonso X', *Traditio*, XXVII (1971), p. 393, n. 54.

[46] Burgo de Osma, Biblioteca del Cabildo, cód. 8, fo. 201v: 'Anno domini M.CC. septuagesimo nono jueves, xiiij dias por andar del mes de Octubre. El Prior don Estevan e el Cabildo dela Eglesia de Osma ovieron su tractado sobre la respuesta e el Conseio que darien al Infante don Sancho en Razon delos Articulos que enbio el Papa al Rey por el estado dela Eglesia e dela tierra. E el acuerdo que ovieron e el mandamiento que dieron a los procuradores que dixiessen fue esto. Que bien sabien el Rey e don Sancho que lo que el Papa dizie que verdat era e derecho e pues que verdat e derecho era que les conseiavan e les pidien mercet que fiziessen lo que el Papa tenie por bien por que non pudiesse venir ende periglo. Aun dixieron mas a los procuradores que si todos los otros fuessen contrarios desto que ellos non mudassen esta respuesta. En esta acuerdo fueron presentes el Prior e don Garçi Uanes Arcidiano de Osma e don Julian Perez Arcidiano de Asça e don Domingo Miguel Capiscol que fue depues requerido e otorgo *(sic)* e don Fferran Abbat Sacristan que fue present e don Guillem Capellan mayor …' Notice of this document was provided by T. Rojo Orcajo, 'Catálogo descríptivo de los códices que se conservan en la Santa Iglesia Catedral de Burgo de Osma', *Boletín de la R. Academia de la Historia*, CXIV (1929), p. 715. Cf. Linehan, 'The Synod of Segovia (1166)', *BMCL*, n.s. X (1980). Economic pressures may have strengthened their resolve: for evidence regarding the rapid price rises of the years 1278–81, see M. del Carmen Carlé, 'El precio de la vida en Castilla del Rey Sabio al Emplazado', *Cuadernos de Historia de España*, XV (1951), p. 139.

Compostela and León writ large. Coming from that area of the centre of the kingdom which for half a century or more had borne such heavy financial burdens, it represents the widespread discontent of precisely that region which Sancho would court in 1282, and was indeed already courting in 1279, by masquerading as the champion of *libertas ecclesiastica*.[47] At the very end of 1279 he was still at work collecting evidence bearing on the episcopal grievances, possibly with a view to preparing a consolidated reply for the pope. It is not known whether any such reply was ever sent. No trace of one has survived. What, however, is certain is that for all his feigned tenderness to churchmen, Sancho was already developing fast as his father's son, the man who as king would harass the Church quite as remorselessly as Alfonso had ever done.[48]

Recent work has represented the twenty to thirty years after the death of Alfonso X as a period during which the Castilian nobility recovered the share in government of which Alfonso had deprived it.[49] The record of the Salamanca assembly of 1310 suggests that churchmen experienced no such revival – if revival be the word.[50] The evidence presented by the bishop of Cuenca at the Council of Vienne in 1311–12 shows that little had changed since 1279.[51] And little would change thereafter, because the Vienne decrees concerning those very abuses which had been catalogued on the earlier occasion would remain a dead letter in Castile–León.[52] Although on his return from Vienne Arch-

---

[47] He arbitrated the Zamora dispute of the bishop and chapter who, through the exiled archbishop of Compostela, had complained to Nicholas III in May 1278 that sundry named civic officials were subverting *libertas ecclesiastica* by preventing them from tending their vines and selling their wine: a settlement from which the laymen subsequently resiled (AC Zamora, 11(D–1)i.13; 11(D–1)ii.10). See also Martín Martín *et al.*, *Documentos de Salamanca*, nos. 365–7, 369; A. López Ferreiro, *Historia de la Santa Iglesia de Santiago de Compostela*, V (Santiago, 1902), appendix, pp. 112–13; L. Fernández Martín, 'La participación de los monasterios en la *Hermandad* de los reinos de Castilla, León y Galicia (1282–1284)', *Hispania Sacra*, XXV (1972), pp. 5–35.

[48] An indication of future developments was provided as early as December 1279 by Sancho's demand that representatives of the *conceio* of Burgos should come to him with 'carta blanca seellada, con uestro sseello colgado, para afirmar las cosas que acá ffueren ffechas' (Ballesteros, 'Burgos y la rebelión', p. 144): the exaction of blank charters from the prelates had figured in the *gravamina* (item D), and the charge had elicited no response from Sancho. And by December 1284 Sancho IV was taking the part of the friars against 'los obispos e los clerigos': M. Rodríguez Pazos, 'Privilegios de Sancho IV a los franciscanos de la provincia de Santiago (1284) y de Castilla (1285), *Archivo Ibero-Americano*, XXXVI (1976), p. 534. Cf. H. Grassotti, *Las instituciones feudo-vasalláticas en León y Castilla* (Spoleto, 1969), pp. 789ff., 1000ff.

[49] Jimeno Casalduero, *La imagen*, pp. 45–62; C. González Mínguez, *Fernando IV de Castilla (1295–1312): la guerra civil y el predominio de la nobleza* (Vitoria, 1976), p. 205ff., 330ff.

[50] See above, n. 1.

[51] F. Ehrle, 'Ein Bruchstück der Acten des Concils von Vienne', *Archiv für Literatur- und Kirchengeschichte des Mittelalters*, IV (1888), p. 370.   [52] Cf. J. Lecler, *Vienne* (Paris, 1964), pp. 113ff.

bishop Rodrigo of Compostela summoned a provincial council 'for the maintenance and defence of ourselves and of our churches' and – in a letter the tone of which was one of cautious daring – urged Gonzalo of Toledo to do likewise and to prepare for an imminent meeting of the Cortes by discussing with him matters of common concern,[53] it was not an updated version of the 1279 *gravamina* that occupied the attention of the Zamora Council of 1313, but the Jews and legislation for their containment allegedly promulgated at Vienne.[54] And it was backward, to that single dark detail, and forward, to the darker decades ahead that Rodrigo and his suffragans referred. Like most of his episcopal colleagues both then and earlier, Rodrigo represented the interests of his God and his king as coterminous,[55] and on this occasion as on so many others a king who was professedly committed to the task of extending the boundaries of Christendom declined to subscribe to this comfortable arrangement. For when, other than in such relatively rare circumstances as those that obtained in the early 1280s did kings, or would-be kings, or even child-kings, need to ingratiate themselves with Castilian churchmen? Evidently not in 1313 at the beginning of a period of royal minority the civil disorders of which rendered churchmen particularly susceptible to secular attack.[56] Yet precisely what it was, in terms of political power and influence, that their predecessors may have possessed before it was lost by the churchmen of Castile-León in the course of the thirteenth century: that has yet to be established.[57]

53 'Et creemos Sennor que sia bem que vos fezessedes con vossos soffragannos vosso aiuntamento ante das Cortes pora aver acordo sobraquellas cousas que fazian mester avos et anos et a nossas Iglesias desse mostraren ennas Cortes': Madrid, Archivo Histórico Nacional, 7216/2, *papel* unnumbered doc: publ. from a faulty eighteenth-century copy by J. Tejada y Ramiro, *Colección de cánones y de todos los concilios de la Iglesia española*, v (Madrid, 1855), p. 679. Note the terminology – *aiuntamento*: his own Zamora Council he describes as 'nosso ajuntamento et conçello provinçial'.

54 Tejada y Ramiro, *loc. cit.*, pp. 674–8. Cf. C.-J. Hefele (trans. H. Leclercq), *Histoire des conciles*, VI.ii (Paris, 1915), pp. 672–717; E. Müller, *Das Konzil von Vienne 1311–1312: seine Quellen und seine Geschichte* (Münster in W., 1934), pp. 685–8.

55 'Et aeste tempo Sennor seiamos todos huna cousa pora sserviço de dios et del Rey': as n. 53 above.

56 On 7 December 1312, six days after Rodrigo of Compostela wrote his letter, the regent María de Molina was pressing for a meeting of the Cortes: A. Giménez Soler, *Don Juan Manuel* (Zaragoza, 1932), p. 418. The Jewish legislation of the Palencia Cortes (June 1313) fell far short of what the Zamora Council had prescribed in the previous January. In the context of tax-collecting, indeed, the clergy and the Jews were lumped together with 'otros ommes rreboltosos': *Cortes de León y de Castilla*, I, pp. 224, 226ff.

57 For some observations regarding the kingdom of León, see R. A. Fletcher, 'Regalian right in twelfth-century Spain: the case of Archbishop Martín of Santiago de Compostela', *JEH*, XXVIII (1977), pp. 337–60, esp. pp. 357–9, and the same author's *The Episcopate in the Kingdom of León in the Twelfth Century* (Oxford, 1978), pp. 80–1.

APPENDIX

TOLEDO, ARCHIVO DE LA CATEDRAL, X.I.B.I.4

In the document the Latin *gravamina*, the Spanish translation of them, and the draft replies are all copied *seriatim*. In what follows I have rearranged the text for ease of identification by bringing together the Latin and Spanish passages bearing on each individual *gravamen*, and for the same reason have supplied further lettering – B', B'', L-P – which is lacking in the text.

The following conventions have been adopted:

italic: doubtful reading

( ): word or words supplied

[ ]: word or words illegible

Deletions and insertions in the draft reply are not normally noted.

My thanks are due to Don Ramón Gonzálvez, canon archivist of Toledo Cathedral, for assistance in locating the document and for permitting photographs to be taken of it, and to Professor C. C. Smith (St Catharine's College Cambridge) for his help in deciphering the Spanish passages.

Este traslado nos dio el arcidiano Pay Dacana e^a trexolo de casa del Rey e fue trasladado dela carta del papa que levo el obispo de Rieto por que sopiessemos meior guardar al Rey e tractar en la corte algunas cosas a su servicio.

Estos son los mayorales articulos sobre que el papa enbia al Obispo de Rieto al Rey de Castiella e de Leon.

A Primera mientre delas tercias delas eglesias que el Rey tiene por fuerça e a tenido ya muchos annos.

Al primer articolo esta podrie seer carrera de avenencia que aya el Rey las tercias en su vida por otorgamiento dela eglesia e depues de sus dias que nunquam por^b sus herederos sean tomadas sin licencia dela eglesia de primera e de esto que assegure el Rey e Don Sancho en aquella manera que conviene.

B Lo segundo dela guarda delas eglesias que vagan e de algunas dignidades e delos bienes que tenia delas eglasias cathedrales e Reglares.

Al segund articolo semeiarie esto que otorgasse la eglesia al Rey por las necessidades en que es que en su vida oviesse por razon dela guarda delas eglesias que vagan los frutas e las rendas dela mesa delos obispos mas el mueble que finca del obispo muerto quier en sus casas quier en su camara, que non sea tomado mas sea todo guardado pora conplir manda del obispo o poral successor que uviere.

B' El tercero articolo es delos agraviamientos fechos por el e por razon del al Arcobispo e ala eglesia de Santiago en las tierras e en los vasallos en el qual se contienen estos articolos que son de suso escriptos, sacado otros muchos que serie grave cosa aver remembrança.

---

a The conjunctive ⁊ has been rendered 'e' throughout.   *b* por [el m: *del.*]

Primera ment que demanda el Rey omenage al Arcobispo de Santiago el qual non el nin los otros Arçobispos que fueron ante del nunquam fizieron.

Otrossi que el Arcobispo quiere aver la piertega que el Rey tiene por fuerça e contra derecho e en grande danno dela Eglesia de Santiago.

Otrossi que se tien por agravado sobre sennorio dela Çibdad de Santiago e que non puede usar del e sobre los dannos fechos al Arçobispo por razon dela discordia que fue entrel e el Rey e sobre otros dannos que fueron fechos al Arçobispo por razon dela discordia que fue entrel e los omnes dela Çiudat de Santiago, a sugestion delos quales el Rey fizo fazer dannos sin cuento non tan solament al Arçobispo e ala eglesia mas alos que tienen con ellos e los ayudan.

Otrossi que el Rey que agrava al Arçobispo e ala eglesia de Santiago en muchas guisas en los puertos e enlos vassallos e que fizo fazer muchos dannos e muchas fuerças alas eglesias e alas personas delas eglesias que son subiectas al Arçobispo e ala eglesia. Ca tiene el Rey enbargado e ocupado todo el Arçobispado o por si o por otro e a dos annos que fizo delas rendas asu voluntad.

Otrossi que los castiellos e las fortalezas e las villas e las possessiones e los Celleros que la eglesia de Santiago a en muchos logares que son ocupados e enbargados por el Rey o por su mandado. E çertas otra cosa que no semeia de creer que las offrendas que vienen o que vinieron al Abad de Santiago desdel tiempo que lo el Rey tiene enbargado en aca que las reciben los legos e que fazan dellas asu voluntad. Onde acaesce que los Romeros *despreçiando* esto assi como cosa desguisada dexan de aver devocion e de yr en Romeria ala eglesia sobredicha.

Otrossi que los bienes dela eglesia e los bienes de aquellos que tienen con la eglesia e que la ayudan e demas los fructos e las rendas delos personadgos e delas raciones e delos otros beneficios que vagaron e vagan del sobredicho tiempo a aca que estan enbargadas por mandado del Rey e fazen dello a su voluntad. E commo quier que sea de doler delas cosas sobredichas mayor mente es de llorar del periglo delas almas dela Çiudat e del Arcobispado sobredichos, las quales almas son por esta razon en periglo de perdicion perdurable. E por aventura muchos dellos son dannados por esta razon.

Estas cosas son sacadas breve miente de otras muchas e fastas sin cuento por que el Rey que deve seer çierto de su fecho non se morasse por muchas palabras o por grand escriptura, ala dignidad e ala persona del qual el Obispo aviendo reverençia en quanto ael conviene es apareiado de conplir por palaura lo que mingua en este escripto en logares e en tienpos convenibles.

B'' El quarto articolo es delos agraviamientos e delos tuertos que son fechos por el Rey o por razon del al Obispo e ala eglesia de Leon, las quales cosas mas son manifiestas por fama publica e por vista del fecho la qual non se podrie encubrir por ninguna guisa, que por demonstramiento de çierto e de special demostrador, como el sobredicho obispo aviendo reverencia al Rey a ya avido verguença e temor de fazer appella del o de enbiarla por mandadero. En pero manifiesta cosa es que el fuyendo la persecucion del Rey que mendiga e anda desterrado en tierras estrannas, cuyos bienes e los dela eglesia sobredicha son enbargadas por mandado del Rey a muy grande danno del obispo e dela eglesia, e non se puede escusar delas cosas sobredichas *ante* es la

opinion del Rey muy agraviada porend que sea dicho que el aya puesto plazo sennalado al Obispo sobredicho que tornasse a su eglesia e sino dend adelante quel Rey yria
contra el. Como tales cosas como estas tengan e encierren en si servidumbre de la
persona e dela eglesia sobredichas.

Quintus articulus principalis est de [ ] forte in iniuriis gravaminibus et pressuris
prelatorum et clericorum personarum (ecclesiarum regu)larium et secularium vassal-
lorum et bonorum ad ipsas personas spectantium, de quibus gravaminibus iniuriis et
pressuris causa brevitatis et vitande prolixitatis quaedam presentibus duximus
annectenda.

Hic intermittitur grave iugum et honus populi ne hoc audito superbiat contra
regem; qui super hoc dicto regi plene locutus fuerit quod debebat, et rex respondit
quod non potuerat aliud olim facere quamvis proponeret corrigere in futurum.

El quinto articolo es de agraviamientos de muchos maneras e sin cuento de *punnas*
delos prelados e delos clerigos e delas personas delas eglesias reglares e seglares e delos
vassallos e delos bienes que pertenescen a estas personas, delos quales agraviamientos e
delos tuertos e delas punnas oir razon delo dezir mas breve ment de muchas que son
pusiemos aqui algunas.

Estas cosas son las que descenden delos sobredichos articolos mayorales.

C Primum gravamen est quod quamcito vacat aliqua ecclesia regni sui statim fundit
preces pro aliquo eligendo seu postulando, quod si preces non sufficiunt addicit minas
et tandem in ecclesiis regularibus vel secularibus inponit quos vult pro sue beneplacito
voluntatis. Et quod peius est intrusis vel impressis facit omnes proventus vacantis
ecclesie vel partem ipsorum ministrari, parte sibi altera reservata, et tali accione
ecclesie destruuntur.

El primer articolo es que luego que vaga alguna eglesia desu reyno enbiar rogar por
alguien quel eslean o que demanden por prelado, e si el ruego non abasta annade
amenazas, e ala postre mete en las eglesias reglares e seglares los que el quiere segund
la su voluntad. E lo que es peor cosa, que faze dar alos que assi son metidos todas las
rendas dela eglesia que vaga o partida dellas e la otra parte recabela pora si, e por tal
razon destruyense las eglesias.

Al otro articolo ⟨...⟩ que es que el Rey inecta por algunos que sean esleydos alas
eglesias e alas vezes que ameneça, non se otra avenencia sinno que si *non* es assi es bien
e si assi es non sea daqui adelant.

D Secundum est quod a prelatis et personis ecclesiasticis et vassallis colonis et serrariis
eorum per varios modos exactiones et subsidia extorquantur et ipsis frequenter onera
gravia, angarie et perangarie imponuntur. Facit etiam dominus Rex sigillari paginas
vacuas per prelatos et perhibere testimonium de hiis que nec viderunt nec sciverunt.

El segundo articolo es que delos prelados e delas personas delas eglesias e delos
vassallos de sus omnes por desvariadas maneras saca dellos por fuerça pedidos e
ayudas e muchas veçes son puestos a esto por fuerça e malament e en grand punna
muchos agraviamientos. E faze aun el Rey alos prelados que seellen cartas blancas e
que den testimonio delas cosas que non veen nin saben.

Al otro articolo que el Rey saca pedidos e ayudas de prelados clerigos e vassallos delas eglesias por muchas guisas e por fuerça, non se otra avenencia sinno que non se faga por ninguna manera. Ca esto es cosa que aun que los prelados fuessen requeridos e quisiessen consentir non lo pueden fazer menos de licencia dela eglesia de Roma. Ca los prelados non son sennores pora poder esto otorgar mas solament procuradores. Pues mucho menos se deve esto fazer los prelados non seyendo requeridos.

E Tertium est quod privilegia et libertates ecclesiarum et ecclesiasticarum personarum, sive habeant hec a iure sive a predecessoribus dicti Regis vel etiam ab eodem Rege concessa, per actum contrarium infringuntur. Ita quod frequenter dicte persone aliquando contra iura quandoque vero contra suorum privilegiorum tenorem trahuntur ad iudicium seculare, immo quod gravius est capiuntur et incarcerantur et occiduntur eedem persone per iudices seculares de mandato vel auctoritate regis predicti, et in tantum est in regno dicti regis libertas ecclesiastica cavillata quod thesauri ecclesie fracti sunt in locis pluribus violenter.

El tercero articolo es que los privilegios e las liberdades delas eglesias e delas personas dellas, quier los ayan de derecho o por los anteçessores del rey o que los aya el mismo otorgados, que son quebrantados por fecho contrallo e en tal manera que muchas vezes los clerigos e las personas sobredichas son traydas a juyzio delos seglares, alas vezes contra derecho, alas vezes contra sus privilegios. E çertas lo que mas grave cosa es que los juezes seglares penden e meten enlas carçeres e matan estas personas. E esto acaesce muchas vezes por pesquisas que fazen encubiertamente los Alcaldes seglares contra los clerigos e contra las personas delas eglesias por mandado del Rey, non lo otorgando ellos nin seyendo vençidos en juyzio. E assi es la franqueza dela iglesia minguada enlos reynos del Rey. E que los tesoros delas eglesias son quebrantados por fuerça en muchos logares e los conceios son lamados que vayan contra las personas delas eglesias e contra sus vassallos e contra aquellos que tienen con ellos assi como enemigos.

Al otro articolo quanto al pender delas personas delos clerigos non veo y avenencia si non que non se faga o sinno fuesse preso en el fecho e citacion que se de luego ala iustiçia clerigal e que nel Rey nin los legos *ensufran*, pues mucho menos en iusticiarle a menos de seer judgado e degradado por su prelado. Esso mismo en razon de llamar los clerigos ante juez seglar. Ca non sabemos caso ninguno en que esto deva seer, quier sea la demanda personal, quier real, quier sea mueble, quier rayz, quier sobre demanda *spiritual* quier episcopal. Ca todos los bienes delos clerigos aun que sean temporales todos son de suso dela eglesia sinon fuesse por aventura demanda de ffeudo e de particion entre herederos. Esso mismo en razon de fazer pesquisa contra los clerigos, ca quier non puede seer juez non puede pesquisa fazer. Esso mismo en razon de los thesoros delas eglesias que se quebrantan. Esso mismo en razon de llamar e assonar los conceios contra las eglesias. En todas estas cosas non ay avenencia otra sinon parar ende mano, mayormente que en todas estas cosas es fazer libertad dela eglesia e todos los que esto fazen son descomulgados.

F Item si ecclesie vel ecclesiastice persone *regulares vel seculares* acquirunt vel acquisiverunt vassallos possessiones et bona exempta *communia* prius ab omni fisco vel onere dominus rex facit quod dicti vassalli possessiones et bona fiunt sibi tributaria et censsualia. Nec obstat etiam si ecclesia super talibus sit legitima prescriptione munita vel habeant (*sic*) super eas idonea munimenta. Sed quod mirabilius est coget possessores titulum sue possessionis ostendere contra iura.

Otrossi que si las eglesias o los clerigos o las personas delas eglesias reglares o seglares ganan o ganaron vassallos possessiones o bienes que eran ante francos de todo pecho de Rey que faze e que costrinne que los vassallos e las possessiones e los bienes sean pecheros. E non lo dexa pora que la eglesia sobre tales cosas aya legitima prescripcion o aya sobrestas cosas convenibles cartas. Elo que es mayor maravilla que costrinne contra derecho los possessores que muestren el titulo de su possession.

Al otro articolo semeiarie esto que por razon delas possessiones que fueron ante liberas por passar ala eglesia non fiziessen los clerigos por ellas pechar nin aun por las otras que fueron pecheras, si por privilegio que oviessen las ovieron quier ante delas cortes de Naiara quier despues. Mas en razon delas pechas que passaron alas eglesias e alos clerigos sin privilegio semeiarie esta carrera que pues los otros reyes lo suffrieron fasta aqui e la eglesia fue *confirmada* en possession desta libertad fasta agora, mayor mient como estas possessiones sean muy pocas e todas las possessiones tales que agora han fincassen en las eglesias e en los clerigos liberas, e daqui adelant non pudiessen comprar sin mandado del Rey o si comprassen pechassen por ellas. Pero si alguno por su alma assi como por anniversario dexasse alguna rayz ala eglesia por reverencia dela eglesia e por favor del alma fincasse quita e libera ala eglesia. Otrossi la heredad que los clerigos ganassen por otra manera e non por compra assi como por herencia o por manda o por donadio de parient o damigo por que si las quisiessen mas vender que pechar por ellas recibien grand menoscabo en venderlas tan assi a essora^e pusiesseles el Rey plazo fasta quando las deviess*en* vender, e si las non vendiess*en* fasta aquel plazo que pechassen por ellas e encaramient non. E si en razon delas heredades que han por herencia de padre o de madre o de parient fuesse la merced mayor que en su vida non pechasse el clerigo por ella, razon que serie guisado, ca aun non ha grand tiempo que non solament su persona mas el padre e la madre escusava. Elo que dixo de suso que tales heredades como estas son muy pocas entendiesse e esto que todas las eglesias catedrales en Castiella han privilegia que ellas e los canonigos dellas puedan comprar e ganiar (*sic*) por quel quier titulo, pues non finca la gracia si non en las possessiones que ganaron clerigos parrochiales e aldeanos e por verdad estas son muy pocas en Castiella.

G Item instituit auctoritate propria novum ordinem seu religionem quod esse de iure non potest, cuius occasione ecclesie multipliciter aggravantur.

Otrossi que establesçio por su auctoridat nueva orden a religion, la qual cosa non pode seer con derecho por razon dela qual los clerigos son mucho agraviados.

El otro articolo dela orden nueva: *gap*

H Item impetratis ab apostolica sede privilegiis vel obtentis utitur etiam ultra concessionis tempus pro sue beneplacito voluntatis, non facta de ipsis originalibus copia illis ad quos privilegia dicta spectant, et ut ex talibus privilegiis maius commodum assequatur alias ordinariorum indulgencias in terra sua frequenter non patitur publi-

c tan assi era a so ora

cari. Decimas quoque ad tempus sibi concessas extorqueri facit ab illis personis qui ab ipsarum solutione per declarationem summi pontificis sunt exempte.

Otrossi que delos privilegios ganados del papa usa a su voluntad mayor tiempo de quanto los otorgado, non dando traslado dellos a aquellos aquien pertenescen. E por que de tales privilegios aya mayor pro non consiente algunas vezes que por su tierra anden otros perdones ordinarios. E las decimas quele son otorgados por tiempo sennalado toma las daquellas personas que son end quitas por la declaracion del papa.

El otro articolo en razon de usar delos privilegios mayor tiempo que deve, e otras delas decimas: *gap*

I Item prelatis et capitulis terre sue non est liberum[d] convenire ut tractarent de premissis at aliis gravaminibus quae ipsis et aliis personis ecclesiasticis pro tempore inferuntur, nec exire extra regnum vel extrahere inde pecuniam pro necessitatibus variis que occurrunt etiam de bonis ecclesiasticis acquisitam libere permittuntur.

Otrossi que los prelados e los cabildos de su tierra non se osan ayuntar pora fablar e tractar destas cosas sobredichas e de otros agraviamientos que los fazie a ellos e alas personas delas eglesias. E non osan nin pueden salir del reyno nin sacar el aver ganado delos bienes delas eglesias pora aquellas cosas que an mester.

El otro en razon delos prelados que no se osan ayuntar ni osan salir del reyno nin sacar aver, a que non se avenencia ninguna ca es contra libertad de sancta eglesia e grand servidumbre delos clerigos e grand periudicio dela eglesia de Roma a que han de venir liberament los prelados e los otros cristianos por sus necessidades e de sus eglesias e de sus almas: *gap*

K Item judei[e] christianis in officiis et exactionibus preponuntur, ex quo perveniunt multa mala inter que id est principuum (*sic*), quod christiani multi ut favorem habeant judeorum subiciuntur eis et eorum ritibus et traditionibus corrumpuntur.

Otrossi que los judios son puestos sobre los cristianos en los offiçios e enlas collechas,[f] dela qual cosa vienen muchos males entre los quales es mayor mal quelos cristianos son subiectos a ellos e son corrumpidos por sus costumbres e por sus malos husos. Al otro de los judios que se ponen sobre los cristianos: *gap*

L Item de spiritualibus causis et processibus se multipliciter intromittens et legata ad pias causas sine cause cognitione usurpans facit auctoritate propria inquisitiones fieri contra clericos et laycos de usuris et fere contractum quemlibet usurarium judicans extorquet a dictis personis pecuniam sicut placet, prelatorum vel interdicti sententias servari nec in certis casibus non permittans (*sic*) ita quod excommunicationis exceptio a paucis annis citra non admittitur in sua curia et suorum, et qui eam observant vel observari mandant spoliantur bonis et de personis aliquando capiuntur.

Otrossi que se entremete en muchas maneras delos pleytos spirituales e las mandas que se fazen a casas de piedad, tomalos contra derecho sin connoscimiento de pleyto. E manda fazer por su auctoridat pesquisas contra los clerigos e sobre los legos sobre fecho delas husuras e fastas cada un contracto judga por usurario e saca por fuerca delas dichas personas aver segund su voluntad e non dexa aguardar sinon en ciertas

d suppl. liberum   *e* judeis   *f* cogechas

cosas las sentencias que fazen los prelados de descomunion o de demedo de pocos
annos en aca no es recebida en su corte e delos suyos sinon en çiertas cosas, e a aquellos
que la aguardan o que mandan^g guardar tomanles lo que an e alas vezes pendenlos.

M Item propter auctoritatem ecclesiasticam modis premissis et aliis impeditam, nam
(*sic*) prelati non possunt suum officium libere exercere immo viles et ydiote penitus in:
gap. Matrimonia multa in casibus illicitis contrahuntur, claves ecclesie contempnantur.
Attribuuntur non Deo qui est natura naturans sed *nature* ab ipso naturate fere omnia a
quibusdam qui, asserentes deum non esse ad fallax astronomorum et augurum vel
aiusperitum judicium, procedunt quasi in omnibus factis suis.

Otrossi por que la auctoridad dela eglesia es enbargada por las maneras sobredichas
e por otras los prelados non pueden de su officio usar libre mente, mas viles e non
letrados son metidos enlas eglesias. E fazen se casamientos e matrimonios en casos non
convenibles e que son menospreciados las laves dela eglesia e que se fazen otras cosas
non convenibles.

N Item privilegia etiam ab ipso et predecessoribus suis ecclesiis et personis ecclesiasticis
vassallis colonis et serrariis eorum concessa non observant eisdem et exigens a talibus
martinega compellunt eos ad exercitium et ad diversas tallias et exactiones et censsus
solvendos, ita quod vassalli et huiusmodi serrarii et coloni coguntur dimittere dominium prelatorum et exire regnum vel subicere se dominio laycorum.

Otrossi segund que sobredicho es non aguarda los privilegios que el e los otros sos
antecessores dieron alas eglesias e alas personas delas eglesias e asus vassallos e asus omnes
demandandoles martiniega o costreyendo les yr en hueste e pechar pechos de muchas
maneras por que estos sus vassallos e sus omnes an de dexar el sennorio delos prelados
e salir del reyno a meter en sennorio delos legos.

O Item clerici et ecclesiastice persone trahuntur frequenter in petitorio et possessorio
ad seculare judicium violenter nec ibi possunt si aliquos conveniant expediri et fere
in omnibus tributis et exactionibus sicut laici talliantur.

Otrossi los clerigos e las personas delas eglesias non tan solamente son traydos
muchas vegadas a juyzio delos seglares por fuerça en razon desus possessiones e de
otras demandas que les fazen. Mas si ellos demandan alli a algunos non son librados.
E fastas en todos los pechos son pecheros assi como los legos.

P Item imponit nova pedagia et tributa locis et portibus spectantibus etiam ad
ecclesias pleno iure.

Otrossi pone nuevos peages e pechos alos lugares e alos puertos que pertieniscen
(*sic*) de derecho ala eglesia.

g madan

OCKHAM AND THE BIRTH OF
INDIVIDUAL RIGHTS*

by ARTHUR STEPHEN MCGRADE

PERHAPS THE ONLY THING more frustrating than the combination of politics and philosophy is their separation. The idea of a society dominated by philosophy epitomises rigidity, and certainly philosophy does not flourish when it is dominated by society. Yet a social order which cannot sustain deep critical examination of its institutions and values courts corruption, and a philosopher who can discuss profoundly everything in heaven and earth except the human world he lives in is alienated – he 'has problems'. The later Middle Ages afford abundant material for observing all of these frustrations, but there is no case in which they are presented more acutely than that of Ockham. And there is no point at which the classical problem of clearing up the relationship of Ockham's philosophy to his politics – a preoccupation of Ockham scholars if not of their subject – can be brought to sharper focus than that provided by Ockham's conception of individual rights. It has been argued by the French historian of the philosophy of law, Michel Villey, that Ockham's formal definitions of the legal rights of use and ownership inaugurate a veritable Copernican revolution in jurisprudence and political thought, a shift of basic orientation from an objective to a subjective view of economic, social, and even ethical legitimacy.[1] But the subjectivity of Ockham's conception of rights and the rest of his political thought can be properly appreciated, according to Professor Villey, only by reference to the radical individualism of his nominalist philosophy, a philosophy which on the

---

* I am much indebted to Professor Leonard Boyle of the Pontifical Institute of Mediaeval Studies, University of Toronto, and to my colleagues in philosophy at the University of Connecticut for their comments on an earlier version of this paper.

[1] Michel Villey, 'La Genèse du droit subjectif chez Guillaume d'Occam', *Archives de Philosophie du Droit*, IX (1964), pp. 97–127. Also see L. Vereecke, 'Individu et communauté selon Guillaume d'Ockham', *Studia Moralia*, III (1965), pp. 150–77. Both of these essays depend on Georges de Lagarde's extensive, brilliant, and much debated study of Ockham and his times, *La Naissance de l'esprit laïque au déclin du moyen-âge*, 1st edn, 6 vols (Paris, 1934–46); new edn, 5 vols (Paris, 1956–70).

surface has nothing at all to do with politics. The place to deal in detail with Ockham's conception of rights would be in a thorough study of the important legal dimension of his political writings, but I agree with Professor Villey that the significance to be attributed to Ockham's definitions will depend to a great degree on how we take them and his other political ideas in relation to his philosophy. I doubt that a global interpretation of nominalism provides a good basis for a global interpretation of Ockham's political thought, but we may still look to specific aspects of Ockham's metaphysics, epistemology or (as in this essay) his logic for at least a partial explanation of various points in his polemical works. Indeed, a more modest approach may not only shed light on the sorts of relations that properly may obtain between philosophy and politics, both in Ockham and generally, but may also help explain why more ambitious attempts run into difficulties of their own.

POWER AND THE INDIVIDUAL

Here are the key definitions of rights of use and ownership (in rough translation):

right of use (*ius utendi*): a licit power of using an external object, the unwarranted denial of which can be prosecuted in a court of law.[2]

ownership (*dominium*): a principal power of laying claim to a thing in court and of using it in any way not prohibited by natural law.[3]

The putatively revolutionary feature of these definitions is their identification of a right with some kind of *power* of the person having it. Whereas powers of various kinds had, of course, been exercised in the world long before Ockham, Professor Villey finds that these powers were typically regarded by Greek philosophers, Roman jurists, and later commentators as pre- or extra-juridical *facts*, natural liberties for

[2] Ockham, *Opus Nonaginta Dierum*, ed. R. F. Bennett and J. G. Sikes, ch. 2: *OP*, I (Manchester, 1940), p. 304.

[3] *Ibid.*, p. 310. Ockham recognises that there are other important senses of *dominium* besides this one. It is in this sense of the term, however, that *dominium* seemed to him to be an issue in the controversy over Franciscan poverty, use, and property with which the *Opus Nonaginta Dierum* is concerned. For a slightly earlier use of a similar conception of ownership in an important political work also influenced by the Franciscan concern with poverty, see Marsilius of Padua, *Defensor Pacis*, II.12.13 (trans. Alan Gewirth, *Marsilius of Padua: The Defender of Peace*, II (New York, 1956), p. 192). On the philosophical significance of sharply distinguishing various senses of such terms as *dominium* or, on the other hand, of using broad analogical concepts regarding similarities among the various forms of mastery (e.g. of an owner over his property, a lord over his servant or vassal, soul over body, or God over creation), see R. P. McKeon, 'The development of the concept of property in political philosophy: a study of the background of the constitution', *Ethics*, XLVIII (1938), pp. 297–366.

which it was the function of jurisprudence to determine just limits in accordance with an objectively conceived, impersonal common good. In this view, powers are not sanctified as *rights*. The title of right is reserved for those harmonious proportions or relations among persons and things which are just in the abstract and reflect a natural or cosmic order. A right is that which is just, a just share of the common good. The view put forward in Ockham's definitions, reflected elsewhere in his political writings, and rendered repellently intelligible, it would seem, by his philosophical nominalism, is just the opposite. In seeing rights as powers, Ockham locates every right, as it were, in the very essence of the subject whose right it is, whether that subject be God, mankind, a king or parliament, or the individual citizen; such public norms as may seem to have objective validity are merely offshoots or conventional constructions of these various subjects; and hence political thought and action is totally concerned with the conflict, balancing, acquisition, delegation, and more or less chaotic interplay of various subjective powers.

The relations among facts, powers, and rights are such basic and perennial philosophical problems that it would be strange if they did not bear somehow on the correct interpretation of a major philosopher's discussions of law and government. Ockham, however, was by no means unusual among his contemporaries in viewing power as a central topic in political thought[4] or in often employing a concept of

---

[4] On the pervasiveness of power in the titles and contents of fourteenth century political writings, see Gewirth, *Marsilius of Padua*, 1 (New York, 1951), pp. 7–9. As Gewirth notes, indeed, it was the claims and arguments in behalf of *papal* power which 'brought the whole conception of political power to an unparalleled degree of development . . . a detailed consideration of almost every conceivable question bearing upon political power: its nature, kinds, sources, locus, justification, conditions, limits' (pp. 7–8). On power (sovereignty) and knowledge (infallibility) as alternative principles of papal authority in the period, see Brian Tierney, *Origins of Papal Infallibility: 1150–1350* (Leiden, 1972). Of course, 'power' is not a simple idea. In some sense, it was held by an idealist like Plato to be a mark of real things or, as Jowett has it, a definition of being (*Sophist*, 247e). F. M. Cornford (*Plato's Theory of Knowledge* (New York, 1957), pp. v–vi) objects to Jowett's rendering and to the interpretation of Plato that Whitehead drew from it, but the issue goes beyond accuracy of translation to philosophical adequacy of conception. Plato may well have thought that power as *he* conceived of it (in the *Gorgias*, for example) was indeed definitive of true reality. Care is also needed in determining the place of power in Aristotle. Aristotle discusses the virtue of justice in detail in the *Nicomachean Ethics* and points to the occasional effectiveness of appeals to natural law in the *Rhetoric*, but his *Politics* allows for a considerable relativity of justice to the existing distribution of power in a community and includes an astute analysis of revolution which is sometimes cited as an important source for the concentrated attention to power in the late Middle Ages and Renaissance. A profound discussion of these themes, full of insights into classical, early medieval, and Renaissance culture and political thought, is R. D. Cumming, *Human Nature and History: A Study of the Development of Liberal Political Thought*, 2 vols (Chicago, 1969).

power which included the notion of legal or political authority.[5] If anything truly radical is to be found in this area of his thought, it must concern not simply the political importance or the juridical nature of power but its location, the question of who has power, or better yet, the question of what *sort* of entity *could* have power. It is at this point that Ockham's nominalism seems potentially illuminating, for when we consider that the papal power exalted by such hierocratic writers as Aegidius Romanus and Augustinus Triumphus was by no means a straightforward attribute of the individual pope, but belonged rather to the papal office, and that the relation between a pope and the papal office was like the participation relation between a particular and an eternal Idea in Platonic metaphysics, we may well expect to find that Ockham's staunch nominalist *rejection* of Platonic Ideas or anything like them in his earlier philosophical and theological work at Oxford had an effect on *his* conception of powers or rights or offices.

This sort of reflection is both traditional and plausible, but it can produce illusions. Thus, for example, if we are too quick to draw political conclusions from the exclusive reality of individuals and the unreality of universals in Ockham's academic writings, we may fail to notice that it was John XXII, not Ockham, who insisted that only individual Franciscans were true persons and that the Franciscan order was only a *persona repraesentata* or *imaginaria*.[6] Or again, if we are overly intent on seeing Ockham's nominalism as a basis for modern doctrines of individual rights, we may fail to give due weight to the starting point of his whole involvement in political affairs, his commitment to Franciscan poverty as a basis for the highest state of Christian life, his insistence on the theological right of the Franciscans *not* to have legal rights or private (or even common) property.[7] Whatever sort of individualism there may be in Ockham, it is not that of the Protestant

---

5 Aegidius Romanus, for example, clearly regarded the pope's *plenitudo potestatis* as something which legitimated virtually any action the papacy might wish to take. The pope's power, like God's, gave weight, measure, and number to all other authority without itself being weighed measured, or numbered; *De Ecclesiastica Potestate*, ed. R. Scholz (Weimar, 1929), p. 206. In philosophy Aegidius was a speculative metaphysician of the type Ockham most disliked.

6 Ockham contended, *against* this view, that if the Franciscan order was only an imaginary person, then so was the Church, but this would imply the blasphemous conclusion that the Church could not exercise real power: *Opus Nonaginta Dierum*, c. 6: *OP*, I, pp. 372–3; and c. 62; *OP*, II (Manchester, 1963), p. 568. Cf. Ockham's rejection in chs. 67–73 of John's denial of reality to actions.

7 More specifically, Ockham insisted that the friars' exercise of *natural* rights to use material things not be made to depend on positive legal 'civil' rights but be left to depend on freely given 'licenses' revocable at the will of the grantor.

ethic or the spirit of capitalism. I know of no infallible device for maintaining perspective when passing from Ockham's philosophy to his politics, but we seem less likely to go wrong if we begin by looking at his work in non-political disciplines in its own terms. If a neat over-all picture emerges at the end, well and good, but at least to begin with we should have the patience to try to follow Ockham through such mazes as the problem of universals as if we were as interested in them as he was, and as if we were interested in them in the same technical theological, philosophical, or logical way as he was. To do this with the problem of universals is beyond my power and would be a long and difficult task, but I can give some indication of the approach I have in mind by taking as a starting point a limited but central part of Ockham's work in logic.

LOGICAL INDIVIDUALISM FROM 'A' TO 'O' AND BEYOND

The goal of much of Ockham's work in logic was the discovery of equivalences between propositions containing universals or general terms and propositions whose content is specified entirely by singular or discrete terms.[8] He was looking, that is, for propositions between which valid inferences could be made in either direction, propositions which mutually implied one another, as, for example, 'That man is Cicero' and 'Cicero is that man', may in suitable circumstances mutually imply one another (here all the terms are singular, they refer to individuals; let us call such propositions individual propositions), or 'No dogs are cats' and 'No cats are dogs' mutually imply one another (here all the terms are general; let us call such propositions general propositions). Now Ockham's project, intriguing and technically complex as it may become, is simply to find, or show how one *could* find, for every general proposition – for every proposition composed of general terms – an equivalent individual proposition – a proposition which contains no general terms at all.

---

[8] My discussion of this aspect of Ockham's logic largely follows Robert Price, 'William of Ockham and *suppositio personalis*', *Franciscan Studies*, xxx (1970), pp. 131–40; and Michael J. Loux, trans. and ed., *Ockham's Theory of Terms: Part I of the Summa Logicae* (Notre Dame, Indiana, 1974). Also see John Swiniarski, 'A new presentation of Ockham's theory of supposition with an evaluation of some contemporary criticisms', *Franciscan Studies*, xxx (1970), pp. 181–217, and Gordon Leff, *William of Ockham: The Metamorphosis of Scholastic Discourse* (Manchester, 1975), pp. 135–9. Leff is surely right in emphasising in his massive study both the thoroughness of Ockham's epistemological and ontological individualism and its objective, non-sceptical character. On Ockham's notion of logical equivalence, see Marilyn McCord Adams, 'Did Ockham know of material and strict implication?' *Franciscan Studies*, xxxiii (1973), pp. 5–37.

To see how this works, let us consider his treatment of two types of proposition from the traditional Aristotelian square of opposition. We may use 'All crows are black' as an example of the universal affirmative, or *A*, proposition and 'Some dog is not black' as an example of the particular negative, or *O*, proposition. We note first that the subject terms in these propositions, 'crows' and 'dog', are both general terms. We must therefore look for propositions in which exactly what is said in our examples by using these terms can be said by using singular terms, terms designating individual crows and dogs. 'This crow', 'that crow', 'this dog', 'that dog', 'Fido', 'Lassie', and so on are the sorts of terms needed for this purpose. Let us assume, then, that there are two and only two crows – call them 'this crow' and 'that crow'. Then 'All crows are black' will be equivalent to 'This crow is black *and* that crow is black.' That is, the universal proposition about all crows is equivalent to a *conjunction* of singular propositions about individual crows. The universal proposition is true if and only if the conjunction of singular propositions is true, and this is the case if and only if *each* of the conjuncts – the singular propositions forming the conjunction – is true. What could be simpler? In similar fashion, if we assume that there are just two dogs, Fido and Lassie, 'Some dog is not black' will be equivalent to the *disjunction* of singular propositions, 'Fido is not black *or* Lassie is not black,' where the disjunction is true if *any* of the disjuncts is true.

Now 'crows' and 'dogs' are not the only general terms in our sample *A* and *O* propositions. The predicate terms as well as the subjects of *A*, *E*, *I*, and *O* propositions are universal, too. What is a logical individualist to do about this? The proper treatment of predicates and predication is among the central tasks for any adequate theory of logic or language there may be, past, present, or future, and it is an especially challenging and fascinating task for nominalists, of whatever century. Ockham's approach is characteristically bold. It consists of a reduction of predicative propositions to assertions or negations of identity between individuals. Think of 'That man is Cicero' as a model. Here 'that man' and 'Cicero' are both singular terms (a good sign), the 'is' is the 'is' of identity, and the proposition asserts that the individual referred to by 'that man' in the situation at hand is the same as the individual referred to by 'Cicero'. Ockham's approach to predicative statements is to treat them on the model of just such identity statements. It is easy to see where this leads in the case of 'All crows are black.'

Let us assume again that there exist two and only two crows ('this crow' and 'that crow'), and let us, a bit more daringly, assume that there are exactly *three* black things in the universe. As these are individual black things, we can appropriately use singular terms to refer to them – 'Blackie$_1$', 'Blackie$_2$', and 'Blackie$_3$'. Clearly, then, in this somewhat limited universe, 'All crows are black' will be equivalent to the following conjuction of disjunctions:

> This crow is Blackie$_1$ *or* this crow is Blackie$_2$ *or* this crow is Blackie$_3$
>
> *and*
>
> that crow is Blackie$_1$ *or* that crow is Blackie$_2$ *or* that crow is Blackie$_3$.

Our O proposition, 'Some dogs are not black,' naturally enough, turns into a denial of identity (a 'negentity,' as Price puts it) with the 'ands' and 'ors' of the previous pattern trading places. (This is not surprising, since A and O are contradictories in the traditional square.) Thus, assuming again that Fido and Lassie are the only dogs and that Blackie$_1$ Blackie$_2$, and Blackie$_3$ are the only black things, we can say that 'Some dog is not black' is equivalent to:

> Fido isn't Blackie$_1$ *and* Fido isn't Blackie$_2$ *and* Fido isn't Blackie$_3$.
>
> *or*
>
> Lassie isn't Blackie$_1$ *and* Lassie isn't Blackie$_2$ *and* Lassie isn't Blackie$_3$.

I shall argue in the next section that there are political morals to be drawn from the very complexity of Ockham's working out of individualism in logic. I trust that it begins to be apparent by now that there *is* much complexity in Ockham's logical project. We have been living in a small world in the last page or so: two crows, two dogs, and three black things (four or five things in all, depending on whether one of the dogs is black), but specifying the conjunctions or disjunctions of identities and negentities equivalent to a couple of simple general propositions in that world has been a moderately complicated task in itself, and in doing even this we have taken for granted a fair amount of logical machinery for which an account could very well be asked. There could be question, for example, about the notion of equivalence used in these transformations of general into individual propositions, and we have not explained what identity and negentity are – what it means for an individual referred to by one expression to be the same as, or other than, an individual referred to by another expression; nor have we made explicit the assumptions about names or name-like expressions underlying our use of such tags as 'this crow' and 'that crow' or 'Blackie₁' and 'Blackie₂' as translations for 'crows' or 'black'. On this last point, Price has achieved a significant advance in clarity and accuracy by presenting Ockham's project in terms of a semantical interpretation of quantification over sorted individuals, an approach to Aristotelian logics first suggested by the Cambridge logician, Timothy Smiley, in 1962.[9] But getting clear what is involved in an individualistic account of our two model propositions is only the first step in carrying out Ockham's project. Although the idea of identifying universals with sets of individuals and the goal of determining what *claims* are being made about individuals remain dominant themes, Ockham's development of these themes has a complexity which deserves attention in its own right. But I must simply refer the reader to the good work of Price and Michael Loux for details.

POLITICAL REPERCUSSIONS OF OCKHAM'S LOGICAL INDIVIDUALISM?

Nothing is easier than jumping from such points as these about Ockham's logic to conclusions about how he should have proceeded in politics. Clearly, he should have proceeded by treating statements about social or political groups as statements about the individuals composing those groups, he should have emphasised the need to get clear exactly what is claimed about, or for, individuals in political discourse, and he should have shown a special awareness of how complex a task it is to go from general statements about groups to genuinely equivalent sets of statements about individuals. In this section I shall present what seem to me to be examples of Ockham doing each of these things, but I would like to begin by pointing out that there is no logical or moral necessity that there be any such

---

[9] Timothy Smiley, 'Syllogism and quantification', *Journal of Symbolic Logic*, XXVII (1962), pp. 58–62. Price points out ('William of Ockham and *suppositio personalis*', p. 132) that the treatment of general terms as equivalents to lists of singular terms presupposes that the lists are 'long enough' to do the jobs traditionally done by the associated general terms. I think he must be right in assuming here that the lists needed are denumerably infinite in length. Loux, on the other hand, seems to think Ockham's project of reducing the general to the singular works only for general terms with finite domains (*Ockham's Theory of Terms*, p. 31). This is awkward, since, as Loux himself points out (p. 46, n. 13 (to p. 31)), Ockham surely would have accepted the Aristotelian principle that the individuals of a species are (or at least could be) infinite.

examples. As Ockham remarks in a chapter of the *Summa Totius Logicae* on logically improper uses of terms, most terms *are* used improperly or equivocally in different places by highly reputable authors.[10] Now he himself had urgent practical goals: the overthrow of three popes and the preservation of Ludwig of Bavaria's empire, among other things. We should not take it for granted that he took it for granted that an application of his highly technical earlier work on the *Sentences* of Peter Lombard or the logic of Aristotle was the best thing he could do to achieve these goals. But perhaps we will have a better basis for assessing whatever connections there may be between Ockham's logic and his politics if we get down to political cases.

To do this, we must first see that there can be political, or communal, cases for a nominalist. We must see that the individualising approach to propositions with general terms surveyed above by no means annihilates the classes of being signified by those terms. To understand 'All Franciscans wear grey' as equivalent to 'Roger Bacon wears grey *and* Bonaventure wears grey *and* Matthew of Aquasparta wears grey *and* Duns Scotus wears grey *and* Ockham wears grey *and* Philotheus Boehner wears grey, and so on' is not to do away with the reality of the Franciscan Order but to identify the reality of the Order in some way with the reality of the individuals constituting it. In this example, furthermore, the individual friars are not 'isolated', nor does the equivalence between general and singular propositions hold if we consider only 'the' individual or a few individuals. For the general proposition to be true, Bacon *and* Bonaventure *and* the others must all wear grey. They are all of them logically together in the proposition, and it is not clear to a nominalist that there would be more or better togetherness if we imagined the Franciscan Order to be a different sort of entity, an abstract individual or a supra-individual being over and against the individual friars composing the Order. Accordingly, we should not expect Ockham to forbear talking about communities such as religious orders, peoples, political bodies, or the Church, nor should we suppose that when he does talk about such things he does not take them seriously or literally as communities. What we should watch for instead are statements about groups that can most naturally be understood as equivalent to statements of some sort about their members and an avoidance of statements that seem to conceive of groups in

[10] Loux, *Ockham's Theory of Terms*, p. 220.

terms of essences, relations, or abstract wholes having a reality over and above their members.

The clearest indication of which I am aware that Ockham did indeed regard political communities as identical with the individuals composing them is the sort of argument he typically gives in favour of one or another form of government. Especially in the secular sphere, he assesses governments instrumentally, in terms of their effectiveness in taking appropriate action for or, very often, against certain classes of individuals. A unified secular government would be best for the world, he argues, because by such a regime evildoers could be coerced more easily, beneficially, effectively, justly, and severely, and good people could live more quietly among the bad; discord among mortals would be more effectively abolished if all were subject to one secular ruler; disputes and litigations are more conveniently decided if the parties have a common judge or ruler; if all rulers were subject to an emperor, not only inferiors but superiors too could be corrected for wrongdoing.[11] In all of these arguments, it seems to me, we are dealing with a view of communal life as made up of interactions among concrete individuals, which can be facilitated or impeded by political action (particular action by particular rulers, one imagines), but which do not derive their essential character from anything supra-individual. And I know of no Ockhamist arguments which do call for us to assume a supra-individualistic conception of what a community is. Another sign of this aspect of political individualism in Ockham is his striking concern with personal liberty.[12]

If a community is identical with its members, a statement about the community will be equivalent to some statement or statements about the members. But *what* statements about individuals are implied by *what* statements about their communities? The most vivid illustrations of what social statements can 'mean for the individual' in Ockham's thought are to be found in his most protracted and disquieting polemical work, the first part of the *Dialogus*. 1 *Dialogus* is about heresy,

[11] These arguments from the first book of the second tractate of Part III of Ockham's *Dialogus* are presented and discussed in my *The Political Thought of William of Ockham* (Cambridge, 1974), pp. 110–11 and 116–17. For a similar treatment of ecclesiastical government, see pp. 154–67.

[12] *Ibid.*, pp. 119–21, 140–49. In contrast with writers who regard freedom as something to be found through participation in a supra-individualistic corporate whole, Ockham clearly regarded it as a matter of individual freedom of action, thus suggesting, it seems to me, that corporate wholes *are* the individuals composing them and that a free society is one composed of free individuals.

and most especially about the problem of papal heresy. As one example
of the way in which Ockham's manner of thinking could lead him to
lay strong claims upon individuals, I would cite his relentless survey in
1 *Dialogus* 6 and 7 of the responsibilities of the various members of the
Church or of a Christian society for resisting or punishing papal heresy.
It looks very much as if he had in mind some such scheme of inference
as the following: 'The Church must resist papal heresy; therefore, this
Christian must resist, *and* that Christian must resist, *and* this other
Christian must resist, and so on.' And it is noteworthy that although
most of the discussion concerns the responsibilities which individuals
have in this matter in virtue of holding one or another office or place,
the obligation is eventually laid by Ockham on the individual Christian
as such.[13] As a still clearer illustration of an Ockhamist descent from
general to individual, I would cite the discussion earlier in 1 *Dialogus*
of the question: who can become a heretic? The discussion is largely
based on Christ's promise to his disciples at the end of the Gospel of
Matthew: 'I am with you to the end of the world.' Now Ockham
argues that Christ was speaking to the disciples here as to the whole
Church and that his promise should thus be taken to mean that the
Christian faith will endure in the Church to the end of the world. But
what does such a promise to the whole Church mean? Under what
particular conditions should we say that it is fulfilled? The fundamental
argument used by Ockham in dealing with this question is that what
has been promised to the whole Church should not be attributed
without some special reason to any one part of the Church, whether
it be pope, cardinals, pope and cardinals together, the Roman church,
the clergy, all male Christians, or even, it would seem, all baptised
adults.[14] It is not necessary that any one Christian be incapable of

---

[13] *Ibid.*, pp. 68–73. A good impression of the shape of Book 7 is given by the student's list of
topics I have cited on p. 48, n. 9.

[14] See, for example, 1 *Dialogus*, Book 5, vii (fo.38rb in the Gregg Press facsimile (London, 1962)
of vol. 1 (Lyon, 1494) of J. Trechsel's edition of Ockham's *Opera Plurima*): 'De una sola ecclesia
militante dicitur quod non potest errare contra fidem, collegium autem cardinalium non est
ista ecclesia: licet sit pars huius ecclesie sicut etiam ecclesia parisiensis est pars istius ecclesie,
igitur congregatio cardinalium potest errare contra fidem. Confirmatur haec ratio, quia quod
competit toti ecclesie non est attribuendum parti ecclesie: etiam principali nisi hoc possit per
rationem necessariam vel auctoritatem apertam ostendi: collegium autem cardinalium est pars
ecclesie quae errare non potest contra fidem, ergo non posse errare contra fidem non debet
attribui collegio cardinalium, cum nec per rationem necessariam: nec per auctoritatem apertam
possit ostendi.' The *una sola ecclesia militans* Ockham has in mind is the whole congregation of
believers: 'Ad probandum ecclesiam romanam contra fidem posse errare: nonnulli plures
rationes adducunt. Quorundam autem ratio fundamentalis est quidam ratio saepe tacta superius
ad alias assertiones ostendendas: quae talis est. Illud quod promittitur toti et nulli parti non

erring, for if any one should abandon the faith, God can bring it about that another one will remain in it.[15] This is to say that the indefectibility promised by Christ to the Church is not to be thought of as an indefectibility of an individual or some few determinate members of the Church. But nor is this indefectibility to be thought of as an attribute of a supra-individual entity above all the members. The situation, rather, is one which can be described with a scheme of equivalence such as the following: 'Christ is with the Church' means (at any one

debuit alicui parti attribui: etiam principaliori. Sed numquam errare contra fidem *toti congregationi fidelium* promissum fuit a christo et nulli parti fuit hoc promissum a christo, igitur non debet hoc alicui particulari ecclesie catholicorum attribui, cum ergo romana ecclesia sit pars ecclesie et non sit tota ecclesia non posse errare contra fidem non est attribuendum romane ecclesia.' 1 *Dialogus* 5, xxii, fo. 43va. For other applications of this distinction between whole and part, see 1 *Dialogus* 5, xxv, fo. 46ra (*Prima ratio*); xxix, fo. 48ra (*Prima ratio*); xxxii, fo. 50rb (*Prima ratio*); xxxv, fo. 51rb–va (*Quinta ratio*). On '*ecclesia*' as designating the collection of (individual) believers, see 1 *Dialogus* 5, xxxi, fo. 49va: 'Secundo modo accipitur hoc nomen ecclesia pro congregatione christianorum fidelium generali vel particulari: quae tam viros quam mulieres comprehendere potest.' *Ecclesia* is used in this sense and in the sense of a material house in Scripture, according to Ockham, but in canon law the term has other significations. The question of the inerrancy of the Roman church is affected by the ambiguity of the term *romana ecclesia*. 'Nonnumquam tota congregatio fidelium nomine romane ecclesie importatur. Et de ecclesia romana illo ultimo modo dicta dicunt quod non potest errare, de papa autem et cardinalibus, de tota romana diocesi quae est distincta ab aliis diodesibus in provinciis aliis constitutis, concedunt quod potest errare contra fidem.' 1 *Dialogus* 5, xi, fo. 49va.

15 Ockham develops this line of thought in response to an argument for papal inerrancy based on the Church's need for certain judgment about matters of faith. The passages are interesting in several ways. 'In illa communitate non potest esse iudicium certum sine vacillatione de dubiis quae emergunt circa quae dubia et fundamenta eorum quilibet in illa communitate existens potest errare, sed in ecclesia militante est iudicium certum absque vacillatione de dubiis quae circa fidem emergunt, aliter eis nulli determinationi diffinitioni seu declarationi ecclesie militantis circa ea quae fidei sunt esset firmiter adherendum, quia illi qui potest errare non est indubitata fide credendum, igitur non quilibet in ecclesia militante potest errare, igitur est aliquis in ecclesia militante qui errare non potest et non alius quam papa, igitur papa circa ea quae fidei sunt non potest errare.' 1 *Dialogus* 5, iv, fos. 35vb–36ra. Ockham's response to this argument: 'In illa communitate quae non est sibi ipsi relicta, sed est preservata ab eo qui errare non potest, potest esse iudicium certum de dubiis, licet quilibet de illa communitate sigillatim possit errare: et hoc, quia nullus eorum specialiter preservatur quin possit errare sicut communitas preservatur, sic est de ecclesia militante, quia quilibet in ecclesia militante in manu consilii sui relinquitur ut secundum sue voluntatis arbitrium manere possit in fide gratia affinitate divina vel a fide catholica deviare, communitas autem christianorum sic preservatur a deo quod si unus a fide exorbitaverit alius firmus in fide divino munere permanebit, unde si papa contra fidem erraverit alius christianus vir vel mulier minime a fide recedet. *Disc.* Nonne talis modus arguendi valet, quilibet christianus potest errare contra fidem, igitur tota christianorum communitas potest errare contra fidem. *Mag.* Talis modus arguendi (ut multi dicunt) non valet sed est fallacia figure dictionis quia saepe a nomine quod non est collectivum ad nomen collectivum est fallacia figure dictionis sicut hoc, quilibetde populo potest sustentari de uno pane in die, igitur populus potest sustentari de uno pane in die. Et sicut hic utraque pars contradictionis potest esse vera, igitur contradictoria possunt esse vera. *Disc.* Non placet mihi: quod circa rationalem scientiam te diffundas, ideo refer quomodo ad alias rationes respondetur.' 1 *Dialogus* 5, v, fo. 36va. The same logical point comes up in a political context at III *Dialogus* 1, 2, xvii, fos. 196vb–197ra, where Ockham gives an unusually detailed logic lesson about it (on this passage, see my *The Political Thought of William of Ockham*, p. 183, n. 32).

time) 'Christ is with this Christian *or* Christ is with that Christian *or* Christ is with this other Christian, and so on.'

Although 1 *Dialogus* is an exhaustively and exhaustingly complicated work, the passage from universal to individual in the preceding examples is rather straightforward. It would be surprising, in the light of our brief look at his logical individualism, if this were always the case with Ockham's political thought. Even at the simplest stage of analysis, we found that the identification of a group or class with its members did not mean for Ockham that all statements about the group were to be taken as equivalent to the same sort of statements about the members. In some cases a statement with a collective or general subject called for a more or less lengthy conjunction of individual propositions to say the same thing, in other cases a disjunction was required, or a conjunction of disjunctions, and so on. If we had gone on to consider Ockham's treatment of other sorts of propositions or the various categories of predicates, still more complicated patterns of equivalence would have emerged. Such complexity may have its reflections in politics. Ockham argues that monarchy is regularly the best form of government both for the world and for parts of the world, both in secular affairs and in spiritual matters, but, he contends, this is not always the case. It can happen, due to the necessities of times and circumstances, that some other constitution will be more expedient for the communities of mortals or believers involved.[16] Although he exalted voluntary poverty as the highest form of Christian life, he did not regard private property as an evil in itself, and he placed a high value on personal liberty; on the other hand, however, he held that the natural rights to available material resources possessed by individuals in extreme need were not abolished by prior legitimate property assignments of those resources to others; he accepted the view that the goods of the Church in some sense belonged to the poor, and he clearly thought of

---

[16] On the variability of expedient constitutional forms in Ockham's thought, see *The Political Thought of William of Ockham*, pp. 122–7, 161–7. It is certainly correct to speak of contingency here, in the sense that the best form of government is *contingent on* existing circumstances. We should hesitate, however, to regard an emphasis on this sort of contingency as a break with the rationalism of earlier scholastics. In so far as Ockham had a sense of history, he may well have been struck by the changes and chances of human affairs, but he did not simply acquiesce in them. A whole branch of natural law, as he saw it, was concerned with determining objectively correct, rationally evident responses to arbitrarily given circumstances. On this branch of natural law, see *The Political Thought of William of Ockham*, pp. 182–4. On the rationally constructive character of his political thought in general, see pp. 214–20. H. S. Offler has edited a key natural law passage in 'The three modes of natural law in Ockham: a revision of the text', *Franciscan Studies*, xxxvii (1977), pp. 207-18.

preserving the common good as a reasonable cause for which governments might override the legitimate rights of their subjects.[17] He
argued at considerable length that the government of secular and
spiritual matters should normally be in separate hands but insisted that
'casually' – in special cases – the pope might be subject to the emperor
or, contrariwise, the emperor be politically subordinate to the pope.[18]
These contrasts have sometimes proved aggravating to modern scholars,
but I would like to propose that they are altogether natural reflections of
the complexity Ockham was prepared to encounter in any project of
reducing universal propositions to singular identities and negentities.

The idea is simply that a world of individuals is very complicated.
The exercise of rights legitimately enjoyed by the individuals making
up a society at one time may lead to a situation in which undeserved,
unbearable, and unnecessary hardship is experienced by some individuals of the society at another time. Ockham might have been as
astonished at the thought that one could infallibly avoid this by
advance planning and the establishment of a perfect constitution as by
the reflection that one had to put up with such situations when they
arose simply because they had been, in a sense, unavoidable. So a
government is needed strong enough to trample on the rights of some
individuals occasionally if an acceptable approximation to the common
good, to which all reasonable individuals are committed, is to be
maintained. But the difficulty of coming up with a distribution of goods
and powers at one time that will forever keep a community acceptably
near the best situation available to it (as a group) also suggests the
occasional need for revolution, for change of government. What I am
suggesting is that the logical habit of understanding general propositions
as equivalent to very complex sets of individual propositions makes it
easier to see that the 'fit' or political equivalence between common
good and private rights or between government and society is also a
very complex matter. It is natural to wish that things were simpler or
human beings better, so that neither strong government nor revolution
was ever needed, but wishing doesn't make it so.

[17] On the rights of those in extreme need to the property of others, see *Opus Nonaginta Dierum*,
c. 65: *OP*, II, pp. 577–8. On the sense in which the *superflua* of the rich and the goods of the
Church belong to the poor, *ibid.*, p. 576. On the pope's power in special cases to transfer
empires and kingdoms, to deprive any layman of his temporal rights and goods, or to do 'all
things' in spiritual matters, see III *Dialogus* I, I, xvi, fo. 188vab. On the emperor's 'plenitude of
power' in secular affairs (limited by divine and natural law and respect for the common good),
III *Dialogus* II, 2, xxv–xxvi, fos. 257va–258va.

[18] On the pope's casual temporal power, see preceding note. On the supreme secular ruler's
casual power over the pope, *Octo Quaestiones*, ed. J. G. Sikes, III, p. 12; *OP*, I, pp. 121–2.

CONCLUSION

What are we to make of these affinities? What do these more or less clear political reflections of his logical nominalism show us about the subjectivity or individualism of Ockham's conception of rights? And what, if anything, does all of this in Ockham suggest about the general relations of politics and philosophy? Since we have discovered only reflections of Ockham's logic in his politics and not a political theory constructed on an explicitly nominalistic conceptual base, our first conclusion must be that Ockham himself evidently did not think it crucial that his readers accept logical individualism in order to give proper consideration to his arguments and conclusions in politics. We might suppose that this was merely a matter of tactics. After all, his early theological and philosophical work was highly controversial in academic circles during his lifetime. A prudent nominalist living in a world of philosophical realists and hoping to achieve important practical goals would perhaps not wish to grind too many axes at once. If he could find political arguments both consistent with his own principles and capable of convincing a realist, he might leave to another day the more congenial task of disputing with the realist about the correct ultimate reasons justifying their practical common front. There may be something to this supposition. It is at least a pleasant fancy to imagine Ockham, in a happier time than his career in public life gave him, commenting on Aristotle's *Politics*, deploying invincible arguments to show that the Philosopher held, or at least should have held, a distinctively nominalistic conception of the *polis* and the common good. It would be a great mistake, however, to let this fancy carry us to a starkly factional view of the political positions implicit in different schools of medieval philosophy and theology. On the one hand, not every logical individualist would necessarily agree with Ockham's concrete political conclusions, for some might argue that he came up with the *wrong* equivalences between general and individual propositions in politics. Nor, on the other philosophical hand, would a Platonic realist necessarily disagree with Ockham on every matter of practical concern. Just as Ptolemaic and Copernican astronomical theories agree in most of their observational consequences, so a realist and a nominalist might sincerely agree in some of their practical political positions (for example, in supporting one form of government over another – monarchy, say, over direct democracy). So we should not think of nominalism as rigidly determining a programme or moral content for politics. The most that we are entitled to say, on the basis of the present study at any rate, is that Ockham's political works resulted partly from a way of looking at things which came quite naturally to a logician whose preferred response to general propositions was to search for adequate individual equivalents to them.[19]

These considerations about the general political import of Ockham's logical individualism throw light on the 'subjectivity' of his conception of individual rights. We noted earlier that Ockham became involved in political affairs in the first place because of the need he saw to defend the Franciscan ideal of a life without property or legal involvements as the highest state of Christian perfection. The model Ockhamist individual, then, is one who virtually ceases to be an individual in the acquisitive, right-possessing, power-claiming senses of individualism central to modern secular thought. Furthermore, both Ockham's defence of Franciscan poverty and the positions he developed later in his career as a political writer were based to a large extent on appeals to universally accepted Christian principles or to rationality and natural law.[20] These features of Ockham's thought are inexplicable if we think of nominalism as entailing a substitution of human agreement for cosmic order and private opinion for objective knowledge. From what we have seen above, however, it appears that the main point of Ockham's individualism is not so much to give individuals political power or to celebrate the fact that individuals naturally have powers of various other kinds before anyone gives them political power. There is some of the former and a good deal of the latter in Ockham, but the main point is, rather, that it matters in politics *how things stand* with individuals – with all the individuals involved in human communities. This is not to say that the truth or falsity of propositions in legal and

---

[19] The monarchy supported by a nominalist might, of course, differ in important ways from that desired by a realist (on this and many other points concerning the relations between philosophy and politics, see Alan Gewirth's illuminating essay, 'Philosophy and political thought in the fourteenth century', in F. L. Utley, ed., *The Forward Movement of the Fourteenth Century* (Columbus, Ohio, 1961), pp. 125–164, especially pp. 125–7, 130–3, and 151–4), but it would be wrong to assume *a priori* that such differences must be irreconcilable in practice.

[20] *The Political Thought of William of Ockham*, pp. 173–96. See now Kevin McDonnell, 'Does William of Ockham have a theory of natural law?', *Franciscan Studies*, XXXIV (1974), pp. 383–92. Ockham's ethics continues to be a challenging subject but one which now receives subtler treatment than used to be accorded it. See especially Linwood Urban, 'William of Ockham's theological ethics', *Franciscan Studies*, XXXIII (1973), pp. 310–50; David W. Clark, 'Voluntarism and rationalism in the ethics of Ockham', *Franciscan Studies*, XXXI (1971), pp. 72–87, and 'William of Ockham on right reason', *Speculum*, XLVIII (1973), pp. 13–36; and Gordon Leff, *William of Ockham*, pp. 476–92.

political theory is to be determined *by* individuals, but that such propositions are to be understood and judged as being *about* individuals. The proper object of political argument, we might say, is a statement putting together in an objectively correct way all the individuals of which our practical human world is composed. Such a reduction of political discourse to sets of individual propositions may, of course, be impossible, even in principle, for anything we have seen to the contrary. The philosophical realist or holist may be right. It may be impossible, indeed, to make sense of even one individual proposition without presupposing an ontology of Forms or essences or social wholes. But the search for such equivalences is something even a realist may wish to encourage, for when such searching is carried on with an appreciation of the complexities it involves, it does not give subjective, arbitrary, and chaotic power to 'the' individual but concrete effectiveness to the universal and ideal.

As to the general relations of philosophy and politics, the moral to be drawn from this brief investigation of Ockham would seem to be that philosophy is and ought to be a cause, but only a partial cause, of reasonable activity in politics. Anything worth asserting in philosophy is, after all, also worth disputing. When either realism or nominalism becomes a dogma, it loses all philosophical value (including the value of making a philosophical contribution to politics), and hence, although a prudent philosopher will demand of himself that his participation in communal affairs comport well with his philosophical principles, he will not demand allegiance to those principles from others as the sole legitimate basis for their co-operation. From either the standpoint of a detached observer of human affairs or that of a participant in them, it may be equally misleading to regard a constitution, culture, or movement as properly the implementation of a single set of ideas as it is to treat such things as disconnected from any serious ideas at all. In Western political thought and action, one does encounter imprudent philosophers and thoughtless politicians, frequently, but both our understanding and our action might improve if we did not so often take these types as the norm. The frustrations of combining or separating politics and philosophy can be treated best by doing both.

PUBLIC EXPEDIENCY AND NATURAL LAW: A FOURTEENTH-CENTURY DISCUSSION ON THE ORIGINS OF GOVERNMENT AND PROPERTY

by BRIAN TIERNEY

The Sum of the Matter betwixt Mr. *Hoadly* and Me is this, I think it most Natural that *Authority* shou'd *Descend*, that is, be *Derived* from a *Superiour* to an *Inferiour*, from *God* to *Fathers* and *Kings*, and from *Kings* and *Fathers* to *Sons* and *Servants*: But Mr. *Hoadly* wou'd have it *Ascend*, from *Sons* to *Fathers* and from *Subjects* to *Sovereigns*; nay to *God* Himself, whose *Kingship* the Men of the *Rights* say, is *Derived* to *Him* from the *People*! And the *Argument* does Naturally Carry it all that Way. For if *Authority* does *Ascend* it must *Ascend* to the *Height*.[1]

THIS PARADOX was presented by Charles Leslie, a brilliant contemporary critic of John Locke's theory of natural law and natural rights. Walter Ullmann, with his characteristic learning and insight, has shown us in many distinguished studies how the problem of ascending and descending powers discussed here by Leslie had already been posed centuries earlier in the religious and political thought of the Middle Ages.[2] Indeed the English seventeenth-century debate echoed strangely – as it were in a different key – a theme that had already been clearly enunciated in Western political theory in the years around 1300. Moreover the earlier debate, like the later one, concerned not only political authority but also property rights, 'dominion' understood to mean both jurisdiction and ownership. The really complicated problems arose, as Michael Wilks has pointed out, when constitutional theorists began to argue that such rights came from both God and the people, that they somehow ascended and descended at the same time.[3]

In this paper we shall be concerned with an aspect of the medieval debate. But we must note at the outset that the resemblances between the discussions of the early fourteenth century and those of the late

---

[1] Charles Leslie, *The Finishing Stroke, Being a Vindication of the Patriarchal Scheme of Government* (London, 1711), p. 87, quoted by John Dunn, *The Political Thought of John Locke* (Cambridge, 1969), p. 63, n. 1.

[2] My own first attempt at historical writing, written under Dr Ullmann's supervision nearly thirty years ago, dealt with the best-known medieval exponent of the 'ascending' thesis, Marsilius of Padua.

[3] M. Wilks, *The Problem of Sovereignty in the Later Middle Ages* (Cambridge, 1963), p. 202.

seventeenth century are not merely coincidental. Throughout the whole medieval period the 'descending' thesis was implicit in the accepted Christian conception of the universe to this extent at least: no one denied that licit dominion came ultimately from God. But from about 1250 onward the problem arose of combining this apparently self-evident doctrine with new versions of the 'ascending' thesis based on the Aristotelian teaching that society and the state were natural to man. In the ensuing discussions, a cluster of ideas emerged that would have a continuous history of development in Western constitutional thought down to the time of Leslie and Locke.

Early modern debates on the origins of government and property centred around three themes: divine right, natural law, and public utility. Proponents of divine right, like Leslie, maintained that all licit rights of jurisdiction and ownership were derived from God directly or through his agents on earth.[4] Natural law theorists, like Locke, argued that legitimate government was based on consent and that legitimate property rights arose whenever a man mixed his own labour with material things. Such arguments did not convince the theorists of divine right. How could any man be licitly subjected to another, they asked, unless God, the lord of all, had established rulers among men? And how could any man licitly claim property for himself unless God, the owner of all, had granted the property to him?[5] (Arguing against Locke's labour theory of acquisition, his critics pointed out that even a man's own person belonged to God.) At a later stage of the discussion, utilitarian thinkers attacked the whole doctrine of natural rights and natural law from a more radical perspective. Beccaria argued that human law, especially penal law, could not and should not seek to exemplify abstract principles of natural justice but should aim solely at promoting public utility. And Bentham, rejecting all theories of natural rights, constructed an alternative doctrine of government by consent based on the utilitarian principle that only the whole community would most clearly perceive and most effectively pursue its own self-interest.

Historians have often noted that both the natural law theories and the divine right theories of the early modern world had medieval antecedents. Medieval anticipations of later utilitarian doctrines have

---

[4] For these views and Locke's counter-arguments see John Locke, *Two Treatises of Government*, ed. P. Laslett (Cambridge, 1967), pp. 174–89, 213–17.

[5] *Ibid.*, p. 111.

been less often noticed (though legal historians at least will be aware that the concepts of *utilitas publica*, *necessitas*, and *status regni* (or *status ecclesiae*) were very familiar to medieval Roman and canon lawyers). The work to be considered below, a fourteenth-century *Tractatus de Legibus* attributed to Durandus of St Pourçain, is interesting for its persistent emphasis on utilitarian arguments.[6] The author quoted often from Aristotle and Thomas Aquinas (as well as from Roman and canon law) but he did not present just one more medieval natural-law theory of the state. On the contrary his work is most interesting at the points where he anticipated later criticisms of such theories. The *Tractatus* shows how far a medieval author could go in constructing a purely utilitarian theory of law, government and property, and also the difficulties of conducting such an enterprise within a framework of medieval presuppositions. The discussion moved from a conventional account of *ius naturale* and *ius gentium* to a highly pragmatic theory of human legislation. When applied to problems of political theory, the author's arguments led to a nuanced doctrine of government by consent and, most interestingly, to an unusually detailed consideration of property rights in natural law and in civil law. We shall consider these topics in turn.

[6] The arguments against Durandus's authorship were given by J. Koch, *Durandus de S. Porciano*, *O.P.* (Münster, 1927), pp. 177–8. His discussion is persuasive but not conclusive. Koch presents the following six arguments. (I have added responses to them.) (1) The treatise is more loosely organised than Durandus's other works. But it seems doubtful that the surviving text presents the full work as the author wrote it. See (5) below. (2) The author seems more a jurist than a philosopher. But there is no display of juristic learning in the work. It includes only well-known texts of Roman and canon law which are found in other fourteenth-century works on political theory written by philosophers. (3) The author expresses views that are not found in Durandus's other works. But this point lacks substance. Even medieval authors did not invariably repeat themselves. (4) The author refers to the *populus romanus* and *res publica* which suggests that he was Italian. But he also presents an argument for hereditary monarchy which might suggest that he was French. (5) The author often states that he has discussed controversial points elsewhere and sometimes no such discussions can be found in Durandus's certainly authoritative works. This is important but not decisive. The author sometimes uses indeterminate phrases like *probavi alias*, but sometimes writes more explicitly, e.g. *ut supra innui* (fo. 15vb), *dixi in hac materia* (fo. 16ra), *ut superius dicebatur* (fo. 17ra). It is not always possible to find corresponding passages in the surviving text of the *Tractatus*. Possibly all references to discussions 'elsewhere' refer to missing sections of the *Tractatus* itself. Of course they could also refer to some lost work of Durandus. (6) The author quotes Thomas Aquinas extensively. But he often disagrees with Thomas's views. Johannes de Turrecremata, who probably acquired the Vatican MS about 1420 (Koch, *Durandus*, p. 177, n. 1), attributed the work to Durandus. See his *Repertorium super Decretum* (Venice, 1578), ad Dist. 1 c. 9. It seems that the question of authorship should be regarded as still open. Certainly the tone and substance of the treatise seem in keeping with Durandus's cognomen (*Doctor Resolutissimus*) and with his epitaph (*durus Durandus*). The *Tractatus* was printed by J. Barbier (Paris, 1506), fo. 10r–23r. In the following notes I have collated the printed text with MS Vatican Barb. lat.869, pp. 77–93 (omitting very minor variations of spelling and word order).

Thomas Aquinas defined natural law as a 'participation of reason in the eternal law'. He regarded *ius gentium* as a form of human law, closely related to natural law and derived immediately from its principles. All positive human law, he maintained, was derived from natural law either as a conclusion from a premise or as a determination of something left indifferent in natural law.[7] The author of the *Tractatus de Legibus* agreed with Thomas about the definition of natural law. But since *ius gentium* was defined in the Digest precisely as 'what natural reason has established among all men' he could see no grounds for distinguishing between *ius gentium* and *ius naturale*. Both were common to all men and were immutable. Both were based on 'natural reason', on 'nature itself considered absolutely', on the intrinsic 'nature of a thing', or on the nature of the case, we might say (*natura rei*). Accordingly, for him, *iura gentium et iura naturalia non distinguuntur*.[8] This departure from Thomas's classification was perhaps more a matter of words than a serious disagreement in substance. (The author agreed with Thomas that *ius gentium* was different from the 'primeval' natural law which applied to animals as well as to men.[9]) The real difference came with the treatment of human law. The author of the *Tractatus* accepted the common opinion that human law, unlike natural law, varied with time and place, but he did not agree with Thomas that human law was derived from natural law. On the contrary it was based on a different foundation. 'Civil law does not take nature (*natura rei*) as its foundation, but rather public expediency, so that there public expediency occurs as the whole cause of establishing its conclusions.' Accordingly *ius naturale* and *ius gentium* were 'formally distinguished from civil law'.[10]

These propositions were set out at the beginning of the treatise. From there onward the whole argument was conducted in terms of

---

[7] *Divi Thomas Aquinatis Opera Omnia*, ed. L. Vives (Paris, 1874–1889), *Summa Theologiae*, 1a2ae.91.2, 1a2ae.95.4, 1a2ae.95.2. All subsequent quotations from Aquinas are taken from this edition.

[8] 'Ius gentium secundum legem descriptionem est illud quod ratio naturalis constituit inter omnes homines.' (fo. 10ra) (cf. *Dig.* 1.1.9); '. . . talia recipiunt natura rei pro fundamento . . .' (fo. 10va); 'Prima conclusio est quod iura gentium et iura naturalia non distinguuntur . . . iuris naturalis et iuris gentium fundamentum est natura ipsa absolute considerata' (fo. 10vb).

[9] *Tractatus*, fo. 10vb. Cf. *Summa Theologiae*, 2a2ae.57.3. The problems of definition arose from the differing usages of the terms *ius naturale* and *ius gentium* that occur in the Institutes and Digest.

[10] 'Ius ciuile uero non accipit sic naturam rei pro fundamento illo (primo, MS 77b) sed magis expedientiam publicam ita quod expedentia publica concurrit ibi pro totali cause in constituendo istas conclusiones' (fo. 10va) (cf. *Dig.* 1.1.11).

public expediency. The words *expediens, expedientia, utilitas* are scattered over every page of the treatise. (The specific phrase *expedientia publica* occurs more than thirty times.) As a first example of his doctrine the author considered a point of penal practice. Natural law indicated that a criminal should be punished, but it did not specify the precise punishment, e.g. that a thief should be hanged. The specification of the punishment belonged to human law.[11] This is of course a familiar medieval example. Thomas Aquinas also used it. But the author of the *Tractatus* pressed his argument in an unusual way by insisting that human law had to mete out a punishment determined solely by public expediency. Let us suppose, he suggested, a polity in which there were few men and an abundance of goods. In those circumstances it would not be necessary to hang thieves. Some other penalty could be assigned. But if there was a large population and a shortage of material goods, then it would be expedient to hang thieves for even small offences. Later the author noted that in some places men were more prone to theft than in others and that it would be expedient to punish them more severely in such places.[12]

The example of theft was only an illustration in a general theory of penal law based on expediency. The author did not deny that a given offence merited a particular degree of punishment from the nature of the offence itself. But he held that it was no business of the human judge to enter into such calculations. One could argue that divine judgment and divine punishment were necessary precisely because human judgments could not concern themselves with abstract justice. Emperors could not be 'true punishers' (as God was). There was 'no way in the world' that they could know the proper penalty that should be assigned in a particular case.[13] Human law measured punishment according to public expediency, divine law according to justice.[14]

The author also applied his theory of expediency rather oddly to

---

11 'Nam aliqua expediunt uno tempore que non expediunt alio, ut quando est raritas hominum in policia et sunt bona ad uitam super excrescentia non impedit (expedit, MS 77b) tunc quod pro furto aliquis suspandatur sed debet aliter castigari. Et aliter quando est multitudo hominum quasi super excrescens et bona terre pauca, expedit quod suspendatur etiam pro modico furto' (fo. 10va). The author often used the word *policia* in preference to *civitas* or *respublica*.

12 'homines in aliquo loco sunt magis inclinati ad furtum quam in alio (loco *add.* MS 85b), ergo expedit quod puniantur magis scilicet per suspendium' (fo. 17ra).

13 'imperatores puniunt homines pro suis delictis qui non sunt punitores ueri, nam per nullam rationem mundi possunt cognoscere certum gradum pene imponende . . .' (fo. 16va).

14 'Nam lex humana . . . in punitionibus faciendis mensurat secundum expedientiam publicam . . . et quantum exigit expedenta publica . . . Sed lex diuina imponit penam delinquenti ut aliquid iustum . . .' (fo. 19vb).

marriage law. Marriage could be viewed on several levels. The actual act of generation pertained to the primeval natural law common to men and animals. Consent in marriage pertained to the *ius gentium* (the natural law proper to man). But the indissolubility of marriage was a provision of civil law introduced for the sake of public expediency. It did not have its origin in the 'nature of the thing'. Rather nature suggested that an infertile marriage should be dissolved. But a man would more readily undertake noble deeds for his own good and the good of the state if he had someone to share his misfortunes (should any befall him) and to succour him in time of need.[15] In a later discussion the author suggested that, if a population grew too large in relation to the available resources, marriage might be prohibited for a time.[16]

Some precepts of natural law were indeed included in human legislation, the author acknowledged, but this was because they promoted the health of the state. In such cases it might be said that the legislator acted only as a teacher declaring the law, but this was not the whole truth, for the emperor's declaration had binding force, unlike that of any private doctor.[17] Still such enactments did not derive their justice solely from the emperor's promulgation; they could be seen to be just beforehand by natural reason. Other laws, however, acquired a quality of justice only from the fact that they had been promulgated.[18] In general, civil procedure was not regulated by natural reason but, to borrow the phrase of a later jurist, by 'the artificial reason of the law'. For instance, natural reason could not prove that the evidence of two witnesses established a fact as true; such evidence had to be accepted

---

[15] 'Item est actus iuris ciuilis quantum ad aliqua ibi introducta propter expedientiam publicam ut quod non sit separatio uiri a muliere. Hoc non est secundum natura rei . . . Attamen propter expedientiam publicam est introducta impossibilitas separationis. Nam uir citius facta laudabilia ad bonum suum et policie aggredietur si sciat aliquem participare in suis infortuniis supposito quod aliqua sibi contingat (continguant, MS 79a) et qui succurret sue necessitati' (fo. 11vb).

[16] 'Nona conclusio est quod in conclusionibus iuris naturalis sunt gradus ita quod alique conclusiones sunt magis naturalis aliis . . . Uellent aliqui dicere quod posset recipere mutationem, ut si multitudo hominum esset super excrescens secundum quantitatem bonorum deberet usque ad tempus prohiberi ad matrimonium. Quid hic dicendum non assero. Et secundum hoc sequitur quod alique conclusiones iuris gentium debent magis dici (dici magis esse, MS 80a) naturales quam alique que sunt de iure naturali primeuo . . . ut ista conclusio quod deus sit diligendus' (fo. 13va).

[17] 'inter ea que facienda sunt in policia ad saluandum policiam quedam sunt que essent facienda secundum se . . . non per consuetudinem set magis naturaliter indita rei' (fo. 10ra); 'Quia diximus quod in conclusionibus iuris naturalis non interuenit imperator nisi per modum doctoris declarantis. Hoc posset male intelligi . . . nam sue declarationi oportet stare quod non esset de alio . . .' (fo. 12vb).

[18] The author specifically discussed the law of *usucapio* as legislation based on public expediency rather than on natural reason (fo. 12va).

as if it were true for the sake of public expediency.[19] Legal science was
not a subordinate branch of moral philosophy. It was an autonomous
discipline deriving its conclusions, not from one first principle (*bonum
humanum*) as many doctors taught, but from two basic principles – the
good and the expedient.[20]

We need not pursue all the applications of the doctrine of expediency that occur throughout the *Tractatus*.[21] The underlying
argument was always the same, that expediency required the elaboration of a structure of purely human legislation which was not deduced
or deducible from natural law. Yet the author insisted that men living
within such a framework of human laws continued to be bound by
natural law before God.[22] For him, we might say, *expedientia non tollit
naturam*. The author of the *Tractatus* did not acknowledge any opposition between the two basic principles upon which all law was founded
in his theory – nature and expediency. Rather he argued that the two
principles could be reconciled in a broader generalisation – that men
should always do what was pleasing to God. The conclusions of law
established what was pleasing to God in two ways, immediately from
natural law, and mediately from considerations of public expediency.
Laws based on expediency were pleasing to God because it pleased
God that those things be done which promoted the well-being of the
whole.[23]

This may seem an optimistic conclusion. Common sense suggests
that sometimes the demands of expediency might conflict with the
precepts of natural law. It remains to consider how far this difficulty
did arise in connection with the two problems raised at the outset of

---

[19] 'sed solum talia recipiuntur ac si essent uera propter expedientiam publicam' (fo. 12rb).

[20] 'ista principia scilicet bonum ex natura rei et expedientia publica fundant omnes conclusiones
morales siue legales sint siue non . . . Et ex hoc improbaui quod communiter dicitur a doctoribus
quod ipsa legalis scientia est subalternata morali philosophie . . .' (fos. 15vb–16ra). 'bonum
humanum . . . non est subiectum in legali scientia licet communiter asseratur . . . bonum et
expedientia publica assumuntur ut subiectum ad demonstrandas omnes conclusiones legales'
(fo. 16rb).

[21] E.g. servitude based on public expediency (fo. 11vb); exceptions to natural law for reasons of
expediency (fo. 15vb); validity of customs based on expediency (fo. 19vb). The author acknowledged that in practice some human laws were neither natural nor expedient. The definition of
ius, he wrote, described what laws ought to be, not what they always were (fo. 11ra). Further
discussion of the legislator's will as source of human law at fos. 13rb, 16vb.

[22] Even the emperor was so bound, 'a legibus iuris naturalis imperator non est absolutus . . .'
(fo. 12vb).

[23] 'illa (principia) reducuntur in unum primum, scilicet in amabilitatem diuinam . . . Et ideo de
his dicitur quod sunt quedam diuina prouidentia constitute . . . alia uero per medium scilicet
per expedientiam publicam. Unde amabile est deo quod fiat illud quod est ad salutem totius . . .'
(fo. 16vb).

this paper, the origin of human government and the origin of private property. Were such institutions rooted in natural law or in expediency, in nature or in convention? Evidently the thought of our author could have been developed in either direction. We may add that his teaching on the will of God as the ultimate source of all law could have been developed into a 'descending' theory, his teaching on human nature and human needs into an 'ascending' theory.

Let us begin with the origin of licit government. Thomas Aquinas had provided no definitive solution to the problem of political obligation. Rather he hinted at two quite different solutions, both of which were developed independently by the philosophers of the next generation. In some contexts Thomas wrote that men were inherently unequal, ranked in a hierarchy that was part of the hierarchical order of the whole universe. The right of some men to rule others could then be based on their status in the hierarchy.[24] And since the whole hierarchy depended on God it was not difficult to develop from this side of Thomas's thought a thoroughly theocratic 'descending' theory of government like that of Aegidius Romanus. But in other contexts Thomas wrote that all men were by nature equal.[25] One could deduce from these texts that licit authority could only be based on consent and so arrive at the radical 'ascending' theory of popular sovereignty later developed by Marsilius of Padua.

The author of the *Tractatus de Legibus* took an intermediate position. His discussion favoured an 'ascending' thesis but it was complicated by his usual concern for the dual claims of nature and expediency. On one point he was quite clear. The constituting of a ruler was not a matter of natural law but of civil law.[26] In defending this view the author

---

[24] *Summa Contra Gentiles* 3.81, 'Quia vero homo habet intellectum et sensum et corporalem virtutem, haec in ipso ad invicem ordinantur, secundum divinae Providentiae dispositionem ad similitudinem ordinis qui in universo invenitur ... Ex eadem ratione et inter ipsos homines ordo invenitur; nam illi qui intellectu praeeminent naturalitur dominantur.' See also *Summa Theol.* 1.96.4, 2a2ae.104.1, *II Sent.* 44.1.3; *De Regno* 1.9.

[25] *Summa Theol.* 1.109.2, 'Ad tertium dicendum quod daemones non sunt aequales secundum naturam; unde in eis non est naturalis praelatio; quod in hominibus non contingit, qui natura sunt pares'; 2a2ae.10.11 'dominium et praelatio introducta sunt ex iure humano ...'; 2a2ae.12.2 'dominium introductum est de iure gentium ...'. On natural equality see also 2a2ae.104.5; *II Sent.* 6.1.4; and, on servitude as a product of human law, *Summa Theol.* 1a2ae.94.5; *IV Sent.* 36.1.2. Modern authors, by emphasising one set of texts or the other have been able to present Aquinas as an extreme theocrat or an extreme democrat.

[26] The author did not emphasise even the natural origin of society as such. Indeed his remarks sometimes have an almost Hobbesian flavor. 'Item nisi essent iudices statim homines procederent ad bella (arma, MS 79b)' (fo. 12rb). Again, unless a threat of divine punishment existed 'homines ... intantum sunt nati ad sequendum suos motus quod nunquam submitterent se ad uoluntatem alicuius principis immo sine freno sequerentur concupiscentias suas' (fo. 19rb).

addressed himself to the question that Thomas had left open. What if there were one man in a society clearly superior to all others? It would be natural, he replied, that such a man should be honoured and followed in some things, but not that he should be sole ruler in the sense that all men had to obey his laws in all matters.[27] The argument on this point was not based on natural liberty and equality as in the more radical theories of the time but on an old-fashioned Aristotelian position. It was conceivable that some one man might know more than any other individual about the direction of public affairs, but not that one man should know more than the whole collectivity of men, including himself and others. Therefore it was inherent in the nature of things that rights of government should reside in the whole community.[28] But at once the claims of expediency arose. All the members could not assemble together and if they did assemble they would hardly agree. It was expedient therefore to transfer power to a ruler.[29]

The next question followed inevitably. Was this 'translation of power' revocable? The answer seems inevitable too given the whole structure of the argument. The ruler's power was immediately revocable if it ceased to serve the end of public expediency.[30] It was not to be lightly revoked on account of personal defect in the ruler – change of rulers might do more harm than good – but a ruler was to be deposed if his offence was such as to 'infect the whole polity', if for instance he became a heretic.

The author also considered the relative merits of elective and hereditary rulership. Again his argument balanced the natural against the expedient. It was 'more natural', he wrote, that succession should

---

[27] 'Decima conclusio est quod constitutio principis non est naturalis sed ciuilis. Uerum est quod si esset unus homo in mundo omnibus hominibus melior (melior omnibus, MS 80a) bonum est secundum constitutionem naturale quod ipse plus honoretur et quod ipse principaretur quantum ad quedam. Sed quod ipse simpliciter principetur et quod alii omnes eius obediant legibus in omnibus non est secundum naturam rei' (fo. 13vb).

[28] 'Nam licet sit unus homo in mundo melius cognoscens illa que possunt esse ad directionem populi, tamen non (nullus, MS 80b) est in mundo qui simpliciter omnia ita (omnia illa possit esse ita, MS 80b) possit cognoscere sicut faceret tota collectio hominum ipsius et aliorum. Et ideo magis esset secundum naturam rei quod totus populus haberet rationem principis. Et esset simile ac si esset unum animal habens ualde multos oculos . . .' (fo. 13vb). Cf. Aristotle, *Politics*, 3.11.2 (1281b).

[29] 'Tamen propter expediens quia non possunt congregari omnes et congregati uix consentirent fuit expedientius contrarium' (fo. 13vb).

[30] 'Translatio potestatis translate in imperatorem est reuocabilis ex una causa . . . statim quod cessaret expedientia posset reuocari, ut puta si essent pauci homines equalis sciencie qui faciliter congregarentur et faciliter conuenirent' (fo. 13vb). The author noted that future generations were bound by the initial consent of the populus. 'Et ita populus sequens reputatur idem cum populo preterito' (fo. 17va).

be by election, for natural reason indicated that the best man should rule and election was better adapted to secure this result than hereditary right. He brushed aside the argument that, because a good man would generate a good heir, hereditary kingship was really more natural. (Astrological influences might interfere with the act of generation.) 'And so', the author concluded, 'election is always more natural.' But then came the usual qualification. Perhaps in his own time hereditary rule was more expedient because, if men could not come together to elect, they might remain without a head.[31]

There is evidently a tension here between the 'ascending' and 'descending' theses and between the claims of the natural and the expedient. An argument for natural popular sovereignty ends in a defence of expedient hereditary monarchy. But the tension is not too disruptive. The 'natural' right of a people to govern itself is not extinguished by the 'expedient' transfer of power to a ruler since the people never lose the natural right to revoke that power. Here again we might adapt St Thomas and say, *expedientia non tollit naturam*.

The situation is more complicated when we turn to the problem of property. The author devoted substantial sections of his work to this question and they contain some of his most idiosyncratic arguments. Virtually all medieval thinkers adhered to the common Stoic–Patristic tradition which described 'the common possession of all things' as a tenet of natural law. Obviously then a problem arose of explaining how private property could licitly be established by human law. Thomas Aquinas offered one widely accepted solution. He argued thus. The statement that by natural law all things are possessed in common meant only that natural law did not assign specific possessions to particular men. There was no positive precept of natural law which forbade such division. Hence the right of individual ownership was not contrary to natural law, but was rather an addition to it devised by human reason.[32] The author of the *Tractatus de Legibus* presented a quite different argument. The idea that individual property rights exist in

---

[31] 'Duodecima conclusio est quod constitutio principis per electionem est magis naturalis quam per progeniei successionem ... semper est electio magis naturalis licet forsan alia magis sit expediens pro hoc tempore quia homines non possunt conuenire ad electionem et ita remanerent membra sine capite' (fo. 14ra).

[32] *Summa Theol.* 2a2ae.66.2. Thomas held that the use of property (as distinct from possession) remained common according to natural law in the sense that a man was required to share goods with those in need. On canonistic doctrines see my *Medieval Poor Law* (Berkeley and Los Angeles, 1959). A good general survey of medieval doctrines in this area is provided by G. Couvreur, *Les Pauvres ont-ils des droits?* (Rome, 1961).

natural law is sometimes supposed to be a contribution of the natural rights school of the seventeenth century. In fact our author presented such a doctrine three centuries earlier. His theory was a very odd one however. The author did not argue, like so many later thinkers, that human law was created to preserve natural rights. On the contrary, he asserted that the requirements of public expediency required human law to set up a system of civil rights in property quite different from the rights that existed under natural law.

The author's fundamental premise was that rightful ownership was based on virtue, so his theory could find a place in the broad spectrum of medieval doctrines of dominion founded on grace.[33] In his first approach to the problem he wrote that, although division of property as it actually existed in the world was not based on natural law, still natural law did indeed define individual rights of ownership. For, according to natural law, property ought to be subjected to the will of good men rather than bad (and, the author added, a man was called the owner of a thing precisely when it was subjected to his will so that he could claim it against others). But it was not in accord with nature, rather against nature, that a bad man should claim goods as his own against a better one. That claim could only be based on public ex-pediency. The text of the Digest stating that division of property was introduced by the *ius gentium* had to be understood therefore in the sense that *ius gentium* (which the author equated with natural law, as we have noted) upheld the right of the good against the bad, but not vice versa. Also natural reason urged that, other things being equal, a man could claim as his own what he acquired by his own labour.[34]

In a later discussion the author summed up his teaching thus: *In rebus naturalibus melior ... potest dici dominus rerum diuisim et distinctim et alii non sic.* For instance, if there were two men and only sufficient resources to support one, the better man would have a 'distinct and separate right' against the other by natural law. The reason for this was

---

[33] The most obvious source for such a doctrine would be Augustine's phrase, 'iure divino ... cuncta justorum sunt' (Ep. 93c.12, PL xxxiii. 345), but the author does not cite this.

[34] 'Bene (Unde, MS 79a) apparet secundum naturam rei quod debet esse aliqua distinctio quantum ad hoc quod res magis submittantur uoluntati meliorum quam peiorum. Sed quod pessimus possit distinguere res suas contra meliorem non apparet quod illud possit dici secundum naturam rei ... Et sic (Ideo, MS 79a) intelligendum est (est *om.* MS 79a) quod est fundata propter expedientiam publicam ... Et cum dicitur *ff de iusticia et iure* 1. ex hoc iure quod distinctio dominiorum est ex iure gentium intelligo ... quantum ad hoc quod melior potest condistinguere aliquam rem contra minus bonum et uti ea ... Item cum aliquid est acquisitum ex industria mea naturalis ratio dictat quod ego possum illud condistinguere contra alium ubi cetera paria essent' (fo. 12ra).

simple. God was the lord of all things; God loved the better man more; therefore God would want him to use the goods in question.[35] The argument that the other man might have acquired a natural right by his labour had no force here, for God always had a superior right. Subsequently the author wrote that God had dominion even over our own persons,[36] thus anticipating one of the arguments that, centuries later, would be directed against Locke's labour theory of property. The author also maintained that a bad man claiming a property right against a good one in time of necessity was a thief and a murderer.[37]

How then could one defend the traditional teaching, 'By natural law all things are common'? They were common, the author replied, in the sense that they were distributed from a common source, God, who was no respecter of persons. That is to say, no one was excluded from acquiring a just title to property by natural law. If a better man had a greater right, the worse man had only to improve himself. As soon as he became as good as the other he acquired an equal right and, if he became better, he acquired a superior right. Property was also common by natural law in the sense that natural law rejected the division of property that actually existed among men.[38]

Let us turn next to property in civil law. The author's teaching was summed up towards the end of the treatise. 'Although things are common by natural law as set out above, nevertheless because of men's wickedness it was expedient for the state (reipublice) that rights of ownership (dominia) be distinguished.'[39] In several preceding discussions

---

[35] 'Dico quod magis bonus . . . habet unum ius distinctum et diuisum contra alium' (fo. 14rb).

[36] 'Nec obstat quod res sit acquisita industria alterius quia deus semper magis habet ius in re . . .' (fo. 14rb). 'Unde sicut de rebus ita nec de se ipso plenum et totale habet dominium (plenum . . . dominium *om.* MS 83a) quia omnia sunt dei' (fo. 14ra).

[37] 'Tertia conclusio est quod minus bonus diuidens rem quam habet contra magis bonum in casu necessitas est uere fur . . . et uere homicida' (fo. 14vb). Cicero had posed the question whether a wise man in great need could take the goods of some idle, worthless person (*De Officiis*, 3.6) and decided that he could do so, not for his own sake but for the sake of the common weal. For medieval discussion of this text see Couvreur, *Les Pauvres*, pp. 22–9. The doctrines evolved from it are quite different from those of the *Tractatus de Legibus*.

[38] 'Qualiter ergo intelligendum est quod res sunt communes . . . sunt communes quia exhibende sunt per receptum (respectum, MS 82a) ad medium commune scilicet deum qui est totum ens et (qui MS 82a) non est acceptor personarum. Et ideo si ille melior habeat plus iuris quam alius, faciat se alius meliorem, et si ad equalitatem bonitatis se reducat habeat ius equale. Si autem (autem *om.* MS 82a) ad maiorem, habebit ius (ius *om.* MS 82a) maius, et sic (etc, MS 82a) in aliis. Item sunt communes per negationem distinctionis que nunc est secundum qua minus bonus diuidit rem suam contra magis bonum' (fo. 14rb).

[39] 'licet enim res sint communes inspecto iure naturale eo modo quo in superioribus est declaratum, tamen expediens fuit reipublice occasione malicie hominum quod dominia rerum distinguerentur' (fo. 22vb).

the author had made it clear that the rights guaranteed by civil law could not be the same as those that arose from natural law. The emperor could not discriminate among so many men to determine the relative goodness of each. But the well-being of the polity required that the emperor or people make some division. Otherwise each man would claim to be better than others and often the strong would kill the weak. It was opportune therefore to so divide things that a man who was able to acquire more should have more.[40] Such a division was accordingly made 'by the consent of men or of one acting on behalf of the community'.[41] The division might assign property rights to good men or bad. But normally the less good men would have greater riches because they were more solicitous about acquiring material things.[42] The constant assumption of the argument was that rights in civil law could not and would not coincide with rights in natural law. There were two different structures of rights, one 'descending' from God, the other 'ascending' from popular consent.

The author applied his ideas in a variety of ways. He accepted the common view that in time of necessity superfluities were common according to natural law. (That is to say, even a good man could not claim his superfluous possessions against those in extreme want.) This led him to develop an interesting theory of poor relief.[43] The author also showed how, on his theory, it would be possible – though not expedient – for the pope to claim a universal right of dominion.[44]

[40] 'Non enim sufficeret imperator ad considerandum circa quemlibet hominem ille habebit tantum, alius tantum propter multitudinem super excrescentem hominum et quia difficile esset cognoscere circa quodlibet indiuiduum gradum quem habet in genere boni' (fo. 12ra). 'Unde in tanto populo ut nunc est non posset fieri ut semper melior haberet plus iuris in rebus. Quilibet enim assereret (se esse *add.* MS 82b) meliorem et alii minus boni qui sepius corpore sunt robustiores, alios interficerent. Ergo oportuit ut distinguerentur res ita quod qui posset plus acquirere plus habet . . .' (fo. 14va).

[41] 'ex consensu hominum uel alicuius habentis vicem populi fuerunt distincta dominia' (fo. 22ra).

[42] 'minus boni regulariter habundant pecuniis quia magis solliciti sunt circa acquisitionem rerum (rerum *om.* MS 82b)' (fo. 14vb). This served as a proof that usury was against natural law. The man in need who had to borrow money would normally be better than the rich man who lent. But by natural law the money belonged to the better man. Therefore it was wrong to charge him usury.

[43] Officials should be appointed in each city to help those in extreme need. Fear of want made men cowardly and it ought to be alleviated. In the last resort it was licit for one in extreme need to steal (fo. 22ra). If a man fell into want through his own fault, to help him might encourage idleness. But if there were signs of penitence the man should be helped. He might reform and become useful to the state. Public authorities could punish the idle (fo. 22vb).

[44] Jesus Christ was lord of all things by natural law but not by civil law (fo. 14ra). Similarly the pope was lord of all by natural law but this did not prejudice the temporal lordship of kings (fo. 14rb). It was possible that the most perfect man might choose for a time to be lord of all by civil law as well as by natural law (fo. 15rb). But regularly the pope ought not have

It would be interesting to explore all these ramifications of thought. But our main concern is with the tension between natural law and public expediency in the system of the *Tractatus*. On one point the author was entirely in agreement with later exponents of natural rights theories. 'The Obligations of the Law of Nature cease not in Society', observed Locke.[45] So too, in the thought of our medieval author, the natural right of ownership pertaining to a good man was 'a divine right, wholly immutable' which could not be changed 'by the act of the ruler or of anyone else'.[46] Moreover, laws of the emperor contrary to natural law were not to be observed. This may seem to contradict the whole doctrine of property rights in civil law that we have so far described. But, the author explained, imperial laws decreed only that goods should be treated for purposes of civil administration as if they were held separately, since public expediency required this. The emperor's laws did not deny that it was intrinsically good for a man to know his own natural status and refuse to claim his property against a better man. Human law did not destroy the rights and duties that existed before God.[47]

The system seems neatly balanced so far between nature and expediency, between moral rights and legal rights. But when the author tried to work out the detailed implications of his arguments he encountered severe difficulties. These were especially apparent when he discussed the problem whether a man could licitly assert rights derived from natural law against the rights of another derived from civil law. If a better man seized the property of a less good man, property which both needed equally, did he commit an offence?[48] Obviously he did according to civil law. The judge would hang him, our author observed quite contentedly. Without temporal punishments for offences

civil dominion. He would inspire more confidence as an exemplar if he lived modestly. Men needed both kings and pontiffs and it was better if their functions were not confused (fo. 17rb).

45 John Locke, *Two Treatises*, II.xi. 135 (ed. Laslett, p. 375).

46 '... illud ius est ius diuinum totaliter immutabile ita quod facto principis uel alicuius alterius non potest mutari ...' (fo. 14va).

47 'imperator condendo leges suas, si esset contrarius legi naturali, leges suas non essent tenende ... non dicunt quominus semper bonum est quod quilibet congnoscat statum suum naturalem et non condiuidat res suas contra meliorem eo. Sed dicunt quod expediencia publica exigit quod proinde obseruentur ac si essent distincta quantum ad executiones faciendas' (fo. 15va); 'Et aduertendum quod imperator non remouet illud ius quod causabitur in ordine ad deum necque illud ligamen' (fo. 14vb).

48 'Sed pone quod (quod *om.* MS 92a) unus bonus habet unam rem (rem *om.* MS 92a) que precise est sibi necessaria, uenit magis bonus qui similiter est in articulo necessitatis, nunquid potest ab alio furari uel subrepere?' (fo. 22rb).

against civil law there would be constant dissensions and fighting among men. The people might even depose a prince who refused to punish such offences. But, the author observed, some would hold that the better man in our example did not offend before God. This implied, however, that civil laws were not binding *in foro conscientiae*.[49] Hence others would argue that, since God had given the better man strength to support himself, and the existing system of property rights was established by popular consent, he did indeed sin. But then again it might be argued that God sometimes gave much greater strength to the less good man and this could only be so that he should support both himself and the better man too.[50] The argument continued indecisively with further points of casuistry.[51] It is not a very satisfying discussion.

Indeed, at this point a real conflict arose in the author's thought that he was not able to resolve satisfactorily. Evidently, on his theory, any attempt to maintain natural rights in a civil society would lead to anarchy. Civil law could not abolish such rights but equally it could not permit them to be asserted. Still more confusingly, it was not even clear whether the assertion of natural rights against civil rights was morally justified. We are not dealing here with the situation envisaged by Thomas Aquinas – a definition in human law of a matter left undetermined by natural law. In this area natural law had made its determinations and human law imposed a conflicting set of obligations. At the end of his treatise the author explicitly rejected the argument of Aquinas that no positive precept of natural law required goods to be held in common. Natural law did require common ownership in the peculiar sense that the author had given to the phrase.[52] His very last

---

49 'Hic uellent forsan aliqui dicere quod posset. Et dicerent quod duplex est furtum, quoddam punibile eternaliter . . . Aliud est furtum punibile solum temporaliter ut in hoc casu. Unde iudex suspenderet eum et puniret temporaliter quia secundum hoc contingeret multociens nisi essent punitiones quod alicui (quia aliqui MS 92a) subirent necessitates et essent dissensiones et bella inter homines uel forsan quod populus procederet ad depositionem principis nisi ipsum puniret. Sed secundum hoc leges ciuiles etiam quantum ad prohibita non ligarent in foro conscientiae' (fo. 22rb).

50 'Uel dicatur quod non poterit iuste auferre ita quod utroque modo erit furtum uerum. Nam licet sit melior tamen ex quo deus dedit uirtutem prouisiuam ad conseruationem sui esse (utrique add MS 92a) et diuisi (diuisim, MS 92a) sunt dominia de consensu populi . . . magis uidetur amabile deo quod ipse moriatur . . . Sed illud non uidetur ualere quia interdum minus bono communicata est maior prouisiua potentia et magis bono nulla uel quasi, et non uidetur hoc aliud esse nisi ut ille prouideat sibi et alii magis bono' (fo. 22va).

51 E.g. if two men were starving could the better one 'use' the other (as food?).

52 'Dicunt aliqui quod res non sunt communes iure naturali positiue sed solum negatiue pro quanto oppositum scilicet distinctio diuiciarum non est de iure naturali. Non credo hoc uerum nam per rationem naturalem supra est probata communitas rerum secundum intellectum ibi expositum' (fo. 23ra) (see above, n. 38).

argument restated the underlying tension of the whole treatise. 'It is true that by natural law things are common. Nevertheless it is expedient that some division be made.'[53]

We shall not be surprised that the author of the *Tractatus de Legibus* failed to achieve an altogether harmonious synthesis if we remember how many different elements of thought he tried to include in one systematic treatise. The author tried to combine a doctrine of divinely sanctioned natural law with a theory of public utility that, in later times, would provide a potent weapon for critics of all natural law doctrines. He was equally concerned with the theoretical doctrine of government by consent and with the practical demands of expediency in shaping the form of a particular polity. Moreover the author was as interested in natural rights as in natural law. He saw the force of the Lockean argument about labour as a source of natural right in property but casually dismissed it with the same arguments that Locke's critics would use centuries later. He wanted to give due weight to both the 'ascending' and 'descending' theories of government and property.

We cannot regard the author of the *Tractatus* as a 'forerunner' of any one particular system of modern thought. But he did present various strands of argument that would be woven into different patterns in the theories of many later and more famous political thinkers. Walter Ullmann has given us the salutary reminder that, before the rediscovery of Aristotle's *Politics*, medieval men had no more idea of the state than they had of the steam engine. It is only a small footnote to his thought to add that, once they did recover the concept of the state, the men of the later Middle Ages began at once to identify and to attack the central problems that would preoccupy Western political theorists for the next several hundred years.

[53] 'Ergo hoc est uerum quod iure naturali res sunt communes. Tamen expediens est quod ibi sit aliqualis distinctio scilicet illa que dicta est supra' (fo. 23rb).

THE KING'S HALL, CAMBRIDGE, AND ENGLISH MEDIEVAL COLLEGIATE HISTORY

by ALAN B. COBBAN

THE ROYAL COLLEGE of the King's Hall, Cambridge, whose origins date from *c.*1317 and which became an endowed collegiate society in 1337, is indeed an institution *sui generis* among English academic corporations of the Middle Ages.[1] It had its genesis in the Society of the King's Scholars which was an arm of Edward II's chapel royal planted in the University of Cambridge. For over two centuries the King's Hall was supported by direct exchequer grant and successive English kings kept the patronage entirely in their own control, every fellow and warden being a Crown appointee, a circumstance which set the King's Hall apart constitutionally from all other English secular colleges with royal associations.[2] Moreover, Edward II's Society of the King's Scholars brought into being the first royal colony of clerks to be domiciled in an English university and thus inaugurated the institutional link between the royal household and the English universities. Although this link was expanded to embrace all 'royal' colleges at Oxford and Cambridge, the relation of the King's Hall to the royal household remained one of particular intimacy throughout the medieval period.

Until the foundation of New College, Oxford, in 1379, the King's Hall and Merton College, Oxford, stood in the forefront of the academic scene as the largest and most celebrated of the English secular colleges.[3] At Cambridge, the King's Hall retained its primatial position until rivalled by King's College from the mid-fifteenth century: even so, and until its dissolution in 1546 to give way to Henry VIII's foundation, Trinity College, it was still commonly regarded by contemporary

---

[1] See A. B. Cobban, *The King's Hall within the University of Cambridge in the later Middle Ages* (Cambridge, 1969) (cited hereafter as *The King's Hall.*) For its general academic and governmental significance see esp. ch. 1.

[2] On the constitutional aspects see *ibid.*, ch. 5.

[3] For details of numbers at the King's Hall and other English secular colleges see *ibid.*, pp. 44–6 and A. B. Cobban, *The Medieval Universities: Their Development and Organization* (London, 1975), pp. 138–9.

opinion as the 'oracle' of Cambridge University.[4] As an adjunct to the royal household and to the court circle it is fascinating that civil law was the principal superior faculty concentration at the King's Hall and that from the early fourteenth century English kings had deliberately fostered this discipline at the college. Under royal patronage the college became the most important single cradle of civil law graduates in Cambridge, producing, for example, about one fifth of the university's known total of legists in the period between *c.*1350 and *c.*1450.[5] This suggests that the King's Hall was intended by the monarchy as one of the several agencies used by the Crown to promote civil law studies in medieval England, a policy which, apart from the production of civilians to satisfy England's military diplomacy and conciliarist needs, was also designed to engender a climate of legal thought generally favourable to the accentuation of royal prerogative power. Although All Souls was probably the most significant of the Oxford colleges in this respect, it would appear that the King's Hall made a proportionately higher contribution to the output of university civil lawyers than any other English secular college.

The role of the King's Hall with regard to the growth of collegiate tutorial and lecture systems, which were fundamental to the transformation of medieval Oxford and Cambridge from universities of a centripetal to a centrifugal character, was given prominence in my doctoral thesis accepted in 1965 and later in my book on the King's Hall published in 1969. Extensive archival research in Oxford colleges in recent years, while serving to reinforce the original conclusions concerning the King's Hall and collegiate teaching, has, at the same time, fleshed them out and refined the perspective. And it is on this teaching aspect that this brief essay will now concentrate.

The growth of decentralised teaching in the medieval English universities, which so completely transformed their nature, had a tripartite institutional source. It was an amalgam of the tutorial and lecturing facilities which evolved in the monastic colleges, in the halls or hostels, and in the secular colleges. It would appear that such facilities were established first in the monastic colleges and in the halls, and it is highly probable that these influenced the teaching and tutorial arrangements of the secular colleges, which, by the time of the Reformation, had become the primary teaching units in the English universities.

[4] See Cobban, *The King's Hall*, p. 46, n. 1.
[5] On civil law at the King's Hall see *ibid.*, pp. 255–8.

Considerations of space preclude an examination of the monastic and aularian contribution to teaching forms;[6] and for the purposes of the present discussion it has to be assumed that the former was of some significance and the latter was substantial and that combined they provided an influential backcloth against which secular collegiate teaching emerged and crystallised.

In the majority of the early English secular colleges, which were graduate societies designed not to give a general arts education but a diet of advanced arts and superior faculty studies, there were arrangements whereby the senior members would aid and teach younger colleagues who were incorporated fellows possessed of at least an arts degree.[7] These supervisory provisions were so informal that they scarcely amounted to a system: and there is no suggestion, at this juncture, that the younger fellows would vest control of their finances in the hands of senior colleagues; and thus there is no trace in the early stages of English secular collegiate development of the controlling financial aspect of the tutorial system. What is here displayed is the simplest kind of tutorial organisation, wholly informal, unpaid, and confined solely to members of the college. In the late thirteenth and fourteenth centuries there is no evidence in the secular colleges of the internal lectures found in the contemporary monastic colleges and halls.

It is still valid to conclude that the King's Hall, Cambridge, and not New College, Oxford, was the first English college to incorporate a sizeable undergraduate element which, at the same time, formed an integral part of the institution. The general situation would appear to be that, prior to the foundation of New College in 1379, several English secular colleges made a nominal gesture towards undergraduate intake but that little of consequence materialised from this.[8] More importantly, Merton College, Oxford, made provision for categories of students who were perhaps gravitating towards undergraduate status: clearly, this fact should not be minimised, but it must be stressed that these groups of students were housed mostly outside the college and were not incorporated undergraduate fellows after the

---

[6] For the contribution of the Oxford monastic colleges and halls to tutorial and lecture forms see A. B. Cobban, 'Decentralized Teaching in the Medieval English Universities', *History of Education*, v (1976), pp. 193–4, 199–200.

[7] See e.g. the supervisory arrangements at Merton College prescribed in the statutes of 1270 in *Statutes of the Colleges of Oxford* (Oxford and London, 1853), I, ch. 2, p. 12 (cited hereafter as *Statutes*); and for similar arrangements at Peterhouse, Cambridge, see *Documents relating to the University and Colleges of Cambridge* (London, 1852), II, p. 12.

[8] The evidence is discussed by Cobban, *The King's Hall*, pp. 50–3.

manner of the King's Hall and New College.[9] It is therefore apparent that, as a college which accommodated an association of university scholars engaged in study from undergraduate to doctoral level, the King's Hall must be deemed the archetypal mixed secular collegiate society. Such an academic framework may well have encouraged the early growth of internal teaching facilities: whatever the case, among the unusually copious records of the King's Hall there is no reference to tutorial or lecturing arrangements in the fourteenth century.

The first traceable development in this matter of collegiate teaching which can definitely be established, and leaving aside the special instance of Merton College, is the salaried tutorial system devised by William of Wykeham for New College towards the end of the fourteenth century. This system involved setting apart a sum of 100s. from college funds as payment for fellows or scholars who were to act as tutors (*informatores*) to younger fellows or scholars during their first three years of residence.[10] Neither in the New College statutes nor in the domestic records of the late fourteenth and fifteenth centuries is there any indication that these tutorial facilities were extended to students who were not college members (that is, to undergraduate commoners). An examination of the New College Bursars' and Receipt Rolls to 1500 reveals that instruction by fellows of the college, as *informatores*, was afforded only to fellows and scholars on the foundation.[11] Moreover, there is nothing to show that the finances of Wykeham's tutees were controlled by the fellows or senior scholars who acted as their tutors. From the cumulative data of the New College Bursars' and Receipt Rolls it seems that *informatores* should be taken in the sense of tutors and not of lecturers as is sometimes suggested.[12]

The temptation to exaggerate Wykeham's contribution to the college tutorial system must be resisted. In effect, Wykeham formalised and buttressed by payment the informal unremunerated tutorial practices to be found in the earlier secular colleges, his arrangements being confined to members on the foundation. If the tutorial system were to grow it would be essential to open up college teaching to

---

[9] See Cobban, 'Decentralized Teaching', p. 198.   [10] *Statutes*, I, ch. 5, p. 54.

[11] I have consulted all the New College Bursars' and Receipt Rolls between 1376–7 and 1498–9 (deposited in New College Muniment Tower): a guide to these records has been compiled by F. W. Steer, *The Archives of New College, Oxford* (London and Chichester, 1974). Further details of the New College tutorial arrangements are given by Cobban, 'Decentralized Teaching', p. 196.

[12] See e.g. the discussion by M. H. Curtis, *Oxford and Cambridge in Transition 1558–1642* (Oxford, 1959), pp. 102–3, 284, n. G.

undergraduate commoners who were not foundation members. It cannot be determined that the King's Hall ever possessed a salaried tutorial system in the Wykehamite sense, but from the 1430s there is sustained evidence that the college made tutorial facilities available to private pupils who were introduced from outside and who did not have fellowship status: moreover, it is established that those fellows who acted as tutors to pupils of this kind were accountable to the college administration for the expenses incurred by their charges.[13] The King's Hall evidence delineates a situation whereby several of the fellows stood in the relation of *in loco parentis* to a number of pupils for whose finances they had assumed responsibility. At least four of the seventeen known fellows who acted as tutors supervised two or more pupils at a time: but the supervision of a single pupil was the more usual pattern. Some of the fellow-tutors retained pupils for several years; others kept pupils for parts of one or two academic sessions. It is unlikely that the tuition of private pupils (*pupilli*) at the King's Hall ever amounted to a regular system. The intermittent nature of the data for undergraduate commoners indicates that the initiative lay with the individual fellow who wished to supplement his income with tutorial fees rather than with the college as a collectivity. This situation implies that every graduate fellow was a potential tutor and that tutoring work was geared to an open competitive market with no attempt yet made to confine tutorial functions to a few fellows appointed by the college governing body, an elastic arrangement still operating in several of the post-Reformation Cambridge colleges including Gonville and Caius and Trinity.[14] For the English secular colleges this King's Hall material furnishes some of the earliest known evidence concerning that form of tutorial organisation embracing undergraduates introduced into the college for instruction, with the accompanying regulation of the pupil's finances vested in the hands of a number of fellow-tutors. It is possible that there were similar tutorial births in English colleges before their appearance at the King's Hall in the early fifteenth century, but the many sets of college records examined have not yielded much concrete information on this elusive point. In this connection, however, the

---

13 For a full analysis of the King's Hall tutorial evidence relating to undergraduate commoners see Cobban, *The King's Hall*, pp. 67 ff.

14 For tutorial arrangements at Gonville and Caius in the late sixteenth and seventeenth centuries see J. Venn, *Biographical History of Gonville and Caius College*, III (Cambridge, 1901), pp. 251–2; and for similar provisions at Trinity see W. W. Rouse Ball, *Cambridge Papers* (London, 1918), ch. 2, esp. pp. 31–6.

special circumstances prevailing at Merton College, Oxford, must be mentioned. Walter de Merton had made provision for the grammatical instruction of a number of *parvuli*, needy and orphan children of the founder's kin, the most promising of whom might be advanced to the status of scholar:[15] the *parvuli* remained the special care of the warden, and were treated as part of his household, but they lived, for the most part, outside the college in rented hospices with their own instructors.[16] From the combined testimony of the sub-wardens' rolls and the later separate rolls for these *pueri de genere fundatoris*[17] it seems clear that a kind of tutorial system was in operation, involving grammar masters, sub-wardens, and perhaps one or two fellows of the college, whereby these boys of the founder's kin received a measure of academic, financial and moral supervision. Similar considerations apply to Merton's other category of external scholars, *scolares in villa degentes*, the poor secondary scholars who seem to have been studying grammar under a master and, at times, one or two fellows of the college: and also to their successors from *c*.1380, the maintained poor scholars or portionists of John Wylyot, a fellow and sub-warden of Merton.[18] These Mertonian groups of scholars were neither undergraduate fellows nor, because they were supported, were they undergraduate commoners in the usual sense: but that they were regulated by a form of tutorial organisation is a circumstance of undeniable interest in English academic history.

The admission of undergraduate commoners for tutorial purposes at the King's Hall is an event of primary academic import. It can no longer be asserted that the entry of undergraduate commoners is an innovation associated with William Waynflete's Magdalen College, Oxford, founded in 1448, where the founder's statutes of 1479/80 made allowance for the admission of up to twenty commoners who were to be the sons of nobles or other worthy persons and were to live in college at their own expense under the direction of a tutor.[19] Whatever

---

[15] *Statutes*, I, ch. 2, p. 6 (code of 1264). The provision is repeated in the code of 1270 where the maximum number of *parvuli* is given as both thirteen and fifteen: *ibid.*, p. 17. In the code of 1274 the maximum is given as thirteen: *ibid.*, p. 36.

[16] See J. R. L. Highfield, ed., *The Early Rolls of Merton College, Oxford*, Oxf. Hist. Soc., n.s. XVIII (1964), p. 72.

[17] See e.g. Merton Rolls, 3973e, 3973f, 3974, 3974d, 3974e, 3976, 4116, 4117 (deposited in Merton College Muniments). Merton Roll 4117 for 1459–60 is particularly interesting as it lists the expenses of Thomas Lee, a scholar of the founder's kin, and it indicates that his finances were vested in the regulating hands of the sub-warden, John Yonge, as tutor (*creditor*).

[18] On the *scolares in villa* and Wylyot's portionists see Highfield, *Early Rolls*, pp. 72–4.

[19] *Statutes*, II, ch. 8, p. 60: the commoners were to be *sub tutela et regimine creditorum vulgariter creancers nuncupatorum*.

impact Waynflete's 'commoner' provisions may have had on later collegiate life, there can be no doubt that undergraduate commoners formed part of the complement of the King's Hall at least some fifty years previously. (Graduate commoners were present at the King's Hall from the first half of the fourteenth century.) Moreover, from the Magdalen domestic records of the fifteenth century it seems that before *c.*1500 undergraduate commoners were not resident in the college in any numbers, although they probably included John Colet, the humanist scholar and re-founder of St Paul's School, London, Richard Fox, the future bishop of Winchester and founder of the humanist haven, Corpus Christi College, Oxford, and Richard Whittinton, the distinguished grammarian.[20]

The apparent dearth of undergraduate commoners is one of the more arresting features of the Oxford colleges of the later medieval period. The more usual commoner element at Oxford comprised mature and mainly graduate commoners. University College, Oxford, is particularly interesting in having an impressively large number of regular mature commoners: in the University College Bursars' Rolls at least 187 commoners are named between 1385–6 and 1495–6.[21] The dimensions of the University College commoner population approach the order of magnitude of that of the King's Hall, both being unusually large for their respective universities. But apart from the odd undergraduate commoner of noble lineage who lived in college with his private tutor,[22] University College accommodated commoners of the mature type. And before their statutory inception at Magdalen there is not much evidence of colonies of undergraduate commoners in Oxford colleges. There is here, however, a caveat to be entered. Several of the Oxford colleges probably lodged a number of undergraduate commoners in halls closely associated with or annexed to the college: Merton and Oriel appear to have done so, Merton using Postmasters Hall and Oriel utilising Bedel Hall and St Mary

---

[20] This conclusion concerning the paucity of commoners is based upon an analysis of the Magdalen College Bursars' Book for 1476/7–86 and the *Libri Computi* for 1481–8 and 1490–1510 (deposited in Magdalen College Muniments). J. R. Bloxam's notes on Magdalen commoners between 1460 and 1600 are of some slight assistance: Magdalen College Library, D. 7. 10.

[21] This information has been extracted from University College's magnificent series of Bursars' Rolls which begin in 1381–2 (deposited in University College Muniments).

[22] E.g. Robert Hungerford, later Lord Hungerford and Moleyns, was resident for three terms in 1437–8, and aged about 9 or 10 when living in college; and John Tiptoft, the future 'humanist' earl of Worcester, who resided between 1440–1 and 1443–4, was aged between about 13 and 16.

Hall.[23] As aularian students, the occupants of such halls would be governed by the official university statutes pertaining to halls and to curricular matters, and this may account for the paucity of references to undergraduate commoners in Oxford collegiate records. But even making allowance for this aularian commoner outlet, the infrequency with which undergraduate commoners occur in Oxford college documentation is a noticeable fact which should make us wary of exaggerating the extent of the undergraduate migration from the halls to the colleges before the sixteenth century.

The transformation of the English colleges from the 'graduate' norm to societies of graduates and undergraduates living a life in common brought with it the birth of the college lecture. A sign of things to come is found in the Oxford statute of 1409 which stipulated that those about to determine as bachelors were to have heard appropriate lectures given in the colleges or halls.[24] It is difficult to say if lectures were being delivered in any Oxford college as early as 1409. As previously mentioned, it seems that Wykeham's *informatores* at New College should be taken in the sense of tutors rather than lecturers. Whether or not there were lectures in secular colleges by 1409 (as in the monastic colleges and in the halls) the earliest concrete evidence of the college lecture would appear to be found at the Cambridge college of Godshouse which possessed its own lecturer or reader (*lector*) probably from its foundation in 1439. But Godshouse, later refounded as Christ's College, was an exceptional kind of college.[25] According to the founder, William Byngham, the *raison d'être* for the college was to alleviate the famine of grammar masters in the country and in the English universities by training undergraduates for the degree of master of grammar with a view to their becoming teachers in England's languishing grammar schools: and their training was entrusted to a reader or lecturer elected by the college. The Godshouse *lector* cannot be equated exactly with the later endowed lectureships which were established in English secular colleges first as a supplement to and then in competition with the lectures of the regent masters in the university schools. Arising from the particular grammatical needs of Godshouse

---

[23] On Bedel Hall and St Mary Hall see W. A. Pantin, 'The Halls and Schools of Medieval Oxford: an Attempt at Reconstruction', *Oxford Studies presented to Daniel Callus*, Oxf. Hist. Soc., n.s. XVI (1964), pp. 31ff., at pp. 41–6.

[24] *Statuta Antiqua Universitatis Oxoniensis*, ed. S. Gibson (Oxford, 1931), p. 200.

[25] On Godshouse see Cobban, *The King's Hall*, pp. 79–80; A. H. Lloyd, *The Early History of Christ's College, Cambridge* (Cambridge, 1934).

the provision of a *lector* was a *sine qua non* if the purpose of the foundation were to be implemented. For this reason, the Godshouse lecturer
does not easily fit into the mainstream development of the English
college lectureship.

The more characteristic type of endowed lectureship seems to have
made its *début* at Magdalen College, Oxford, where, by the statutes of
1479/80, provision was made for three lectureships: one in theology
and the other two in natural and moral philosophy respectively. All
three lecture courses were to be free and open to the entire university
community including members of the regular orders.[26] It may well be
that these lectureships were instituted slightly before the statutes of
1479/80 as the Magdalen College Bursars' Book of 1476/7–86 records
payments for these lecturers beginning apparantly *c*.1476–7.[27] In
addition, lecturers in logic appear on a regular basis from 1481–2.
There are annual entries for the stipends of the three statutory lecturers
in the Magdalen *Libri Computi* for 1481–8 and for 1490–1510.[28] In some
years the lectures in theology and philosophy were shared between two
lecturers but a single *lector* was the more usual pattern: in logic, however, two or three lecturers might be employed annually. From 1484–5
the surnames of the lecturers are normally supplied, and it is clear that
there was a fair measure of continuity in lecturer personnel. The
stipends of the *lectores* in the Magdalen records correspond to the
statutory rates: the theology *lector* was the most highly paid at £10 per
annum and the philosophy lecturers received £6.13s.4d. each; the
stipend of the logic lecturer, who is not specified in the statutes, was
£5 a year.

Shortly after the prototypal lectures at Magdalen, an endowed
lectureship in canon law was launched at the King's Hall, Cambridge,
towards the close of the fifteenth century. The lectureship, the outcome
of a legacy bequeathed to the King's Hall by Robert Bellamy, DCnL,
a fellow of the college from 1464–5 until his death in 1492, was to be of
a semi-public nature: Bellamy decreed that it was to be open and free
to the King's Hall fellows and to all other poor clerks studying in
Cambridge University, but that scholars outside the college with
sufficient financial support were to be excluded unless by special permission of the lecturer.[29] The first known Bellamy lecturer was master

---

[26] *Statutes*, II, ch. 8, pp. 47–9.   [27] Magdalen College Bursars' Book, 1476/7–86, fo. 5.
[28] Magdalen College *Libri Computi*, 1481–8, fos. 13v, 16, 43, 69v, 98v, 116, 141v, 173v; *Libri Computi*, 1490–1510, fos. 5v, 15v, 24, 38, 59v–60, 77, 92.
[29] On the Bellamy lectureship see Cobban, *The King's Hall*, pp. 77–9, 82.

Collett, a fellow of the college, whose stipend for a term in 1502–3 was 20s. It is probable that the lectureship was discontinued from 1528–9 but, if not, it would certainly have been abolished in 1535 when the study of canon law was suppressed at the English universities. The Bellamy lectureship in canon law clearly ranks among the earliest of English college lectureships. If the Godshouse *lector* is treated as an exceptional case, it follows that the King's Hall was the second of the English secular colleges known to have possessed a lectureship of a public (or at least semi-public) nature, and the first to furnish one in canon law.

But this lectureship in canon law was not the only contribution which the King's Hall made towards the growth of lecturing facilities at Cambridge. There is transient evidence that the college participated in the promotion of humanist studies in the university by staging, in the early sixteenth century, lectures in what appears to be elementary Greek.[30] It cannot be determined if the lectures were of a public or semi-public nature or if they were wholly confined to members of the college. This King's Hall evidence for Greek instruction occurs in 1517–18, five years after the first official course of Greek lectures at Oxford[31] and a year or so before regular Greek lectures were instituted at Cambridge;[32] and it occurs in the year following the foundation of Corpus Christi College, Oxford, and six years after that of St John's College, Cambridge, both of which, along with Magdalen College grammar school, were the influential university seats of humanist studies in England in the early sixteenth century. Thus, the King's Hall's flirtation with Greek is an interesting early example of an attempt made by an English college to further Greek studies through the medium of the lecture. In addition, it is noteworthy that, as a result of royal injunctions of 1535, the King's Hall instituted public lectures in Greek and Hebrew to be delivered in the university schools at the college's expense;[33] these lectures, which commenced in 1535–6, were still functioning in 1543–4 and must be seen as part of the abortive royal drive to shore up the crumbling wall of public instruction in the English universities. Also, the performance of classical plays, including the comedies of Terence, in the King's Hall in the early sixteenth century, has a certain interest both within a dramatic context and in the

---

[30] See *ibid.*, pp. 82–3.
[31] J. K. McConica, *English Humanists and Reformation Politics* (Oxford, 1965), p. 83.
[32] Regular public lectures in the humanities at Cambridge were provided from c.1518: *ibid.*, p. 80.
[33] See Cobban, *The King's Hall*, pp. 84–5.

realm of humanist studies.[34] The comedies of Terence were relatively new to Cambridge society when these productions were being staged in the King's Hall, although they had been part of the official grammar curriculum at Oxford from the opening years of the sixteenth century.

The emergence of tutorial and lecturing facilities in the halls and secular colleges had the effect of rendering the undergraduates less reliant upon the ordinary lectures of the regent masters, although, at Oxford, students were required to attend university lectures until at least the mid-sixteenth century.[35] The entrenchment of the endowed college lectureship heralded the progressive decline of public university instruction even if the full impact was delayed until well into the sixteenth century. Emulating the Magdalen and the King's Hall pattern, subsequent college lectureships were mostly of a public or semi-public nature, the statutes of the new foundations making provision for lectures *ab initio*, while most of the older colleges revised their constitutions to keep pace with what was tantamount to an academic revolution. Of the new colleges there was, however, one interesting exception: St Catharine's College, Cambridge, which opened in 1473, remained, during its formative years, a graduate society specialising in philosophy and theology and did not, in the late fifteenth and early sixteenth centuries, employ the services of college lecturers.[36]

Salaried lectureships[37] had been progressively adopted in the universities of southern Europe in the course of the thirteenth and fourteenth centuries: but the emergence of *nuclei* of salaried teachers in some of the northern universities was a late medieval development and Oxford and Cambridge were among the last to come to terms with this movement. This meant that for about three hundred years the English universities relied in large measure upon the necessary regency system, an economical method of lecturer recruitment whereby every new master of arts or doctor of theology or law had to teach for about two years. This system tended to promote excessive academic mobility and a bias towards the young and inexperienced teacher although these defects would be qualified by the proportion of lecturers who could remain at university for several years supported in part by a college fellowship or

---

[34] See *ibid.*, pp. 227–9.
[35] See W. A. Pantin, *Oxford Life in Oxford Archives* (Oxford, 1972), p. 36.
[36] See Cobban, 'Origins: Robert Wodelarke and St Catharine's', in *St Catharine's College 1473–1973*, ed. E. E. Rich (Leeds, 1973), pp. 1ff., at pp. 30–1 and *passim*.
[37] For the growth of the salaried lectureship in European universities see Cobban, *The Medieval Universities*, pp. 154–7.

by an ecclesiastical benefice or by a religious order. In the English situation the problem of lecturer stability was solved primarily through the medium of the secular colleges which became the central *foci* of endowed teaching. The college lectureship was the chief agency by which Oxford and Cambridge were translated into decentralised universities based upon the collegiate unit, a movement more diffused in England than at Paris University where a similar development occurred.[38] At Oxford and Cambridge even modest colleges would provide nuclear teaching although they might have recourse to drawing upon the instructional aid of colleges designed on a more grandiose teaching scale. In general, however, England avoided the two-tier collegiate situation of late medieval Paris wherein the majority of the colleges were educationally dependent on a minority of prominent institutions.

It is true that a belated attempt was made to halt the decentralising process by regenerating English university teaching through the sporadic funding of salaried lecturers who would form part of the university's contingent of teachers and not part of the college network.[39] Events were set in motion with the Lady Margaret Beaufort Chairs of Divinity permanently established at Oxford and Cambridge by 1503, although, as readerships, they had probably been in operation from 1497. Her lead was followed by Sir Robert Rede, Chief Justice of Common Pleas, who, in his will of *c.*1519, left money for three Cambridge readerships in philosophy, logic and rhetoric. The movement was crowned with the establishment at both universities of Henry VIII's Regius Chairs of Divinity, Civil Law, Physics, Hebrew and Greek. But despite these impressive-looking efforts to prop up public university instruction, they proved in the event to be palliatives, a series of cosmetics both too late and too little to prevent the centre of teaching gravity from moving relentlessly and fixedly to the college sector.

In the broad perspective of English academic history, and insofar as individual colleges served to shape and promote the college-orientated English universities, it may be argued that the King's Hall, Cambridge, occupies a not unimportant role. As the prototype *par excellence* of the mixed collegiate society, incorporating undergraduate members on the

---

[38] *Ibid.*, pp. 131–2.
[39] For this movement see Curtis, *Oxford and Cambridge in Transition*, p. 101, with notes; also Cobban, *The King's Hall*, pp. 81–2.

foundation and which became the distinguishing hallmark of the colleges of post-Reformation England, this royal enterprise cannot but have been an influential point of reference. And the King's Hall evidence for the admission of undergraduate commoners and the tutorial arrangements, dating from the 1430s, made for their academic and financial supervision, combined with that for the second known college lectureship of a mainly public character, and taken in conjunction with the early sixteenth-century data for the staging of internal Greek lectures and Latin plays and for lectures in Greek and Hebrew delivered in the university schools, would all seem to indicate that the King's Hall stood in the forefront of educational change, finely attuned and adaptable to the academic needs of the age. When, to this university contribution, is added the functioning of the King's Hall as an educational supplement to the royal household and to the court, it is clear that this regal Cambridge foundation must be reckoned among the more distinctive of English secular colleges of the medieval period.

A FOURTEENTH-CENTURY CONTRIBUTION TO THE THEORY OF CITIZENSHIP: POLITICAL MAN AND THE PROBLEM OF CREATED CITIZENSHIP IN THE THOUGHT OF BALDUS DE UBALDIS

by JOSEPH P. CANNING

I

ONE of the major bodies of sources for the reconstruction of the history of medieval political thought is provided by the works of the medieval jurists, both civilians and canonists. This essay is concerned with the political ideas of one of these jurists, the Italian Baldus de Ubaldis (d. 1400). Baldus and his colleague and teacher, Bartolus of Sassoferrato, were the most famous and influential of the Commentators (or Postglossators). Originating in the second half of the thirteenth century, this school of jurists dominated Roman Law studies from the early fourteenth century until the late sixteenth, although in the later period their predominance was disputed by the emergence of legal humanism. Baldus was also a canonist of renown. Both within his lifetime and beyond he achieved a European-wide fame. In Italy itself the great influence of Baldus's ideas was assured both by the emphasis which Italian university education placed on legal studies, and by the revered status which the courts accorded to his works together with those of Bartolus.[1]

That one should turn to a jurist such as Baldus for a contribution to

---

[1] Despite the importance of Baldus's work there has been a marked paucity of modern studies of his writings. For instance, only three monographs devoted to aspects of his ideas have been produced: J. P. Canning, 'The Political Thought of Baldus de Ubaldis' (unpublished Cambridge Ph.D. dissertation, 1974); N. Horn, *Aequitas in den Lehren des Baldus*, Forschungen zur neueren Privatrechtsgeschichte, XI (Cologne–Graz, 1968); and J. A. Wahl, 'Baldus de Ubaldis' Concept of State: a Study in Fourteenth-Century Legal Theory' (unpublished University of St Louis Ph.D. dissertation, 1968). See also *L'opera di Baldo, per cura dell'Università di Perugia* (Perugia, 1901), a collection of essays to mark the five-hundredth anniversary of Baldus's death. For a list of a number of articles devoted to Baldus see Horn, 'Die legistische Literatur der Kommentatoren und der Ausbreitung des gelehrten Rechts', in H. Coing, ed, *Handbuch der Quellen und Literatur der neueren europäischen Privatrechtsgeschichte, I – Mittelalter, 1100–1500* (Munich, 1973), p. 273.

the development of political thought should cause no surprise. So much of late medieval political theory was couched in juristic language; and furthermore the jurists gave extensive treatment to so many questions which may be considered as aspects of political thought. Baldus's own political theory is important, both because of the intrinsic interest of his ideas, and because of the influence which these ideas exercised on his contemporaries and later generations of jurists and political thinkers. Baldus's political thought is, indeed, distinguished by the broad sweep of topics which he considers: in this respect his treatment is more extensive than that of Bartolus. In his political theory Baldus examines both government by the people and monarchy. Although his ideas concerning monarchy are very important, his major contribution is to the theory of government by the people, and it is within this area that the particular subject of this essay lies: namely Baldus's contribution to the theory of citizenship.

II

In his treatment of popular[2] government Baldus seeks primarily to provide a theory to describe and account for the phenomenon of the independent Italian city-republics. In so doing Baldus, like Bartolus, attributes legal sovereignty to the autonomous city-community.[3] Bartolus had shown his originality in being the first jurist to uphold the view that the exercise of consent by the people, in the making of their customs and statutes, entailed the possession of legal sovereignty by the people.[4] He saw that the acceptance of consent as a law-creating element indicated that the ultimate power to make law rested in the hands of the people; and that the whole theocratic system, in which the divinely appointed superior makes law by his will, was thus excluded. Bartolus, by realising the full implications of consent as the constitutive element of law, was able to establish the conception of the *civitas que non recognoscit superiorem*,[5] which is in the position of a *populus liber*, and to which, as a sign of its sovereignty, he attributes the powers of the

---

[2] Throughout this essay I use the term, 'popular', in the sense of 'of' or 'by the people'.

[3] See Canning, 'Baldus', pp. 47–78.

[4] For Bartolus's political theory see especially C. N. S. Woolf, *Bartolus of Sassoferrato – his Position in the History of Medieval Political Thought* (Cambridge, 1913); and W. Ullmann, 'De Bartoli sententia: *concilium repraesentat mentem populi*', in *Bartolo da Sassoferrato – studi e documenti per il VI centenario* (2 vols., Milan, 1962), II, pp. 707–33.

[5] Bartolus *ad* D.1.1.9, fo. 85r–v (ed. Lyon, 1510).

princeps within its own territory (*civitas sibi princeps*).[6] Baldus incorporates and develops all these ideas of Bartolus, and includes some new ones of his own; but his most original contribution to the juristic theory of popular government lies in his development of the theme of citizenship. Baldus examines the status of the individual, who, as a member of an independent city-*populus*, is the bearer of political rights and duties, and governs himself through the exercise of his own consent. Bartolus in his theory of popular government demonstrates purely in juristic terms the independence of the *populus* and the *civitas*, and accords some attention to the *civis* as such, and to the concept of *civilitas*; Baldus, however, goes beyond his master by giving a more extensive treatment to the citizen, and to the concept of *civilitas* itself.

From at least the sixteenth century Baldus had a reputation of being the Commentator who made most use of philosophy.[7] In his theory of citizenship in particular he applies his knowledge of philosophy to produce highly creative results. Baldus is not content to erect a theory of citizenship and of popular government couched purely in juristic terms; rather he attempts to present a philosophical conception of man in society, in order to provide the foundation for the construction of a legal theory of citizenship and government by popular consent. To this end he adopts the concept of natural man, who becomes political in community – a concept which is the common coin of medieval political thought from the time of Aquinas, and which is ultimately derived from Aristotle. It does appear that, in terms of jurisprudence, Baldus in constructing a theory of citizenship based upon this conception of political man is expressing a thesis which is entirely novel. Within jurisprudence Baldus innovates; in the context of fourteenth-century political thought as a whole he gives further juristic definition and precision to aspects of the fundamental concept of citizenship. A claim may be made for great originality on Baldus's part for the extent to which, in his theory of popular government, he harnesses political conceptions of an ultimately Aristotelian parentage to medieval legal ideas of government. Baldus thus makes advances in jurisprudence in the process of exploring, where Bartolus did not, areas of thought fundamental to the theory of popular government.

[6] *Idem ad* D.4.4.3, fo. 117r (ead. ed.). For similar passages from Bartolus, see Woolf, *Bartolus*, pp. 155–8.

[7] See N. Horn, 'Philosophie in der Jurisprudenz der Kommentatoren: Baldus Philosophus', *Ius Commune*, I (1967), pp. 104–49; F. Calasso, *Medio evo del diritto*, I: *Le fonti* (Milan, 1954), p. 578; and W. Ullmann's review of Horn, *Aequitas*, in *RHD*, XXXVII (1969), p. 281: 'That his [i.e. Baldus's] jurisprudence was suffused with philosophical and ethical elements is undeniable.'

Baldus introduces this concept of natural, political man in a passage of great importance. He has been discussing the nature of the *populus*, and continues:

Dic incidenter quod homo potest tripliciter considerari. Vno modo prout est per se quoddam individuum ex anima et corpore naturaliter constitutum, ut (D.21.2.56, 2). Secundo modo potest considerari prout est quoddam corpus iconomicum, id est, princeps familie, ut (D.50.16.195, 1), sicut est paterfamilias et abbas monasterii. *Tertio modo potest considerari prout est quoddam corpus civile seu politicum* sicut est episcopus civitatis et potestas, et hoc si consideretur in preeminentia. *Sed si consideratur in congregatione tunc homo naturalis efficeretur politicus, et ex multis aggregatis fit populus,* ut (D.41.3.30). Iste populus quandoque muris cingitur, et incolit civitatem; et idem proprie dicitur politicus a polis quod est civitas. Alius est populus rusticanus qui habitat in castris vel villis, et ibi habet suum domicilium, ut supra (C.6.23.31).[8]

This is a passage into which a wealth of meaning has been compressed; its significance is that it presents a number of concepts fundamental to his theory of citizenship.

Baldus describes the citizen as *homo naturalis*. He intends this to signify, in this context, man as he is made up of body and soul (*ex anima et corpore naturaliter constitutum*). This definition is important for what it does not include: man is not considered here in his supranatural or theological aspect. In discussing man living in the *civitas*, making up the *populus*, no reference is made to his membership of the Christian community: man, the citizen, is simply man in his 'natural' state living in a city. His supranatural aspect is not under consideration. The concepts which the term, *natura*, and its derivatives denote in Baldus's works vary in meaning in different places; and the precise meaning attached to them is often obscure. The meaning of *homo naturalis* here is admittedly vague; but the consideration of man in community without recourse to theology is of crucial importance. Within the theocratic system the individual in society is in the first place a Christian, a *fidelis*; and the *fidelis* is necessarily subject to his superior, who gains his power from God, and gives to the subject whatever rights the latter possesses. As a result of his adoption of a 'natural' view Baldus makes possible the elaboration of a concept of the citizen, whose rights do not come from any superior, but are inherent. The *civis* had indeed featured in the writings of civilians before Bartolus,

[8] C.7.53.5. Unless otherwise stated I have used the [Lyon], 1498, edition of Baldus's commentaries on the *Digesta*, and on *Codex*, I-IX; the Pavia, 1495, edition of his commentary on the Feudal Law; and the Lyon, 1551, edition of his commentary on the *Decretales*.

but had no connotation of active citizenship in the sense of the possession of full and indigenous political rights and duties – the *civis* belonged
to a *civitas* subject to a superior.[9]

The theocratic conception of the government of society depended
upon a 'total' view of man. The resurrection of Aristotelian political
ideas produced the dissolution of this 'total' view, what Walter
Ullmann has called the 'atomization' of man:[10] it was now possible to
distinguish between the different characteristics possessed by man in his
various activities. *Homo iconomicus* could be differentiated from *homo
politicus*: most important of all *homo christianus* could be considered
separately from *homo politicus*. That is to say natural man could be
considered as existing, as a citizen, on a political plane, a plane which
was quite distinct from that of his life as a Christian. It became possible,
therefore, to bypass the postulates of the theocratic system, which was
operative only within a Christian framework. Baldus in his commentary on C.7.53.5 adopts these divisions of the activities of natural
man: he is an individual; he is (and here Baldus follows Aristotle's
description of man's major activities)[11] an economic body (*corpus
iconomicum*); and he is a civil or political entity (*corpus civile seu politicum*)
– that is to say, a citizen. Thus Baldus maintains that man in the society
of a city becomes a particular kind of human being: a citizen. The
individual assumes in congregation a specific characteristic which he
lacks in isolation. This fragmentation of man by Baldus and his conception of a separate political field of activity for natural man provide
the context for the development of a theory of active citizenship – the
antithesis of the existence of the subject. Elsewhere Baldus, in defining
the *causa finalis* of jurisprudence, uses the same tripartite division of
human activity:

Causa finalis (artis nostre) est triplex, scilicet in homine, ad hominem, et ad rempublicam. In homine, ut bonus sit; et hoc pertinet ad ethicam. Ad hominem, ut quis
bene regat familiam; et hoc pertinet ad economicam. Ad rempublicam, ut respublica
salubriter regatur; et hoc pertinet ad politicam, supra in (D.Const., 'Omnem', 11).[12]

In his commentary on C.7.53.5 Baldus presents a fundamental aspect
of citizenship: the citizen is natural man in congregation, and specifically

---

[9] For an exception see Jacobus de Ravannis *ad* C.7.33.12, fo. 344v (ed. Paris, 1519): 'hodie
vacante imperio civitates regunt seipsas; et una civitas regit seipsam, nec habet superiorem'.
[10] *A History of Political Thought: the Middle Ages* (London, 1965), pp. 169–70.
[11] Aristotle, for instance, devotes to economics the greater part of *Politics*, Book I, with which as
we shall see Baldus is familiar: economics is a necessary introduction to politics (1253b).
[12] D.1.1.Rubr., n. 20.

in a *populus*, which inhabits a city. A *populus* inhabiting a *castrum* or *villa* is not political.[13] Baldus thus sets the scale of political activity by indicating in general terms the size and kind of group in which it takes place. He does not incidentally express any opinions on the desirable size of a city, but merely declares:

Dicit Aristotiles, communis custodia regni et civitatis est non sinere illum crescere preter commensurationem.[14]

He does not, however, adopt any of Aristotle's recommendations concerning the optimal extent of a city.

It does appear that Baldus was the first jurist to utilise the ultimately Aristotelian conception of political man as citizen. Previous jurists do mention Aristotle's *Politics*, and make some very small use of it.[15] But the point is that previous and contemporary jurists develop no theory of citizenship from Aristotle's *Politics*. Lucas de Penna, who was Baldus's contemporary, but who appears to have worked completely separately from him, does, indeed, in an important passage use the term 'political', but not in any sense related to citizenship and government by the people.[16]

Baldus's conception of the nature of law itself is affected by his idea of political man. In a juristic general statement Baldus indicates that law should be in harmony with the needs of political man:

Nota ibi 'naturalia et civilia' quod homo naturaliter est animal civile; et lex similis debet esse homini bene composito et civili.[17]

In saying that man is by nature a civil animal, he adopts one of the most well-known, if not hackneyed, phrases in Aristotle's *Politics*.[18] (In William of Moerbeke's translation *civile* renders πολιτικόν;[19] and, as we have seen, Baldus equates *civile* with *politicum*). In terms of

---

13 This contrast between the political life of the city-*populus*, and the non-political life of the country-dwellers reflects the general condition in fourteenth-century Italy, in which the city ruled its subject *contado*. Cp. Baldus *ad* X.1.31.3 (below, p. 207).

14 *Feud.*, II, 53 (fo. 77r). Cf. Aristotle, *Politics*, 1325b ff.

15 Albericus de Rosciate, for instance, refers to *Pol.*, II, c. 4, in his commentaries on D.1.1.1, 2 and D.3.4.1. Bartolus refers to *Pol.*, III, in his tract, *De regimine civitatis*, pp. 417–18 (ed. Basel, 1589).

16 See Lucas *ad* C.11.59.7, n. 8, p. 563 (ed. Lyon, 1597): 'Inter principem et rempublicam matrimonium morale contrahitur et politicum'; *ibid.*, p. 564; 'Moraliter et politice homines coniunguntur reipublice, que corpus est, cuius caput est princeps'; and *ad* C.12.43.3, n. 12 (p. 897): 'Sicut anima est salus et vita corporis, sic rex et huiusmodi principes, si recte principantur, sunt salus et vita regnorum, ut patet per Aristotelem 4. Politic.'

17 D.1.3.2, n. 3. Cf. D.1.3.2: 'Lex est omnium divinarum et humanarum rerum notitia . . . regula est iustorum et iniustorum et eorum que natura civilia sunt', fo. 8r (ed. Venice, 1494).

18 1253a: 'ὁ ἄνθρωπος φύσει πολιτικὸν ζῷον'.

19 William of Moerbeke translates the phrase as, 'homo natura civile animal est' (ed. Susemihl).

fourteenth-century political thought the use of this phrase alone would be unremarkable; as regards jurisprudence, however, its employment is an innovation. The true importance of Baldus's introduction here of this Aristotelian concept lies in his application of it to the law.[20] Aquinas and Marsilius had, of course, used both legal ideas of government and Aristotelian political concepts. They, however, approached law from political philosophy; Baldus has his own contribution to make, because he approaches political theory from law with an expert knowledge of the latter, which Thomas and Marsilius lacked.[21] This passage provides a basis for the juristic elaboration of the theme of citizenship by appealing to nature as the source of the legal norms which govern the life of political man, and by thus supplanting theocratic conceptions: the law affecting the individual's place in society does not find its origin in the will of a divinely appointed ruler.

In this passage there is contained a play on the word '*civilis*': *lex* is 'civil' in an Aristotelian sense; it is also 'civil' in the sense that enacted law is, in the terminology of Roman law, part of *ius civile*.[22] This illustrates the semantic ease with which Baldus is able to combine Aristotelian political concepts with Roman law ideas of government. He is aided in this by the community of terms, such as *civis*, *civitas*, and *civilis*, existing between Roman law and medieval versions of Aristotelian political ideas.[23] William of Moerbeke, for instance, when translating Aristotle's *Politics*, was constrained in his rendering of Greek concepts by the concepts and terms available to him in Latin. Apart

---

[20] From the context of Baldus's statement it is clear that he is not discussing a particular *lex*, but *lex* in the sense of human enacted law in general: 'Hic ponitur diffinitio Greca. Nota quod lex est inventio et donum dei. Item nota quod lex est princeps, dux et regula. Nota quod et iusticia et iniusticia indigent ordine. Nota ibi "naturalia et civilia" ...'.

[21] For Aquinas's use of Roman Law, see J.-M. Aubert, *Le Droit romain dans l'œuvre de S. Thomas* (Paris, 1955). See especially Aubert's conclusion: 'Ainsi, sans être dans son œuvre un juriste à proprement parler, et malgré les déficiences imputables à une carence de formation juridique, saint Thomas se situe cependent admirablement dans la ligne spirituelle des grands romanistes médiévaux qui, au dire de Sohm, ont été les fondateurs de la science moderne du droit' (pp. 138–9). For Marsilius's knowledge of Roman and canon law see A. Gewirth, *Marsilius of Padua – the Defender of Peace* (2 vols., New York, 1951 and 1956), I, pp. 248ff.; E. Lewis, 'The "Positivism" of Marsiglio of Padua', *Speculum*, XXXVIII (1963), pp. 541–82; and M. J. Wilks, 'Corporation and Representation in the Defensor Pacis', *Studia Gratiana*, ed. J. Forchielli and A. M. Stickler, XV (1972), pp. 251–92 (and esp. pp. 254–5).

[22] See, for instance, D.1.1.9: 'quod quisque populus ipse sibi ius constituit, id ipsius proprium civitatis est vocaturque ius civile, quasi ius proprium ipsius civitatis'.

[23] Because of this community of terms it is very difficult to determine whether there is any germ of a conception of political man living in a political community, in Raynerius de Forlì *Rep. ad* D.1.1.9, n. 10, in Albericus de Rosciate, *Commentariorum Pars Prima super Digesto Veteri* (Lyon, 1545), fo. 17v.

from transliterations, like *politia* and *politicus*, William in translating such terms as πόλις, πολίτης, and πολιτικός also had recourse to the only Latin terms available, namely *civitas, civis,* and *civilis*.[24] Thus *civis* came to bear Aristotelian connotations.

Baldus's statement, '*lex similis debet esse homini bene composito et civili*', illustrates his conception of the relationship between enacted law and political society. In the context of a city or a *populus* a system of civil law (that is the law made by the city or *populus*) is understood as existing within a political order. Baldus expresses this elsewhere in a complicated passage in which the play on the legal and political meanings of 'civil' again appears:

Vbi vero est tribunal, ibi aliquam politicam et regulam necesse est esse que dici potest ius civile, id est ius vivendi sub quadam specie civilitatis.[25]

Civilitas is a term which in Baldus's works usually signifies citizenship; here it appears to mean something like 'civil order', with both legal and political connotations. Thus *ius civile* as the *ius vivendi sub quadam specie civilitatis* signifies the law according to which one lives in a civil or political order or system. Law provides a structure for political life.

Baldus's concept of man as a civil or political animal is part of his wider view of man as a social animal: the citizen is a particular kind of social man. For his conception of man as a social animal Baldus is indebted to Aquinas. He does not, however, acknowledge Aquinas as the source of the idea, but attributes it to Aristotle, referring to *Politics*, Book I. This appears in a passage in which Baldus maintains that because man is a social animal, law must be suited to man in society:

Quia homo est animal sociale, ut in primo Politicorum, competunt sibi iura, que societatis sunt, et iura civitatis sue.[26]

This complements his conception of political man as being subject to political legal norms.

Aristotle, of course, did not call man a 'social animal'. The concept is not to be found in the Greek text of the *Politics* nor in William of Moerbeke's translation. Aquinas introduced the concept of man as a

---

[24] Out of a host of examples, see especially William, *ed. cit.*, pp. 150–1.

[25] *Feud.*, I, 8 (Additio), fo. 19v (ed. Lyon, 1585).

[26] D.1.1.1,1 (Additio), n. 4 (ed. Venice, 1616). Cf. also *idem ad* X.2.1.10, n. 1 (fo. 188r). Cp. Lucas de Penna *ad* C.10.38.1, nn. 5–6, p. 221 (*ed. cit.*): 'Et homo sociale animal communi bono genitus est, dicit Seneca, lib. de clementia.'

sociale animal, and quoted as his source *Politics*, Book I, thus putting his own gloss on Aristotle:

Homo est naturaliter animal politicum et sociale, ut probatur in I Politicorum.[27]

Aquinas's definition of man as a 'political and social animal', and his attribution of the source of this concept to Book I of the *Politics*, were extremely well known, and easily accessible to Baldus. It is also possible that Baldus obtained this idea from Aquinas's commentary on Book I of the *Politics*. Upon this text in William of Moerbeke's translation:

Ex hiis igitur manifestum, quod eorum quae natura civitas est, et quod homo natura civile animal est,[28]

Aquinas comments:

Deinde cum dicit 'ex iis igitur'
Ostendit, quod homo sit naturaliter civile animal. Et primo concludit hoc ex naturalitate civitatis. Secundo probat hoc per operationem propriam ipsius, ibi, 'Ex quo patet sociale animal etc.'.[29]

Again Aquinas introduces his own interpretation of the words of Aristotle.

In sum, the major significance of Baldus's use of the concept of natural man, who becomes political in the city-community is this: such a community, being composed of men of this kind, is not dependent upon any other human agency (that is, a superior) for its existence or for its legal and political rights. Baldus has thus provided a philosophical foundation for his juristic elaboration of the theme of the city-community as an autogenous, fully independent and self-governing corporation of citizens. It is true that Baldus in a highly important passage in his commentary on *l. Omnes populi* also appeals to the *ius*

[27] *Summa Theologiae*, 1a2ae, q.72, art. 4, ed. J. Fearson (London, 1969). Cf. also *S.T.*, 1a2ae, q. 95, art. 4: 'Homo est naturaliter animal sociabile, ut probatur in I Politicorum', ed. T. Gilby (London, 1966). Aquinas is normally understood to have introduced the concept of man as a social animal. Albertus Magnus, however, also uses the term, and attributes it as well to Aristotle: 'Vlterius quaeritur utrum aliqua animalia debeant vivere in societate. (1) Videtur, quod non. Nam *"homo est animal civile" et sociale per Philosophum I Politicae*, et ideo vita hominis regitur per politicam et oeconomicam. Si ergo omnia animalia essent sociabilia, haberent regi per politicam et oeconomicam, quod non est verum, quia politica est virtus humana', *Quaestiones de Animalibus*, I, qu. 8, ed. E. Filthaut (Münster, 1955), p. 85. According to Filthaut (p. xlvi), Albert's *Quaestiones de Animalibus* were probably first delivered in 1258, and were written down in the form in which we have them 'multo ante a. 1300'. With this amount of uncertainty it is impossible to say whether Albert was the first to call man a social animal.
[28] *Ed. cit.*, p. 7.
[29] *Pol.*, I, lectio I, n. 34, ed. Spiazzi, p. 11.

gentium as an explanation of why the people is not dependent on a superior for its genesis and government:

Nota ergo quod populi possunt sibi facere statuta. . . . Modo restat videre numquid in tali statuto requiratur auctoritas superioris. Videtur quod non quia populi sunt de iure gentium ergo regimen populi est de iure gentium, ut supra (D.1.1.5). Sed regimen non potest esse sine legibus et statutis. Ergo eo ipso quod populus habet esse habet per consequens regimen in suo esse, sicut omne animal regitur a suo spiritu proprio et anima.[30]

This is, however, a good example of Baldus's arguing on a purely juristic level, and should not be seen as being in conflict with his philosophical argument. Indeed the general problem posed for the interpreter of Baldus's political thought is that he elaborates the details of his theory of popular government in juristic terms, while this whole juristic edifice is constructed upon the philosophical foundation of his concept of natural, political man. This has two implications. Firstly, the content of Baldus's conceptions of citizenship can only be discovered from an examination of his treatment, conducted in juristic terms, of the various aspects of the city-community: its corporate nature, its organisation and structure of government, and the extent and limitations of its powers. Secondly, Baldus's juristic theory of popular government is complete within its own terms, but he is not satisfied with juristic constructions, such as those employed by Bartolus, demonstrating the sovereignty of the people. In his recourse to the *ius gentium* in his commentary on D.1.1.9, he exhausts the possibilities of juristic language for providing a fundamental explanation for popular sovereignty, and also in his usage of the concept of natural, political man stretches out into political philosophy to provide a foundation for his juristic theory.

Precisely because, however, Baldus elaborates his theory of popular government in juristic terms, his conception of political man, despite its importance, is tantalising. Baldus does little to explore further the conceptual possibilities opened up for jurisprudence by the adoption of the idea of natural man, who becomes political in the city-community. Apart from one example of a highly important application of the concept of political man to corporation-theory,[31] Baldus uses the concept, 'political', only on a few other occasions, all except one of

---

[30] D.1.1.9, nn. 3–4.
[31] C.7.53.5 (the passage in question occurs later in Baldus's commentary than the passage cited above, p. 200). For a full discussion of this passage see Canning, 'Baldus', pp. 127–9.

which serve only to indicate that politics is concerned with the government of the community.[32] At the profound level of the concept of natural, political man, and the relationship between him and law, Baldus rests content with what has already been quoted. He is not seeking to construct his theory of popular government in the language of political science.

In these remaining passages, in which Baldus employs the term 'political', no particular form of political government is envisaged by him. Only once does he intimate that politics is concerned with active participation in government by the community; and this he indicates in a somewhat obtuse way:

> Quedam sunt universitates, que habent regimen active, id est que habent regere; quedam passive tantum, id est que habent regi et non regere, ut rustici qui non participant politica, nam agricole non participant politica secundum Aristotelem.[33]

Here the theme of active citizenship could be developed using the language of political science; but this Baldus does not do. Perhaps Baldus missed his opportunity; perhaps, as a jurist, he felt that in going as far as he did in introducing concepts from political science he had gone far enough. It is important to remember that Baldus aimed at a juristic elaboration of popular government; but it is difficult not to wish that he had developed further his introduction of political conceptions into jurisprudence.

III

Although Baldus's conception of natural man's becoming political in the city-community constitutes his major contribution to the juristic theory of citizenship, he also accords a deep treatment to the specific problem of the person, who is created a citizen by legal enactment. This is a question to which the late medieval jurists gave a lot of attention. Their *consilia* reveal that problems concerning the status of created citizens were common. Indeed their theories concerning the legal status of the created citizen were of far more than academic interest, because in practical terms so many of the legal rights and

---

[32] For full details see Canning, 'Baldus', pp. 92–7. The exception is contained in Baldus *ad* D.1.1.1 (Additio), n. 7, fo. 8r (ed. Lyon, 1585), where he discusses the subject matter of jurisprudence: 'Subiectum est homo, qui per scientiam acquirit politicam, id est moralem, qualitatem seu philosophiam, per quam perfecte cognoscit, separat iustum a contrario, quia indicat quod iustum est.'

[33] X.1.31.3, n. 5 (fo. 151r). As regards Aristotle's exclusion of farmers from political life Baldus may well have in mind *Pol.* 1268a and 1328b–1329b.

duties of the created citizen depended upon the interpretation which the courts, in the light of the opinions of jurists, placed upon the content of acquired citizen status. Baldus himself gives an extensive, overt, and deep elaboration of the question of created citizenship. Indeed, it is here that Baldus gives his most detailed treatment of the concept of *civilitas* itself.[34]

For Baldus citizenship is not only the political aspect of the life of natural man; it is also a legal status. This status can be attained either by right of birth (*civilitas naturalis* or *originalis*), or by legal enactment (*civilitas civilis*). Both forms of citizenship are for Baldus full citizenship. The *civis naturalis*, the native citizen, is 'natural' in a different sense from the *homo naturalis*, who becomes political in the city-community. The reason is simple: the adjective, *naturalis*, may indicate both the element of birth (a root meaning of *natura*), and the attributes and activities of man viewed solely within the context of his existence in this world. Nevertheless Baldus's concept of *civilitas naturalis*, native citizenship, clearly fits in with his overall conception of natural, political man, because it indicates that citizen rights are inborn and inherent, and thus not given to the citizen by anyone else, such as a superior. Nor need there be any conflict involved between Baldus's concept of created citizenship and that of natural, political man. Baldus accepts that citizenship is an expression of man's nature; but this proposition does not dictate the possession of the citizenship of any particular city. It is perfectly possible for man's political nature to be expressed through citizenship granted by a city other than that of his birth – Baldus nowhere suggests otherwise. Furthermore, where the

---

34 This essay concentrates on the most important aspects of Baldus's theory of created citizenship. I propose to produce soon an extensive treatment of this topic. Already Baldus's ideas in this respect have attracted some interest: see J. Kirshner, '"Ars imitatur naturam": A Consilium of Baldus on Naturalization in Florence', *Viator*, v (1974), pp. 289-331; and J. Rummer, 'A Fourteenth-Century Legal Opinion', *The Quarterly Journal of the Library of Congress*, xxv (1968), pp. 179-93 (this is concerned with an autograph *consilium* of Baldus). For other jurists' theories of created citizenship see Kirshner, 'Paolo di Castro on *Cives ex Privilegio*: a Controversy over the Legal Qualifications for Public Office in Early Fifteenth-Century Florence', in *Renaissance Studies in Honor of Hans Baron*, ed. A. Molho and J. A. Tedeschi (De Kalb, Illinois, 1971), pp. 227-64; and *idem*, ' "Civitas sibi faciat civem": Bartolus of Sassoferrato's Doctrine of the Making of a Citizen', *Speculum*, xlviii (1973), pp. 694-713. For the general importance of citizenship in later medieval Italy (including discussions of created citizenship) see P. Riesenberg, 'Civism and Roman Law in Fourteenth-Century Italian Society', in *Economy, Society, and Government in Medieval Italy*, ed. D. Herlihy, R. S. Lopez and V. Slessarev (Ohio, 1969), pp. 237-54; *idem*, 'Citizenship and Equality in Late Medieval Italy', *Studia Gratiana*, xv (1972), pp. 425-39; and *idem*, 'Citizenship at Law in Late Medieval Italy', *Viator*, v (1974), pp. 333-46. Still very useful as a general treatment is D. Bizzari, 'Ricerche sul diritto di cittadinanza nella costituzione comunale', *Studi Senesi*, xxxii (1916), pp. 19-136.

city is independent, the ability to create citizens, and thus determine its own membership, is an aspect of its autonomy.

It had been Bartolus's achievement to demonstrate within juristic terms the full validity of created citizenship. Baldus substantially develops his master's work. Bartolus maintained that there were two *species* of citizen, original and created.[35] In seeking to determine the validity of created citizenship Bartolus proceded, as Baldus was also to do, to isolate the concept of citizenship itself. Bartolus's solution was thoroughly juristic: citizenship is a legal status created by the civil law. Thus both original citizenship and that resulting from legal enactment are on a par. Birth is no more than a qualification for citizenship. All citizens, in short, are made so by the law:

Est ergo constitutio iuris civilis que facit aliquem civem propter originem vel propter dignitatem vel propter adoptionem, ut (C.10.40.7). Vnde non est dicendum quod quidam sunt cives naturaliter, quidam civiliter. Immo est dicendum quod omnes sunt cives civiliter: aliqui tamen propter naturalem originem, aliqui propter aliam causam. Vnde si civitas facit statutum quod quicunque habet ibi domum sit civis, vere erit civis, ut (D.50.16.139 & 190; D.1.5.17).[36]

Thus Bartolus's two *species*, original and non-original, are differentiated by the qualification for citizenship (birth or another cause), and have in common the constitutive element of citizenship – the enactment of the civil law. It is not surprising that Bartolus, since he argues within a juristic frame of reference, comes to this solution. For him citizenship is a legal status created by human positive law. In the context of the *civitas que non recognoscit superiorem* the citizen-body would thus create citizenship. Furthermore Bartolus maintained that the formula, *habeatur pro cive*, so commonly applied to the new citizen in the city-legislation creating him such, signified truth rather than fiction when applied to what can be true and proper, and that therefore the created citizen received a true citizenship rather than a merely fictive one.[37]

35 See, for instance, Bartolus *ad* C.10.40.7.
36 Bartolus, *Cons.*, I, 62 (I have used Kirshner's text: *Speculum*, XLVIII (1973), p. 713).
37 D.41.3.15, nn. 35–36: 'Pone ergo statuit civitas, quod nullus possit effici civis nisi de voluntate maioris consilii, ipse presens in consilio recipiatur ut alii cives . . . In reformatione continetur quod habeatur pro cive talis qui erat presens in consilio. Et tunc aut dixit, quod habeatur pro cive quoad quedam tantum, et est civis secundum fictionem, arg. (D.14.6.2); aut dixit, quod habeatur pro cive quoad omnia, et tunc erit civis secundum veritatem, argu. eorum que supra dicta sunt. Et si opponis mihi quod ista oratio "habeatur pro cive etc." denotat fictionem, ut (D.35.1.24), respondeo quod denotantia fictionem et improprietatem, si apponantur in lege iuxta id quod potest esse verum secundum veritatem et proprietatem, magis dicuntur verba proprietatis et veritatis expressiva, quam improprietatis vel fictionis significativa, ut dicimus de verbo "quasi" (D.24.3.7; D.47.10.17,5; D.2.15.1).'

Baldus also, in the construction of his major argument concerning created citizenship, adopts the conceptual tools of *genus–species*, and *fictio–veritas*. But whereas Bartolus simply considers whether the created citizen is a true one or not, Baldus goes further and explores the sense in which the created citizen, while he is truly a citizen, is only fictively an original one. That is to say, Baldus seeks to explain how both forms of citizenship are valid, and how they relate to each other. To do this he designates *civilitas* itself as *genus*. Thus natural and created citizenship are *species* of citizenship. Created citizenship is, therefore, truly citizenship in that it as *species* is contained within its *genus*; but it can only fictively be considered as the other *species* (natural citizenship). Thus created citizenship is truly *civilitas civilis*, but only fictively *civilitas naturalis et originalis*. Perhaps the neatest expression of Baldus's argument is to be found in a passage dealing with another form of citizenship other than by birth – citizenship by prescription:

Dubitatur an quis possit prescribere civilitatem et privilegia civium alicuius terre. Videtur quod sic, excepta origine que prescribi non potest; sed commoda originis bene possunt prescribi, et erit simul iste civis verus et fictus originarius, id est in hac specie civilitatis, que naturalis sive in naturali est, et verus in vero iure civilitatis in genere (D.41.3.15) per Bartolum.[38]

It is noteworthy that here and elsewhere Baldus gives as a source for his argument the commentary of Bartolus on D.41.3.15. Baldus, however, develops the argument by maintaining, firstly, that the formula, *habeatur pro cive*, does, indeed, signify that a created citizen is a true one, because it is true that citizenship in a civil sense can be created; but secondly, that the formula can only denote fiction in so far as the created citizen is described as an original one (as in the phrase common in city-legislation, *habeatur pro cive vero et originario*), because it is not true in fact that the created citizen is a native of his new city. That is to say, the created citizen is truly a citizen as regards his

[38] X.2.26.Rubr., n. 23 (fo. 325r). See also *idem ad* C.6.8.2: 'Et facit ad statutum quod comitativi habeantur pro civitatensibus. Nam hoc nomen "civitatensibus" ponitur naturaliter; et ius originis non potest mutari nisi per fictionem, ut (D.50.1.6; et C.10.40.9). Sed Bartolus dicit quod istud statutum in veritate disponit, non in fictione (D.41.3.15). Sed tu dic quod duplex est civilitas, scilicet originaria, et quoad istam est fictio, et civilitas in genere, et quoad istam est veritas, quia predicatur de multis speciebus, et ideo species contenta sub genere ex propria natura generis inest ei secundum veritatem, ergo etc., ut (C.10.40.7).' I have adopted the reading, 'ex propria natura' from the Lyon, 1585, edition in place of 'prior a natura' in the [Lyon, 1498], edition.

citizenship as such, but can only ever fictively be considered an original citizen.[39]

Baldus's interpretation of the formula, *habeatur pro cive*, becomes very clear in the next stage of his treatment of the theme of created citizenship. Baldus goes further in isolating the concept of citizenship from the means by which it is obtained: he calls this core of citizenship *pura* or *mera civilitas* – citizenship pure and simple. It is this which is the common element of both natural and created citizenship:

Et facit arg. ad forenses qui recipiuntur in cives originarios, quia hoc est per fictionem: pura enim civilitas potest induci per veritatem, sed originaria non, ut (D.50.1.6); pares ergo erunt per omnia iste civilitates.[40]

Thus in a discussion of the formula, *habeatur pro cive*, Baldus maintains that the created citizen, whereas in terms of origin he is a citizen only fictively, is however a true one as regards *mera civilitas*:

Verbum 'habeatur' positum super vero significat veritatem, quod si super ficto significat fictionem. Et facit ad questionem statuti dicentis quod mercatores forenses pro civibus habeantur, quia denotat similitudinem non unitatem, quia contra naturam sermo prolatus fictionem inducit . . . *Si igitur gentem consideres, id est patriam, fictio est; si meram civilitatem, potest esse veritas*, ut hic et no. per Bartolum (D.41.3.15).[41]

The concepts of *civilitas in genere*, and of *pura* or *mera civilitas*, mark the highest degree of abstraction which Baldus attains in his treatment of the relationship between created and natural citizenship: these are the high points of his discussion. Furthermore in the context of his theory of citizenship as a whole they are the most striking examples of his powers of abstraction. The comparison with other jurists is revealing. Baldus is here in a class of his own in the profundity which he attains in his consideration of the abstract concept, *civilitas* itself, as distinct from the more corporeal phenomenon of the *civis*.

I have here presented the major parts of Baldus's theory of created citizenship. There are other aspects, such as the concepts of adoptive citizenship, and *civilitas accidentalis*, together with the relationship of

---

[39] See Baldus *ad* D.3.2.6,1 (fo. 148r): 'Si statutum dicit quod aliquis intelligatur esse civis, importat veritatem quoad civilitatem civilem, sed non quoad civilitatem originis, que requirit verum naturale principium, ut (D.41.3.15). Vnde dato quod statutum diceret ita quod intelligatur esse et sit originarius civis, tamen quoad naturalem et originalem civilitatem ista verba non important nisi fictionem, quia non habet tantam potestatem lex vel statutum quod possit tollere facti veritatem, ut (D.49.15.12,2). Vbi ergo verba possunt adaptari ad veritatem important veritatem, ubi non possunt adaptari ad veritatem important fictionem.' The text of the [Lyon], 1498, edition contains 'quo civilitatem', which I have emended.

[40] D.12.1.14 (Lectura antiqua). [41] X.1.6.6, n. 4 (fo. 77v).

created citizenship to corporation-theory, and Baldus's treatment of the status of the citizenship obtained by a foreign woman who marries a citizen. I have not been able to include these in the scope of this essay, because given the limited space available it has seemed preferable to concentrate on the major issues.

Because of its central position, Baldus's theory of citizenship forms a good introduction to his political ideas. The major aspects of his theory of citizenship, as treated in this essay, hold a key position in his theory of popular government. Baldus's works do, indeed, contain much more information on the general topic of citizenship than is included here; but his introduction of the concept of natural, political man, and his ideas concerning created citizenship are certainly his most important contribution to the juristic theory of citizenship. His contribution is characterised by a profundity of mind and intellectual versatility, as revealed in his capacity to explore the very boundaries of the possibilities contained in juristic conceptions, and to make use of the conceptual opportunities provided by philosophical ideas.

WHAT WAS CONCILIARISM?
CONCILIAR THEORY IN HISTORICAL PERSPECTIVE

by A. J. BLACK

IN A WAY, the terms 'conciliar movement' and 'conciliarism' are mis-
nomers, if we take them to imply that developments of ecclesiastical
theory and policy between 1378 and 1512 – or, if one likes, between
the mid-thirteenth century and the Reformation – were strange and
new, eccentric to the mainstream of Catholic Christianity, and wholly
determined by the needs of the time and a particular *Zeitgeist*. For
councils of various kinds and a conciliar tradition had existed in the
early Church, grew up alongside episcopacy, patriarchate and papacy,
flourished especially in the third, fourth and fifth centuries, remained
an integral part of both eastern and western ecclesiology; and, besides,
flourished again in various forms in the post-Reformation Churches,
and are in a state of considerable vitality today. The conciliarists saw
themselves as traditionalists, not revolutionaries; and, as with Protestantism, a study of earlier periods in ecclesiastical history gives some
credibility to this self-image.

Much of the interest in the conciliar movement on the part of
modern historians has come from those concerned, on the one hand,
with the *Vorreformation*, and, on the other hand, with parliamentarism
and constitutionalism. In the case of the former, the conciliar movement
has the disadvantage of falling between two stools: historians sympathetic to Protestantism and sensitive to the rise of the 'modern, secular
state' see it as a kind of Decembrist revolt, good as far as it went but
unable to go far enough without destroying its own premises, namely
the notion of the universal Church and of Catholic tradition.[1] Those
sympathetic to Roman Catholicism have tended to see it as well-
meaning, perhaps, but erroneous; to regard it as a good Whig would

---

[1] E.g. J. Haller, 'Die Kirchenreform auf dem Konzil zu Basel', *Korrespondenzblatt des Gesamt-
vereins der deutschen Geschichte- und Altertums-vereins*, LVIII (1910), pp. 9–26; J. K. Cameron,
'Conciliarism in theory and practice' (Dissertation, Hartford, 1952). This view seems to be
implicit in M. Wilks, *The Problem of Sovereignty in the Later Middle Ages* (Cambridge, 1963),
e.g. pp. 521–3.

regard the Jacobite rising of 1745, an episode best forgotten and not likely to be repeated.[2] Those interested in parliamentarism, on the other hand, emphasise the elements in conciliar thought and practice for which analogues can be found in secular politics, such as the theory of representation and constitutional checks on monarchical power.[3] Marsilius and Cusa have, justifiably, been given accredited status in 'the history of political thought'; and connections have been sought between the conciliar theorists and the constitutionalists of sixteenth- and seventeenth-century France, England and Scotland.[4] There are, indeed, interesting parallels between the movement of thought during Constance and Basle and the movement of thought during the English and French revolutions. In each case, what started as an attempt to reintroduce the norms of the 'true' constitution, to create a balance between monarch and assembly, ended up by asserting unequivocally the sovereignty of the assembly; in each case, appeals to tradition were joined or even replaced by appeals to natural right, and so – as we find in Cusa and Segovia, in Harrington and Locke – to the erection of general political theories of a rationalistic kind. Monarchical thought moved similarly towards rationality and generality, as in both Torquemada and Hobbes.

Recent developments in the Roman Catholic Church are giving rise to yet another approach, which moves away from the pre-reform or counter-Reformation views and is analogous to the parliamentarist approach. Thinkers such as de Vooght[5] and Küng[6] see the Council of Constance and its apologists as upholding in a dark time certain central principles of Catholic ecclesiology, which are only now gaining hard-won acceptance among Catholic theologians. This does less violence to the ideas of the conciliarists, for their interpreters are in this case

[2] E.g. N. Valois, *Le Pape et le concile (1378–1450)* (2 vols., Paris, 1909); H. Jedin, *Bischöfliches Konzil oder Kirchenparlament* (Stuttgart–Basel, 1963); J. Gill, *Constance et Bâle–Florence* (Paris, 1965).

[3] E.g. J. N. Figgis, *Studies in Political Thought from Gerson to Grotius* (Cambridge, 1916), pp. 31–47; H. Laski in *Cambridge Med. History*, VIII (Cambridge, 1936), p. 638; F. Oakley, 'On the road from Constance to 1688', *Journal of British Studies*, I (1962), pp. 1–32; A. Black, 'The political ideas of conciliarism and papalism, 1430–50', *JEH*, XX (1969), pp. 45–65.

[4] F. Oakley, 'Constance to 1688'; *idem*, 'Figgis, Constance and the divines of Paris', *American Historical Review*, LXXV (1969), pp. 368–86; Z. Rueger, 'Gerson, the conciliar movement and the right of resistance (1642–4)', *Journal of the History of Ideas*, XXV (1964), pp. 467–80.

[5] P. de Vooght, *Les Pouvoirs du concile et l'autorité du pape au concile de Constance* (Paris, 1965); *idem*, 'Le conciliarisme aux conciles de Constance et de Bâle', in *Le Concile et les conciles*, ed. B. Botte *et al.* (Chevetogne, 1960), pp. 143–81; *idem*, 'Le Conciliarisme aux conciles de Constance et de Bâle: compléments et précisions', *Irenikon*, XXXVI (1963), pp. 61–75.

[6] H. Küng, *Structures of the Church* (London, 1967); *idem*, *Infallible?* (London, 1972).

treading the intellectual path they themselves trod. Part of the way towards such a reinterpretation was blazed by Tierney, when he showed how much conciliar theorising owed to ideas of collective government deeply embedded within medieval canon law,[7] and, it may be added, within the tradition of the pre-medieval Church. For, however much conciliar theory employed concepts of general political usage such as natural right and consent, however much its conclusions may be 'read off' on the template of secular constitutionalism, and however much some of its exponents themselves wrote on human government in general, the primary concern of the conciliarists (if we except Marsilius) was with the *ecclesia*, and they themselves believed that what they were engaged in was theology and ecclesiastical juris-prudence.[8] To interpret their thought as 'political thought', one has to pre-select a rather minute proportion of their arguments and citations.

Yet the balance of interpretation is still not right; the conciliar movement as a whole is still not adequately understood for what it was. First, we have still to identify the particular mix of situational and intellectual factors, and also of faith and reasoning, which went to make up conciliarism. Secondly, we have still to give due weight to the Basle phase. To take the first question, it is true that conciliarism as a move-ment drew its impetus from the contemporary demand for unity, reform and decentralisation. It was a reaction to the centralisation and monarchical claims of the papacy, it was fuelled in its formative stages by ecclesiastical nationalism, and it arose immediately out of the refusal of rival popes to settle their differences by other means. It was also an expression, particularly attractive to reformers, university clergy and, for different reasons, some secular powers, of the late-medieval urge for a return to apostolic ideals.[9]

Whatever the nature of their material support, however, the ideas to which the conciliar theorists turned, and which they developed, were not solely the product of the medieval environment. For example, it used to be held that conciliar ideology was decisively influenced by Marsilius and Ockham; then Tierney showed how much it owed to the corporation theory of medieval canonists; but it is necessary to add that, in its florescence (roughly 1408–42), it was primarily a theological movement of thought. In its early stages conciliarism was very greatly

[7] B. Tierney, *Foundations of the Conciliar Theory* (Cambridge, repr. 1968).
[8] See below, pp. 216–17.
[9] G. Leff, 'The apostolic ideal in later medieval ecclesiology', *JTS*, n.s. xviii (1967), pp. 58–82.

indebted to the Paduan and to Ockham – we need only cite Gelnhausen, Langenstein, the early d'Ailly and Niem.[10] These thinkers tended, in varying degrees, to see the council in quasi-parliamentary terms, as representing the Church in the sense of representing the views and interests of its members, lay as well as clerical, with some electoral element. They also gave the secular powers a prominent part in conciliar convocation; Niem, following Marsilius, wished the secular powers to take the initiative in reforming the Church; some delegates to the council, it was said, could well be selected (as Ockham suggested, and as often happened in the early phases of both Constance and Basle) by national synods under royal influence. In other words, there was a strong secularist element and a particular cultural flavour in early conciliarism. But from 1408 onwards (with the exception of Niem and, to a slight degree, Cusa)[11] the Marsilian–Ockhamist element is replaced by orthodox theology and ecclesiastical jurisprudence. Zabarella, Gerson, the later d'Ailly and virtually all the Basle thinkers were conciliarists of a different genre from their immediate predecessors. With the exception of Zabarella, they dismissed secular intervention in either the convocation or proceedings of the council; in other words, they detached themselves from the secularising element in earlier conciliarism. And they argued their case in terms of canon law and scripture, fields in which they were truly creative thinkers.

Zabarella and, during Basle, Tudeschi, argued for conciliar sovereignty in legal terms, though they did so not so much in their formal commentaries as in *ad hoc* publicistic treatises.[12] The corporational element remained vital in all subsequent conciliar theory, but we should also note that it was derived not solely, and during Basle I think not even primarily, from the canon law texts and commentaries, but rather from contemporary corporational practices, of which members of the councils had so much personal experience.[13] But it is a great mistake to deduce from Tierney's discoveries that conciliar thought during Constance and Basle was primarily juristic. It comprised, rather, a *theology* of the Church. From Gerson onwards, and most markedly in

---

[10] For an admirable discussion of the primary and secondary sources on these, see Cameron, 'Conciliarism in theory and practice'.

[11] P. Sigmund, 'The influence of Marsilius on 15th-century conciliarism', *Journal of the History of Ideas*, XXIII (1962), pp. 392–402.

[12] W. Ullmann, *Origins of the Great Schism* (London, repr. 1972), pp. 191–231; Tierney, *Foundations*, pp. 220–37; K. Nörr, *Kirche und Konzil bei Nicolaus de Tudeschis* (Cologne–Graz, 1964).

[13] Compare, for example, Segovia in *MC*, III, pp. 720–1 with the description of Paris University's government in A. Cobban, *The Medieval Universities* (London, 1975), pp. 85–6.

Segovia, we hear the rebuke that the canonists have misunderstood the structure of ecclesiastical authority by introducing notions derived from secular, Roman law; we hear the call to return to scripture and patristic tradition.[14] In certain passages, Gerson and Segovia say explicitly that there can be no analogy between the church and secular society, because the former was the unique creation of a special divine providence;[15] its norms, Segovia insists, must be the norms of the gospel alone, that is of fraternal decision-making, with 'authority' meaning 'service'.[16] Their argument is based on St Paul's analogy between the Christian community and the human body (1 Cor. 12.12–14, 18–21; Eph. 4.12, 16; Col. 2.9), from which it is deduced that supreme power belongs only to the whole body working together; on the bestowal of power upon all the apostles together (Matt. 18.18; John 20.23); upon the dominical precept to 'tell the community (*dic ecclesie*)' if a brother errs persistently (Matt. 18.15–20); and, during Basle, on St Paul's statements that teachers, pastors, prophets and others, as well as the apostles, make up the body of Christ (1 Cor. 12.28; Eph. 4.11), from which it is deduced that theologians and other clergy may have a share, beside the bishops, in conciliar decision-making.

In other words, as the conciliar movement went on, it gained an intellectual, and we may say a moral and spiritual, momentum of its own. This both separated it from the Marsilian–secularist heritage, and made it independent of canonist doctrine. With the exception of Tudeschi (who, in fact, was sometimes equivocal) all the creative Basle thinkers were theologians. This momentum further separated the ideal interests of the conciliar reformers from the territorial interests of the major secular powers. This was already evident in the later stages of Constance, but its implications were only fully made clear at Basle.

The study of the conciliar movement has tended to focus upon the years 1378–1418, and has paid relatively little attention to the Council of Basle and, in particular, to its theorists. Basle was above all a council of reform and constitutional change; and it, still more than its predecessors, has been accused of inadequacy by pro-Protestant historians, of excess by pro-Catholic ones. It failed; and the reasons for its failure have been found in its internal structure, its factionalism. With the

---

[14] Gerson, *Oeuvres Complètes*, ed. M. Glorieux, VI (Tournai, 1965), p. 227; Segovia in *MC*, III, pp. 647–50, 792, 845, 937–8.

[15] Gerson, *OC*, VI, 132; Segovia in *MC*, III, pp. 603, 707, 764–5.

[16] A. Black, *Monarchy and Community* (Cambridge, 1970), pp. 22–3, 35, 38.

admirable exception of de Vooght,[17] the recent Catholic renaissance in conciliar studies has also so far virtually ignored Basle. There is not even an adequate history of the council. Johann Haller, having overseen the editing of many of its most extensive records[18] and inspired numerous monographs, never completed his history of Basle, which was to have been the culmination of his *Papsttum und Kirchenreform* (Berlin, 1903). The need for a full history of Basle is perhaps most acute in the area of its internal structure, composition and decision-making processes. The best studies here remain G. Pérouse's *Le Cardinal Aleman, président du concile de Bâle, et la fin du grand schisme* (Paris, 1905); and P. Lazarus's *Das Basler Konzil, seine Berufung und seine Leitung, seine Gliederung und seine Behördenorganisation* (Berlin, 1912); Haller himself still provides some of the most interesting hypotheses, as well as very valuable criticism of the sources.[19] A useful recent study is D. L. Bilderback's thesis, 'The membership of the council of Basel' (Seattle, 1966), still for some reason unpublished.[20] During 1432–6 it was a truly impressive assembly, as well-attended, even by bishops, and as representative of the church, as Constance had been. Its internal constitution, while complex, worked sufficiently well for it to produce numerous far-reaching reform decrees;[21] and it came close to resolving the Catholic–Hussite controversy.[22] Lower clergy were not numerically preponderant prior to 1436, and even thereafter leadership remained with senior prelates and university doctors, with ordinary clergy as back-benchers.[23] It is amazing that this brilliant essay in republican government – the great

[17] Above, p. 214, n. 5.

[18] *Concilium Basiliense*, ed. J. Haller *et al.* (8 vols., Basle, 1896–1936); cf. A. Meijknecht, 'Le Concile de Bâle: aperçu général sur les sources', *RHE*, LXV (1970), pp. 465–73.

[19] See his introduction to *Concilium Basiliense*, I; 'Die Kirchenreform'; *idem*, 'Beiträge zur Geschichte des Basler Konzils', *Zeitschrift für Geschichte des Oberrheins*, n. F., XVI (1901), pp. 48ff.; for further literature, E. Delaruelle *et al.*, *L'Église au temps du grand schisme et de la crise conciliaire (1378–1449)* (2 vols., Paris, 1962–4), pp. 227–8.

[20] Cf. D. Bilderback, 'Eugene IV and the first dissolution of the Council of Basel', *Church History*, XXXVI (1967), pp. 1–14; *idem*, 'Proctorial representation', *Annuarium historiae conciliorum*, I (1969), pp. 140–52; A. Schofield, 'The first English delegation', *JEH*, XII (1961), pp. 167–96; *idem*, 'The second English delegation', *JEH*, XVII (1966), pp. 29ff.; C. Hanna, *Die sudwestdeutschen Diözesen und das Baseler Konzil* (Borna–Leipzig, 1929); H. Stutt, *Die nordwestdeutschen Diözesen und das Baseler Konzil* (Erlangen, 1928).

[21] R. Zwoelfer, 'Die Reform der Kirchenverfassung auf dem Konzil zu Basel', *Basler Zeitschrift für Geschichte und Altertumskunde*, XXVIII (1929), pp. 144–247, and XXIX (1930), pp. 2–58.

[22] E. F. Jacob, 'The Bohemians at the council of Basel, 1433', *Prague Essays*, ed. R. Seton-Watson (Oxford, 1949), pp. 81–123.

[23] D. Bilderback, 'Membership', esp. pp. 175–7; P. Ourliac, 'La Sociologie du concile de Bâle', *RHE*, LVI (1961), pp. 2–32 (substantially reproduced in Delaruelle *et al.*, *L'Église*, pp. 237ff.), and J. Gill, 'The representation of the *universitas fidelium*', *SCH*, VII (1971), pp. 187ff., are somewhat misleading.

constitutional invention of the day, Segovia called it – remains so under-researched.

The reasons for the failure of Basle lie as much outside as they do inside the council, and here ecclesiological dispute was as important a factor as personal and national politics. The development of theological conciliarism, which was most expertly wrought by Gerson and Segovia, had led away from the quasi-parliamentary notion of the council (that it represented the church electorally, as suggested by Marsilius and, at times, Ockham) either towards an episcopalist or towards a collectivist notion. The former notion, entertained by Gerson[24] and (after Basle disbanded) Segovia,[25] located ecclesiastical sovereignty with the episcopate-in-council; here again medieval corporation theory made its impact, but we must not forget that the 'collegiate' notion of the local episcopate went back to subapostolic times, notably at Rome itself.[26] This was the theory dominant at Constance. The collectivist notion, which was dominant during Basle, ascribed sovereignty more loosely to the church-as-a-whole-in-council. To the scriptural arguments it was now possible to add the authority of *Haec Sancta* and *Frequens*; the former was repromulgated in June 1434 and July 1439,[27] the latter in 1431–2, with the added clause that a council could not be dissolved without its own consent.[28]

The strength of the Basle theory lay in its assertion of the fraternal, communal, corporational ethic and constitution within the council itself; again, the New Testament was the starting point, canon law providing precedents at the capitular level. One has, again, the impression that it was the experience of capitular and university government, at least as much as academic canon law, that inspired such practices as majority voting, the equality of all incorporated members, and the division of the council into 'deputations', analogous to university faculties, rather than into 'nations'. For the canonists could never justify the equal participation of lower clergy alongside bishops. The theologians of Paris played the major part in creating the amazingly subtle and democratic constitution of Basle.[29] The weakness of the Basle theory was that, having abandoned both electoral and *ex officio*

---

[24] *OC*, VI, pp. 114, 222.

[25] *De magna auctoritate episcoporum in generali concilio*, Universitätsbibliothek, Basle, B.V. 15.

[26] B. Streeter, *The Primitive Church* (London, 1929), pp. 182, 216; H. Chadwick, *The Early Church* (London, 1967), p. 50.

[27] Mansi, XXIX, pp. 91, 181–2.

[28] Mansi, XXIX, pp. 5–6, 21–2.   [29] Lazarus, *Das Basler Konzil*, pp. 112ff.

representation, it could only justify in theological or philosophical terms the council's claim to represent the Church by appeal to hazy 'realist' concepts of the body assembled as a whole, its potency activated, its matter given form, by the council.[30]

Basle's real problems were, first, that the papacy would never accept its claims; while Eugenius IV happily co-operated with a council that was not conciliarist (Ferrara–Florence), and Basle would retain a papacy that was a subordinate executive organ, the ideological division was insurmountable. Secondly, the secular powers, on whom the councils had come to rely for their *de facto* support among the clergy and peoples of Europe, were not interested in pressing the claims of an exclusively clerical and determinedly autonomous council. Haller went too far in suggesting that Basle was the instrument and mouthpiece of the 'particularist' and secularising interests of the national or regional states;[31] it failed precisely because it refused to accommodate the secular powers. The majority faction was dominated by French clergy, high and low, but these were not acting in unison with the French government, rather the contrary, and already by 1436 Charles VII was abandoning Basle.[32] The Hapsburg alliance with the papacy from 1443[33] onwards was a crucial factor in bringing Germany eventually back into at least formal allegiance to Rome. But Haller was right in saying that the conciliar controversy, particularly during the 'princely neutrality' of the 1440s, precipitated the trend towards ecclesiastical nationalism; and Bilderback, who follows Haller on this, is right in pointing out that, once the powers had got what they could out of Basle, they abandoned it.[34] By 1450 ecclesiastical regionalism was so entrenched that *de facto* the papacy recognised it to a large degree. This, coupled with the subsequent implausibility of reforming the universal church from within, was Basle's contribution to the Reformation.

With the political demise of Basle, the conciliar movement of thought ceased to have widespread appeal, retreated to its original fastness of Paris University, and ceased to develop. But it nevertheless left a distinctive imprint on subsequent Catholic ecclesiology: the right of a council to depose a heretical or schismatic pope was admitted, in various formulae, not only by the remaining conciliarists but also by

---

30 Black, *Monarchy*, pp. 17ff., *idem*, *Council and Commune* (London, 1979), pp. 113ff.
31 'Die Kirchenreform', pp. 21, 25.
32 R. Wittram, *Die französische Politik auf dem Basler Konzil* (Riga, 1927), pp. 83–4.
33 H. Angemeier, 'Das Reich und der Konziliarismus', *HZ*, CXCII (1961), pp. 529–83.
34 Bilderback, 'Membership', pp. 119–23, 173, 179–80.

Torquemada,[35] Biel, Cajetan, Thomas More,[36] Suárez, Bellarmine,[37] and so on. Even today Küng and Rahner are, in their different ways, in part the intellectual and spiritual heirs of Zabarella, Gerson, Velde and Segovia;[38] and, to take but one isolated example, the recent Anglican–Roman Catholic statement on authority shows that conciliar theory was no isolated, time-bound phenomenon.[39] But first let us consider the contribution of conciliarism to later political theory.

It is not enough to point to similarities between conciliarist thought and later parliamentarist or constitutionalist thought, with the implication that the latter derived from the former; for parliaments and constitutionalism antedate the conciliar movement by a century or two. There were points of coincidence, for example in the appeal to natural right and *Widerstandsrecht* in the schism period, and again in Segovia's theory of 'parliamentary monarchy'.[40] But what, if anything, did conciliarism contribute to the fund of political ideas? To begin with, it contributed nothing new to the theory of representation, nor to the practice of representative assemblies; indeed, as regards electoral representation, the councils lagged somewhat behind contemporary secular practice. But, just as papal absolutism contributed to the development of absolutist theories in secular government,[41] so it may have been that, during its florescence, conciliarism gave by its example some encouragement to the theory and practice of parliamentary assemblies, the development of which in certain German principalities during the Basle period is particularly striking.[42] The main innovation would appear to be the establishment, by *Frequens* and the Basle decrees, of positive constitutional law prescribing regular meetings of the assembly, a practice hitherto adopted, so far as I know, only in Aragon–Catalonia. As regards constitutionalism, the conciliarists may be said to have advanced on their secular counterparts by establishing a judicial

---

[35] U. Horst, 'Grenzen der päpstlichen Autorität: konziliare Elemente in der Ekklesiologie des Johann Torquemada', *Freiburger Zeitschrift für Philos. u. Theol.*, XIX (1972), pp. 361–88.

[36] D. Hay, 'A note on More and the general council', *Moreana*, XV (1967), pp. 249–51.

[37] Küng, *Structures*, pp. 253ff.; cf. U. Horst, 'Papst-Unfehlbarkeit-Konzil', in *Thomas von Aquino*, ed. W. Eckert (Mainz, 1974), pp. 779–822.

[38] H. Küng, above, p. 214, n. 6; K. Rahner and J. Ratzinger, *The Episcopate and the Primacy* (Freiburg, 1962); K. Rahner, *Theological Investigations*, VI (Baltimore–London, 1969). Cf. F. Oakley, *Council over Pope?* (New York, 1969); H. Schneider, 'Concilium supra papam?' (Dissertation, Göttingen, 1973).

[39] *Authority in the Church*, Anglican–R.C. International Commission (London, 1977).

[40] Black, *Monarchy*, pp. 44ff.; *idem, Council*, pp. 191–3.

[41] K. Eckermann, *Studien zur Geschichte des monarchischen Gedankens im 15. Jahrhundert* (Berlin, 1933), esp. pp. 45–6, 53–4; Black, *Monarchy*, pp. 105ff., 112ff.

[42] F. Carsten, *Princes and Parliaments in Germany* (Oxford, 1959), pp. 196–8, 264–5, 354.

procedure by which an erring monarch might be judged and deposed; this was, of course, a refinement of existing canonist notions regarding a heretical or schismatic pope, and precedents might also be found in the milieu of some city-states.

On the whole, one suspects that conciliarism contributed something to the de-sacralisation of monarchy, a development of portentous importance for the European polities, and one which was to be taken much further in the sixteenth century, partly under Protestant influence but with the precedent of conciliarism also sometimes invoked, as Oakley has shown.[43] If even a pope was not immune from judgment ... Yet it remains significant that the Englishman Fortescue put forward his parliamentarist–constitutionalist ideas without any recognisable debt to the conciliarists.

The most striking development of political theory by conciliarists lay in their application of civic–republican and communal–corporational ideas to the large-scale polity. Conciliarism included, among many other things, the first attempt to apply some of the norms of civic-republican government on a wider scale. The idea of the sovereignty of the people 'legitimately assembled', and of the superiority of the assembly *qua* legislature over the magistracy *qua* executive – both of them elements in the republican tradition derived from Bartolus[44] and Marsilius respectively – were expounded and implemented by Basle, culminating in the deposition of Eugenius IV in 1439; and the conciliar pope, Felix V, found himself in an exceedingly dependent position. By doing this, conciliarism, mainly in the Basle period, anticipated, though it cannot be said to have influenced, the similar application of republican ideas to large polities in mid-seventeenth-century England and late-eighteenth-century France.

Conciliarism also saw the first attempt to apply the norms hitherto existing in certain corporations, such as majority voting, equality within the assembly, and a kind of fraternal or democratic ethic that had arisen in certain face-to-face societies (such as the guild and confraternity – the latter explicitly cited by Gerson),[45] to a large-scale polity. This development too went furthest at Basle, and was expressed in terms of a general political ideology by Segovia.[46] Authority was conceived as belonging to the association as a whole, so that majority

---

[43] Above, p. 214, n. 4.
[44] W. Ullmann, 'De Bartoli sententia: *concilium representat mentem populi*', *Bartolo da Sassoferrato: Studi e Documenti*, II (Milan, 1962), pp. 707–33.   [45] *OC*, VI, p. 134.
[46] Black, *Monarchy*, pp. 25–8, 142–4, 148–50; *idem, Council*, pp. 138–93.

decision-making and rectorial accountability were mandatory. But, in the case of both republican and corporational thought, conciliarism applied these models *effectively* only within the council and to the pope–council relationship; the community at large, though reference was often enough made to it, was in effect left out in the cold. In this respect, conciliarism must be regarded as an arrested as well as an abortive development.

In the realm of the theology of the Church, conciliarism affirmed the principle of 'conciliarity', itself as old as the Christian Church, at a time when the juridical theory of papal absolutism was at its zenith. The courtly culture of renaissance Italy ran directly counter to the corporational, guild-like instincts of the north-European Church, particularly in the urban centres; and it was this Church which, particularly at Basle, worked up the principles of the *universitas* and the *vita communis* into an alternative vision of the *ecclesia universalis*. On the other hand, as has been said, conciliarism went far beyond such culturally specific attributes: it also reaffirmed certain ecclesial values and organisational principles which flourished in the early and patristic Church, but which had been partially eclipsed by the combined juridicisation (by the canonists) and mystification (by theologians such as Bonaventure and Aquinas) of ecclesiology. The conciliarists, particularly during Basle but following the great Gerson, began to see the Church less as a juridical and more as a caritative structure; this trend was typified by their appeal to Matt. 20.25–8, Luke 22.26–7 and 1 Peter 5.3. The Basileans especially emphasised the ministerial or servile character of ecclesial authority; in his far-reaching discussion of authority, Segovia notes that the word itself occurs only once in the New Testament, and then in the sense of moral authority.[47] The principles of brotherhood and charity were often on the lips of Basilean apologists as they defended the communal organisation of their council. On the other hand, the conciliarists were prevented by their own priorities of structural reform from sliding away into fanciful notions of a merely spiritual communion of souls, which would either leave the field of government to the papalists or abandon the Catholic notion of visible unity and teaching authority altogether. They were constitutionalists, and it was not only personal lives and local churches but the practical government of the universal Church which they wished to reshape in the light of their ethical norms; alongside their idealism, they wished to retain a

[47] *MC*, III, pp. 840–6.

juridical order capable of sustaining the visible unity of the church. Their notion of juridical collectivism, which Vatican II calls 'collegiality',[48] was related to the central Christian idea of the brotherhood of believers: it is the brotherhood or collegiality of bishops (Constance) or of priests (Basle) which is the locus of ecclesiastical sovereignty. Velde further anticipated modern Catholic ecclesiology – or re-affirmed ancient ecclesiology – by arguing that the power of jurisdiction was inseparable from, and dependent upon, the power of order, thus knocking a central pillar from the papalist edifice.[49] Thus, the theological contribution of conciliarism is wider than the recent preoccupation with the status of *Haec Sancta* has allowed.[50]

From the conciliar period we may conclude that far-reaching reform and structural reorientation were impossible in the late-medieval church without a major external shock, both because of the ingrained conventions of papalism and because of the nationalisation of ecclesiastical control. Looking beyond the confines of this particular period in European history, we may say that the conciliarists were right in asserting that the principle of absolute monarchy was incompatible with the gospel. But they also had this advantage over Protestantism, that their ecclesiology embodied and made room for the postulate of ecclesiastical unity.

[48] Y. Congar and J. Dupont, *La Collégialité épiscopale* (Paris, 1965); B. Tierney, 'Collegiality in the Middle Ages', *Concilium* VII (1965), pp. 5–14.

[49] Heimerich van de Velde (Campo), *De eccles. pot.*, Cusanus-Bibliothek, Bernkastel-Kues, Cod. Cus., 106, fos. 89v–90r, 160r, 161r, 163v; cf. Wilks, *Problem*, pp. 375–7.

[50] A. Franzen and W. Müller, eds., *Das Konzil von Konstanz* (Freiburg, 1964); R. Baümer, 'Die Interpretation und Verbindlichkeit der konstanzer Dekrete', *Theol-praktische Quartalschrift*, CXVI (1968), pp. 44–53; W. Brandmüller, 'Besitzt das Dekret "Haec Sancta" dogmatischer Verbindlichkeit?', *Römische Quartalschrift*, LXII (1967), pp. 1–17; I. Pichler, *Die Verbindlichkeit der konstanzer Dekrete* (Vienna, 1967); B. Tierney, 'Hermeneutics and history: the problem of *Haec Sancta*', *Essays in Medieval History* presented to Bertie Wilkinson, ed. T. A. Sandquist and M. R. Powicke (Toronto, 1968), pp. 354–70.

THE PROBLEM OF THE CARDINALATE
IN THE GREAT SCHISM

by R. N. Swanson

BY THE MIDDLE of the fourteenth century, the ecclesiological tensions which had earlier tormented the Church had subsided into some sort of compromise, conceding to the cardinals a pivotal role as intermediaries between the *plena potestas* of the pope as personification of the *ecclesia*, and the *plena potestas* of the *congregatio fidelium* as its manifestation. Concurrently, practical governmental requirements allowed the cardinals another intermediate position, with their oligarchic aspirations and activities interposing between the papal monarchy and the generality of the Church. Both positions were essentially artificial, their continuance depending on the cardinals not overstepping the bounds of an undefined acceptability. Yet this they did in 1378 when, after electing Urban VI as pope, they sought to replace him by Clement VII, and expected the Church to accept him unquestioningly. During the debates of the resulting schism, which lasted forty years, the constitutional position of the cardinals was much discussed, with occasional demands for their total abolition.[1]

But although the furore which broke out immediately after the events of 1378 challenged and partially undermined the cardinals' ecclesiastical position, this was not destroyed. They soon reasserted themselves and, at the Council of Pisa of 1409, fully implemented their gubernatorial and representative functions, being closely involved in the process of constitutional redefinition which was intended to reunite the Church.

However, the cardinals do not seem to have participated much in the tractarian controversies which contributed to this process. Even in the earliest stages of the dispute, from 1378 to about 1383, their involvement was virtually limited to factual statements which others treated

---

[1] F. Oakley, *The Political Thought of Pierre d'Ailly* (New Haven and London, 1964), pp. 328–9. See also for a general discussion of the role of the cardinals in the church, G. Alberigo, *Cardinalato e collegialità* (Florence, 1969).

as source material. However, Petrus Flandrin and Petrus Amelius did produce more theoretical works,[2] while Pedro de Luna proved an energetic advocate of Clement VII in the Iberian peninsula.[3] Thereafter, until the Council of Pisa, almost the only tract produced by a cardinal was the strong defence of Benedict XIII written by Martín de Salva in the late 1390s.[4]

Despite their silence, the cardinals were not passive, their activity increasing after the election of Boniface IX as Roman pope in 1389. By 1394 Pedro de Luna had accepted the Parisian arguments for double abdication as the best solution to the problem;[5] while in the same year Parisian entreaties to the Avignon cardinals to take action[6] apparently bore fruit when, on the death of Clement VII, his cardinals bound themselves and their new pope, Benedict XIII (previously Pedro de Luna), to work for union by all possible means, including cession.[7] This acceptance of the *via cessionis* was confirmed by the cardinals' later actions, collaborating with the French Crown towards its implementation.[8] As the French policy developed into a call for subtraction of obedience, this co-operation rapidly changed to dependence: although individuals at the crucial Parisian council of 1398 wished the cardinals to govern the Church after subtraction,[9] the cardinals themselves were too tied to Charles VI to act unilaterally. Therefore, when the king withdrew obedience in 1398, they followed suit.[10] But attempts to influence the French actually to depose Benedict were repulsed,[11] so that when he regained his liberty in 1403 the cardinals rapidly restored their obedience.[12]

Thereafter, the initiative passed to the cardinals of the Romanist College. They followed the Avignonese precedent after the death of

2 Printed in F. P. Bliemetzrieder, *Literarische Polemik zu Beginn des grossen abendländischen Schismas* (Vienna, 1910), pp. 3–111.
3 L. Suárez Fernández, *Castilla, el cisma, y la crisis conciliar (1378–1440)* (Madrid, 1960), pp. 15–20, 146–9.
4 Paris, BN, MS lat.1475, fos. 33r–53r.
5 N. Valois, *La France et le grand schisme d'occident* (4 vols., Paris, 1896–1904), II, pp. 423–4; H. Denifle and E. Chatelain, *Chartularium Universitatis Parisiensis* (4 vols., Paris, 1889–97), no. 1673.
6 Valois, *La France*, II, p. 426.
7 M. Souchon, *Die Papstwahlen in der Zeit des grossen Schismas* (2 vols., Brunswick, 1898), I, pp. 296–300.
8 See their declaration when a French embassy visited Avignon in 1395: L. Bellaguet, ed., *Chronique du religieux de St Denys* (6 vols., Paris, 1839–52), II, pp. 308–13.
9 E.g., Robert du Quesnoy (Paris, Archives Nationales, J.518, fo. 373v).
10 Bellaguet, *Chronique*, II, pp. 652–3; Valois, *La France*, III, pp. 191–4.
11 Bellaguet, *Chronique*, II, pp. 677–83.
12 Valois, *La France*, III, pp. 329–33.

Boniface IX in 1404, imposing a similar oath on their new pontiff, Innocent VII. Gregory XII was treated likewise on his election in 1406.[13] These oaths were not to be taken lightly. Innocent VII himself led the search for union, summoning a conference at Rome;[14] but his death prevented any outcome. His cardinals were also active, especially Balthasar Cossa, legate in Bologna and later pope John XXIII of the Pisan line. In 1405 he persuaded the Ferraran lawyer Petrus de Ancharano to produce his first major work on the schism, apparently with the connivance of Antonius de Butrio, a leading contemporary academic.[15] Cossa's continuing unionist activity was praised by Matthaeus de Matasellanis in 1409,[16] in which year he was also the addressee of a tract by Dominicus de Sancto Geminiano.[17]

Apart from the oaths imposed on the popes, however, Roman collegiate activity was of little importance until 1407. Then, after the collapse of negotiations between the rivals, and provoked by Gregory XII's determination to ignore the conclave agreement, the cardinals finally acted. On their initiative, the University of Bologna became the centre of a debate on the electoral capitulation, and on the possibility of a union of both Colleges to summon a united general council.[18] The discussions were probably encouraged by Cossa, while among those delivering opinions were Ancharano and Butrio, Paulus de Castro, and Bartholomaeus de Saliceto.[19] But the debate was not restricted to Bologna: the Paduan Franciscus de Zabarella produced both a tract on the powers of the cardinals, and the final section of his *Tractatus de Schismate*,[20] while there are also signs of extensive debate at Florence,

---

[13] Souchon, *Die Papstwahlen*, I, pp. 280–95.

[14] A. Theiner, ed., *Caesaris S.R.E. Card. Baronii ... Annales Ecclesiastici* (37 vols., Bar-le-Duc, 1864–83), a.1404, nos. 11–13.

[15] For MSS, see Souchon, *Die Papstwahlen*, II, p. 243, n. 2. Not all contain the beginning of the tract which indicates that it was compiled at Cossa's request. It does appear in the copy in Florence, Biblioteca Medicea Laurenziana, MS Plut. xx. 39, fos. 77r–109r, which also contains the notice of Butrio's approval at fo. 109r.   [16] Paris, BN, MS lat.17184, fo. 256r.

[17] Vatican, Biblioteca Apostolica, MS Vat. lat.4039, fos. 243–6.

[18] What appears to be the document from the cardinals initiating these discussions is in J. Vincke, *Schriftstücke zum Pisaner Konzil* (Bonn, 1942), pp. 29–30.

[19] For tracts by Butrio, Castro, and Matasellanis, see A. Bzovius, *Annalium Ecclesiasticorum*, xv (Cologne, 1622), pp. 266–71; for that by Saliceto see Vincke, *Schriftstücke*, pp. 30–2. Ancharano's first tract in response to the cardinals is in Florence, MS *cit.*, n. 15, fos. 117v–120v. There were also several anonymous contributions. That the debates were encouraged by Cossa may be inferred from the accusations of the anti-conciliarists that he had forced the academics to adopt the required line; see e.g. J. Weizsäcker, *Deutsche Reichstagsakten unter König Ruprecht*, III, Deutsche Reichstagsakten, vi (Gotha, 1888), pp. 401–2, 695.

[20] The first work is in Vatican, Biblioteca Apostolica, MS Vat. lat.3477, fos. 32r–35v. The third section of the *Tractatus de Schismate* is in S. Schardius, *De iurisdictione, auctoritate, et praeeminentia imperiali* (Basle, 1576), pp. 698–711.

where Lorenzo di Ridolfis produced two lengthy *consilia* favouring the cardinals.[21]

This theorising produced the legal formulation that the rivals, by their persistence in schism, had become heretics and were no longer popes. In such circumstances the leadership of the Church devolved upon the cardinals, who should summon a council to complete the process of removal before electing another pope. Although elements of this formula had appeared in the 1390s, this was their first coherent combination. Reasserting the oligarchic and hierarchical view of the ecclesiastical constitution,[22] the scheme vindicated the cardinals and restored their position. Although others were often accorded the power of summons in a descending hierarchy of authorities, there was no populism involved. The cardinals alone were to initiate the process of summoning what became the Council of Pisa.[23] Moreover, they alone would elect the next pope: although the council would have to confirm the rivals' self-deposition, it was for the cardinals to choose a successor.

But the election of Alexander V did not terminate the schism; the constitutional uncertainty remained. In seeking to obliterate the dispute, the lawyers had merely recreated the situation of July 1378, when Baldus de Ubaldis argued for a general council, but insisted that it could only be summoned by the legitimate pope – for him, Urban VI.[24] Benedict XIII and Gregory XII both held this view in 1409, and held their own assemblies at Perpignan and Cividale, while the rebellious cardinals transformed Pisa into another Anagni.

Instigating debates had been merely part of the increasing activity of the cardinals after 1407 in the politics of the schism. The mission of Cardinal Uguccione to England in late 1408 had exemplified their diplomatic involvement;[27] while in the renewed tractarian warfare after the council, the rival cardinals Orsini and Dominici were particularly active.[26] Moreover, until the end of the Council of Constance, the cardinals were closely involved in the constitutional developments. Several of the earlier theorists became cardinals after Pisa, and continued to write about the Church and the schism. But their changed

---

[21] The first *consilium* is in Vincke, *Schriftstücke*, pp. 122–34; the second in Vatican, Biblioteca Apostolica, MS Vat. lat.5608, fos. 184–202. For the Florentine debates, see L. Martines, *Lawyers and Statecraft in Renaissance Florence* (Princeton, 1968), pp. 289–95.

[22] Schardius, *De iurisdictione*, p. 701.

[23] *Ibid.*, p. 700.

[24] Bzovius, *Annalium*, xv, p. 68.

[25] V. H. Galbraith, ed., *The St Albans Chronicle, 1406–20* (Oxford, 1937), pp. 31–9, 136–52.

[26] Vincke, *Schriftstücke*, pp. 40–69, 75–104.

The cardinalate in the Great Schism

personal status occasionally altered their attitudes, as shown by Pierre d'Ailly's contrasting views on the cardinalate expressed in his *De materia concilii generalis* of 1403, and his *Tractatus de reformatione ecclesie* of 1416.[27] The problem of the cardinalate was highlighted at Constance, where the determination of the participants that this time the Church would be reunited proved too strong a challenge: the cardinals' rights as sole papal electors were overthrown in the conclave which elected Martin V, where they were joined by representatives of the participating nations.[28]

This challenge to the electoral powers of the cardinals had been latent throughout the schism. Originally, the dispute was seen as a simple contest between individuals, of whom one was obviously pope. A concern for straightforward judgment therefore dominated the search for a solution at this stage, generally revealed in a *Gott-mit-uns* appeal to secular intervention, or a call for some form of judicial commission, usually a general council. In these projects, the cardinals were often denied any determinative function: Henry of Langenstein specifically rejected any judgment by them in his *Epistola pacis*,[29] while Conrad of Gelnhausen emphasised their inferiority to the whole Church assembled in council.[30] The view of the schism as a conflict between individuals lingered throughout the dispute, with a sizeable neutralist party seeking a solution by some form of *via juris*.[31] However, this approach became less feasible as the schism became more entrenched, when concern shifted from simple judgment to the removal of the rivals and a fresh start. With this progression, a new problem arose of providing the next pope.[32]

This problem was rarely discussed before 1394, but the possibility of conflict over the cardinals' electoral rights was foreseen in the so-called *Tetragonus Aristotelis* letters, produced c.1382.[33] The anonymous author

[27] Oakley, *Political Thought*, pp. 119, n. 20, 251, 346–7.
[28] Valois, *La France*, IV, pp. 392–405.   [29] Paris, BN, MS Lat.14644, fos. 154v–155v.
[30] Bliemetzrieder, *Literarische Polemik*, pp. 122–3, 128–9.
[31] E.g. Munich, Bayerische Staatsbibliothek, MS Clm. 7006, fo. 127v. In 1396, Stephanus de Labarella called for a definitive decision which would obviate all future difficulties (Grenoble, Bibliothèque Municipale, MS 117, fo. 101r), and Pierre d'Ailly also argued for a final determination in 1403 (F. Ehrle, ed., *Martin de Alpartils Chronica actitatorum temporibus domini Benedicti XIII* (Paderborn, 1906), pp. 498–9, 501–2).
[32] *Ibid.*, p. 484. There was also a small group, characterised by one writer as the Wycliffites and Lollards in England, and the Fraticelli in Italy, for whom the issue of the papacy did not arise, they being content to allow the divisions within the Church to continue indefinitely (Munich, MS *cit.*, n. 31, fo. 127r).
[33] Edited in F. M. Bartoš, *Tetragonus Aristotelis, konciliaristick ý prosen s počátku velikého církeuního rozkolu* (Prague, 1916), pp. 12–42.

urged the *Romana generalitas* (interpreted as the local church of Rome, although acting for the totality of Christendom) to join the emperor in overthrowing the pretensions of the cardinals,[34] employing a historical justification derived from the period when the Roman clergy, rather than the cardinals, had chosen the pope.[35]

The nature of the development of the debate in subsequent years is well illustrated in Henry of Langenstein's *Epistola de cathedra Petri*, produced in 1395–6. He considered four schemes for reunion, of which the first, a judicial commission, catered for the neutralists and, to some extent, for the popes themselves. His second plan required the resignation of the rivals, after they had annulled any pronouncements against the opposing cardinals, both Colleges then uniting for an election. This left the cardinals' electoral rights intact; but Langenstein's other proposals offered a direct challenge. One argued that a general council, representing the whole Church, should elect; the other that the popes should resign after transferring the electoral power to representatives of the obediences (not cardinals), who would then choose the undoubted pontiff.[36] Various other authors suggested other methods, including that of choosing the future pope by lot.[37]

The developing general consensus did not seek to deprive the cardinals of their electoral rights altogether, but there still remained the problem of which cardinals could elect. Logically, as Nicholas Radcliffe noted *c.*1396, doubts about the legitimacy of the rivals must lead to doubts about the cardinals created by them: which meant that only the cardinals surviving from the pontificate of Gregory XI were legally entitled to elect. They were all adherents of Benedict XIII, and likely to elect one of his party, which would be no solution at all.[38] Moreover, this view on the legitimacy of the cardinals could be applied retro-

[34] *Ibid.*, p. 34. [35] *Ibid.*, p. 23.
[36] A. Kneer, *Die Entstehung der konziliaren Theorie* (Rome, 1893), pp. 135–7.
[37] Ehrle, *Alpartils Chronica*, pp. 487, 498.
[38] London, BL, MS Royal 6.D.x., fo. 279r: 'Si dominus papa bonifacius et antipapa simul cederent, vel presumaretur ex hoc quod neuter eorum fuit summus pontifex, vel saltem hesitaretur quis eorum habuit verum et inconcussum titulum in papatu . . . evidenter infertur, quod conformiter presumpcio magna foret de eorum cardinalibus, creatis ab eis post incepcionem scismatice pravitatis, quod non habuerunt verum titulum sui status. Cum igitur ad veros cardinales ius pertineat summum pontificem eligendi, sequi videtur quod utroque cedente presumpcio magna foret quod ad illos cardinales dumtaxat ius pertineret summum pontificem eligendi qui iam supersunt, et cardinales ante incepcionem scismaticis [*sic*] extiterunt. Cum igitur omnes illi fere antipape adherent, et autores et patratores scismatis extiterunt, si dominus noster bonifacius simul cum antipapa cederet, verissimile foret quod ipsi eligerent antipapam, vel aliquem sibi hacte[n]us adherentem, et sic foret novissimus error peior priore.'

spectively to the election of Benedict himself, producing a major change in the definition of his legitimacy. He could ignore the schism between Urban VI and Clement VII and claim to be the successor to Gregory XI, precisely because all the surviving cardinals had participated in his election. This theory was put forward by Radulph of Oulmont in 1397,[39] and was adopted and extended by Benedict himself after the Council of Pisa.[40] Later still Antonius de Piscibus, writing at Benedict's behest, suggested that, even if he did resign to obliterate the schism, he alone as the sole cardinal surviving from the College of Gregory XI was entitled to elect the successor.[41] This redefinition of Benedictine legitimacy allowed his obedience to continue even after his death in 1423, with the election (although itself disputed) of Clement VIII.[42]

While the Benedictines could thus stand aloof from the controversies of the schism, the proposal for the union of both Colleges of Cardinals was gaining increasing support, but not without encountering difficulties. From 1395 to 1403 there are signs of considerable support for a scheme which would simply allow the schism to die out, both popes retaining their obediences, the survivor being recognised as sole pontiff, and the Colleges then uniting under him.[43] This scheme, however, met with vigorous opposition.[44] A variant appeared in Zabarella's suggestion that the popes should bind their cardinals not to elect until both papacies were vacant, proceeding then to a united election, due provision having been made for the administration of the vacant

---

[39] Oxford, Balliol College, MS 165B, p. 222: 'Eleccio dominj benedicti XIII in papam fuit et est sancta et valida, ponito eciam quod eleccio Clementis vij nulla fuisset. Patet, quia sede vaccante per mortem Clementis, vel saltem gregorij xj, fuit a veris cardinalibus concorditer electus; et eleccio bonifacij intrusi non potuit impedire. Patet ... quia cardinales creati per Innocentem vj, per urbanum v, et gregorium xj, de quibus non est dubium quin veri sunt cardinales, in ipsum consenserunt.'

[40] Basle, Öffentliche Bibliothek der Universität, MS A.vi.17, fos. 64r–v: 'Successores Urbani fuerunt electi a solis Cardinalibus vel anticardinalibus dubijs per ipsum Urbanum promotis. Nam, post eleccionem Clementis, nullus Cardinalium indubitatorum adhesit Urbano; unde nullus eorum eleccionj sui successoris interfuit. Sed papa Benedictus, successor Clementis, fuit concorditer electus ab omnibus indubitatis Cardinalibus; et eciam a dubitatis per dominum Clementem promotis. Licet ergo negetur eundem Benedictum potuisse elegi in papam indubium a dubijs Cardinalibus, necessario tamen opportet fateri eum per eleccionem Cardinalium indubitatorum esse papam indubium, et de Jure pro tali habendum a cunctis fidelibus pendente huius scismatis dubio.'

[41] C. Schmitt, 'Un Défenseur attardé de Benoît XIII: Antoine "de Piscibus", O.F.M.', in Isidorus a Villapadierna, O.F.M.Cap., ed., *Miscellanea Melchior de Pobladura* (2 vols., Rome, 1964), I, pp. 288–9.

[42] For these events, see Valois, *La France*, IV, pp. 454–8.

[43] Munich, MS *cit.*, n. 31, fo. 125r; Ehrle, *Alpartils Chronica*, pp. 484–5, 502–4.

[44] Oxford, MS *cit.*, n. 39, p. 14; Munich, MS *cit.*, n. 31, fo. 125v.

obedience in the meantime.[45] Although idiosyncratic, this proposal did avoid one danger facing any proposal for removing the rivals: that the cardinals might still elect separate successors.[46]

For partisanship remained an important factor in the discussions of the proposed election. As the University of Oxford asked in 1396, if the power to elect belonged only to the 'true' cardinals, which side would confess its illegitimacy? And, if the Colleges did join, how were they to reach agreement?[47] These partisan difficulties were reflected in contemporary individual statements. In 1395 Nicholas of Fakenham argued that the schism was due solely to the anticardinals, and would not end until they had been dealt with;[48] while in the same year Pierre d'Ailly strongly opposed any arrangement reducing the number of Benedictine cardinals in a united conclave to give each side equal representation. This would merely give the Italians the majority, allowing the election of an Italian pope, and thereby fulfilling the ambition which had originally caused the schism.[49]

Although most writers apparently accepted that the cardinals should elect, against them could be placed various challenges to the electoral powers of the then cardinals. For one thing, it could be claimed that none of them was capable of electing: if the popes were schismatic heretics, what of their erstwhile adherents – whether as supporters or rebels?[50] In 1380, Conrad of Gelnhausen had listed several situations in which there might be no cardinals capable of electing (although not including this particular case), and had suggested that in such circumstances their electoral powers passed to the general council.[51] Pierre d'Ailly concocted a similar list in 1396, adding that as the cardinals derived their electoral powers from the council, that body could reclaim them – an assertion which was challenged by one of his opponents.[52] There are signs of some discussion of this challenge to the

45 Schardius, De iurisdictione, pp. 697–8.
46 As Oxford had complained in 1396: G. Ouy, 'Gerson et l'Angleterre à propos d'un texte polémique retrouvé du Chancelier de Paris contre l'Université d'Oxford, 1396', in A. H. T. Levi, ed., Humanism in France at the End of the Middle Ages and in the Early Renaissance (Manchester and New York, 1970), p. 58.
47 Ibid., pp. 58–9.
48 F. P. Bliemetzrieder, 'Traktat des Minoritenprovinzials von England, Fr. Nikolaus de Fakenham (1395), über das grosse abendländischen Schisma', Archivum Franciscanum Historicum, II (1910), pp. 88–91.
49 Ehrle, Alpartils Chronica, p. 473.
50 Stephanus de Labarella mentioned this difficulty as applied to the via cessionis: Grenoble, Bibliothèque Municipale, MS 117, fo. 98v.
51 Bliemetzrieder, Literarische Polemik, p. 131.
52 Ehrle, Alpartils Chronica, pp. 483, 490.

cardinals' rights *c.*1395;[53] while in 1403 d'Ailly developed his theory of the representative role of the cardinals in papal elections into a demand for a thorough revision of their status and the method of their creation.[54]

This ecclesiological version of the cardinals' representative role was countered by the historical derivation which made them more specifically representative of the local Roman church in the election of its bishop.[55] This local church could similarly reclaim its electoral powers, as the compiler of the *Tetragonus Aristotelis* letters had suggested. This idea was also being canvassed *c.*1395,[56] but the extent of its support is uncertain. However, Oxford University mentioned it in 1396, after suggesting that the logical consequence of the papal resignations would be resignation by the cardinals, leaving the church with no machinery for a papal election.[57] But Pierre d'Ailly forcefully rejected any scheme for so localised an election.[58]

Finally, among the challenges to the electoral powers of the cardinals, there were the vague proposals for their transference to some other representative group. But such schemes – of which d'Ailly suggested several types in 1403[59] – were only intended to apply in this one instance, and there is little sign of their general acceptance. In any case, all the challenges to the cardinals proved failures. The Clementists would never have tolerated any solution produced by the Romans or Italians alone;[60] while the absence of any machinery to summon a council without papal approval eliminated that possibility. Only when the cardinals recovered the initiative was the necessary procedure formulated, the resulting assembly being sufficiently under their control to prove no danger to their prerogatives. As for the system of election by representatives, apart from inherent difficulties concerning personnel, there was no political will to tamper so blatantly with the ecclesiastical constitution.

And even with the overt failure of the Pisan settlement, the cardinals' powers remained unchallenged. The obstinate persistence of the Benedictine and Gregorian obediences after Pisa was almost ignored, provoking little more than pious hopes that the schism would

---

53 Munich, MS *cit.*, n. 31, fo. 125r.
54 Oakley, *Political Thought*, pp. 322–3.
55 *Ibid.*, pp. 143–4.
56 Munich, MS *cit.*, n. 31, fo. 125r.
57 Ouy, 'Gerson et l'Angleterre', p. 61.
58 Ehrle, *Alpartils Chronica*, p. 483.
59 *Ibid.*, p. 474.
60 This antagonism was apparent both in d'Ailly's 1395 schedule (above, n. 49), and in Henry de Vienne's ballot at the Parisian Council of 1398, deliberately excluding the Romans from his proposed programme of diplomatic activity (Paris, Archives Nationales, J.518, fo. 402r).

eventually die out.[61] But the continuance of the schism placed the constitutionalists in a quandary, from which the only visible escape was a repetition of the Pisan experience: John XXIII should summon a council, and would abdicate after Benedict and Gregory had been deposed, another election then being held. Although John hoped that the Council of Constance would act to confirm his own papacy, he was soon disillusioned: several of the embassies arrived at the council prepared for another election, and the scramble for benefices which would follow.[62] But the discussions continued, and the programme altered. The cardinals had already failed once, and the increasingly populist conciliarism of Constance finally produced the effective challenge to their status embodied in the arrangements at the election of Martin V.

Yet even so, the reunification was not total. Indeed, the slow process whereby Martin V eventually gained almost universal recognition perhaps represented a more effective threat to the powers of the cardinalate than the events of Constance. Although most countries accepted Martin immediately, there were two cases which revealed difficulties. Scotland, the last state recognising Benedict XIII, accepted Martin V only after a national council at Perth in October 1418. The procedure resembled that proposed by the extreme conciliarists: within the national context, the electoral powers were apparently considered as residing in the full *ecclesia* which, after deposing Benedict, chose Martin V as pope. Both sides recognised the abnormality of this procedure: later contacts between Scotland and the papacy left the issue of the termination of Benedict's pontificate and the inception of Martin's almost deliberately vague.[63]

In France, the procedure had been rather different. A strong movement for the immediate acceptance of Martin V had been deliberately obstructed by the Crown. The principle of *cuius regio, eius religio*, a potent force in French policy throughout the schism, was obvious in the government's insistence on assurances of Martin's legitimacy –

---

[61] As in the remarks of a respondent to Benedict XIII (Basle, Öffentliche Bibliothek der Universität, MS A.vi.17, fo. 86v): 'Spes est magna quod finaliter tota Christianitas paulatim ad obedientiam electi in pisis, vel successorum suorum, reducetur; maxime defuncto dicto domino gregorio qui nullum, ut dicitur, secum habet cardinales, et dominus B. paucos qui forssan ipso defuncto nolent eligere, et si vellent non permitteretur eis; et isto saltim modo spero istud scisma finiri.'

[62] For such preparations among the University delegations, see my article, 'The University of Cologne and the Great Schism', *JEH*, xxviii (1977), p. 13, n. 9.

[63] See my article, 'The University of St Andrews and the Great Schism, 1410–1419', *JEH*, xxvi (1975), pp. 236–42.

which effectively meant reaching an acceptable compromise on royal influence over the French Church – before permitting recognition.[64]

The submission of Clement VIII to Martin V in 1429 completed the process begun at Constance in November 1417. But even then, the old Benedictine definition of legitimacy was not abandoned: Clement asserted his rights to the end, and only after he had resigned did his cardinals elect Martin as their pope.[65] Not until the election of Eugenius IV and the restoration of an undeniably legitimate succession did the cardinals fully recover their electoral powers; but even so, the difficulties over their ecclesiastical responsibilities and position lingered on. The election of Felix V at Basle posed an obvious threat to their rights; while the issue of the relationship between pope and cardinals frequently revived in disputes over electoral capitulations, the crises coming to a head in 1511 when some of the cardinals adopted a position relative to Julius II which looked ominously like that immediately preceding the election of Clement VII in 1378.[66] Despite the numerous attempts to settle the issue of the constitutional status of the cardinals during the Great Schism, it was clearly a problem which still required solution.

[64] Valois, *La France*, IV, pp. 421–9.
[65] *Ibid.*, IV, p. 473.
[66] W. Ullmann, 'The legal validity of the papal electoral pacts', *Ephemerides Juris Canonici*, XII (1956), pp. 253–69; W. Ullmann, 'Julius II and the schismatic cardinals', *SCH*, IX (1972), pp. 177–93.

PAULUS VLADIMIRI'S ATTACK ON
THE JUST WAR:
A CASE STUDY IN LEGAL POLEMICS

by FREDERICK H. RUSSELL*

LATE IN 1414 Paulus Vladimiri, the rector of the University of Cracow, set out for the Council of Constance to do intellectual battle with the Teutonic Order. The council was to adjudicate the dispute between Poland and the Order. Paulus would later explain his plan of attack thus:[1]

> Since a war ... is not made just otherwise than from its circumstances, ... hence it is not possible to know this (that the war is a just one) by a doctrinal investigation [*processus doctrinalis*] in which one proceeds, not from particular things but from universal and more well-known ones, not by experience but in the natural light of the intellect. Therefore if it is to be known to all whether a war is just or unjust, this must be carried out by another process, viz., a judicial investigation [*iudicialis indago*], and it must be proved by legitimate witnesses who know such individual facts as justify that war.

Paulus would use both *processus doctrinalis* and *iudicialis indago* in his long battle to condemn the practices of the Order of Crucifers and to justify Polish policy. Both he and the defenders of the Order invoked the commonly accepted concept of the just war to support their respective positions. This study explores Paulus Vladimiri's proposed modifications of the just war theory and some of the problems intellectuals encountered when they sought to define and apply religio-political doctrines to European society.

Thirteenth-century canonists and theologians had developed formulas for determining whether a war was just. The canonist Raymond

---

* The author wishes to express his appreciation to Professor James Muldoon of Rutgers University, Professor Kenneth Pennington Jr of Syracuse University and Professor Charles Donahue Jr of the University of Michigan for their helpful suggestions offered during the writing of this paper. The present paper is a revised and expanded version of one first read at the Twelfth Conference on Medieval Studies at Western Michigan University in May 1977.

[1] *Iste Tractatus* (1417), in L. Ehrlich, ed., *Pisma Wybrane Pawła Włodkowica/Works of Paul Wladimiri (A Selection)* (3 vols., Warsaw, 1966–9), II, pp. 182f., whence the translation; also in S. F. Belch, *Paulus Vladimiri and his Doctrine concerning International Law and Politics* (2 vols., The Hague, 1965), II, p. 994. Cf. H. Boockmann, *Johannes Falkenberg, der deutsche Orden und die polnische Politik* (Göttingen, 1975), p. 258, n. 341.

of Peñafort considered a war just when it met all five requirements of *persona, res, causa, animus* and *auctoritas*. Warriors were to be laymen, not clerics; the fundamental causes (*res*) included recovery of stolen property and defence of the *patria*; the immediate cause was the necessity of waging war; just warriors were to exhibit piety, justice, and obedience, and to shun hatred, cruelty and cupidity; and the war had to be waged on princely or ecclesiastical authority.[2] More simply, Aquinas required that a just war be waged on princely authority, for a just cause, and with a righteous intention. Ambushes were licit and wars could in cases of necessity be waged even on feast days.[3]

In the century and a half before Constance the just war concept had received little significant elaboration. In a rough and ready way, a war was deemed just when waged for an ostensible just cause by a power claiming the requisite authority. Yet in the face of the crusading movement learned observers had arrived at no common opinion about the relation of crusades to the just war and the special legal status of the military orders.[4] Problems concerning the legitimacy of infidel dominion and of pagan participation in just wars remained unresolved.[5] Medieval Christendom had been unable to agree upon any means of securing binding adjudication of the justice of a particular war.[6] With Europe racked by war, it was high time for a full debate on the problems of warfare when the representatives assembled at Constance.

[2] *Summa de Casibus* (Rome, 1603), 2. 5. 12. 17, p. 184ab. Theories of the just war and the crusades have recently been examined by J. Brundage, 'Holy War and the Medieval Lawyers', in T. P. Murphy, ed., *The Holy War* (Columbus, Ohio, 1976), pp. 99–140 and F. H. Russell, *The Just War in the Middle Ages* (Cambridge, 1975). For thirteenth-century canon law formulations, see *ibid.*, pp. 128–31.

[3] Aquinas, *Summa Theologiae* 2a2ae, q. 40, art. 1, resp.; art. 3, resp.; art. 4, resp. Cf. Russell, *Just War*, pp. 267–72.

[4] Cf. *ibid.*, pp. 207, 294–6. Hostiensis did seem to justify defence of the Holy Land by Hospitallers and Templars: *Lectura* (Venice, 1581), ad x. 5. 6. 17, no. 2, p. 33. Aquinas gave a generalised justification of military orders: *Summa* 2a2ae, q. 188, art. 3, resp. Yet neither of these passages constitutes a precise justification of the crusading mission of the Orders.

[5] Cf. J. Muldoon, ' "Extra Ecclesiam non est imperium." The Canonists and the Legitimacy of Secular Power', *Studia Gratiana*, IX (1966), pp. 553–80; K. Pennington Jr, 'Bartolomé de Las Casas and the Tradition of Medieval Law', *Church History*, XXXIX (1970), pp. 149–61; M. Wilks, *The Problem of Sovereignty in the Later Middle Ages* (Cambridge, 1963), pp. 413–16.

[6] Cf. J. Gaudemet, 'La Rôle de la papauté dans le règlement des conflits entre états aux XIIIe et XIVe siècles', *Recueils de la Société Jean Bodin*, XV (1961), pp. 79–106. In the fourteenth century, papal arbitral proceedings between Poland and the Order had usually found for Poland, but the papacy had been unable to secure the Order's compliance with its decisions: P. Knoll, *The Rise of the Polish Monarchy* (Chicago, 1972), pp. 103–7.

I

The Teutonic Order had since the thirteenth century gradually extended its sway along the Baltic littoral, defeating, subjugating and converting the heathen inhabitants. In the fourteenth century wars between Poland and the Order had broken out, and papal attempts at arbitration had been generally unsuccessful. A Polish dynastic crisis, combined with Poland's military position in 1386, resulted in the marriage of Queen Jadwiga to Ladislas Jagiello, the pagan grand duke of Lithuania. Ladislas agreed to convert to Christianity and to work for the conversion of the Lithuanians. Stretching almost from the Baltic to the Black Sea, Poland–Lithuania included pagan tribes and Orthodox Christians as well as Christians of Roman allegiance. After some attempts at compromise, confrontations between Poland and the Order came to a head at the battle of Grunwald (or Tannenberg) in 1410. Polish forces, fighting alongside Hussite Bohemians, Lithuanians, Samogitians, schismatic Ruthenians, Mongols, Cossacks and even Tartars, inflicted a heavy defeat on the Order. In 1411 the papally sponsored Peace of Thorn was concluded, but Poland remained unsatisfied. Both sides were to present their claims at Constance. Poland was pursuing an opportunistic foreign policy bent on acquiring the Order's lands.[7] The Council presented an unusual opportunity for intellectuals to influence one of the major issues of the day.

As part of Poland's resurgence, Casimir the Great in 1364 founded the University of Cracow on the Italian model. The study of canon law was stressed, to enable Poland to play a role in European diplomacy. The foundation languished, but in 1400 the university was refounded on the French model. This time theology was stressed, so that native Lithuanians could be trained to instruct their neophyte people. The history of the fledgling university reflects the contemporary history of Poland itself.[8]

[7] A general bibliography on the Order and Poland in Western languages includes: *Cambridge Medieval History*, VII (1932), ch. ix, and VIII (1936), ch. xviii; K. Setton and H. Hazard, eds, *A History of the Crusades*, III (Madison, Wisconsin, 1975), ch. xvi; W. Urban, *The Baltic Crusade* (De Kalb, Illinois, 1975); *Cambridge History of Poland* (2 vols., Cambridge, 1950); A. Gieysztor et al., eds., *History of Poland* (Warsaw, 1968), chs. i–vi; Z. Wojciechowski, *L'État polonais au moyen âge* (Paris, 1949); and Knoll (as above, n. 6.). For an example of the harsh realities of German–Slav conflict, see W. Urban, 'Martin of Golin', *Lituanus*, XXII (1976), pp. 45–59.

[8] For the history of the University of Cracow, see H. Rashdall, *The Universities of Europe in the Middle Ages* (rev. ed., Oxford, 1936), II, pp. 289–94; K. Morawski, *Histoire de l'Université de Cracovie* (3 vols., Paris, 1900), esp. I, pp. 20, 42, 75f.; A. Vetulani, 'Les Origines de l'université de Cracovie', *Acta Poloniae Historica*, XIII (1966), pp. 14–40; P. Knoll, 'Casimir the Great and

Paulus Vladimiri (or Pawła Włodkowica) served as rector of this university in 1414 and 1415. He had previously studied in Prague and Padua, having attended the lectures of Zabarella and Petrus de Ancharano, and had represented Poland at the papal court. At Constance he represented both university and king, and saw further diplomatic service in Italy, dying in 1434. He produced numerous and lengthy *Streitschriften* devoted to the destruction of the Teutonic Order's claims. His activity is the intellectual analogue of Poland's battle at Grunwald.[9]

II

In 1415 Paulus's first treatise attacking the Order recalled Raymond's criteria for the just war and concluded that an unjust war gave rise to no legitimate dominion.[10] Two years later he fleshed out his critique. The Order's wars lacked proper authority since papal and imperial privileges were either forged or granted erroneously. The true object of the Crucifers' wars was acquisition of infidels' lands and their subjugation and extermination. The Order fought not by necessity but voluntarily. The Crucifers acted out of greed, *libido dominandi* and a desire to subjugate, ravish and occupy the lands of infidels, and as clerics the Crucifers were prohibited from waging wars. By fighting without express papal permission they rendered themselves false monks and were guilty of individual and corporate selfishness.[11] After invoking

the University of Cracow', *Jahrbücher für Geschichte Osteuropas*, XVI (1968), pp. 232–49; and *idem*, 'Learning in late Piast Poland', *Proceedings of the American Philosophical Society*, CXX (April 1976), pp. 136–57.

[9] The life and works of Paulus have only recently come under scrutiny, and it is too early to attempt a comprehensive assessment of his intellectual contributions. Fundamental to this task is Belch's monumental work (above, n. 1; but see H. Kaminsky's review in *Speculum*, XLII (1967), pp. 918–20). For Paulus's life, see Belch, *Paulus*, ch. ii and Ehrlich, *Works*, I, xi–xiv. Belch's work contains some of Paulus's treatises as well as those of some of his adversaries, notably Johannes Urbach. Ehrlich's edition contains most of the treatises with Polish and English translations on the facing page and copious annotation. There remain serious textual problems. Here the treatises will be cited according to Ehrlich's edition, with cross-references to Belch's edition where possible. In his work on Falkenberg (above, n. 1) Boockmann makes some important points about Paulus. Also important is E. Schulz, 'Paulus Vladimiri und das jagiellonische Polen. Eine Untersuchung zu den Wirkungen der italienischen Rechtswissenschaft auf den jagiellonischen Staat' (Dissertation, Göttingen, 1951). Articles that bear on Paulus's activity include R. Bierzanek, 'Les Conceptions de la paix chez les auteurs polonais de la fin du moyen âge et de la Renaissance', *Recueils de la Société Jean Bodin*, XV (1961), pp. 171–97; K. Grzybowski, 'The Polish Doctrine of the Law of War in the Fifteenth Century', *The Jurist*, XVIII (1958), pp. 386–411; and F. Kapelinski, 'Paulus Wladimiri (1369–1435), défenseur de la tolérance religieuse', *Revue internationale d'histoire politique et constitutionelle* n.s. XIX–XX (1955), pp. 201–14.

[10] *Saevientibus*, Ehrlich, *Works*, I, pp. 66f., 73f.; and Belch, *Paulus*, I, pp. 824, 829f. Cf. *Ad Aperiendam*, Ehrlich, *Works*, II, pp. 38f. [11] *Quoniam Error*, Ehrlich, *Works*, II, pp. 378–81.

the Thomistic requirements, Paulus added a new criterion for the just war that was based upon his criticism of the Order. There must be at least a summary legal examination (*cognicio*) followed by a declaration (*declaracio legitima*) that the requirements had been met. As corollaries to this position Paulus claimed that unless a legal declaration determined that the three requirements had been met, infidels could not justly be deprived of dominion, and that unless someone under attack, even an infidel, knew the just cause of the attack, he might justly resist the attack because of the natural right of self-defence.[12]

In a letter of 1432 to the bishop of Cracow, Paulus argued that the Order violated the *animus* criterion because it was motivated by revenge. Since the pope had not done justice in the Polish dispute, he was guilty of homicide. The Order had renounced dominion but still illegally occupied territory. Its supposed privileges had allowed it to acquire Prussia, Livonia and Samogitia and to subject non-Christians to its unjust tyranny. The Order was acting with audacity rather than authority against both infidels and Christians.[13]

This employment of Raymond's just war formula contributed to a strong but, on the whole, unexceptional diatribe that confronted the Order's claims with a biased interpretation of its actions. By the fifteenth century the Teutonic Order had the weight of theory, privileges, official toleration and two centuries of success on its side.[14] Paulus had his work cut out for him. A mechanical application of the formula needed supplementation by a wide-ranging argumentation to which Paulus devoted much ink and sweat. He had to attack the status of the Order and simultaneously to justify Polish conduct against it, in order to destroy its temporal rule. To be successful in the *iudicialis indago* Paulus had to show that the Order had denied due process of law to its enemies, thereby violating existing canon law, and that Poland's

---

[12] *Ibid.*, Ehrlich, *Works*, II, pp. 308–10, 313f.; and Belch, *Paulus*, II, pp. 896–904. Cf. Ehrlich, *Works*, I, p. lvi and Belch, *Paulus*, I, pp. 235, 706, 729, 770; II, p. 894. There are doubts concerning the authorship of these passages; cf. Belch, *Paulus*, II, pp. 892–5; Boockmann, *Falkenberg*, p. 259, n. 942; E. Weise, ed., *Die Staatsschriften des Deutschen Ordens in Preussen im 15. Jahrhundert*, I (Göttingen, 1970), pp. 271–3. On internal and stylistic grounds I take the passage in Ehrlich, *Works*, II, pp. 303–11 (Belch's no. 5) to have been written by Paulus, but based on an earlier version submitted to him by his former teacher Maurice of Prague, found in Ehrlich, *Works*, II, pp. 311–15 and Belch's no. 4.

[13] *Ad Episcopum Cracoviensem*, Ehrlich, *Works*, III, pp. 220f. and Belch, *Paulus*, II, p. 1100.

[14] The validity of papal and imperial privileges granted to the Order is a distinct issue not examined here in detail. Ideally, a medieval court should have pronounced judgment. Paulus minutely analysed these privileges. Honorius III alone issued 113 bulls favouring the Order that Innocent had approved in 1199, thus making it the equal of the older crusading orders: Setton, *Crusades*, III, p. 567.

alliances with non-Christians were licit according to that law. Hence his arguments were necessarily conservative.

In Paulus's view, the major chink in the intellectual armour of the Order was its lack of explicit legal approval. One line of attack was to demonstrate that papal privileges used by the Order only applied to its former activity in the Holy Land. Both papal and imperial privileges were irrelevant when applied to its activity along the Baltic. Since the original purpose of the Order was to run a hospital in Jerusalem, fighting was an illicit task for its clerics, and since that hospital no longer existed, the original justification of the Order was no longer valid.[15] The Order had, moreover, been only tacitly approved by the papacy, even though 'importunate solicitations' had led successive popes to make imprudent grants that knowledge of the facts would have forestalled. Just because the Order had received these grants did not mean that it enjoyed express papal approval.[16]

In many places Paulus claimed that the Teutonic Order was an offshoot of the Templars which the papacy had abolished when this order no longer fulfilled its original purpose.[17] The Crucifers of Prussia were unlike the Hospitallers, who were specially deputised to defend the Holy Land. Since they had not undergone a change in function, the Church tolerated their warfare while approving their tending of the infirm. By contrast, the Teutonic Order no longer ran a hospital, if indeed it ever had, but in its own interest continued to carry on offensive war against the dominions of others. Hence the two orders were different in purpose, and so the justification of the Hospitallers could not be transferred to the Teutonic Order. While the Hospitallers made war by necessity, the Crucifers of Prussia did so voluntarily. All letters endowing the Teutonic Order with privileges from whatever source had been obtained surreptitiously and were null, invalid and false. Anyone who invoked these letters was guilty of forgery.[18]

---

[15] *Ad Aperiendam*, Ehrlich, *Works*, I, pp. 150–4, 250.

[16] *Ibid.*, I, pp. 180, 183; cf. above, n. 11. According to Paulus, the letters of Alexander IV had been obtained surreptitiously and for no good cause, and so the falsity of the cause falsified the whole disposition favouring the Order: *ibid.*, II, pp. 2, 35. In a tactful attempt to soften his criticism of the papacy, Paulus pointed out that the papacy was too distant from Poland to be expected to have firm knowledge of affairs there. Thus Alexander IV at Perugia or Anagni was variously seen as fifty or one hundred days' travelling time from Livonia or Prussia: *ibid.*, II, pp. 32, 240f. Hence it was reckless, even though the papacy had been misled, to attribute the errors of the Order to the Church at large: *ibid.*, II, pp. 380f.

[17] *Ad Aperiendam*, *ibid.*, I, pp. 183, 202, 211, 218–20.

[18] *Ibid.*, I, pp. 167–70, II, pp. 5–10, 99f., 254f. The Polish grants to the Order were invalid because of the doctrine of inalienability: *Ad Videndum*, *ibid.*, III, p. 142.

Imperial grants to the Crucifers were likewise invalid. For example, Frederick II's grants of lands were null because they were not within imperial jurisdiction. Since the reason for the grants was the propagation of the faith the matter properly belonged to ecclesiastical jurisdiction.[19] Most imperial grants were made for the Order's foundation in Jerusalem, not for its holdings in Prussia. Since that foundation had been destroyed, so also were the privileges attached to it.[20] Paulus accused the Order of seeking to escape from both spiritual and temporal jurisdiction by its contradictory claims that its possessions were imperial gifts and that its possessions were ecclesiastical dependencies. Great confusion was the inevitable result.[21] Further, emperors such as Frederick II were excommunicated and condemned as enemies of the Church and heretics when they made donations to the Order, so their donations were invalid for that reason.[22] Since all grants were either false or erroneous, the Order had no legal existence and could not exercise legitimate dominion. Lands subject to the Order were unjustly detained by it.[23] The real aims of the Order were homicide, robbery, theft, and slavery. Not a true *religio*, the Order should be damned by canon, civil, natural and divine law.[24]

When Paulus turned to justify the legitimacy of infidel dominion and Poland's use of infidel troops, he was able to argue on more traditional grounds. Even if the Order's privileges were genuine, they were invalid. The pope had no just cause to authorise the Crucifers to seize the lands of infidels.[25] The faithful were deceived by such letters.[26] Neither propagation of the faith nor even the papal plenitude of power was sufficient to legitimate donations since dominion could not be taken away even from infidels without just cause. These assertions

---

[19] *Ad Aperiendam, ibid.*, II, p. 121; *Quoniam Error, ibid.*, II, pp. 238– 361.

[20] *Ad Aperiendam, ibid.*, II, p. 146.

[21] *Ad Aperiendam, ibid.*, I, pp. 218f.: '... isti templarii nullum in temporalibus volunt habere iudicem: Ecclesiam non quia dicunt quod ex donacione imperatoris habent Prussiam et alia temporalia, imperatorem non quia ducunt quod eadem bona eque habent et ita eciam bene ab ecclesia: et sic nervi testiculorum Leviathan perplexi sunt.' Cf. Job 40.12.

[22] *Ad Videndum, ibid.*, III, p. 149.

[23] *Ad Aperiendam, ibid.*, I, p. 201, II, p. 77; *Quoniam Error, ibid.*, II, pp. 256, 269.

[24] *Ad Aperiendam, ibid.*, I, p. 189. Paulus also condemned the Order's practice of conducting semi-annual *Reisen* or expeditions against infidels on the feasts of Purification and Assumption. His argument, based on Aquinas, concluded that since the Crucifers fought voluntarily rather than from necessity, they should especially not fight on feast days: *Saevientibus, ibid.*, I, pp. 68–72 and Belch, *Paulus*, II, pp. 825–8; *Opinio Hostiensis*, Ehrlich, *Works*, I, p. 132f. and Belch, *Paulus*, II, p. 881; *Ad Aperiendam*, Ehrlich, *Works*, I, p. 202.

[25] *Opinio Hostiensis*, Ehrlich, *Works*, I, pp. 124f.; and Belch, *Paulus*, II, pp. 873f.

[26] *Ad Aperiendam*, Ehrlich, *Works*, I, p. 201.

were based on a commentary of Innocent IV (to x.3.34.8) that allowed peaceful infidels to exercise legitimate dominion.[27] Innocent's opinion had been followed by Johannes Andreae, Zabarella and Petrus de Ancharano; it was contested by Hostiensis who argued that with the coming of Christ all legitimate dominion had been transferred to Christian rulers. In his treatise, most widely read at Constance, the *Opinio Hostiensis* of 1415, and elsewhere, Paulus condemned Hostiensis's position.[28] The Crucifers had failed to advise infidel rulers of the justice of the Order's cause and had not issued a formal declaration of war. Since the Order had deprived infidels of their legal rights, Paulus urged the Council to compel the Order to restore its conquests.[29]

As if these charges were not enough, Paulus even accused the Order of heresy. His arguments did not attempt to convict the Crucifers of asserting perverse dogma in the usual sense, but were aimed rather at the Order's acts and defence of them at Constance. The Order was heretical because in waging unjust wars it sinned against charity.[30] If the Order's wars deprived infidel rulers of legitimate dominion, they were unjust because they lacked any just cause and were prohibited by divine law. Since propagation of the faith was the ostensible but illicit cause of these wars, to justify them was moreover an error amounting to heresy.[31]

On the other hand, the Order's spokesmen at Constance claimed that Poland had acted illegally and immorally by using infidel troops against the Order. Yet both Oldradus and Johannes Andreae had considered as licit the use by Christians of infidels in a just war against other Christians. Following these canonists Paulus argued that peaceful infidels who were otherwise not at war with Christians could so aid Christians. If guile, ambushes and clever ruses were licit, and if Christians could aid infidels in just wars, Christians could make common cause with excommunicates and infidels in cases of necessity.[32]

---

[27] *Ibid.*, I, pp. 233f., 238. Cf. above, n. 5.

[28] E.g. *Saevientibus, ibid.*, I, pp. 12–14 and Belch, *Paulus*, II, pp. 799–801.

[29] *Quoniam Error*, Ehrlich, *Works*, II, pp. 308–11. Cf. above, n. 12.

[30] *Ad Aperiendam, ibid.*, I, pp. 197, 210. By the Order's 'Prussian heresy' Paulus seems to mean their unjust usurpations, the blasphemy of fighting on feast days, and illicit violence done to fellow creatures of God: *Ad Aperiendam, ibid.*, I, pp. 201f., 206f.; *Quoniam Error, ibid.*, II, p. 310. Cf. Belch, *Paulus*, ch. xviii, esp. p. 695.

[31] *Quoniam Error*, in Ehrlich, *Works*, II, pp. 303–13.

[32] *Saevientibus, ibid.*, I, pp. 75–7 and Belch, *Paulus*, II, pp. 830f. Paulus did not say straight out that excommunicates could be used in a just war, but he did cite a canon (x. 5. 39. 34) stating that in case of necessity Christians could communicate with excommunicates. At the council he obviously did not wish to emphasise this contention, but simply used whatever canonical notions would support his arguments. Paulus's compatriot and fellow Cracow canonist Stanislas of Scarbimiria was more direct in justifying the use of heathens in a just war waged by

III

As sampled here, Paulus's opinions constituted a broadside against the Teutonic Order buttressed by an overabundance of legal citations. But how convincing were they? After all, it was possible to draw entirely different conclusions from the diversity of facts, law and theology. Realising the threat to its credibility posed by Paulus, the Order has- tened to commission spokesmen for its position.[33] Foremost among these was the German Dominican, Johannes Falkenberg, whose vigorous treatises, such as his *Satira* of 1412, excited debates at the council. Falkenberg claimed that Poland was hindering the Order's task of extending and defending the faith, and in intemperate language called for the destruction of Poland's king and kingdom and for com- pensation to the Order for the damages caused by Poland. For his *Satira* Falkenberg was condemned at the council and by a later papal inquest.[34] In Paulus's *Iste Tractatus* and *Quoniam Error* of 1417 he treated Falkenberg's theological defence of the Order and his attack upon Polish policy as the logical conclusion of Hostiensis's position on infidel dominion.[35]

From Paulus's perspective a far more dangerous treatise was put forth in 1416 by the canonist Johannes Urbach, who met Vladimiri on their common ground of canon law.[36] From the same assumptions and

Christians against other Christians. In his sermon *De Bellis Justis*, composed between 1410 and 1414, he argued that pagans could punish unjust Christians, that if ambushes and siege machines were licit in a just war, so was the use of men of whatever stripe, and that pagans could wage just wars against Christians: L. Ehrlich, ed., *Polski wykład prawa wojny XV wieku* (Warsaw, 1955), pp. 126–36. Even more unrestrained was an anonymous tract entitled 'Revocatur in dubium', which argued that Poland could use the aid of heretics in a defensive war: *ibid.*, pp. 198–202. (There is a summary in English of the two works in *ibid.*, pp. 250–63.) On these two tracts, cf. Boockmann, *Falkenberg*, pp. 171, 174–7. This line of reasoning understandably was unacceptable to the delegates at Constance. Its dangers were confirmed early in the 1430s, when a Hussite army supporting Poland against the Order penetrated as far as the West Prussian Baltic coast: Setton, *Crusades*, II, p. 643.

33 Recent works on these spokesmen include Weise, *Staatsschriften*; *idem*, *Die Amtsgewalt von Papst und Kaiser und die Ostmission* (Marburg, 1971); and Boockmann, *Falkenberg*. Much more study is needed, for the textual diffusion and even the positions of the various authors remain unclear.

34 For the career of Falkenberg and the newly discovered text of his *Satira*, see Boockmann, *Falkenberg* (cf. K. Pennington Jr's review in *Speculum*, LII (1977)). In effect Falkenberg equated the Order with the Church (c. 6, pp. 329–32), and claimed that to attack the 'Church' with infidel aid constituted heresy (cc. 7–8, pp. 332–8).

35 Cf. Belch, *Paulus*, II, p. 1008.

36 For Urbach's career, see H. Boockmann, 'Aus dem Handakten des Kanonisten Johannes Urbach', *Deutsches Archiv*, XXVIII (1972), pp. 497–532 and *Falkenberg*, pp. 22–4. Other render- ings of his name include Vrebach and Frebach. The text of his *Tractatus de Statu Fratrum Ordinis Theutonicorum* is in Belch, *Paulus*, II, pp. 1116–80, and Weisse, *Staatsschriften*, I, pp. 318–80.

sources Urbach argued systematically and cogently that the Order was both licit and acting lawfully, and that Poland was the unjust aggressor. In short, Urbach agreed doctrinally with Paulus, but reached opposite conclusions.

The second part of Paulus's *Quoniam Error* was devoted to a point-by-point refutation of Urbach's eighteen conclusions. In his second conclusion Urbach denied the possibility of legitimate infidel dominion. Paulus countered that this smacked of the Wycliffite heresy, previously condemned by the council, that legitimate dominion was grounded on Christian faith.[37] Urbach's fifteenth conclusion argued that Christians might seek aid from infidels for simple defence but not for attack, vengeance or offensive warfare. Vladimiri responded that Urbach tacitly implied that Poland had gone beyond these limits by using infidels and schismatics at Grunwald. Urbach's position was moreover erroneous in law, injurious to Poland, and internally inconsistent. Since offensive war was categorically condemned, Urbach's distinction was useless. Furthermore, no competent tribunal had convicted Poland, and canon law allowed the faithful to communicate with infidels.[38] The debate thus turned on whether peaceful relations between Christians and infidels were licit or even possible.

On the basis of textual argumentation it would be difficult to award victory in the Urbach–Vladimiri battle, for both argued their cases impeccably. The respective arguments tended to degenerate into a citation-mongering verbal bombast that demonstrates the medieval adage that 'authorities have wax noses that can be bent in diverse directions'. On the level of these *consilia*, the debate was at an impasse, so Paulus invoked another weapon: the facts. As he often emphasised, the facts were on his side. While each of his treatises contained some version of the relevant facts used as a cudgel against the Order's

---

Cf. Belch, *Paulus*, II, pp. 910, 1113; Schulz, 'Paulus', pp. 24–8. According to both Falkenberg and Urbach, Poland as the unjust party was bound to compensate the Order for damages incurred: Paulus, *Quoniam Error*, Ehrlich, *Works*, II, p. 397.

[37] *Quoniam Error*, Ehrlich, *Works*, II, p. 337: 'Igitur inferiores fideles naturaliter subiecti superioribus infidelibus possunt suis superioribus racione infidelitatis subtrahere obedienciam. Tenet consequencia quia infideles propter peccatum infidelitatis desinunt esse domini ex conclusione. Et sic prelatus existens in peccato mortali quo est Deo infidelis desinit esse prelatus et dominus: que omnia sunt articuli Wykleff damnati in Concilio Constanciensi.' Wycliff claimed that legitimate dominion was based on grace, while Paulus attempted to taint Urbach with Wycliffism by attributing to him the claim that legitimate dominion was based on faith. By faith in this context Paulus meant living without mortal sin. The distinction here between faith and grace is a subtle one; for its importance, see J. Muldoon, 'John Wyclif and the Rights of the Infidels: the *Requerimento* re-examined', to appear in *Americas*.

[38] *Quoniam Error*, Ehrlich, *Works*, II, pp. 386–91.

pretensions, this tendency was most clearly contained in his *Articuli contra Cruciferos*.[39] Here he marshalled 155 articles into a diverse bill of particulars that named names, dates, places and treaties in roughly chronological order. Most articles ended with a comment such as 'and so this is true, public and notorious'. Using historical argumentation, biased naturally against the Order, Paulus first surveyed the Crucifers' activities up to 1410, then backtracked to the papal arbitral award of 1339, and finally examined the Order's subsequent crimes and bad faith. Throughout Paulus was concerned to demonstrate the ineffectiveness of the Order's attempts to defend and extend Christianity.[40] The sum total of Vladimiri's rather miscellaneous list of charges argued that the Order was in revolt against both Church and Empire.

Paulus resorted to historical research to counter the systematic arguments advanced by the Order's spokesmen. He charged that Urbach's conclusions were as easily rejected as they were proved.[41] Since he was thus aware that systematic arguments based on common doctrines alone could not prove his case, he invoked the historical record to tip the balance of opinion in his favour. At some points in a systematic argument he would lapse into historical reasoning to prove the iniquity of Urbach's conclusions, as when he invoked Gratian and the *Digest* and then gave a potted history of events leading up to Grunwald.[42] Toward the end of his life Paulus refused to try to resolve the question of whether all men, Christians and unbelievers alike, were legally subject to the Empire, which he would leave to 'vain disputation, since this matter seems to be tenebrous water in the clouds of the air'.[43]

[39] For the date and authorship of this work and its relationship to Paulus's *Quoniam Error* of 1417, see Belch, *Paulus*, I, pp. 177f., II, pp. 906–15 (with a resumé of the contents on pp. 912f.). The text is in *ibid.*, II, pp. 916–88. Cf. Boockmann, *Falkenberg*, p. 228, n. 181.

[40] Paulus focused not on the violence of the pagan Prussians which had occasioned the original attacks of the Order, but rather on the Order's destruction of the Prussians (art. 15). Illiterate in dogma, the Crucifers had not instructed the Prussians in the faith, so the latter preserved their pagan customs. The Order's missionary work was thus ineffective. The Crucifers were greedy (art. 17), they practised simony (arts. 108–10), and they treated Ruthenian schismatics as pagans (art. 18). The conversion of Ladislas and his cousin Witold, along with the Lithuanians, deprived the Order of its just cause for the acquisition of Lithuania, and yet it continued its aggressive wars (art. 20). The Order aimed at the total destruction of Poland (art. 61). Since the Order had broken treaties, Poland was no longer obliged to maintain them (art. 88). For the transformation of the Order from a missionary and crusading institution to the bureaucratic *Ordenstaat*, see P. Knoll, 'Poland as *Antemurale Christianitatis* in the Late Middle Ages', *Catholic Historical Review*, LX (1974), pp. 381–401, at p. 396.

[41] *Quoniam Error*, in Ehrlich, *Works*, II, p. 365.

[42] *Ibid.*, II, pp. 395f.

[43] *Ad Episcopum Cracoviensem*, Ehrlich, *Works*, III, p. 223 and Belch, *Paulus*, II, p. 1101: 'An autem omnes increduli de iure subsint imperio Romano, qui eciam Romanum imperium minime

While these may well be the words of an embittered old man, they indicate Paulus's realisation of the impotence of doctrinal argumentation without an appeal to history.[44]

IV

The ensemble of Paulus's arguments was a bewildering *tour de force* in which accepted authorities were bent to his attempt to call into question the entire ecclesiastical position of the Teutonic Order. The long-neglected duel between Paulus and the defenders of the Order has recently attracted the attention of scholars of diverse persuasions. What was its significance? The suggestions here turn on Paulus's methods of argumentation, his use of historical reasoning, his originality, and his modifications of the just war tradition.

A sincere and well-meaning partisan, Paulus harped on the discrepancies between the professed ideals of Christian society and the practices of the Crucifers. In effect Paulus accused the Order of what sociologists have called 'institutional goal displacement', whereby the

recognoscunt vel eciam omnes Christiani, non diffinio sed vane disputacioni hoc relinquo cum hec materia videatur esse tenebrosa aqua in nubibus aeris. Hoc autem certum teneo Romanum Pontificem tamquam vicarium Christi esse indubitatum iudicem omnium predictorum qui habet indicere bellum eciam incredulis Romanam ecclesiam non recognoscentibus [*sic*] quociens causa racionabilis hoc requirit.' Earlier Paulus was willing to restrict significantly the jurisdiction of the empire, when he observed that if it was impossible for the world to be politically united under one ruler, as was the case at his time, then it was better that there should be no juridical unity either. Consequently the emperor had no right to make war on infidels to secure imperial jurisdiction over them: *Quoniam Error*, Ehrlich, *Works*, II, p. 370: 'Et ideo quia tale dominium [=single world monarchy] de facto haberi non potest, ideo in casu expediens est sicud nunc quod eciam ad tempus de iure cesset. Cum igitur non expedit in hoc casu sub uno principe seculari rem publicam gubernari totius universi, non potest Imperator stante tali casu nunc de iure vel licite movere bellum infidelibus pro ipsorum ad obedienciam reduccione.'

44 It is not claimed here that Paulus resorted to history in direct response to Falkenberg and Urbach, or that Paulus's appeal to history was unique for the time. A survey of the Order's proponents shows that Peter of Wormdith, the procurator of the Order, had already detailed instances in which Poland had broken the Thorn ceasefire of 1411 (Weise, *Staatsschriften*, I, no. 2). At about the same time as Paulus finished his *Articuli*, the Spaniard Andreas de Escobar gave an historical narration of Polish misdeeds (*ibid.*, no. 16), bolstered by many specific observations about the Order's aid to the Poles against the Prussians. For the shortness of his treatment of Poland's hindering of the Order's war against the heathen Andreas excused himself, 'propter defectum librorum quos in hoc sacro concilio Constantiensi non habeo nec habere valeo' (*ibid.*, I, p. 401). Ardicinus of Novara (*ibid.*, no. 9), and Dominicus de Ponte (*ibid.*, no. 10) used canonical arguments to indict Polish policy. After all the sound and fury over doctrine at Constance, the tract of Andreas de Escobar evidenced a return to Peter of Wormdith's arguments based on historical facts as filtered through the eyes of partisan observers. Clearly Paulus was not alone among his contemporaries in sensing the ultimate insufficiency of both doctrinal and historical arguments to convince those in a position to adjudicate the conflict.

248

Order had forsaken its original purpose to become a bureaucratic and territorial state that approached the early modern model of absolutism. Vladimiri's intellectual arsenal included canon and civil law, history and even common sense, and he used these to exploit ambiguities about the extent of papal and imperial jurisdiction. He added a goodly amount of late scholastic dialectical baggage and more than a hint of the Aristotelian–Thomistic notion that human society organised apart from God was legitimate.

Yet Paulus's arguments against the Order's legitimacy are not wholly convincing. His case rested upon his determination that the Order had always waged unjust wars. Given the crusading tradition, this could be and easily was contested. Further, it was more than a little odd to claim that the Order and its wars possessed no legal status after two centuries of existence and general acceptance.[45] After all, the concept of prescription could have been invoked to legitimate the Order's dominion. Similarly strange was the charge of heresy based on the Order's practices rather than on any doctrinal heterodoxy. It was obviously difficult to indict the Order's legal position within Europe by a condemnation of its acts, for this type of argument could cut both ways and could be wielded against just about any institution including the Polish kingdom itself.

While Paulus had the effrontery to claim that the papacy had been misled for two hundred years, in general he was careful to avoid antagonising the pope, the imperial policy or conciliar opinion. Thus he often did not push his ideas to their logical conclusions.[46] When he could find no legal texts to support his contentions directly, he sought refuge in vague and general canons or in biblical passages.[47] That it is sometimes difficult to discern where he stood on specific issues is partly due to his care to avoid any suspicion of heresy. In the charged atmosphere at Constance, where political conflicts were waged by legal and theological arguments, an accusation of heresy was an easy way to damage an adveisary.[48] Very serious constraints were placed on clear

---

[45] There are some grounds for considering certain bulls to be forgeries: Ehrlich, *Works*, I, pp. xvii–xviii, li; Setton, *Crusades*, III, pp. 569, 579; Urban, *Baltic Crusade*, p. 201.

[46] E.g., since Augustine, the just war tradition had maintained that any means could be used to wage a just war. Paulus could have made this point much more trenchantly, had European opinion been prepared to accept the prospect of infidels and heretics fighting alongside Christians in just wars. Cf. above, n. 32.

[47] E.g. *Quoniam Error*, Ehrlich, *Works*, II, pp. 303f., where Paulus argues for peaceful propagation of the faith. Cf. Kapelinski, 'Paulus', p. 208.

[48] Cf. Boockmann, *Falkenberg*, pp. 16f. and above, nn. 16, 32.

9-2

articulation of volatile issues, so Paulus tailored his arguments to fit both his sources and the immediate political situation. As a result, Paulus succumbed to a kind of legalistic and factual overkill, whereby dense verbosity and repetition camouflaged an inability to hit the intended mark the first time. Underneath the weight of words the main points made were few.

What distinguished Paulus's methods from those of Falkenberg and Urbach was his use of history. To legal scholarship he joined a temporal perspective, and resorted to the texture of history to criticise evidence. When it suited his purposes he could be overly literal, as in his treatment of papal letters, yet he could overlook such salient points as the violence of the pagan Prussians and Poles, the mutual provocations and the many instances when Poland co-operated with the Order.[49] While he invoked the concept of inalienability, he neglected to consider Poland's complicity in its own fate. Thus, to say that Paulus thought historically is not to say that his interpretations were valid or even objective. Like the Order itself, Paulus in his own way exploited the inability of papacy and empire to maintain close supervision over it. The archaism of his arguments concerning the validity of the privileges assumed that thirteenth-century arguments could deal adequately with fifteenth-century problems, and that institutions must be frozen in their original mould rather than being capable of expansion and diversification. Again, how many other medieval institutions could have withstood such narrow scrutiny?

The defenders of the Order expressed doubts about the genuineness of the conversion of the Samogitians and Lithuanians. In a way they had a factual dispute with Paulus, for these doubts were at least plausible in view of the recent rapid evolution of the Polish–Lithuanian state. In response, the Lithuanian grand duke Witold sent some sixty Christian Samogitians to Constance.[50] Paulus argued that the two tribes were truly converted to Roman Christianity.[51] For all his faults as an historian, many of them occasioned by his bias in favour of Poland, he was led by the demands of his task to a recognition, albeit hesitant, of the mutability of laws and the relativity of circumstances according to time and place. Hostile actions that may have been appropriate in the

49 The Order in 1401 mediated arrangements strengthening the union between Poland and Lithuania: Weise, *Amtsgewalt*, p. 89, with other examples.
50 Cf. Urban, *Baltic Crusade*, pp. 186, 211; Boockmann, *Falkenberg*, pp. 220, 243; H. Bellée, *Polen und die römische Kurie in den Jahren 1414–1424* (Berlin and Leipzig, 1914), p. 10.
51 *Ad Aperiendam*, Ehrlich, *Works*, II, pp. 61f., 104. Cf. Belch, *Paulus*, I, p. 87.

earlier period of European settlement or in the Holy Land were inappropriate and ineffective in contemporary eastern Europe.[52]

Pro-Polish scholars like Belch and Ehrlich see Paulus as a pathfinder toward modern international law, while Schulz and Kahl on the German side see him as almost devoid of originality.[53] The debate is oversimplified on both sides. No medieval canonist in his right mind would dare claim bold originality for his ideas, but would rather seek to show that his interpretation was at least logically implicit in the received tradition. Paulus had to show both that his interpretation was the only valid one and that it was already established law. The complexities of medieval political thought fostered a rich plasticity that allowed old ideas to take on new meaning. The cogency of Paulus's ideas depended upon his seeming lack of originality. In using arguments from both law and history, Paulus innovated while appealing to sources that conservatives would accept.

By 1400 the just war tradition was full of tensions and unresolved conflicts that Paulus attempted to resolve. For his own reasons he retained such features as the prohibition on clerical warriors, and he strengthened the requirement that a competent tribunal first determine the justice of the cause before hostilities were begun. Neither council nor pope rendered such judgment in the Polish dispute; that was eventually settled on the battlefield rather than in court and was articulated in the second Peace of Thorn in 1466. The council's failure to reach a decision is a problem that merits further examination; the failure itself testified to the weakness of the papacy, empire, conciliarists and the just war theory. Endemic hostility could not be resolved by recourse to basic principles and formal procedures.

The question remains: how did Paulus modify the traditions of the crusade and the just war? The question turns on the conditions under which Paulus would permit the use of force against infidels. Innocent IV allowed warfare against idol-worshippers, those who sinned against natural law, and persecutors of Christian missionaries. Since according to the Church most pagans were idolaters, since the Church defined

---

[52] Cf. the analysis of Gallican historians of the early modern period in D. Kelley, *Foundations of Modern Historical Scholarship. Language, Law and History in the French Renaissance* (New York, 1970), esp. pp. 302–8; and the remarks about the use of historical methods by Paulus's contemporaries in W. Ullmann, *Law and Politics in the Middle Ages* (London, 1975), pp. 290, 296f. Cf. above, n. 40.

[53] Cf. Schulz, 'Paulus', pp. 86f.; H.-D. Kahl, 'Die volkerrechtliche Lösung der "Heidenfrage" bei Paulus Vladimiri von Krakau (†1435) und ihre problemgeschichtliche Einordnung', *Zeitschrift für Ostforschung*, VII (1958), pp. 161–209, at p. 178; Boockmann, *Falkenberg*, pp. 229f.

the content of natural law and the pope judged its infractions, and since few infidels co-operated with canon law by remaining peaceful in the face of incursions by Christian missionaries and adventurers, there were few groups of pagans who could meet Innocent's requirements for Christian toleration of their dominions. To do so, they would have had to forsake their paganism.[54] In grimly adhering to Innocent, Paulus rendered his arguments for toleration almost devoid of practical consequences beyond the immediate situation in eastern Europe.[55] He refused to limit war against infidels only to those instances in which infidels directly attacked the faithful. For example, he would permit an infidel ruler of neophyte Christians to be overthrown.[56] In effect he supported many potential uses of war against infidels who had done violence to Christians. Such incidents occurred often in the course of European expansion. Paulus simply did not face up either to the possible consequences of his position or to the facts of Christian–infidel contacts.[57] In the end he accorded to the pope the right whenever required by a reasonable cause to declare war on unbelievers who did not recognise the authority of the Roman Church.[58]

At Constance Paulus sought the destruction of the Teutonic Order by tearing at its status and exacerbating the fiscal and manpower crises occasioned by its defeat at Grunwald. Indeed, Paulus would have had Poland take over the Order's lands. His goals accorded well with the thrust of Polish policy, for the Peace of Thorn of 1411 provided that Poland and the Order share the newly conquered and converted lands, and John XXIII entrusted the Polish kingdom with the task of 'reducing' pagans and schismatics, granting the use of ecclesiastical revenues for this task. Poland sought to use the crusade tradition as legitimation for its dominion over eastern Europe.[59] Paulus did not

---

[54] In order to be tolerated by Christians, heathen tribes must first have been 'entpaganisiert', shorn of all vestiges of their pagan customs: Kahl, 'Heidenfrage', pp. 169, 173–5, 177.

[55] Dominicus of San Geminiano would refuse to allow the overthrow of peaceful infidel rulers, but in citing him Paulus omitted this restriction: Ad Videndum, Ehrlich, Works, III, pp. 177f. Cf. Belch, Paulus, I, p. 470 and Opinio Hostiensis, Ehrlich, Works, I, p. 124 and Belch, Paulus, II, p. 873.

[56] Saevientibus, Ehrlich, Works, I, p. 38 and Belch, Paulus, II, p. 809. Cf. Schulz, 'Paulus', p. 25.

[57] Had Paulus examined more closely the Christburg peace of 1249 between the pagan Prussians and the Order, he might have perceived more sharply the difficulties of treating infidels peacefully when they attacked missionaries and neophytes: Weise, Amtsgewalt, p. 89. Cf. J. Muldoon, 'A fifteenth-century application of the canonistic theory of the just war', Proceedings of the Fourth International Congress of Medieval Canon Law, 1972, ed. S. Kuttner, (Vatican City, 1976), pp. 467–80, at pp. 478f.

[58] Above, n. 43.   [59] Cf. Boockmann, Falkenberg, pp. 234, 309f.

refuse to invoke Innocent's crusading ideology to support Polish policy. Poland had participated in crusades and would do so again. What Paulus condemned was the Order's brutal warfare for conquest and conversion, but he allowed wars for defence of the faith when infidels did not remain peaceable, as they seldom did. He would restrict the crusade from being waged as the Order waged it, but he did not destroy the crusading idea.

In the Middle Ages there were two accepted means of expanding the frontiers of Christendom, the sword and the word. The Order preferred the former, while Poland, for reasons of its own position, preferred the latter. In arguing against the Order and for Poland, Paulus foreshadowed a just war that froze out pursuit of Christian orthodoxy as an immediate motive for war, while allowing Christian rulers the full right to defend the faith and the faithful. His major difference was not with the Order's apologists, Falkenberg excepted, but with its practices. His use of history was motivated by his conviction that the Order must be judged by its acts, not its professed original intentions.[60] The just war had been freighted with a heavy dose of ideological baggage which Paulus sought to jettison in order to limit the right of his opponents to wage a crusade. He deglamourised the just war as a means of territorial expansion. For him it was an imperfect means of immediate defence against attacks upon territorial integrity and the Christian faith. A war was to be presumed to be unjust unless its justice was formally proved.[61] At the end of his life he rejected warfare in favour of judicial action as a means of resolving disputes, for even just wars produced many misfortunes.[62] Grotius would later refuse to allow propagation of the faith by the sword.[63] The problems Paulus addressed would soon resurface with the European conquest of America. Though no direct influence of his thought has been shown, Paulus adumbrated the doctrines of early modern international law and historical jurisprudence.

[60] Cf. *Ad Aperiendam*, Ehrlich, *Works*, II, pp. 35: 'Sequitur necessario quod ex evidencia istius operis non potest inferri evidencia huius finis. Sed nec eciam iste finis potest dici operantis et bellantis tamquam primum in intencione et ultimum in execucione. Hec autem intencio nisi demonstretur aliquo opere est nobis incognita, cuius solus Deus est cognitor et iudex. . . . Et homo propositum mentemque alterius videre aut cognoscere non potest. . . . Patet ergo huius cause falsitas videlicet quod evidencia huius operis hanc intencionem declaret quod isti Cruciferi hunc finem intenderent.'

[61] *Quoniam Error*, Ehrlich, *Works*, II, p. 241: 'Nec eciam presumitur bellum iustum nisi appareat, ymmo bellum semper presumitur iniustum nisi de iusticia appareat.'

[62] *Ad Episcopum Cracoviensem*, Ehrlich, *Works*, III, pp. 206f., 220, and Belch, *Paulus*, II, pp. 1092f., 1100.

[63] H. Grotius, *De Iure Belli ac Pacis* II, 20, 48, ed. P. Molhuysen (Leiden, 1919), pp. 404f.

Yet in terms of his goals Paulus remained a failure. He aimed at a system of international law defined and enforced by canonical jurisprudence and ecclesiastical authority. His attempts to realise both *processus doctrinalis* and *iudicialis indago* were thwarted by history. If the academics of the theologically oriented University of Paris were unrealistic in proposing solutions to the Hundred Years' War, the more realistic canonist at Cracow was similarly unsuccessful.[64] His failure illustrates the folly of attempting to resolve disputes according to commonly accepted principles. That the attempt to transfer Poland's dispute from battlefield to court failed testifies to the practical limitations of late scholastic dialectic.

[64] Jacques Verger, 'The University of Paris at the End of the Hundred Years' War', in J. Baldwin and R. Goldthwaite, eds, *Universities in Politics. Case Studies from the Late Middle Ages and Early Modern Period* (Baltimore, 1972), pp. 47–78 at pp. 64–6.

BIBLIOGRAPHY OF THE WRITINGS
OF WALTER ULLMAN 1940-1979

compiled by PETER LINEHAN

1940

1. 'Bartolus on customary law', *Juridical Review*, LII (1940), pp. 265–83.

1941

2. 'Der Versuch nach der mittelalterlichen italienischen Lehre', *RHD*, XVII (1941), pp. 28–72.

1942

3. 'Baldus' conception of law', *LQR*, LVIII (1942), pp. 386–99.

1944

4. 'Reflections on medieval torture', *Juridical Review*, LVI (1944), pp. 123–37.
5. 'The mediaeval theory of legal and illegal organizations', *LQR*, LX (1944), pp. 285–91.
6. 'The right of asylum in sixteenth-century theory and practice', *Dublin Review*, CCXV, no. 431 (1944), pp. 103–10.

1945

7. 'A mediaeval philosophy of law', *CHR*, XXXI (1945), pp. 1–30.

1946

8. *The Medieval Idea of Law as represented by Lucas de Penna: a study in fourteenth-century legal scholarship*, with an introduction by H. D. Hazeltine (London, 1946), XXXIX+220 pp.
9. 'Medieval principles of evidence', *LQR*, LXII (1946), pp. 77–87.
10. 'Reflections on mediaeval clerical taxation', *Dublin Review*, CCXVIII, no. 436 (1946), pp. 150–61.
11. 'A medieval document on papal theories of government', *EHR*, LXI (1946), pp. 180–201.

1947

12. 'Medieval hospices', *The Month*, CLXXXIV (1947), pp. 46–9.
13. 'Some medieval principles of criminal procedure', *Juridical Review*, LIX (1947), pp. 1–28.
14. *Review of Symbolae ad ius et historiam antiquitatis pertinentes Julio C. van Oven dedicatae* (Leiden, 1946), *LQR*, LXIII (1947), pp. 386–9.

1948

15. *The Origins of the Great Schism: a study in fourteenth-century ecclesiastical history* (London, 1948), XIV+244 pp.

16. 'The delictal responsibility of medieval corporations', *LQR*, LXIV (1948), pp. 77–96.

17. 'Honorius III and the prohibition of legal studies', *Juridical Review*, LX (1948), pp. 177–86.

1949

18. *Medieval Papalism: the political theories of the medieval canonists* (The Maitland Memorial Lectures 1947–8) (London, 1949), XIV+230 pp.

19. 'The development of the medieval idea of sovereignty', *EHR*, LXIV (1949), pp. 1–33.

20. 'The disputed election of Hugh Balsham, bishop of Ely', *CHJ*, IX (1949), pp. 259–68.

21. 'Medieval views on papal abdication', *Irish Ecclesiastical Record*, LXXI (1949), pp. 125–33.

22. 'A Scottish charter and its place in medieval canon law', *Juridical Review*, LXI (1949), pp. 225–41.

23. *Review* of J. Beneyto, *Los origenes de la ciencia política en España* (Madrid, 1949), *EHR*, LXIV (1949), pp. 541–2.

1950

24. 'The defence of the accused in the medieval Inquisition', *Irish Ecclesiastical Record*, LXXIII (1950), pp. 481–9.

25. *Review* of G. G. Coulton, *Five Centuries of Religion*, IV (Cambridge, 1949), *CR*, LXXII (1950–1), pp. 384–6.

26. *Review* of L. Weckmann, *Las bulas alejandrinas de 1493 y la teoría política del papado medieval* (Mexico, 1949), *EHR*, LXV (1950), pp. 128–9.

1951

27. 'A forgotten dispute at Bridlington Priory and its canonistic setting', *Yorkshire Archaeological Journal*, XXXVII (1951), pp. 456–73.

28. *Review* of G. Lapsley, *Crown, Community and Parliament in the Later Middle Ages* (Oxford, 1951), *RHD*, XIX (1951), pp. 462–5.

29. *Review* of A. Gewirth, *Marsilius of Padua: The Defender of Peace*, I (New York, 1951), *CHR*, XXXVII (1951–2), pp. 321–2.

30. *Review* of A. C. Shannon, *The Popes and Heresy in the Thirteenth Century* (Villanova, 1949), *EHR*, LXVI (1951), pp. 137–8.

1952

31. 'Cardinal Humbert and the *Ecclesia Romana*', *Studi Gregoriani*, IV (1952), pp. 111–27.

32. 'Master Gratian', *The Times*, 15 April 1952.

33. 'Frederick II's opponent Innocent IV as Melchisedek', *Atti del Convegno Internazionale di Studi Federiciani* (Palermo, 1952), pp. 53–81.

Bibliography

34. *Review* of S. Mochi Onory, *Fonti canonistiche dell' idea moderno dello stato* (Milan, 1951), *EHR*, LXVII (1952), pp. 112–13.
35. *Review* of A. P. D'Entrèves, *Dante as a Political Thinker* (Oxford, 1952), *EHR*, LXVII (1952), pp. 434–5.
36. *Review* of J. H. Dahmus, *The Metropolitan Visitations of William Courtenay, Archbishop of Canterbury, 1381–1396* (Urbana, 1950), *CHR*, XXXVIII (1952–3), pp. 321–2.

1953

37. 'The medieval interpretation of Frederick I's Authentic "Habita" ', *L'Europa e il Diritto Romano* (= *Studi in memoria di Paolo Koschaker*), I (Milan, 1953), pp. 101–36.
38. 'The Paleae in Cambridge manuscripts of the Decretum', *Studia Gratiana*, I (1953), pp. 161–216.
39. 'The Origins of the *Ottonianum*', *CHJ*, XI (1953), pp. 114–28.
40. ' "Nos si aliquid incompetenter": some observations on the Register fragments of Leo IV in the Collectio Britannica', *Ephemerides Iuris Canonici*, IX (1953), pp. 3–21.
41. 'The pontificate of Adrian IV', *CHJ*, XI (1953), pp. 233–52.
42. *Review* of C. R. Cheney, ed., and W. H. Semple, trans., *Selected Letters of Pope Innocent III concerning England, 1198–1216* (London, 1953), *CR*, LXXV (1953–4), p. 438.

1954

43. 'Canonistics in England', *Studia Gratiana*, II (1954), pp. 519–28.
44. 'Cardinal Roland and Besançon', *Sacerdozio e Regno da Gregorio VII a Bonifacio VIII* (= *Miscellanea Historiae Pontificiae*, XVIII, 1954), pp. 107–26.
45. *Review* of C. Dawson, gen. ed., *The Makers of Christendom*, I and II (London, 1955), *CR*, LXXVI (1954–5), pp. 128–9.
46. *Review* of W. Holtzmann and E. W. Kemp, eds., *Papal Decretals relating to the Diocese of Lincoln in the Twelfth Century* (Lincoln, 1954), *CR*, LXXVI (1954–5), p. 205.

1955

47. *The Growth of Papal Government in the Middle Ages: a study in the ideological relation of clerical to lay power* (London, 1955), XVIII+482 pp.
48. 'The curial exequies for Edward I and Edward III', *JEH*, VI (1955), pp. 26–36.
49. *Review* of R. Hunt and R. Klibansky, eds., *Medieval and Renaissance Studies*, III (London, 1954), *JTS*, n.s. VI (1955), pp. 143–5.
50. *Review* of F. Kempf, *Papsttum und Kaisertum bei Innocenz III: die geistigen und rechtlichen Grundlagen seiner Thronstreitpolitik* (Rome, 1954), *JEH*, VI (1955), pp. 233–6.
51. *Review* of B. Tierney, *Foundations of the Conciliar Theory: the contribution of the medieval canonists from Gratian to the Great Schism* (Cambridge, 1955), *CR*, LXXVII (1955–6), p. 325.

1956

52. 'The legal validity of the papal electoral pacts', *Ephemerides Iuris Canonici*, XII (1956), pp. 1–35.

53. 'A disputable *consuetudo contra legem* in the later Middle Ages', *South African Law Review* (Memorial volume for Herbert F. Jolowicz, 1956), pp. 85–94.

54. 'Papacy' (from Gregory I to Boniface VIII), *Encyclopaedia Britannica*, new edn (London, 1956).

55. Review of F. Dressler, *Petrus Damiani: Leben und Werk* (Rome, 1954), *JTS*, n.s. VII (1956), pp. 146–8.

56. Review of M. David, *La souveraineté et les limites juridiques du pouvoir monarchique du IX au XV siècle* (Paris, 1954), *EHR*, LXXI (1956), pp. 83–6.

57. Review of T. M. Parker, *Christianity and the State in the Light of History* (London, 1955), *JEH*, VII (1956), pp. 78–82.

58. Review of A. Borst, *Die Katharer* (Stuttgart, 1953), *JEH*, VII (1956), pp. 103–4.

59. Review of W. A. Pantin, *The English Church in the Fourteenth Century* (Cambridge, 1955), *CHR*, XLII (1956–7), pp. 186–8.

1957

60. 'On the use of the term "Romani" in the sources of the earlier Middle Ages', *Studia Patristica* I [= *Texte und Untersuchungen zur Geschichte der altchristlichen Literatur*, LXIV (1957)], pp. 155–63.

61. 'Thomas Becket's miraculous oil', *JTS*, n.s. VIII (1957), pp. 129–33.

62. 'The recognition of St Bridget's Rule by Martin V', *Revue Bénédictine*, LXVII (1957), pp. 190–201.

63. Review of P. Zerbi, *Papato, Impero e 'Respublica Christiana' dal 1187 al 1198* (Milan, 1955), *EHR*, LXXII (1957), pp. 155–7.

64. Review of H. Wolter, *Orderic Vitalis: ein Beitrag zur kluniazensischen Geschichtsschreibung* (Wiesbaden, 1955), *JTS*, n.s. VIII (1957), pp. 183–5.

65. Review of H. S. Offler, ed., *Guillelmi de Ockham: Opera Politica*, III (Manchester, 1956), *EHR*, LXXII (1957), pp. 309–16.

66. Review of P. van den Baar, *Die kirchliche Lehre der Translatio Imperii Romani* (Rome, 1956), *EHR*, LXXII (1957), pp. 522–4.

67. Review of P. Gassó and C. Batlle, eds., *Pelagii I Papae Epistulae quae supersunt (556–561)* (Montserrat, 1956), *JTS*, n.s. VIII (1957), pp. 344–7.

68. Review of J. J. Ryan, *Saint Peter Damian and his Canonical Sources* (Toronto, 1956), *JTS*, n.s. VIII (1957), pp. 353–4.

69. Review of J. Autenrieth, *Die Domschule von Konstanz zur Zeit des Investiturstreits* (Stuttgart, 1956), *JEH*, VIII (1957), pp. 240–1.

70. Review of H. Raab, *Die Concordata Nationis Germanicae in der kanonistischen Diskussion des 17. bis 19. Jahrhunderts* (Mainz, 1956), *MIÖG*, LXV (1957), pp. 240–1.

71. Review of H. Hess, *The Canons of the Council of Sardica, A.D. 343: a landmark in the early development of canon law* (Oxford, 1958), *CR*, LXXIX (1957–8), p. 395.

1958

72. 'Some observations on the medieval evaluation of the "homo naturalis" and the "christianus"', *L'Homme et son destin* (= *Actes du Premier Congrès International de Philosophie Médiévale*) (Louvain, 1958), pp. 145–51.

Bibliography

73. 'St Bernard and the nascent international law', *Cîteaux*, x (1958), pp. 277–87.

74. 'Usage in modern canon law', *Proceedings: International Academy of Comparative Law: Fifth Congress* (Brussels, 1958), pp. 45–65.

75. 'The decline of the Chancellor's authority in medieval Cambridge: a rediscovered statute', *Historical Journal*, I (1958), pp. 176–82.

76. 'The University of Cambridge and the Great Schism', *JTS*, n.s. IX (1958), pp. 53–77.

77. *Review* of P. N. Riesenberg, *Inalienability of Sovereignty in Medieval Political Thought* (New York, 1956), *Medium Aevum*, XXVI (1958), pp. 201–4.

78. *Review* of A. Gewirth, *Marsilius of Padua: The Defender of Peace*, II (New York, 1956), *History*, XLIII (1958), pp. 227–30.

79. *Review* of M. J. Odenheimer, *Der christlich-kirchliche Anteil an der Verdrängung der mittelalterlichen Rechtsstruktur und an der Entstehung der Vorherrschaft des stantlich Gesetzten Rechts im Deutschen und Französischen Rechtsgebiet* (Basel, 1957), *RHD*, XXVI (1958), pp. 360–6.

80. *Review* of E. A. Bruck, *Kirchenväter und soziales Erbrecht: Wanderungen religiöser Ideen durch die Rechte der östlichen und westlichen Welt* (Berlin, 1956), *JTS*, n.s. IX (1958), pp. 388–90.

81. *Review* of C. A. Bouman, *Sacring and Crowning: the development of the Latin ritual for the anointing of kings and the coronation of an emperor before the eleventh century* (Groningen, 1957), *JTS*, n.s. IX (1958), pp. 390–2.

82. *Review* of T. Gilby, *Principality and Power: Aquinas and the Rise of State Theory in the West* (London, 1958), *EHR*, LXXIII (1958), pp. 706–7.

83. *Review* of E. H. Kantorowicz, *The King's Two Bodies. A Study in Medieval Political Theory* (Princeton, 1957), *MIÖG*, LXVI (1958), pp. 364–9.

84. *Review* of T. F. T. Plucknett, *Early English Legal Literature* (Cambridge, 1957), *CR*, LXXX (1958–9), p. 337.

85. ' "Romanus pontifex indubitanter efficitur sanctus": Dictatus papae 23 in retrospect and prospect', *Studi Gregoriani*, VI (1959–61), pp. 229–64.

86–94. 'Adrian IV'; 'Boniface VIII'; 'Church and State'; 'Gregory I'; 'Gregory VII'; 'Gregory IX'; 'Innocent IV'; 'Leo IX'; 'Urban VI': *Collier's Encyclopedia*, new edn (New York, 1959).

95. *Review* of J. B. Morrall, *Political Thought in Medieval Times* (London, 1958), *EHR*, LXXIV (1959), pp. 340–1.

96. *Review* of P. Rabikauskas, *Die römische Kuriale in der päpstlichen Kanzlei* (Rome, 1958), *JEH*, X (1959), pp. 233–4.

97. *Review* of N. F. Cantor, *Church, Kingship and Lay Investiture in England, 1089–1135* (Princeton, 1958), *JEH*, X (1959), pp. 234–7.

1960

98. *Die Machtstellung des Papsttums im Mittelalter. Idee und Geschichte* (mit einem Geleitwort von H. Fichtenau): German trans. of no. 4**7**, revised and with a new preface (Graz-Vienna-Cologne, 1960), XLIII + 682 pp.

99. 'The Medieval Papacy, St Thomas and beyond', *Aquinas Papers* (Publications of the Aquinas Society of London), no. 35 (London, 1960).

100. 'Leo I and the theme of papal primacy', *JTS*, n.s., XI (1960), pp. 25-51.

101. 'The significance of the *Epistola Clementis* in the Pseudo-Clementines', *JTS*, n.s., XI (1960), pp. 295-317.

102. 'Über eine kanonistische Vorlage Friedrichs I.', *ZRG* Kan., XLVI (1960), pp. 430-3.

103. 'Law and the Medieval Historian', *Rapports du XIe Congrès International des Sciences Historiques* (Stockholm, 1960), pp. 34-74.

104. 'Some reflexions on the opposition of Frederick II to the papacy', *Archivio Storico Pugliese*, XIII (1960), pp. 3-26.

105. *Review* of K. Schwarzenberg, *Adler und Drache: der Weltherrschaftsgedanke* (Vienna, 1958), *EHR*, LXXV (1960), p. 321.

106. *Review* of W. Goez, *Translatio Imperii: ein Beitrag zur Geschichte des Geschichts-denkens und der politischen Theorien im Mittelalter und in der frühen Neuzeit* (Tübingen, 1959), *EHR*, LXXV (1960), pp. 333-4.

107. *Review* of D. Geanakoplos, *Emperor Michael Palaeologus and the West, 1258-1282: a study in Byzantine–Latin Relations* (Cambridge, Mass., 1959), *Heythrop Journal*, I (1960), pp. 245-7.

108. *Review* of *Saggi storici intorno al papato* (= *Miscellanea Historiae Pontificiae*, XXI, 1959), *HZ*, CXCI (1960), pp. 620-4.

109. *Review* of J. Huizinga, *Men and Ideas* (London, 1960), *CR*, LXXXII (1960-1), p. 407.

110. *Review* of B. Smalley, *English Friars and Antiquity in the Fourteenth Century* (Oxford, 1960), *Oxford Magazine*, n.s. I (1960-1), pp. 418-19.

1961

111. *Principles of Government and Politics in the Middle Ages* (London, 1961), 322 pp.

112. (Ed.) *Liber Regie Capelle* (Henry Bradshaw Society, XCII) (London, 1961), x+122 pp.

113. 'Some remarks on the significance of the *Epistola Clementis* in the Pseudo-Clementines', *Studia Patristica*, I [= *Texte und Untersuchungen zur Geschichte der altchristlichen Literatur*, LXXIX (1961)], pp. 330-7.

114. 'Eugenius IV, Cardinal Kemp and Archbishop Chichele', *Medieval Studies presented to Aubrey Gwynn, S.J.*, ed. J. A. Watt, J. B. Morrall and F. X. Martin (Dublin, 1961), pp. 359-83.

115. 'The King's Grace', *The Listener*, LXVI (1961), pp. 53-4.

116. 'Medieval populism', *The Listener*, LXVI (1961), pp. 131-3.

117. 'Bartolus and English jurisprudence', *Bartolo da Sassoferrato: studi e documenti per il VI centenario* (Milan, 1961), I, pp. 49-73.

118-21 'Leo III'; 'Magna Carta'; 'Paul I'; 'York, Anonymous': *Lexicon für Theologie und Kirche*, new edn (Freiburg, 1961-7).

122. *Review* of H. Siuts, *Bann und Acht und ihre Grundlagen im Totenglauben* (Berlin, 1959), *EHR*, LXXVI (1961), pp. 118-19.

123. *Review* of L. Buisson, *Potestas und Caritas: die päpstliche Gewalt im Spätmittelalter* (Cologne–Graz, 1959), *EHR*, LXXVI (1961), pp. 324–7.

124. *Review* of S. Gagnér, *Studien zur Ideengeschichte der Gesetzgebung* (Stockholm, 1960), *RHD*, XXIX (1961), pp. 118–29.

125. *Review* of J. B. Morrall, *Gerson and the Great Schism* (Manchester, 1960), *History*, XLVI (1961), pp. 133–4.

126. *Review* of B. Rubin, *Das Zeitalter Justinians*, I (Berlin, 1960), *JEH*, XII (1961), pp. 100–1.

127. *Review* of T. Buyken, *Das römische Recht in den Constitutionen von Melfi* (Cologne–Opladen, 1960), *JEH*, XII (1961), pp. 263–4.

1962

128. *The Growth* . . . (no. 4?) (London, 1962), 2nd edn, XXIV + 489 pp.

129. 'De Bartoli sententia: *Concilium repraesentat mentem populi*', *Bartolo da Sassoferrato: studi e documenti per il VI centenario* (Milan, 1962), II, pp. 707–33.

130. *Review* of E. E. Stengel, *Abhandlungen und Untersuchungen zur Geschichte des Mittelalters* (Cologne–Graz, 1960), *EHR*, LXXVII (1962), pp. 343–4.

131. *Review* of G. B. Ladner, *The Idea of Reform: its impact on Christian thought and action in the Age of the Fathers* (Cambridge, Mass., 1959), *JTS*, n.s. XIII (1962), pp. 190–2.

132. *Review* of F. Merzbacher, *Die Bischofstadt* (Cologne–Opladen, 1961), *JTS*, n.s XIII (1962), p. 193.

133. *Review* of G. Inger, *Das kirchliche Visitationsinstitut im mittelalterlichen Schweden* (Lund, 1961), *JEH*, XIII (1962), pp. 93–4.

134. *Review* of E. Schwartz, *Zur Geschichte der alten Kirche und ihres Rechts* (Berlin, 1960), *JEH*, XIII (1962), pp. 119–20.

135. *Review* of C. Johnson, ed., *Hugh the Chanter: the History of the Church of York* (Edinburgh, 1961), *HZ*, CXCIV (1962), p. 747.

136. *Review* of J. A. Robson, *Wyclif and the Oxford Schools* (Cambridge, 1961), *HZ*, CXCIV (1962), p. 753.

137. *Review* of E. W. Kemp, *Counsel and Consent: aspects of the government of the Church as exemplified in the history of the English provincial synods* (London, 1961), *JTS*, n.s., XIII (1962), pp. 475–6.

1963

138. 'The papacy and the faithful', *Gouvernés et Gouvernants = Recueils de la Société Jean Bodin pour l'histoire comparative des institutions*, XXV (1963), pp. 7–45.

139. *Introduction* to H. C. Lea, *The Inquisition of the Middle Ages* (London, 1963), pp. 11–51.

140. 'The Inquisition: an explanation', *The Listener*, LXIX (1963), 671–3 (broadcast 4 April 1963).

141. 'The Bible and principles of government in the Middle Ages', *Settimane di studio del Centro Italiano di Studi sull' Alto Medioevo*, X (1963), pp. 183–227.

142. 'John of Paris', *The Listener*, LXX (1963), pp. 787–9 (broadcast 12 November 1963).

Bibliography

143. Review of P. Herde, *Beiträge zum päpstlichen Kanzlei- und Urkundenwesen im 13. Jahrhundert* (Kallmünz, 1961), *History*, XLVIII (1963), pp. 55–6.
144. Review of S. Kuttner, *Harmony from Dissonance: an interpretation of medieval canon law* (Latrobe, Pa., 1961), *EHR*, LXXVIII (1963), pp. 359–60.
145. Review of K. Ritzer, *Formen, Riten und religiöses Brauchtum der Eheschliessung in den christlichen Kirchen des ersten Jahrtausend* (Münster, 1962), *JTS*, n.s. XIV (1963), pp. 172–6.
146. Review of A. Krchnák, *De vita et operibus Iohannis de Ragusio* (Rome, 1961), *CHR*, XLIX (1963–4), pp. 96–7.
147. Review of G. Pilati, *Chiesa e stato nei primi quindici seculi: profilo dello svillupo della teoria attraverso le fonti e la bibliografia* (Rome–Paris, 1961), *RHD*, XXXI (1963), pp. 131–6.
148. Review of M. Hellmann, ed., *Corona Regni: Studien über die Krone als Symbol des Staates im späteren Mittelalter* (Weimar, 1961), *EHR*, LXXVIII (1963), p. 564.
149. Review of W. Fesefeldt, *Englische Staatstheorie des 13. Jahrhunderts: Henry de Bracton und sein Werk* (Göttingen, 1962), *RHD*, XXXI (1963), pp. 289–99.
150. Review of A. Largiadèr, *Die Papsturkunden des Staatsarchivs Zürich von Innocenz III. bis Martin V: ein Beitrag zum Censimentum Helveticum* (Zurich, 1963), *JEH*, XIV (1963), pp. 229–30.
151. Review of L. Hödl, *Johannes Quidort von Paris, O.P. (†1306). De confessionibus audiendis* (Munich, 1962), *JEH*, XIV (1963), p. 230.
152. Review of H. Cnattingius, *Studies in the Order of St Bridget of Sweden*, I: *the crisis in the 1420s* (Stockholm, 1963), *JEH*, XIV (1963), p. 261.
153. Review of J. Godfrey, *The Church in Anglo-Saxon England* (Cambridge, 1962), *HZ*, CXCVII (1963), pp. 434–7.

1964

154. 'Der Souveränitätsgedanke in den mittelalterlichen Krönungsordines' in P. Classen and P. Scheibert, eds., *Festschrift für Percy Ernst Schramm* (Wiesbaden, 1964), I, pp. 72–89.
155. 'Reflexions on the medieval empire', *Transactions of the Royal Historical Society*, 5th ser. XIV (1964), pp. 89–109.
156. 'On the heuristic value of medieval chancery products, with special reference to papal documents', *Annali della Fondazione Italiana per la storia amministrativa*, I (1964), pp. 117–34.
157. 'Cardinal Francis Zabarella', *The Listener*, LXXI (1964), pp. 53–5 (broadcast 19 November 1963).
158. Review of J. M. Moynihan, *Papal Immunity and Liability in the Writings of Medieval Canonists* (Rome, 1961), *EHR*, LXXIX (1964), pp. 154–5.
159. Review of *Ius romanum medii aevi*, pars I, a–d (Milan, 1961), *EHR*, LXXIX (1964), p. 155.
160. Review of R. W. Southern, ed., *The Life of St Anselm by Eadmer* (Edinburgh–London, 1963), *HZ*, CXCVIII (1964), p. 210.
161. Review of *Ius romanum medii aevi*, pars V, 2 d, 7–9 (Milan, 1962), *EHR*, LXXIX (1964), pp. 403–4.

Bibliography

162. *Review* of P. E. Sigmund, *Nicholas of Cusa and Medieval Political Thought* (Cambridge, Mass., 1964), *Blackfriars*, XLV (1964), pp. 330–3.

163. *Review* of W. Trusen, *Anfänge des gelehrten Rechts in Deutschland* (Wiesbaden, 1962), *JTS*, n.s. XV (1964), pp. 432–3.

164. *Review* of W. Schlesinger, *Kirchengeschichte Sachsens im Mittelalter*, I and II (Cologne, 1962), *JEH*, XV (1964), p. 272.

165. *Review* of M. Watanabe, *The Political Ideas of Nicholas of Cusa, with special reference to his* De concordantia catholica (Geneva, 1963), *History*, XLIX (1964), pp. 345–6.

166. *Review* of D. Knowles, *The Historian and Character and other Essays* (Cambridge, 1963), *HZ*, CXCIX (1964), pp. 559–61.

1965

167. *A History of Political Thought: the Middle Ages* (Harmondsworth, 1965), 247 pp.

168. *The Growth* . . . (London, 1965), reprint of no. 128.

169. 'The significance of Innocent III's decretal *Vergentis*' in *Études d'histoire du droit canonique dédiées à Gabriel le Bras* (Paris, 1965), pp. 729–41.

170. 'The papacy as an institution of government in the Middle Ages', *SCH*, II (Edinburgh, 1965), pp. 78–101.

171. 'Historical jurisprudence, historical politology and the history of the Middle Ages', *Atti del Primo Congresso Internazionale della Società di Storia del Diritto* (Florence, 1965), pp. 195–224.

172. 'East and West in the Middle Ages', *The Listener*, LXXIII (1965), pp. 51–3, 99–101 (broadcast 28 November and 6 December 1964).

173. *Review* of A. Becker, *Papst Urban II. (1088–1099)*, I (Stuttgart, 1964), *JTS*, n.s. XVI (1965), pp. 236–7.

174. *Review* of H. A. J. Allard, *Die eheliche Lebens- und Liebesgemeinschaft nach Hugo von St. Viktor* (Rome, 1963), *JTS*, n.s. XVI (1965), pp. 237–8.

175. *Review* of K. W. Nörr, *Kirche und Konzil bei Nicolaus de Tudeschis (Panormitanus)* (Cologne, 1964), *JEH*, XVI (1965), pp. 99–100.

176. *Review* of L. Hödl, *Die neuen Quästionen der Gnadentheologie des Johannes von Rupella O.M. (†1245) in Cod. lat. Paris 14726* (Munich, 1964), *JEH*, XVI (1965), pp. 120–1.

177. *Review* of H. Feine, *Kirchliche Rechtsgeschichte: die katholische Kirche*, 4th edn (Cologne–Graz, 1964), *JEH*, XVI (1965), p. 125.

178. *Review* of D. Maffei, *La Lectura super Digesto Veteri di Cino da Pistoia* (Milan, 1963), *EHR*, LXXX (1965), pp. 818–19.

179. *Review* of D. Maffei, *La Donazione di Costantino nei giuristi medievali* (Milan, 1964), *JTS*, n.s. XVI (1965), pp. 526–9.

180. *Review* of A. Gransden, ed., *The Chronicle of Bury St Edmund's* (London, 1964), *HZ*, CCI (1965), p. 467.

181. *Review* of R. Folz, *Le couronnement impérial de Charlemagne* (Paris, 1964), *RBPH*, XLIII (1965), pp. 1069–75.

182. *Review* of G. Musca, *Carlo Magno e l'Inghilterra anglosassone* (Bari, 1964), *HZ*, CCI (1965), pp. 745–6.

1966

183. *The Individual and Society in the Middle Ages* (Baltimore and London, 1966), XIV + 160 pp.

184. *Papst und König im Mittelalter: Grundlagen des Papsttums und der englischen Verfassung des Mittelalters* (mit einem Nachwort von H. Koller), Salzburger Universitätsschriften, Dike, III (Salzburg–Munich, 1966), 93 pp.

185. *Principles of Government and Politics* ... (no. 111) (London, 1966), 2nd edn, 332 pp.

186. 'On the influence of Geoffrey of Monmouth in English history' in C. Bauer, L. Boehm, M. Müller, eds., *Speculum Historiale: Festschrift für Johannes Spörl* (Munich, 1966), pp. 257–76.

187. *Review* of *Ius romanum medii aevi*, pars I, 2a (Milan, 1963), *EHR*, LXXXI (1966), p. 133.

188. *Review* of F. Oakley, *The Political Thought of Pierre d'Ailly: the voluntarist tradition* (New Haven, 1964), *Renaissance News*, IV (1966), pp. 305–7.

189. *Review* of M. Bowsky, ed., *Studies in Medieval and Renaissance History*, I (Nebraska, 1964), *HZ*, CCII (1966), pp. 104–7.

190. *Review* of K. F. Morrison, *The Two Kingdoms: ecclesiology in Carolingian political thought* (Princeton, 1964), *JTS*, n.s. XVII (1966), pp. 191–5.

191. *Review* of T. Nyberg, *Birgittinische Klostergründungen des Mittelalters* (Lund, 1965), *JEH*, XVII (1966), pp. 115–16.

192. *Review* of J. Duvernoy, ed., *Le registre d'inquisition de Jacques Fournier* (3 vols., Toulouse, 1965–6), *Times Literary Supplement*, no. 3354 (1966), p. 517.

193. *Review* of J. Hussey, ed., *The Cambridge Medieval History*, IV: *The Byzantine Empire* (Cambridge, 1966) Pt I, *CR*, LXXXVIII (1966–7), pp. 69–70.

194. *Review* of J. D. Tooke, *The Just War in Aquinas and Grotius* (London, 1965), *EHR*, LXXXI (1966), pp. 823–4.

195. *Review* of E. A. Thompson, *The Visigoths in the time of Ulfila* (Oxford, 1966), *CR*, LXXXVIII (1966–7), p. 85.

196. *Review* of P. R. Coleman-Norton, *Roman State and Christian Church: a collection of legal documents to A.D. 535* (3 vols., London, 1966), *Journal of the Society of Public Teachers of Law*, IX (1966), pp. 276–8.

1967

197. 'The Relevance of Medieval Ecclesiastical History: an inaugural lecture delivered in the University of Cambridge, 8 March 1966' (Cambridge, 1967), 36 pp.

198. *The Origins of the Great Schism* (London–Camden, Conn., 1967), reprint of no. 15.

199. 'The rebirth of the citizen on the eve of the Renaissance period', in A. R. Lewis, ed., *Aspects of the Renaissance: a symposium* (Austin, Texas, 1967), pp. 5–25.

200. 'A decision of the Rota Romana on the benefit of clergy in England', *Studia Gratiana*, XIII (1967) [= *Collectanea Stephan Kuttner*], pp. 455–90.

Bibliography

201. *Review* of S. Kuttner and J. J. Ryan, eds., *Proceedings of the Second International Congress of Medieval Canon Law* (Vatican City, 1965), *JEH*, XVIII (1967), pp. 90–4.

202. *Review* of H. Mayr-Harting, ed., *Acta of the Bishops of Chichester, 1075–1207*, Canterbury and York Society (1964), *JEH*, XVIII (1967), pp. 94–5.

203. *Review* of J. Le Goff, *Das Hochmittelalter* (Frankfurt, 1965), *HZ*, CCIV (1967), pp. 456–7.

204. *Review* of J. C. Holt, *Magna Carta* (Cambridge, 1965), *CHR*, LIII (1967–8), pp. 262–4.

205. *Review* of R. Heinzmann, *Die 'Compilatio quaestionum theologiae secundum Magistrum Martinum'* (Munich, 1964), *JEH*, XVIII (1967), pp. 275–6.

206. *Review* of L. Hödl, *Von der Wirklichkeit und Wirksamkeit des dreieinen Gottes nach der appropriativen Trinitätstheologie des 12. Jahrhunderts* (Munich, 1965), *JEH*, XVIII (1967), p. 276.

207. *Review* of G. Miccoli, *Chiesa Gregoriana: Ricerche sulla riforma del secolo XI* (Florence, 1966), *JTS*, n.s. XVIII (1967), pp. 517–19.

208. *Review* of E. E. Stengel, *Abhandlungen und Untersuchungen zur Geschichte des Kaisergedankens im Mittelalter* (Cologne–Graz, 1965), *RBPH*, XLV (1967), pp. 531–6.

1968

209. *The Medieval Idea of Law* . . . (London, 1968), reprint of no. 8.

210. *A History of Political Thought* . . . (Harmondsworth, 1968), reprint of no. 167.

211. 'A proposito dell' Authentica "Habita": intervento sulla comunicazione di Antonio Marongiu', *Atti del Convegno Internazionale di Studi Accursiani* (Milan, 1968), I, pp. CVI–CVII.

212. 'Dies ortus imperii: a note on the Glossa Ordinaria on C.III.12.7 (5)', *Atti del Convegno Internazionale di Studi Accursiani* (Milan, 1968), pp. 663–96.

213. 'Juristic obstacles to the emergence of the concept of the State in the Middle Ages', *Annali di storia del diritto* (= *Studi in memoria di Francesco Calasso*), XII–XIII (1968–9), pp. 43–64.

214–17 'Conciliar Movement'; 'Great Schism'; 'Martin V'; 'Urban VI': *Catholic Youth Encyclopedia* (New York, 1968).

218–28 'Adrian IV'; 'Avignon Papacy'; 'Caspar, Erich'; 'Cesaropapism'; 'Chichele, Henry'; 'Donation of Constantine'; 'Gregory VII'; 'Innocent III'; 'Kempe, John'; 'Papacy (to 1500)'; 'Western Schism': *New Catholic Encyclopedia* (New York, 1968).

229. *Review* of L. F. J. Meulenberg, *Der Primat der romischen Kirche im Denken und Handeln Gregors VII.* (The Hague, 1965), *JEH*, XIX (1968), pp. 101–4.

230. *Review* of K. Pellens, *Die Texte des Normannischen Anonymus, unter Konsultation der Teilausgaben von H. Böhmer, H. Scherrinsky und G. H. Williams* (Wiesbaden, 1966), *HZ*, CVI (1968), pp. 696–703.

231. *Review* of G. Kisch, *Enea Silvio Piccolomini und die Jurisprudenz* (Basel, 1967), *Renaissance Quarterly*, XXI (1968), pp. 316–17.

232. *Review* of C. R. Cheney and M. G. Cheney, *The Letters of Pope Innocent III, 1198–1216, concerning England and Wales: a calendar with an appendix of texts* (Oxford, 1967), *HZ*, CCVII (1968), p. 727.

1969

233. *The Carolingian Renaissance and the Idea of Kingship* (*The Birkbeck Lectures in Ecclesiastical History 1968–9*) (London, 1969), XIV + 201 pp.

234. *Review* of G. Barraclough, *The Medieval Papacy* (London, 1968), *Catholic Herald*, 21 February 1969.

235. *Review* of E. von Koerber, *Die Staatstheorie des Erasmus von Rotterdam* (Berlin, 1967), *EHR*, LXXXIV (1969), pp. 390–1.

236. *Review* of L. Martines, *Lawyers and Statecraft in Renaissance Florence* (Princeton, 1968), *Renaissance Quarterly*, XXII (1969), pp. 38–40.

237. *Review* of J. T. Sawicki, ed., *Bibliographia synodorum particularium* (Vatican City, 1967), *JEH*, XX (1969), pp. 127–9.

238. *Review* of R. L. Benson, *The Bishop-elect: a study in medieval ecclesiastical office* (Princeton, 1968), *American Historical Review*, LXXIV (1969), p. 1266.

239. *Review* of W. von den Steinen, *Menschen im Mittelalter* (Berne–Munich, 1968), *History*, LIV (1969), p. 256.

240. *Review* of E. F. Jacob, *Archbishop Henry Chichele* (London, 1967), *Medium Aevum*, XXXVIII (1969), pp. 206–7.

241. *Review* of H. A. Oberman, D. E. Zerfoss, W. J. Courtenay, eds., *Defensorium obedientiae apostolicae et alia documenta* (Cambridge, Mass., 1968), *JTS*, n.s. XX (1969), pp. 690–3.

242. *Review* of N. Horn, *Aequitas in den Lehren des Baldus* (Cologne–Graz, 1968), *RHD*, XXXVII (1969), pp. 280–4.

243. *Review* of J. Fleckenstein and K. Schmid, eds., *Adel und Kirche: Festschrift für Gerd Tellenbach* (Freiburg–Basel–Vienna, 1968), *JEH*, XX (1969), pp. 323–7.

244. *Review* of E. Meyer-Martheler, *Römisches Recht in Rätien im frühen und hohen Mittelalter* (Zurich, 1968), *JEH*, XX (1969), p. 369.

245. *Review* of *Individu et société à la Renaissance* (Colloque, 1967) = *Travaux de l'Institut pour l'Étude de la Renaissance et de l'Humanisme* (1967), *RBPH*, XLVII (1969), pp. 1378–81.

1970

246. *The Growth of Papal Government*... (no. 46) (London, 1970), 3rd edn, XXIV + 496 pp.

247. *A History of Political Thought*... (no. 167) (Harmondsworth, 1970), revised edn, 256 pp.

248. *Review* of A. Largiadèr, *Die Papsturkunden der Schweiz von Innocenz III. bis Martin V. ohne Zürich: ein Beitrag zum Censimentum Helveticum*, I: *Von Innocenz III. bis Benedikt XI, 1198 bis 1304* (Zurich, 1968), *JEH*, XXI (1970), pp. 80–1.

249. *Review* of P. B. Roberts, *Stephanus de Lingua-Tonante: studies in the Sermons of Stephen Langton* (Toronto, 1968), *JEH*, XXI (1970), pp. 180–1.

Bibliography

250. *Review of* M. D. Chenu, *Nature, Man and Society in the Twelfth Century*, trans. J. Taylor and L. K. Little (Chicago, 1968), *EHR*, LXXXV (1970), p. 397.

251. *Review of* Y. M.-J. Congar, *L'Ecclésiologie du haut Moyen Âge: de S. Grégoire le Grand à la désunion entre Byzance et Rome* (Paris, 1968), *JTS*, n.s. XXI (1970), pp. 216–26.

252. *Review of* W. Seegrün, *Das Papsttum und Skandinavien bis zur Vollendung der nordischen Kirchenorganisation (1164)*, *CHR*, LVI (1970), pp. 342–3.

253. *Review of* R. Brentano, *Two Churches: England and Italy in the Thirteenth Century* (Princeton, 1968), *RBPH*, xlviii (1970), pp. 74–8.

1971

254.

中世に
おける 個 人 と 社 会

Japanese edition and translation of no. 183 (Tokyo, 1971), 266 pp.

255. *Principios de gobierno y política en la Edad Media*: Spanish trans. of no. III (Madrid, 1971), 322 pp.

256. 'Schranken der Königsgewalt im Mittelalter', *Historisches Jahrbuch*, XCI (1971), pp. 1–21.

257. 'The medieval papal court as an international tribunal', *Virginia Journal of International Law*, XI (1971) [=*Essays presented to H. C. Dillard*], pp. 356–71.

258. 'Public welfare and social legislation in the early medieval councils', *SCH*, VII (Cambridge, 1971), pp. 1–39.

259. *Review of* E. Hlawitschka, *Lotharingien und das Reich an der Schwelle der deutschen Geschichte* (Schriften der MGH, XXI) (Stuttgart, 1968), *EHR*, LXXXVI (1971), pp. 156–7.

260. *Review of* M. B. Hackett, *The Original Statutes of Cambridge University: the text and its history* (Cambridge, 1970), *JEH*, XXII (1971), pp. 134–9.

261. *Review of* G. Oberkofler, *Die geschichtlichen Fächer und der Universität Innsbruck 1850–1945* (Innsbruck, 1969), *Erasmus*, XXIII (1971), pp. 387–92.

262. *Review of* J. W. Baldwin, *Masters, Princes and Merchants: the social views of Peter the Chanter and his circle* (Princeton, 1970), *JTS*, n.s. XXII (1971), pp. 263–9.

263. *Review of* P. Costa, *Iurisdictio: semantica del potere politico nella pubblicistica medievale (1100–1433)* (Milan, 1969), *RHD*, XXXIX (1971), pp. 298–302.

264. *Review of* Y. Renouard, *The Avignonese Papacy*, trans. D. Bethell (London, 1970), *JEH*, XXII (1971), pp. 379–80.

265. *Review of* A. Esch, *Bonifaz IX. und der Kirchenstaat* (Tübingen, 1969), *CHR*, LVII (1971–2), pp. 494–6.

266. *Review of* W. Kölmel, *Regimen christianum: Weg und Ergebnisse des Gewalten-verhältnisses und des Gewaltenverständnisses (8. bis 14. Jahrhundert)* (Berlin, 1970), *Medium Aevum*, XL (1971), pp. 288–90.

267. *Review of* A. Erler, *Aegidius Albornoz als Gesetzgeber des Kirchenstaates* (Berlin, 1970), *Medium Aevum*, XL (1971), pp. 290–1.

268. *Review of* S. Mähl, *Quadriga virtutum* (Cologne-Vienna, 1969), *RBPH*, XLIX (1971), pp. 791–2.

1972

269. *A Short History of the Papacy in the Middle Ages* (London, 1972), 389 pp.

270. *Principi di governo e politica nel medioevo*: Italian trans. of no. 111 (Bologna, 1972), 421 pp.

271. *The Origins of the Great Schism . . .* (Hamden, Conn., 1972), reprint of no. 15, with new introduction, xxviii+ 244 pp.

272. 'The election of bishops and kings of France in the ninth and tenth centuries', *Concilium*, vii (1972), pp. 79–85.

273. 'A note on inalienability in Gregory VII', *Studi Gregoriani*, ix (1972) [Studia in memoriam G. B. Borino], pp. 117–40.

274. 'The cosmic theme of the *Prima Clementis* and its significance for the concept of Roman Rulership', *Studia Patristica* xi [= *Texte und Untersuchungen zur Geschichte der altchristlichen Literatur*, cviii (1972)], pp. 85–91.

275. 'Julius II and the schismatic cardinals', *SCH*, ix (Cambridge, 1972), pp. 177–93.

276. *Review* of P. Herde, *Audientia litterarum contradictarum: Untersuchungen über die päpstlichen Justizbriefe und die päpstliche Delegationsgerichtsbarkeit vom 13. bis zum Beginn des 16. Jahrhunderts* (2 vols., Tübingen, 1970), *JEH*, xxiii (1972), pp. 84–5.

277. *Review* of N. Grass, ed., *Cusanus Gedächtnisschrift* (Innsbruck–Munich, 1970), *JEH*, xxiii (1972), pp. 86–7.

278. *Review* of W. Wehlen, *Geschichtsschreibung und Staatsauffassung im Zeitalter Ludwigs des Frommen* (Lübeck–Hamburg, 1970), *History*, lvii (1972), pp. 112–13.

279. *Review* of G. Kirsch, *Consilia: eine Bibliographie der juristischen Konsiliensammlungen* (Basel, 1970), *Renaissance Quarterly*, xxiv (1972), pp. 530–2.

280. *Review* of J. E. Sayers, *Papal Judges Delegate in the Province of Canterbury, 1198–1254: a study in ecclesiastical jurisdiction and administration* (Oxford, 1971), *JEH*, xxiii (1972), pp. 181–3.

281. *Review* of J. R. Strayer, *On the Medieval Origins of the Modern State* (Princeton, 1971), *Medium Aevum*, xli (1972), pp. 79–80.

282. *Review* of P. Michaud-Quantin, *Universitas: expressions du mouvement communautaire dans le moyen âge latin* (Paris, 1970), *EHR*, lxxxvii (1972), pp. 607–8.

283. *Review* of G. Seebass, *Bibliographica Osiandrica* (Niewkoop, 1971); E. Wolgast, *Die Wittenberger Luther-Ausgabe* (Niewkoop, 1971), *The Library*, 5th ser. xxvii (1972), pp. 148–9.

284. *Review* of E. Peters, *The Shadow-King: 'Rex inutilis' in medieval law and literature, 751–1327* (New Haven, 1970), *CHR*, lviii (1972–3), pp. 264–6.

285. *Review* of J. Deér, *Die heilige Krone Ungarns* (Vienna, 1966), *RBPH*, l (1972), pp. 282–4.

286. *Review* of S. Chodorow, *Christian Political Theory and Church Politics in the Mid-Twelfth Century: the ecclesiology of Gratian's Decretum* (Berkeley, 1972), *CHR*, lviii (1972–3), pp. 596–9.

1973

287. 'The Future of Medieval History: an inaugural lecture delivered in the University of Cambridge, 6 November 1972' (Cambridge, 1973), 30 pp.

Bibliography

288. 'Von Canossa nach Pavia: zum Strukturwandel der Herrschaftsgrundlagen im salischen und staufischen Zeitalter', *Historisches Jahrbuch*, CXIII (1973), pp. 265–300.

289. *Review* of F. Liotta, *La continenza dei chierici nel pensiero canonistico classico* (Milan, 1971), *EHR*, LXXXVIII (1973), pp. 165–6.

290. *Review* of S. Williams. *Codices Pseudo-Isidoriani: a palaeographico-historical study* (New York, 1971), *JEH*, XXIV (1973), p. 217.

291. *Review* of J. A. Watt, trans., *John of Paris, On Royal and Papal Power* (Toronto, 1971), *JEH*, XXIV (1973), p. 218.

292. *Review* of M. Adriaen, ed., *Sancti Gregorii Magni Homiliae in Hiezechihelem prophetam*, Corpus Christianorum, CXLII (Turnhout, 1971), *JTS*, n.s. XXIV (1973), pp. 274–6.

293. *Review* of H. E. J. Cowdrey, ed. and trans., *The Epistolae Vagantes of Pope Gregory VII* (Oxford, 1972), *JTS*, n.s. XXIV (1973), pp. 286–7.

294. *Review* of M. Chibnall, ed. and trans., *The Ecclesiastical History of Orderic Vitalis*, III (Oxford, 1972), *JTS*, n.s. XXIV (1973), pp. 287–8.

295. *Review* of L. E. Boyle, *A Survey of the Vatican Archives and of its Medieval Holdings* (Toronto, 1972), *JEH*, XXIV (1973), pp. 292–3.

296. *Review* of W. Berschin, *Bonizo von Sutri: Leben und Werk* (Berlin, 1972), *JEH*, XXIV (1973), pp. 294–5.

297. *Review* of E. Pitz, *Papstreskript und Kaiserreskript im Mittelalter* (Tübingen, 1971), *EHR*, LXXXVIII (1973), p. 620.

298. *Review* of M. Ascheri, *Un maestro del Mos Italicus: Gianfrancesco Sannazari della Ripa* (Siena, 1970); *ibid.*, *Saggi sul Diplovatazio* (Milan, 1971), *Renaissance Quarterly*, XXVI (1973), pp. 481–3.

299. *Review* of D. Claude, *Adel, Kirche und Königtum in Westgotenreich* (Sigmaringen, 1971), *Historisches Jahrbuch*, CXIII (1973), pp. 409–11.

300. *Review* of E. Boshof, *Das Erzstift Trier und seine Stellung zu Königtum und Papsttum im ausgehenden 10. Jahrhundert* (Cologne, 1972), *Historisches Jahrbuch*, CXIII (1973), pp. 422–4.

301. *Review* of A. E. Vacalopoulos, *Origins of the Greek Nation 1204–1461: the Byzantine period* (New Brunswick, 1970), *Historisches Jahrbuch*, CXIII (1973), pp. 424–5.

1974

302. *Individuo e società nel medioevo:* Italian trans. and revision of no. 183 (Rome–Bari, 1974), XVI+140 pp.

303. *Individuum und Gemeinschaft im Mittelalter:* German trans. and revision of no. 183 (Göttingen, 1974), 143 pp.

304. 中世における 個人 と 社会

Revised Japanese edn of no. 254 (Tokyo, 1974), 270 pp.

305. *A Short History of the Papacy* . . . (no. 269) (London, 1974), 2nd edn, 394 pp.

306. *Principles of Government and Politics* . . . (no. 111) (London, 1974), 3rd edn, 340 pp.

307. 'Die Bulle Unam Sanctam: Rückblick und Ausblick', *Römische Historische Mitteilungen*, XVI (1974), pp. 45–77.
308. 'Leo IX, Saint and Pope', *New Encyclopaedia Britannica*, 15th edn (Chicago, 1974).
309. Review of C. Schneider, *Prophetisches Sacerdotium und heilgeschichtliches Regnum im Dialog 1073–1077* (Munich, 1972), *EHR*, LXXXIX (1974), pp. 152–3.
310. Review of A. M. Stickler, ed., *Studia Gratiana*, XV [=J. R. Strayer and D. E. Queller, eds., *Post Scripta*] (Rome, 1972), *EHR*, LXXXIX (1974), pp. 162–3.
311. Review of J. Alberigo *et al.*, eds., *Conciliorum oecumenicorum decreta*, 3rd edn (Bologna, 1973), *JEH*, XXV (1974), p. 222.
312. Review of R. Somerville, *The Councils of Urban II*, I: *Decreta Claromontensia* (Amsterdam, 1972), *JTS*, n.s. XXV (1974), pp. 204–5.
313. Review of H. Biezais, ed., *The Myth of the State* (Stockholm, 1972), *History*, LIX (1974), p. 165.
314. Review of L. Boisset, *Un concile provincial au treizième siècle: Vienne 1289. Église locale et société* (Paris, 1973), *JTS*, n.s. XXV (1974), pp. 205–6.
315. Review of P. E. Hübinger, *Die letzten Worte Papst Gregors VII.* (Opladen, 1973), *JEH*, XXV (1974), pp. 339–40.
316. Review of *Festschrift für Hermann Heimpel*, II, ed. Max Planck Institut für Geschichte (Göttingen, 1972), *History*, LIX (1974), pp. 328–9.

1975

317. *Law and Politics in the Middle Ages: Introduction to the Sources of Medieval Political Ideas* (London–Cambridge–Ithaca, 1975), 320 pp.
318. *Il papato nel medioevo*: Italian trans. and edition of no. 269 (Rome–Bari, 1975), IX+405 pp.
319. *The Church and the Law in the Earlier Middle Ages*, Collected Studies, I (London, 1975), 406 pp.
320. *A History of Political Thought . . .* (Harmondsworth, 1975), revised new edn of no. 167, 256 pp.
321. 'Zur Entwicklung des Souveränitätsbegriffs im Spätmittelalter', in L. Carlen and F. Steinegger, eds., *Festschrift Nikolaus Grass* (Innsbruck, 1975), II, pp. 9–27.
322. 'A Greek démarche on the eve of the Council of Florence', *JEH*, XXVI (1975), pp. 337–52.
323. Review of R. Brentano, *Rome before Avignon: a social history of thirteenth-century Rome* (London, 1974), *Times Literary Supplement*, no. 3804 (1975), p. 117.
324. Review of *Festschrift für Hermann Heimpel*, III, ed. Max Planck Institut für Geschichte (Göttingen, 1972), *History*, LX (1975), p. 85.
325. Review of J. T. Gilchrist, ed., *Diversorum patrum sententiae siue collectio LXXIV titulos digesta* (Vatican City, 1973), *JEH*, XXVI (1975), pp. 177–8.
326. Review of W. Brandmüller, *Das Konzil von Pavia-Siena 1423–1424*, II: *Quellen* (Münster, 1974), *JEH*, XXVI (1975), pp. 182–4.
327. Review of K. Pellens, *Das Kirchendenken des normannischen Anonymus* (Wiesbaden, 1973), *JTS*, n.s. XXVI (1975), pp. 206–7.

Bibliography

328. *Review* of B. Schimmelpfennig, *Die Zeremonienbücher der Römischen Kurie im Mittelalter* (Tübingen, 1973), *RBPH*, LIII (1975), pp. 104-7.

329. *Review* of A. Marchetto, *Episcopato e primato pontificio nelle decretali pseudo-isidoriane* (Rome, 1972), *EHR*, XC (1975), pp. 627-8.

330. *Review* of H. Löwe, *Von Cassiodor zu Dante* (Berlin-New York, 1973), *EHR*, XC (1975), p. 873.

331. *Review* of D. Unverhau, *Approbatio-Reprobatio: Studien zum päpstlichen Mitspracherecht bei Kaiserkrönung und Königswahl vom Investiturstreit bis zum ersten Prozess Johanns XXII. gegen Ludwigs IV.* (Lübeck, 1973), *EHR*, XC (1975), p. 877.

332. *Review* of A. Bocognano, ed., *Grégoire le Grand: Morales sur Job (XI-XIV)* (= Sources chrétiennes, CCXII) (Paris, 1974), *JTS*, n.s. XXVI (1975), pp. 474-5.

333. *Review* of R. Weiss, *Chlodwigs Taufe: Reims 508. Versuch einer neuen Chronologie für die Regierungzeit des ersten christlichen Frankenkönigs unter Berücksichtigung der politischen und kirchlich-dogmatischen Probleme seiner Zeit* (Bonn-Frankfurt, 1971), *RBPH*, LIII (1975), pp. 552-3.

334. *Review* of J. Deér, *Papsttum und Normannen* (Cologne-Vienna, 1972), *RBPH*, LIII (1975), pp. 555-6.

335. *Review* of L. Duchesne, *Scripta minora: Études de topographie romaine et de géographie ecclésiastique* (Rome, 1973), *RBPH*, LIII (1975), pp. 1287-9.

1976

336. *The Papacy and Political Ideas in the Middle Ages*, Collected Studies, II (London, 1976), 408 pp.

337. 'The constitutional significance of Constantine the Great's settlement', *JEH*, XXVII (1976), pp. 1-16.

338. 'Boniface VIII and his contemporary scholarship', *JTS*, n.s., XXVII (1976), pp. 58-87.

339. 'Dante's *Monarchia* as an illustration of a politico-religious Renovatio', in B. Jaspert and R. Mohr, eds., *Traditio-Krisis-Renovatio aus theologischer Sicht: Festschrift für Winfried Zeller* (Marburg, 1976), pp. 101-13.

340. 'John Baconthorpe as a canonist', in C. N. L. Brooke, D. E. Luscombe, G. H. Martin and D. M. Owen, eds., *Church and Government in the Middle Ages: Essays presented to C. R. Cheney on his 70th birthday* (Cambridge, 1976), pp. 223-46.

341. 'Die Entstehung des Ottonianum', in H. Zimmermann, ed., *Otto der Grosse*, Wege der Forschung, CCCCL (Darmstadt, 1976), pp. 296-324.

342. *Review* of E. Gössmann, *Antiqui und Moderni im Mittelalter: eine geschichtliche Standortbestimmung* (Munich-Vienna, 1974), *JEH*, XXVII (1976), p. 88.

343. *Review* of M. Chibnall, ed. and trans., *The Ecclesiastical History of Orderic Vitalis*, vols. IV and V (Oxford, 1973, 1975), *JTS*, n.s. XXVII (1976), pp. 239-41.

344. *Review* of J. T. Johnson, *Ideology, Reason and the Limitations of War 1200-1740* (Princeton, 1975), *Virginia Journal of International Law*, XVI (1976), pp. 458-62.

345. *Review* of F. Lotter, *Der Brief des Priesters Gerhard an den Erzbischof Friedrich von*

Mainz: ein kanonistisches Gutachten aus frühottonischer Zeit (Sigmaringen, 1975), *JEH*, XXVII (1976), pp. 309–10.

346. *Review* of P. Landau, *Ius patronatus: Studien zur Entwicklung des Patronats im Dekretalenrecht und der Kanonistik des 12. und 13. Jahrhunderts* (Cologne–Vienna, 1975), *EHR*, XCI (1976), pp. 890–1.

347. *Review* of A. Patschovsky, *Die Anfänge einer ständigen Inquisition in Böhmen: ein Prager Inquisitoren-Handbuch aus der ersten Hälfte des 14. Jahrhunderts* (Berlin–New York, 1975), *JEH*, XXVII (1976), pp. 423–5.

348. *Review* of H. E. Troje, *Graeca leguntur: die Aneignung des byzantinischen Rechts und die Entstehung eines humanistischen Corpus iuris civilis in der Jurisprudenz des 16. Jahrhunderts* (Cologne–Vienna, 1971), *Journal of Modern History*, XLVIII (1976), pp. 531–4.

1977

349. *Medieval Foundations of Renaissance Humanism* (London and Ithaca, 1977), xii + 212 pp.

350. *A Short History of the Papacy* . . . (London, 1977), reprint of no. 305.

351. 'Über die rechtliche Bedeutung der spätromischen Kaisertitulatur für das Papsttum', in P. Leisching, F. Pototschnig and R. Potz, eds., *Ex aequo et bono: Willibald M. Plöchl zum 70. Geburtstag* (Innsbruck, 1977), pp. 23–44.

352. *Review* of I. W. Frank, *Der antikonziliaristische Dominikaner Leonhard Huntpichler: ein Beitrag zum Konziliarismus der wiener Universität im 15. Jahrhundert* (Vienna, 1976), *JEH*, XXVIII (1977), pp. 77–80.

353. *Review* of J. Autenrieth and R. Kottje, *Kirchenrechtliche Texte im Bodenseegebiet: Mittelalterliche Überlieferung in Konstanz, auf der Reichenau und in St. Gallen* (Sigmaringen, 1975), *JEH*, XXVIII (1977), pp. 102–3.

354. *Review* of H. Mordek, *Kirchenrecht und Reform im Frankreich: die Collectio Gallica, die älteste systematische Kanonessammlung des fränkischen Gallien: Studien und Edition* (Berlin, 1975), *EHR*, XCII (1977), pp. 359–64.

355. *Review* of H. Fichtenau, *Beiträge zur Mediävistik: Ausgewählte Aufsätze*, I: *Allgemeine Geschichte* (Stuttgart, 1975), *JTS*, n.s. XXVIII (1977), pp. 221–2.

356. *Review* of A. J. Lamping, *Ulrichus Velenus and his Treatise against the Papacy* (Leiden, 1976), *JTS*, n.s. XXVIII (1977), p. 222.

357. *Review* of J. G. A. Pocock, *The Machiavellian Moment: Florentine Political Thought and the Atlantic Republican Tradition* (Princeton, 1975), *Erasmus*, XXIX (1977), pp. 371–6.

1978

358. *Scholarship and Politics in the Middle Ages*, Collected Studies, III (London, 1978), 358 pp.

359. *Kurze Geschichte des Papsttums im Mittelalter:* German trans. and edition of no. 269 (Berlin, 1978), 368 pp.

360. *Principles of Government and Politics* . . . (no. 111) (London, 1978), 4th edn, 347 pp.

361. 'John of Salisbury's Policraticus in the later Middle Ages', in K. Hauck and H. Mordek, eds., *Geschichtsschreibung und geistiges Leben im Mittelalter: Festschrift für Heinz Löwe zum 65. Geburtstag* (Cologne–Vienna, 1978), pp. 519–46.

Bibliography

362. 'Der Grundsatz der Arbeitsteilung bei Gelasius I.', *Historisches Jahrbuch*, XCVII–XCVIII (1978) [= *Gedächtnisband für Johannes Spörl*], pp. 41–70.

363. *Review* of R. Bäumer, ed., *Die Entwicklung des Konziliarismus: Werden und Nachwirken der konziliaren Idee* (Darmstadt, 1976), *JEH*, XXIX (1978), pp. 110–11.

364. *Review* of B. Guillemain, *Machiavel: l'anthropologie politique* (Geneva, 1977), *Erasmus*, XXX (1978), pp. 54–8.

365. *Review* of M. D. Lambert, *Medieval Heresy: Popular Movements from Bogomil to Hus* (London, 1977), *JTS*, n.s. XXIX (1978), pp. 253–5.

366. *Review* of H. Tukay, *Oberschlesien im Spannungsfeld zwischen Deutschland, Polen und Böhmen-Mähren: eine Untersuchung der Kirchenpatrozinien im mittelalterlichen Archidiakonat Oppeln* (Cologne–Vienna, 1976), *JTS*, n.s. XXIX (1978), p. 255.

367. *Review* of H. Fichtenau, *Beiträge zur Mediävistik: Ausgewählte Aufsätze*, II: *Urkundenforschung* (Stuttgart, 1977), *JTS*, n.s. XXIX (1978), pp. 256–7.

368. *Review* of R. Staats, *Theologie der Reichskrone: ottonische 'Renovatio Imperii' im Spiegel einer Insignie* (Stuttgart, 1976), *JTS*, n.s. XXIX (1978), pp. 257–63.

369. *Review* of H. Grundmann, *Ausgewählte Aufsätze*, I: *Religiöse Bewegungen;* II: *Joachim von Fiore* (= Schriften der MGH, 25. 1, 2) (Stuttgart, 1976, 1977), *JEH*, XXIX (1978), pp. 217–19.

370. *Review* of L. Lutz, J. M. McLellan and G. Widhalm, eds., *Lexicon des Mittelalters*, I, 1 (Zurich–Munich, 1977), *JEH*, XXIX (1978), p. 504.

1979

371. *A History of Political Thought* ... (Harmondsworth, 1979), reprint of no. 320.

372. ' "This Realm of England is an Empire" ', *JEH*, XXX (1979) [= *Ecclesia Anglicana: Essays presented to C. W. Dugmore*], pp. 175–203.

373. 'Arthur's homage to King John', *EHR*, XCIV (1979), pp. 356–64.

374. 'Origini medievali del Rinascimento', in G. Laterza, ed., *Il Rinascimento: interpretazioni e problemi, dedicato a Eugenio Garin* (Rome–Bari, 1979), pp. 43–103.

375. 'Roman Public Law and Medieval Monarchy: Norman rulership in Sicily', in W. de Vos *et al.*, eds., *Acta Iuridica: Essays in honour of Ben Beinart*, III (Cape Town, 1979), pp. 157–84.

376. *Review* of M. Kerner, *Johannes von Salisbury und die logische Struktur seines Policraticus* (Wiesbaden, 1977), *Erasmus*, XXXI (1979), pp. 6–9.

377. *Review* of M. Chibnall, ed. and trans., *The Ecclesiastical History of Orderic Vitalis*, VI (Oxford, 1978), *JTS*, n.s. XXX (1979), pp. 353–5.

378. *Review* of G. Fransen and S. Kuttner, eds., *Summa 'Elegantius in iure divino' seu Coloniensis*, II (Vatican City, 1978), *JEH*, XXX (1979), pp. 381–3.

379. *Review* of H. Grundmann, *Ausgewählte Aufsätze*, III: *Bildung und Sprache* (= Schriften der MGH, 25. 3) (Stuttgart, 1978), *JEH*, XXX (1979), pp. 383–5.

380. *Review* of H. Fuhrmann, *Deutsche Geschichte im hohen Mittelalter von der Mitte*

des 11. bis zum Ende des 12. Jahrhunderts (Göttingen, 1978), *JEH*, xxx (1979), pp. 482–5.

381. Review of C. Gallagher, *Canon Law and the Christian Community: the role of law in the Church according to the Summa Aurea of Cardinal Hostiensis* (Rome, 1978), *JEH*, xxx (1979), pp. 488–9.

382. Review of A. E. Bernstein, *Pierre d'Ailly and the Blanchard Affair: University and Chancellor at Paris at the beginning of the Great Schism* (Leiden, 1978), *JTS*, n.s. xxx (1979), pp. 382–4.

383. Review of T. Struve, *Die Entwicklung der organologischen Staatsauffassung im Mittelalter* (Stuttgart, 1978), *ZRG*, Kan. lxvi (1979), pp. 338–50.

384. Review of G. Wesener, *Geschichte der Rechtswissenschaftlichen Fakultät der Universität Graz, I: Römisches Recht und Naturrecht* (Graz, 1978), *RHD*, xlvii (1979), pp. 379–81.